FACTBOOK

Exeter Books
NEW YORK

Editorial
Frances M. Clapham
Christopher Fagg
Fay Franklin
Denise Gardiner
Yvonne Messenger

Compiled by
Norman Barrett

Contributors
Arthur Butterfield
Jean Cooke
Lionel Grigson
Mark Lambert
Theodore Rowland-Entwistle
Christopher Tunney

First published in USA 1980
by Exeter Books
Distributed by Bookthrift, Inc
New York, New York

ISBN 0-89673-055-7
LC 80-80624

Printed and bound in Yugoslavia.

Contents

Our World

Basic facts

Circumference
— equatorial 24,902 miles (40,076km)
— polar 24,860 miles (40,008km)
Diameter
— equatorial 7,927 miles (12,757km)
— polar 7,900 miles (12,714km)
Mass 5,883 million million million tons
Average density 5.52

The symbols and letters on the world maps refer to the tables of extremes and records on pages 3, 4 and 5.

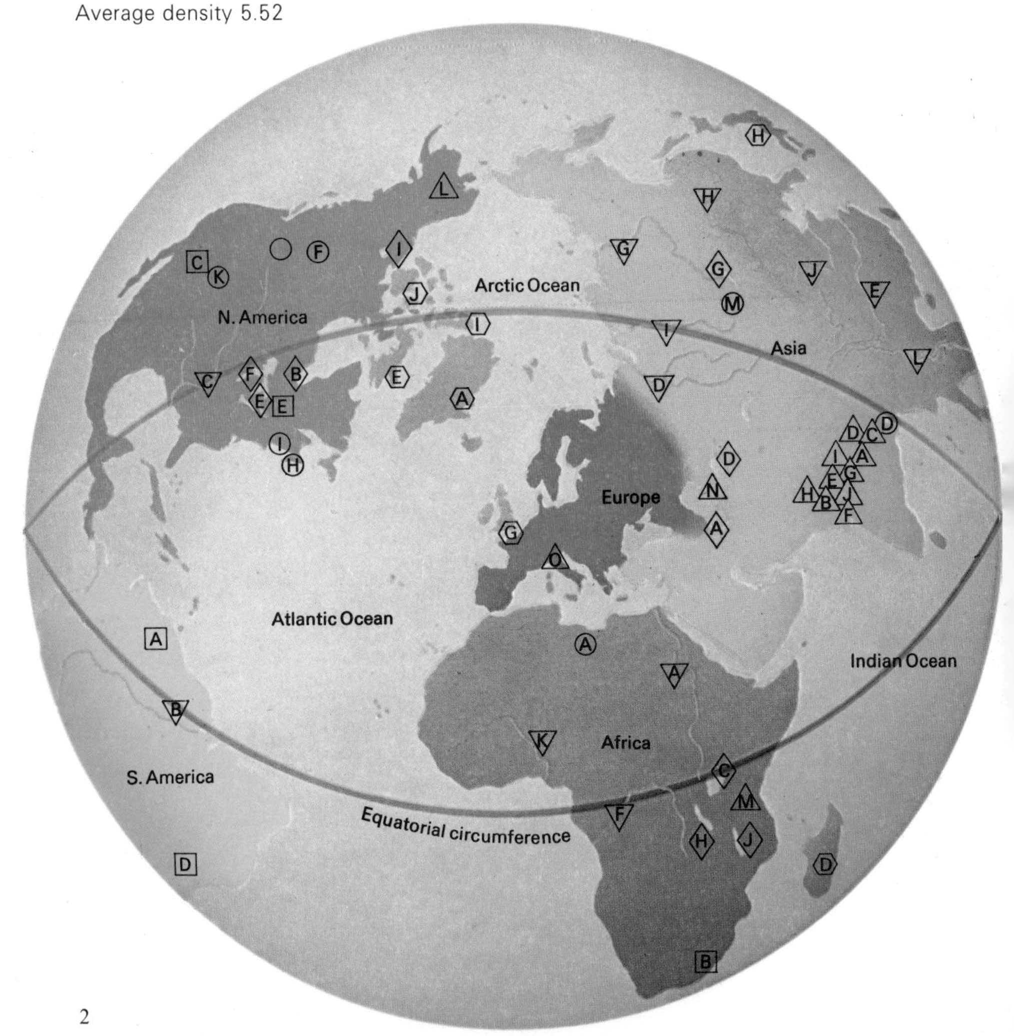

Earth extremes ○

A Hottest shade temperature recorded: 136.4°F (58.0°C) at Al 'Aziziyah, Libya, on 13.9.22
B Coldest temperature recorded: −126.9°F (−88.3°C) at Vostok, Antarctica, on 24.8.60
C Highest annual average rainfall: 460in (11,680mm) at Mt Waialeale, Hawaii
D Most rain in one month: 366.14in (9,300mm) at Cherrapunji, India, in July 1861
E Driest place on earth: Arica, Chile, averages 0.03in (0.76mm) of rain per year.
F Most snow in one year: 1,014in (2,804cm) fell on Tide Lake, Canada, in 1971–2
G Greatest ocean depth: 36,198ft (11,033m) Marianas Trench, Pacific Ocean
H Greatest tides: 53ft (16.2m) Bay of Fundy, Nova Scotia, Canada
I Strongest surface wind recorded: 231 mph (372kph) at Mt Washington, N.H., USA, in 1934
J Deepest gorge: 7,900ft (2,400m) Hells Canyon, Idaho, USA
K Longest gorge: 271 miles (349km) Grand Canyon, Arizona, USA
L Highest lake: Titicaca, Peru/Bolivia, 12,500ft (3,810m) above sea level
M Deepest lake: Baikal, Siberia, USSR, 4,982ft (1,519m)

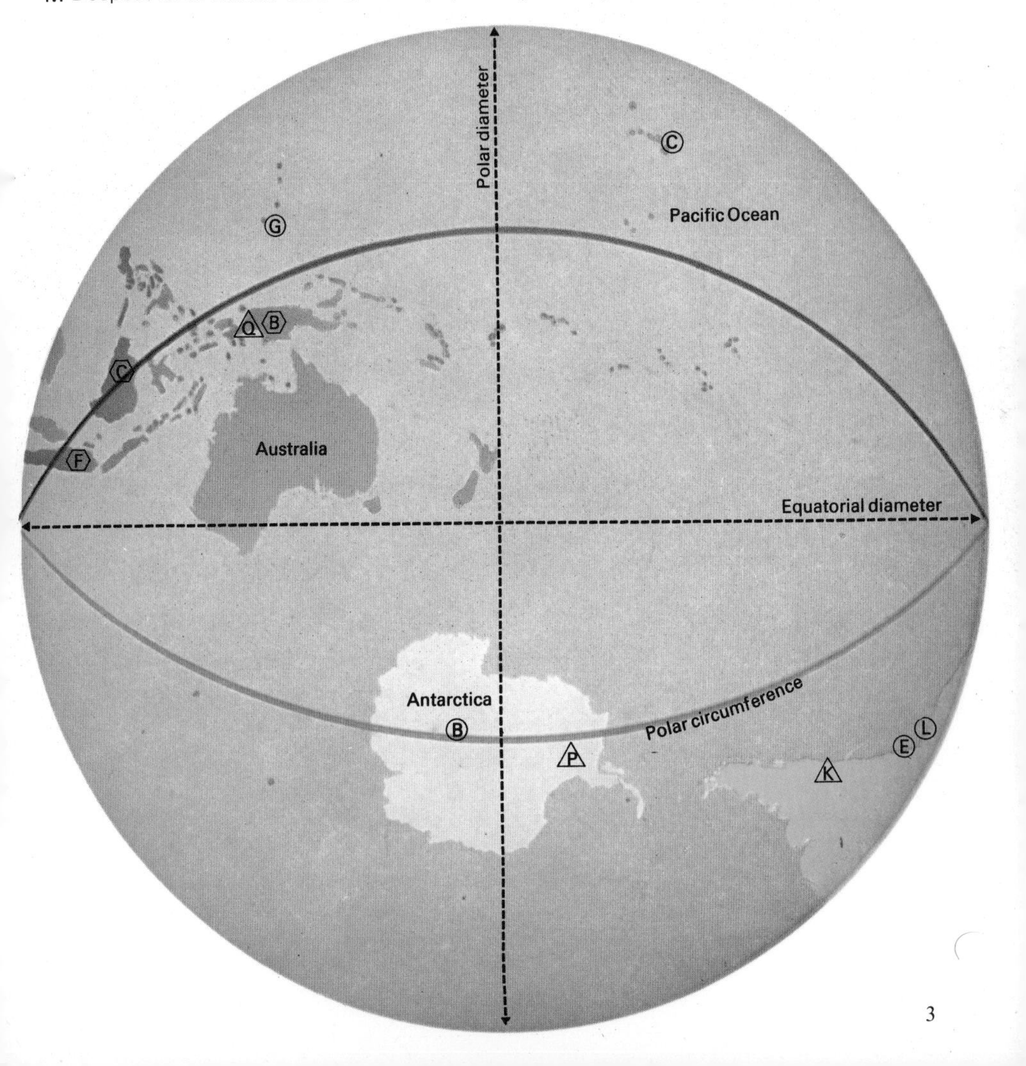

World records (contd.)

Longest rivers ▽

		miles	km
A	Nile (Africa)	4,150	6,679
B	Amazon (S. America)	3,900	6,276
C	Mississippi-Missouri-Red Rock (N. America)	3,872	6,231
D	Ob-Irtysh (USSR)	3,200	5,150
E	Yangtze (China)	3,200	5,150
F	Zaire* (Africa)	3,000	4,828
G	Lena (USSR)	3,000	4,828
H	Amur (Asia)	2,800	4,506
I	Yenisei (USSR)	2,800	4,506
J	Hwang Ho (China)	2,700	4,345
K	Niger (Africa)	2,600	4,184
L	Mekong (SE Asia)	2,600	4,184

*Formerly Congo River

Oceans

	sq miles	sq km
Pacific	70,000,000	181,000,000
Atlantic	41,000,000	106,000,000
Indian	28,375,000	73,490,000
Arctic	5,541,000	14,350,000

Continents

	sq miles	sq km
Asia	16,500,000	42,700,000
Africa	11,530,000	29,860,000
N. America	9,385,000	24,307,000
S. America	7,035,000	18,221,000
Europe	3,800,000	9,800,000
Australia	2,948,000	7,635,000
Antarctica	6,000,000	15,500,000

The great waterfalls of the world are awesome sights.

Largest islands ⬡

		sq miles	sq km
A	Greenland (N. Atlantic)	822,500	2,130,265
B	New Guinea (SW Pacific)	306,600	794,090
C	Borneo (SW Pacific)	289,993	751,078
D	Madagascar (Indian Ocean)	227,678	589,683
E	Baffin I. (Canadian Arctic)	183,810	476,066
F	Sumatra (Indian Ocean)	166,789	431,982
G	Great Britain (N. Atlantic)	88,619	229,522
H	Honshu (NW Pacific)	87,293	226,087
I	Ellesmere (Canadian Arctic)	76,600	198,393
J	Victoria I. (Canadian Arctic)	74,400	192,695

Largest lakes ◇

		sq miles	sq km
A	Caspian Sea (USSR/Iran)	169,381	438,695
B	Superior (USA/Canada)	31,820	82,413
C	Victoria Nyanza (Africa)	26,828	69,484
D	Aral (USSR)	26,166	67,770
E	Huron (USA/Canada)	23,000	59,570
F	Michigan (USA)	22,400	58,016
G	Baikal (USSR)	13,197	34,180
H	Tanganyika (Africa)	12,355	31,999
I	Great Bear (Canada)	12,200	31,598
J	Malawi* (Africa)	11,000	28,490

*Formerly Lake Nyasa

Major waterfalls □

	Highest	feet	metres
A	Angel Falls (Venezuela)	3,212	979
B	Tugela Falls (South Africa)	3,110	948
C	Yosemite Falls (California)	2,425	739
	Greatest Volume	ft^3/sec	m^3/sec
D	Guaira (Brazil/Paraguay)	470,000	13,300
E	Niagara (N. America)	212,200	6,000

Highest mountains △

	feet	metres
Asia		
A Everest (Himalaya—Nepal/Tibet)	29,028	8,848
B Godwin Austen (Karakoram—India)	28,250	8,611
C Kanchenjunga (Himalaya—Nepal/Sikkim)	28,146	8,579
D Makalu (Himalaya—Nepal/Tibet)	27,790	8,470
E Dhaulagiri (Himalaya—Nepal)	26,810	8,172
F Nanga Parbat (Himalaya—India)	26,660	8,126
G Annapurna (Himalaya—Nepal)	26,492	8,075
H Gasherbrum (Karakoram—India)	26,470	8,068
I Gosainthan (Himalaya—Tibet)	26,291	8,013
J Nanda Devi (Himalaya—India)	25,645	7,817
South America		
K Aconcagua (Andes—Argentina)	22,835	6,960
North America		
L McKinley (Alaska—USA)	20,320	6,194
Africa		
M Kilimanjaro (solitary—Tanzania)	19,317	5,888
Europe		
N Elborus (Caucasus—USSR)	18,481	5,633
O Mont Blanc (Alps—France)	15,781	4,810
Antarctica		
P Vinson Massif	16,860	5,139
Oceania		
Q Caestensz (Nassau Range—New Guinea)	16,404	5,000

Table Mountain, overlooking Cape Town, South Africa.

WORLD CLIMATE

The climate in any region is affected by its latitude: that is, how far it is from the Equator. Altitude, ocean currents and winds also affect the climate.

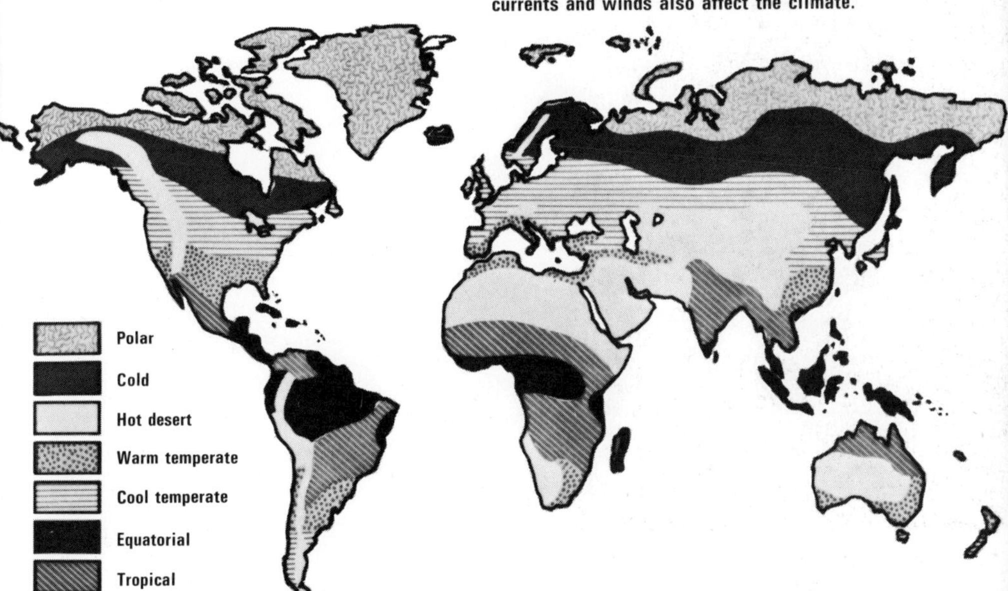

Countries of the World

EUROPE

	Area		Population	Capital
	Sq. miles	Sq. km		
Albania	11,000	28,500	2,548,000	Tirana
Andorra	180	465	29,000	Andorra La Vella
Austria	32,500	84,000	7,520,000	Vienna
Belgium	11,800	30,500	9,889,000	Brussels
Bulgaria	43,000	111,000	8,761,000	Sofia
Cyprus	3,600	9,200	639,000	Nicosia
Czechoslovakia	50,000	130,000	14,918,000	Prague
Denmark	16,500	43,000	5,089,000	Copenhagen
Faroe Islands (Dan.)	540	1,400	41,000	Thorshavn
Finland	130,000	337,000	4,739,000	Helsinki
France	213,000	551,000	53,086,000	Paris
Germany, East	41,500	107,500	16,786,000	East Berlin
Germany, West	96,000	249,000	61,418,000	Bonn
Gibraltar	2	5	30,000	Gibraltar
Greece	51,000	132,000	9,165,000	Athens
Hungary	36,000	93,000	10,654,000	Budapest
Iceland	40,000	103,000	220,000	Reykjavik
Ireland, Republic of	27,000	70,000	3,162,000	Dublin
Italy	116,000	300,000	56,024,000	Rome
Liechtenstein	62	160	24,000	Vaduz
Luxembourg	1,000	2,600	358,000	Luxembourg
Malta	122	316	322,000	Valletta
Monaco	0·7	1·8	25,000	Monaco
Netherlands	15,900	41,200	13,838,000	Amsterdam
Norway	125,000	324,000	4,035,000	Oslo
Poland	121,000	313,000	34,022,000	Warsaw
Portugal	35,400	91,600	9,449,000	Lisbon
Romania	92,000	238,000	21,446,000	Bucharest
San Marino	24	61	20,000	San Marino
Spain	195,000	505,000	36,351,000	Madrid
Sweden	174,000	450,000	8,255,000	Stockholm
Switzerland	16,000	41,000	6,298,000	Bern
Turkey	*See Asia*			
United Kingdom	94,500	245,000	55,928,000	London
USSR	*See Asia*			
Vatican City State	0·17	0·44	648	Vatican City
Yugoslavia	99,000	256,000	21,768,000	Belgrade

NORTH & CENTRAL AMERICA & CARIBBEAN AREA

	Area Sq. miles	Area Sq. km	Population	Capital
Anguilla (Br.)	35	90	5,800	—
Antigua	170	440	71,000	St John's
Bahamas	5,400	14,000	220,000	Nassau
Barbados	166	430	259,000	Bridgetown
Belize	8,900	23,000	144,000	Belmopan
Bermuda	21	53	57,000	Hamilton
Canada	3,852,000	9,976,000	22,992,604	Ottawa
Cayman Islands (Br.)	100	259	14,000	George Town
Costa Rica	19,600	50,800	2,061,000	San José
Cuba	44,000	114,000	9,464,000	Havana
Dominica	290	751	76,000	Roseau
Dominican Republic	18,700	48,400	4,978,000	Santo Domingo
El Salvador	8,000	21,000	4,123,000	San Salvador
Greenland (Dan.)	840,000	2,175,000	50,000	Godthaab
Grenada	133	344	105,000	St George's
Guadeloupe (Fr.)	690	1,790	360,000	Basse-Terre
Guatemala	42,000	109,000	6,436,000	Guatemala City
Haiti	10,700	27,700	4,749,000	Port-au-Prince
Honduras	43,000	111,000	2,831,000	Tegucigalpa
Jamaica	4,400	11,400	2,100,000	Kingston
Martinique (Fr.)	420	1,100	369,000	Fort-de-France
Mexico	760,000	1,970,000	62,329,000	Mexico City
Montserrat (Br.)	39	101	13,000	Plymouth
Netherlands Antilles (Dut.)	380	980	241,000	Willemstad
Nicaragua	57,000	148,000	2,223,000	Managua
Panama	29,200	75,600	1,719,000	Panama City
Panama Canal Zone (US)	647	1,676	44,000	Balboa Heights
Puerto Rico (US)	3,400	8,800	3,213,000	San Juan
St Kitts-Nevis	101	262	66,000	Basseterre
St Lucia	238	616	112,000	Castries
St Pierre & Miquelon (Fr.)	93	241	5,800	St Pierre
St Vincent	150	389	100,000	Kingstown
Trinidad & Tobago	1,980	5,130	1,067,000	Port-of-Spain
Turks & Caicos Is. (Br.)	166	430	6,000	Grand Turk
United States of America	3,615,000	9,363,000	216,450,000	Washington, DC
Virgin Islands (Br.)	59	153	12,000	Road Town
Virgin Islands (US)	133	344	96,000	Charlotte Amalie

AFRICA

	Area		Population	Capital
	Sq. miles	Sq. km		
Algeria	885,400	2,293,000	17,304,000	Algiers
Angola	481,000	1,247,000	6,761,000	S. Paulo de Luanda
Ascension (St Helena)	34	88	1,150	Georgetown
Benin, People's Republic	43,500	112,600	3,197,000	Porto Novo
Botswana	222,000	575,000	693,000	Gaborone
Burundi	10,750	27,800	3,864,000	Bujumbura
Cameroon	183,000	474,000	6,531,000	Yaoundé
Cape Verde Is. (Por.)	1,550	4,000	303,000	Praia
Central African Empire	241,000	625,000	1,637,000	Bangui
Chad	496,000	1,284,000	4,116,000	N'djamena
Comoros	800	2,000	314,000	Moroni
Congo	132,000	342,000	1,390,000	Brazzaville
Djibouti, Republic of	8,900	23,000	108,000	Djibouti
Egypt	386,000	1,000,000	36,656,000	Cairo
Equatorial Guinea	10,800	28,000	316,000	Malabo
Ethiopia	395,000	1,023,000	28,678,000	Addis Ababa
Gabon	103,000	267,000	530,000	Libreville
Gambia	4,300	11,100	538,000	Banjul
Ghana	92,000	238,000	10,309,000	Accra
Guinea	95,000	246,000	4,000,000	Conakry
Guinea-Bissau	14,000	36,000	534,000	Bissau
Ivory Coast	124,000	322,000	6,671,000	Abidjan
Kenya	225,000	583,000	18,847,000	Nairobi
Lesotho	11,700	30,300	1,214,000	Maseru
Liberia	43,700	113,200	1,751,000	Monrovia
Libya	680,000	1,760,000	2,444,000	Tripoli
Malagasy Republic	228,000	591,000	8,266,000	Tananarive
Malawi	45,500	117,800	5,175,000	Lilongwe
Mali	465,000	1,204,000	6,035,000	Bamako
Mauritania	398,000	1,031,000	1,481,000	Nouakchott
Mauritius	720	1,860	895,000	Port Louis
Morocco	177,000	459,000	17,828,000	Rabat
Mozambique	303,000	785,000	9,444,000	Maputo
Namibia	318,000	824,000	852,000	Windhoek
Niger	458,000	1,187,000	4,727,000	Niamey
Nigeria	357,000	924,000	76,742,000	Lagos
Réunion (Fr.)	970	2,500	510,000	St Denis
Rwanda	10,000	26,000	4,289,000	Kigali
St Helena (Br.)	47	122	5,000	Jamestown
São Tomé & Principe	370	960	81,000	São Tomé
Senegal	76,000	198,000	5,085,000	Dakar
Seychelles	107	277	59,000	Victoria
Sierra Leone	28,000	73,000	3,111,000	Freetown
Somalia	246,000	637,000	3,261,000	Mogadishu
South Africa	427,000	1,222,000	26,129,000	Pretoria
Sudan	967,500	2,506,000	16,126,000	Khartoum
Swaziland	6,700	17,400	409,000	Mbabane
Tanzania	365,000	945,000	15,007,000	Dar es Salaam
Togo	21,600	56,000	2,283,000	Lomé
Tristan da Cunha	45	115	292	—
Tunisia	63,000	163,000	5,588,000	Tunis
Uganda	91,400	230,700	11,943,000	Kampala
Upper Volta	106,000	244,000	6,144,000	Ouagadougou
Zaire	905,000	2,344,000	25,629,000	Kinshasa
Zambia	291,000	754,000	5,138,000	Lusaka
Zimbabwe-Rhodesia	151,000	391,000	6,530,000	Salisbury

ASIA

	Area Sq. miles	Area Sq. km	Population	Capital
Afghanistan	250,000	650,000	19,803,000	Kabul
Bahrain	255	660	259,000	Manama
Bangladesh	55,000	143,000	76,200,000	Dacca
Bhutan	18,000	47,000	1,202,000	Thimphu
Brunei	2,230	5,770	170,000	Bandar Seri Begawan
Burma	262,000	678,000	31,240,000	Rangoon
China: People's Republic	3,690,000	9,558,000	838,803,000	Peking
Hong Kong	404	1,046	4,383,000	Victoria
India	1,262,000	3,286,000	605,000,000	New Delhi
Indonesia	735,000	1,900,000	130,597,000	Djakarta
Iran	636,000	1,648,000	32,200,000	Tehran
Iraq	169,000	438,000	11,505,000	Baghdad
Israel	8,000*	20,700*	8,584,000	Jerusalem
Japan	143,000	370,000	114,150,000	Tokyo
Jordan	37,700	97,700	2,779,000	Amman
Kampuchea, Democratic	70,000	180,000	8,354,000	Phnom Penh
Korea: Democratic People's Republic (North)	47,000	122,000	16,246,000	Pyongyang
Korea: Republic of (South)	38,000	99,000	35,860,000	Seoul
Kuwait	7,500	19,000	1,031,000	Kuwait
Laos	91,000	236,000	3,383,000	Vientiane
Lebanon	4,000	10,000	2,961,000	Beirut
Macao (Port.)	6	16	275,000	Macao
Malaysia	128,000	333,000	12,300,000	Kuala Lumpur
Maldives, Republic of	115	298	129,000	Malé
Mongolian People's Republic	600,000	1,500,000	1,488,000	Ulan Bator
Nepal	54,000	140,000	12,904,000	Katmandu
Oman	82,000	212,000	791,000	Muscat
Pakistan	310,000	800,000	70,260,000	Islamabad
Philippines	115,000	300,000	42,513,000	Quezon City
Qatar	4,250	11,000	130,000	Doha
Saudi Arabia	927,000	2,400,000	9,240,000	Riyadh
Singapore	226	584	2,295,000	Singapore
Sri Lanka	25,000	65,000	13,730,000	Colombo
Syria	71,500	185,000	7,596,000	Damascus
Taiwan (Formosa)	13,890	35,970	14,833,000	Taipei
Thailand	200,000	515,000	42,960,000	Bangkok
Turkey	301,000 †	780,000 †	39,180,000	Ankara
United Arab Emirates	32,000	83,000	229,000	—
USSR	8,650,000 ‡	22,300,000 ‡	257,000,000	Moscow
Vietnam	129,000	335,724	46,523,000	Hanoi
Yemen (North)	75,000	195,000	5,237,000	San'a
Yemen PDR (South)	180,000	465,000	1,749,000	Madinat ash Sha'b

* Excluding 26,500 sq. miles (68,500 sq. km) occupied in 1967 war.
† Including 9,100 sq. miles (23,700 sq. km) and 3,000,000 people in Europe.
‡ Including 2,150,000 sq. miles (5,570,000 sq. km) and 185,000,000 people in Europe

Transport in various countries is adapted to the resources available locally. *Above left:* A Tunisian cart is pulled not by horse or donkey, but by a camel, a common beast of burden in many parts of the world. *Below left:* In India a passenger tricycle makes a cheap and efficient taxi, the driver supplying his own 'power', useful when fuel is scarce.

SOUTH AMERICA

	Area Sq. miles	Area Sq. km	Population	Capital
Argentina	1,072,000	2,778,000	25,719,000	Buenos Aires
Bolivia	424,000	1,098,000	4,688,000	La Paz
Brazil	3,286,000	8,511,000	109,181,000	Brasilia
Chile	290,000	750,000	10,454,000	Santiago
Colombia	440,000	1,140,000	24,372,000	Bogotá
Ecuador	105,000	272,000	7,305,000	Quito
Falkland Islands (Br.)	4,700	12,200	2,000	Stanley
French Guiana (Fr.)	35,000	91,000	55,125	Cayenne
Guyana	83,000	215,000	783,000	Georgetown
Paraguay	157,000	407,000	2,724,000	Asunción
Peru	496,000	1,285,000	16,090,000	Lima
Surinam	63,000	163,000	435,000	Paramaribo
Uruguay	72,000	187,000	3,101,000	Montevideo
Venezuela	352,000	912,000	12,361,000	Caracas

In Uruguay, nine-tenths of the land is farmed. However, the number of people actually living on the land is very small, since it is almost entirely pasture for cattle. Most farmers in Uruguay are extremely poor, which has also been responsible for a gradual move to the towns in search of prosperity.

A-Z of earth terms

ablation Wasting and removal of snow and ice, caused by sun, wind, and other factors.
alluvium Silt, sand, and gravel deposited by running water.
alpine Term used to describe any high mountains, their vegetation, wildlife, and climate.
Antarctic The south polar regions; region that lies within Antarctic Circle (latitude 66°32′S).
anticline Arch-like fold in rock layers produced by pressure in Earth's *crust*.
antipodes Two places exactly opposite each other on Earth's surface; in Britain, Australia and New Zealand are called the Antipodes.
archipelago Group of islands in large expanse of water.
Arctic The north polar regions; region that lies within Arctic Circle (latitude 66°32′N).
atoll Circular or horseshoe-shaped *coral* reef round a *lagoon*.
axis Imaginary line joining *poles* through

A group of walruses huddle together for warmth on Arctic pack ice. They rely on the sea beneath for food.

OCEANIA

	Area Sq. miles	Area Sq. km	Population	Capital
Australia	2,968,000	7,687,000	13,548,000	Canberra
Cook Islands	93	241	18,000	Avarua
Fiji	7,050	18,270	580,000	Suva
French Polynesia	1,550	4,000	135,000	Papeete
Gilbert Islands	309	813	58,000	Tarawa
Guam	212	550	104,000	Agaña
Nauru	8	21	8,000	—
New Caledonia	7,350	19,000	135,000	Nouméa
New Hebrides	5,700	14,800	97,000	Vila
New Zealand	104,000	269,000	3,129,000	Wellington
Niue	100	260	4,000	Alofi
Papua New Guinea	178,000	461,000	2,809,000	Port Moresby
Pitcairn Island	1.7	4.4	60	—
Samoa, Eastern (US)	76	197	31,000	Pago Pago
Samoa, Western	1,100	2,850	151,300	Apia
Soloman Islands	11,000	29,000	200,000	Honiara
Tonga	270	700	90,100	Nuku'alofa
Trust Territory of Pacific Is. (US)	700	1,800	102,300	Saipan
Tuvalu	12	30	7,000	—
Wallis and Futuna (Fr.)	100	260	9,000	Matautu

middle of Earth; Earth turns on its axis once every 24 hours.

badlands Any semi-arid, badly eroded region; specifically, area of difficult country in South Dakota.

bar Ridge of mud, sand, gravel, etc., across mouth of river.

barchan Crescent-shaped sand-dune found in some deserts; tips of crescent point down-wind, and gentler slope is on windward side.

barrier reef See *coral*.

basalt Heavy, hard, dark rock made up of solidified *lava* from *volcanoes*; it is one kind of *igneous rock*.

basin Region drained by river and its tributaries.

batholith Mass of *igneous rock* that has formed deep down in the Earth and part of which may be exposed at surface.

bay Wide, open inlet of sea within curving shoreline.

bedding plane Surface or plane that separates two distinct layers of *sedimentary rock*.

bog Area of wet, spongy ground (usually peaty), with decaying vegetation on surface.

Planes of rock have been exposed by the erosion of the sea, so that bedding planes and strata can be seen.

A–Z of Earth terms (contd.)

bore Tidal wave that travels at speed up *estuary*; also called *eagre*.
boulder clay Thick *clay* formed of rock and stones that have been crushed by glaciers and ice-sheets.
bush Any large uncleared area, covered with trees or bushes; specifically, wild areas of South Africa and Australia.
canal Man-made inland waterway used for transport.
canyon Narrow, deep valley with steep sides, cut through soft rock by swift-flowing river in dry region; also called a *gorge*.
cape Headland or mass of hard rock jutting out into sea.
catchment area Area from which river or reservoir draws its water supply; also called *drainage area*.
cave Underground chamber usually formed by sea waves or dissolving action of streams.
chalk Soft, white, *limestone* rock formed millions of years ago from shells and skeletons of minute animals.

Clay has been used by potters since earliest times because it is easy to mould when wet, but dries hard.

channel Bed of a stream; *strait* or narrow sea between two land masses; deepest part of harbour, where ships can navigate.
clay Smooth, impermeable earth formed of finely textured *sedimentary rock*.
conservation Preservation of natural surroundings (plants, animals, soil) from waste, pollution, and destruction, and maintenance of balance of nature.
continents The 7 major unbroken land masses of the Earth: Asia, Africa, Europe, North America, South America, Australia, and Antarctica.
continental drift Movement that, according to some experts, brought continents to their present positions after having broken away from single huge land mass.
continental shelf Ledge or shelf bordering the continents, varying in width up to 100 miles (160 km) out; water is less than 600 ft (180 m) deep.
contour Line on map joining places of same height above sea level.
coral Substance made up of skeletons of millions of tiny sea creatures called *coral polyps*; they build up into ridges called *coral reefs* at or near surface of sea, biggest of which is the *Great Barrier Reef*, off NE coast of Australia.
cordillera (Spanish, 'chain') Series of mountain ranges; specifically Andes in South America, and others in North America.
core Dense, metallic, central mass of the Earth, with diameter of about 4,300 miles (6,900 km).
corrosion Process of wearing down rock surface by friction from material moved by wind, running water, ice, waves, or gravity.
crater Funnel-shaped hollow at top of funnel of a volcano.
crust Outer shell of the Earth, 10 to 30 miles (16 – 48 km) thick.
current Driving force of ocean; movement of water in river; vertical movement of air-mass.
dam Man-made barrier built across river to hold and control flow of water.
delta Fertile, fan-shaped stretch of land at mouth of river, built up of *silt* deposited by the river.
desert Any large area of land with little rainfall – less than 10 in (250 mm) a year – and, as a result, scanty vegetation. Deserts may be hot (e.g. Sahara) or cold (e.g. the Antarctic).

Wind-blown sand has eroded the rock along lines of weakness.

divide See *watershed*.
doldrums Low pressure belt of calms and light surface winds near *equator*.
dune Mound of wind-blown sand formed on beaches and in deserts.
dust Tiny pieces of solid matter that settle only when air is still.
dyke Drainage ditch; man-made embankment to protect low-lying land from flooding; mass of *igneous rock* that cuts across other rocks.
earthquake Shaking or rolling of Earth's crust caused by underground volcanoes or slipping movement of weak part of the Earth.
ecology Study of relationships between living things, and between them and their surroundings.
equator Imaginary line encircling globe at equal distance from North and South poles.
erosion Wearing away of land by water, ice, or wind; does not include *weathering*.
estuary Part of river valley into which sea flows.
fault Break in Earth's *crust* where one rock face has moved out of alignment with the other.

The earthquake which rocked San Francisco in 1906 wrecked 497 buildings and killed 700 people.

A–Z of Earth terms (contd.)

fiord Very deep, long, narrow inlet of sea bounded by steep cliffs; originally scooped out by glaciers.
flood plain Valley floor that is regularly flooded by river and covered with *alluvium*.
fold Bending of rocks produced by pressure from within Earth's *crust* when rocks were soft.
forest Any large continuous stretch of unbroken woodland.
Frigid Zones Regions within the Arctic and Antarctic circles, where weather is never warm.
geodesy Branch of mathematics that deals with measurement of size, shape, and curvature of the Earth or of large parts of it.
geography Study of the Earth's surface, its climate, soils, plants, animals, and peoples.
geology Science that deals with study of the Earth, its history, and the materials that make up its *crust*.
geophysics Science that deals with physics of the Earth; it includes atmosphere, water, earthquakes, and magnetism.
geosyncline Huge downfold or inverted arch in Earth's crust; floor of the trough gradually sinks and fills with sediment.
geyser Fountain of boiling water and steam that shoots out from underground stream at intervals, mostly irregular.
glacier Slow-moving mass of ice that creeps down valley from snow-line towards sea; carries with it quantities of rocks and stones.
gorge See *canyon*.
granite Hard, *igneous rock*, made up mainly of mineral crystals such as feldspar and quartz.
great circle Imaginary line on Earth's surface (e.g. the equator) that divides globe in half.
ground water Rainwater that percolates through Earth's surface and lies in soil and rocks over an impermeable layer.
hemisphere One half of Earth's surface, usually either Northern Hemisphere or Southern Hemisphere, separated by equator.
hinterland Land that lies behind coast or seaport.
Horse Latitudes Atmospheric zones of high pressure on either side of the equator (approximately 30°N to 35°N and 30°S to

35°S), marked by calms and variable light winds; formerly, becalmed sailors in those latitudes threw their cargoes of horses overboard in order to save fresh water.

hot springs Streams of hot water that bubble to the surface in volcanic regions, but do not shoot into the air like *geysers*.

hydrography Science that deals with waters of the Earth's surface.

ice ages Periods when great parts of Earth's surface were covered with ice; they began about 1 million years ago in Pleistocene Epoch.

iceberg Mass of ice floating in sea, after having broken off from *glacier*; about one-ninth of iceberg shows above water's surface.

ice cap Mass of ice that covers polar regions.

igneous rock See *rocks*.

International Date Line Imaginary line drawn for most of its distance along the 180° meridian, marking place where each new calendar day begins. Date immediately to east of line is one day behind date immediately to west.

irrigation Controlled distribution of water to dry areas by means of flooding or via system of ditches and canals.

island Piece of land entirely surrounded by water.

isthmus Narrow strip of land between two seas or oceans, joining two land areas (e.g. Isthmus of Panama).

joint Crack or break in mass of rock; differs from a *fault* in that there is little or no displacement.

jungle Wild, uncultivated land with dense undergrowth; used particularly of monsoon forests.

laccolith Mass of *igneous rock* that in molten state rises up and forces overlying rocks into shape of arch or dome.

lagoon Shallow stretch of salt water partly or wholly cut off from sea by narrow strip of land; sheet of water inside an atoll; stretch of water between mainland and offshore coral reef.

lake Body of water surrounded by land.

latitude Distance of any point on Earth's surface north or south of equator, measured in degrees along a meridian.

A Norwegian fiord, left when the Ice Age ended.

A–Z of Earth terms (contd.)

An erupting volcano throws out lava.

lava Molten rock (*magma*) thrown out onto surface of the Earth by volcanic action.
lignite Low-grade, brownish black coal; intermediate stage between peat and domestic coal.
limestone *Sedimentary rock* consisting mainly of calcium carbonate.
loess Fertile fine silt or dust deposited by wind in interior of Asia and central parts of Europe and United States.
longitude Distance of any point on Earth's surface measured in degrees E or W of prime meridian (0°), on which Greenwich stands.
magma Hot molten material lying below solid rock; *igneous rocks* are formed of magma, and it emerges from a volcano's crater as *lava*.
magnetic poles Poles (ends) of the lines of magnetic force that run north and south through the Earth. North magnetic pole lies in N. America, and south magnetic pole is in Antarctica, each not far from corresponding true pole.
mantle Layer of rocks, about 1,800 miles (2,900 km) thick, lying between *crust* and *core* of the Earth.
massif Central mountainous mass (e.g. Massif Central, in France).
meanders Curves in course of sluggish river flowing across flat country; bank is worn away on concave side and built up by deposits on convex side.
meridian Imaginary circle on Earth's surface that passes through the poles.
metamorphic rocks See *rocks*.
mineral Natural inorganic substance with consistent chemical and physical properties; any substance that is mined.
moraine Rocks and boulders carried by valley glacier; *lateral moraine* forms at sides, *terminal moraine* in front, and *ground moraine* at bottom.
mountain Mass of land that rises more than 2,000 ft (610 m) above its immediate surroundings; may be formed by Earth movements, erosion, or volcanic action.

The Alps, a mountain range in Europe.

Cattle graze on the pampas, watched over by gauchos (South American cowboys).

oasis Fertile part of desert where water is present.
oceans The 5 great sheets of salt water that surround the land masses of the Earth: Pacific, Atlantic, Indian, Arctic, and Antarctic.
pampas Vast treeless grasslands that surround estuary of the Río de la Plata, in South America.
pass Fairly low, narrow gap through mountain range; usually caused by erosion.
peneplain Stretch of land that is almost as level as a *plain*; usually caused by erosion of rivers and rainwater.
peninsula Piece of land almost surrounded by water.
permafrost Permanently frozen subsoil and bedrock, as in the polar regions.
plain Large, generally low-lying area of level or gently rolling land.
plateau Broad, more or less level area of high land.
poles North and south ends of Earth's axis.
pot-hole Hole cut in bed of stream or at foot of waterfall by action of stones carried by water.
prairie Vast, level, treeless grasslands of North America.
quartz Crystalline form of silicon dioxide; hardest of all common minerals, found in many rocks.
rapids Part of river where water is broken because it flows over sudden steepening of river bed or series of rocky outcrops.
rift valley Long, narrow valley formed where land has sunk between two parallel *faults* (e.g. Great Rift Valley that runs from Syria to East Africa).
rivers Large streams of fresh water that flow over land in definite channels and empty into sea, lake, marsh, or another river.
Roaring Forties Ocean region south of latitude 40°S where prevailing north-west to west winds blow fiercely and constantly.
rocks Mass of mineral matter forming part of Earth's crust: *igneous rocks* are formed from solidified molten rock or magma; *metamorphic rocks* are hard, compact rocks whose structure, texture, or composition have at some time been changed by Earth pressures or heat; *sedimentary rocks* are formed of sediment that has been laid down in layers and cemented.
sand Mass of crumbly material made up of tiny fragments of rocks and minerals.
savanna Tropical grassland with clumps of trees.
scrub Coarse grass, bushes, and low stunted trees growing in semi-arid regions on poor soils.
sedimentary rocks See *rocks*.
shale *Sedimentary rock* found in layers and made up of compressed clay.
sierra (Spanish, 'saw') Mountain range with jagged peaks.
sial Comparatively light rocks (mainly granite) of Earth's crust that lie underneath the continents; term comes from *si*lica

Desert sands make up an inhospitable landscape.

A–Z of Earth terms (contd.)

and *al*umina, which are the main components.

silt Fine, muddy earth and sand carried by flowing water and deposited as sediment.

sima Dense rocks that form most of the ocean beds and underly the lighter *sial* masses; named after their main components, *si*lica and *ma*gnesia.

slate Fine-grained *metamorphic rock* that splits easily into layers; formed from *clay* that has been subjected to heat and pressure.

soil Loose surface-layer of the Earth, made up of broken rock and decayed organic matter.

spring Natural flow of water that issues from ground as result of *water table* rising to surface.

steppes Temperate grasslands of Eurasia analogous to *prairies* and *pampas*.

strait Narrow band of water that links two large sea areas (e.g. Strait of Gibraltar).

stratum Layer of *sedimentary rock*.

Soil differs greatly according to factors such as climate and the rock type beneath. Soils have three different layers, or horizons. The A horizon contains much decomposed vegetation. Horizon C is mostly material from the rock beneath, and level B is a mixture of the two.

subsidence Sinking of part of Earth's surface.
subsoil Layer of partly decomposed rock lying between topsoil and bedrock.
swamp Permanently waterlogged stretch of land with growing vegetation (bog has rotting vegetation, marsh is only temporarily waterlogged.
Temperate Zones Mid-latitude zones, about 43° wide, found in both northern and southern *hemispheres* between *Torrid* and *Frigid* zones; seasons are well marked.
tides Regular rise and fall of seas caused by gravitational pull of Moon and Sun; occurs twice a day.
topography Detailed description and representation on map of natural and artificial features of an area.
Torrid Zone Hottest of the three zones of latitude, lying between Tropic of Cancer and Tropic of Capricorn.
tropics *Tropic of Cancer* (23½°N) and Tropic of Capricorn (23½°S), the outer limits of only region where sun shines directly overhead at certain times.
tsunami Japanese term for great destructive sea wave, caused by disturbance of ocean floor; commonly but erroneously called 'tidal wave'.
tundra Treeless Arctic plain that is partly frozen throughout year and lies between polar ice and northern coniferous forests.
valley Long depression between hills or mountains, sometimes with river flowing in it; caused by weathering and erosion, or break in the Earth's crust
volcano Opening in Earth's crust through which lava flows; also, conical hill formed by solidified lava.
waterfall Sudden steep fall of river's course; caused by volcanic action, landslip or differences in hardness of the rock.
watershed Stretch of land that separates sources of two or more river systems; boundary of river basin; also called *divide*.
water table Surface of *ground water*, below which soil is saturated as a result of rainwater trickling through upper layers.
weathering Wearing away of parts of Earth's crust by exposure to atmosphere; may be physical (changes in temperature, etc.) or chemical (oxidation, etc.).
zones The 5 belts into which the Earth may be divided. See *Frigid Zones, Temperate Zones, Torrid Zone*.

The Arctic tundra, where the only plants are lichens, various herbaceous plants, and a few sprawling shrubs.

Weather and Climate

air mass Large body of air with particular characteristics.
anemometer Instrument for measuring speed of the wind.
anticyclone Region of high pressure, usually associated with good weather.
bar Unit of atmospheric pressure (equal to 1,000,000 dynes/sq cm). One bar is equivalent to 750.1 mm mercury in a barometer.
barometer Instrument that measures air pressure and is used to indicate changes in weather.
Beaufort Scale Scale of wind force devised in 1805 by Admiral Sir Francis Beaufort, numbers representing strength of wind in open, 33 ft (10 m) above ground:
blizzard Violent snowstorm with icy winds.
climate The established weather pattern of a region.
cloud Collection of water droplets or ice crystals in the air.

Weather and climate (contd.)

currents Regular systems of movements of water in the oceans.
cyclone Region of low pressure, usually heralding bad weather (called a *depression* in temperate regions).
depression Centre of low pressure, causing wet and windy unsettled weather.
dew Moisture deposited on objects close to the ground when the air condenses.
drought Period of little or no rain that causes crop failure.
fog Low cloud, with visibility reduced to less than 1,000 metres.
föhn Warm, dry wind that blows down the sheltered side of mountains; called *chinook* in North America.
front Boundary between air masses with different temperatures and humidities.
frost Particles of frozen moisture or ice crystals that form when the temperature falls below freezing point (0°C or 32°F).
hail Ice pellets that fall during storms.
humidity The amount of moisture in the air. *Relative humidity* is the amount compared with saturated air.
hurricane Whirling storm with winds blowing violently inwards towards centre of low pressure (the *eye*).
isobar Line on weather map connecting points of equal pressure.
isotherm Line on weather map connecting points of equal temperature.
jet streams Fast-moving currents of air found 6 – 10 miles up in the atmosphere.
lightning Flash caused by electrical discharge in or between clouds or between clouds and earth.
meteorology Study of weather and the atmosphere.
mist Thin cloud at ground level, with visibility reduced to not less than 1,000 metres (see *Fog*).

Meteorologists are greatly helped in their studies by satellite pictures such as this one, showing a cold front along the Florida peninsula.

monsoon A seasonal wind, particularly severe in the region of the Indian Ocean, bringing long periods of heavy rain.
precipitation Any form of moisture, such as rain or snow, that falls to earth from a cloud.
pressure The force exerted by the weight of air over a place on the earth.
rain Water droplets falling to earth from a cloud.
rainbow The coloured arc (red, orange, yellow, green, blue, indigo, violet) that can be seen in the sky as the result of sunlight reflected from raindrops.
rain gauge Instrument for measuring rainfall.
sea breeze Current of cool air from the sea that replaces rising hot air on land.
sleet Partly melted snow or a mixture of snow and rain.
snow Ice crystals that fall from cloud and are still frozen when they reach earth.
storm Violent air disturbance usually accompanied by heavy rain and strong winds.

In the regions of the world where snow falls frequently, people must adapt to survive. In this Swiss village, steeply sloping roofs will not collapse under the weight of a heavy snowfall.

sunshine Light direct from the sun.
thunder The sound of lightning.
thunderstorm Storm with electrical disturbances causing thunder and lightning.
tornado Small but violent storm with whirling winds that can create havoc on the ground.
troposphere Lowest layer of the atmosphere, about 10 miles thick and carries the weather.
water-spout Column of spray on the sea stretching up to low cloud.
weather Condition of the troposphere at a particular place.
wind Movement of air masses over the earth's surface. Winds are denoted by the direction *from* which they blow.

COMMON NAMES OF COUNTRIES

official name	common or alternative name
China, People's Republic of	Communist China, Mainland China, or China
German Democratic Republic	East Germany
Germany, Federal Republic of	West Germany
Ireland, Republic of	Eire
Korea, People's Democratic Republic of	North Korea
Korea, Republic of	South Korea
Mongolian People's Republic	Outer Mongolia
Netherlands, The	Holland
Union of Soviet Socialist Republics (USSR)	Russia or the Soviet Union
United Kingdom of Great Britain & Northern Ireland	Britain, Great Britain, or the United Kingdom

AUSTRALIAN TERRITORIES

	area		
	sq. mi.	sq. km	capital
States			
New South Wales	309,433	801,428	Sydney
Queensland	667,000	1,727,500	Brisbane
South Australia	380,070	984,377	Adelaide
Tasmania	26,383	68,332	Hobart
Victoria	87,884	227,619	Melbourne
Western Australia	975,920	2,527,621	Perth
Territories			
Australian Capital Territory	939	2,432	Canberra
Northern Territory	520,280	1,347,519	Darwin

MOST POPULOUS CITIES

New York (USA)	11,572,000
Tokyo (Japan)	11,403,744
Shanghai (China)	10,820,000
Mexico City (Mexico)	8,589,630
Buenos Aires (Argentina)	8,352,900
Peking (China)	7,570,000
London (UK)	7,379,014
Moscow (USSR)	7,061,000
Los Angeles (USA)	6, 974,103
Chicago (USA)	6,892,509
Bombay (India)	5,970,575

American football is a fast, and often very rough, ball game. The players have to be well padded to protect them from serious injury.

BRITISH ADMINISTRATIVE AREAS

England – *counties*
Avon
Bedfordshire
Berkshire
Buckinghamshire
Cambridgeshire
Cheshire
Cleveland
Cornwall
Cumbria
Derbyshire
Devon
Dorset
Durham
East Sussex
Essex
Gloucestershire
Greater London
Greater Manchester
Hampshire
Hereford & Worcester
Hertfordshire
Humberside
Isle of Wight
Isles of Scilly*
Kent
Lancashire
Leicestershire
Lincolnshire
Merseyside
Norfolk
North Yorkshire
Northamptonshire
Northumberland
Nottinghamshire
Oxfordshire
Salop
Somerset
South Yorkshire
Staffordshire
Suffolk
Surrey
Tyne & Wear
Warwickshire
West Sussex
West Midlands
West Yorkshire
Wiltshire

Wales – *counties*
Clwyd
Dyfed
Gwent
Gwynedd
Mid Glamorgan
Powys
South Glamorgan
West Glamorgan

Scotland
Regions
Borders
Central
Dumfries & Galloway
Fife
Grampian
Highland
Lothian
Strathclyde
Tayside

Island areas
Orkney
Shetland
Western Isles

N. Ireland – *counties*
Antrim
Armagh
Down
Fermanagh
Londonderry
Tyrone

* Separate administration, but not full county status.

Right: **The Grenadier Guards outside Buckingham Palace in London, England, a popular sight with visitors from all countries.**

STATES OF THE UNITED STATES

Alabama
Alaska
Arizona
Arkansas
California
Colorado
Connecticut
Delaware
Florida
Georgia
Hawaii
Idaho
Illinois
Indiana
Iowa
Kansas
Kentucky
Louisiana
Maine
Maryland
Massachusetts
Michigan
Minnesota
Mississippi
Missouri
Montana
Nebraska
Nevada
New Hampshire
New Jersey
New Mexico
New York
N. Carolina
N. Dakota
Ohio
Oklahoma
Oregon
Pennsylvania
Rhode Island
S. Carolina
S. Dakota
Tennessee
Texas
Utah
Vermont
Virginia
Washington
W. Virginia
Wisconsin
Wyoming

Geology

GEOLOGICAL TIME SCALE				
ERAS	**PERIODS**	**EPOCHS**	**millions of years ago**	**life forms**
Cenozoic	Quaternary	Holocene (recent)	2	(end of ice age) development of man
		Pleistocene	7	(ice ages) mammoths, woolly rhinoceroses
	Tertiary	Pliocene	26	mammals spread; earliest men
		Miocene	38	whales and apes
		Oligocene	54	modern types of mammals
		Eocene	65	first horses and elephants
		Palaeocene	136	early mammals
Mesozoic	Cretaceous		193	end of dinosaurs; flowering plants spread
	Jurassic		225	giant dinosaurs; first birds
	Triassic		280	small dinosaurs; first mammals
Palaeozoic	Permian		345	
	Carboniferous (Pennsylvanian and Mississippian)		398	forests formed coal; first reptiles
	Devonian		435	first forests and land animals, amphibians
	Silurian		500	first land plants
	Ordovician		570	first fishes
	Cambrian		1,850	
Precambrian	Proterozoic			sea animals without backbones; seaweeds
	Archaeozoic			first primitive plants and animals
	Azoic		4,000 4,500	(earliest known rocks) (earth formed)

METALS AND THEIR ORES

metal	ores
Aluminium	bauxite, AL_2O_3
Antimony	stibnite, Sb_2S_3
Beryllium	beryl, $3BeO.Al_2O_3.6SiO_2$; chrysoberyl, $BeAl_2O_4$
Bismuth	bismuth glance (bismuthinite), Bi_2S_3; bismite, Bi_2O_3
Calcium	limestone, marble, chalk, all $CaCO_3$; gypsum, alabaster, both $CaSO_4$; fluorspar, CaF_2; rock phosphate, $CaPO_4$
Chromium	chromite, $FeCr_2O_4$
Cobalt	smaltite, $CoAs_2$; cobaltite, CoAsS
Copper	copper pyrites (chalcopyrite), $CuFeS_2$; copper glance (chalcocyte), Cu_2S; cuprite, Cu_2O; bornite, Cu_5FeS_4
Iron	haematite, Fe_2O_3; magnetite, Fe_3O_4; siderite, $FeCO_3$; (iron pyrites, FeS_2)
Lead	galena, PbS; cerussite, $PbCO_3$; massicot, PbO
Lithium	spodumene, LiAl $(SiO_3)_2$
Magnesium	magnesite, dolomite, both $MgCO_3$; kieserite, $MgSO_4.H_2O$; carnallite, $KCl.MgCl_2.6H_2O$
Manganese	pyrolusite, MnO_2; hausmannite, Mn_3O_4
Mercury	cinnabar, HgS
Nickel	millerite, NiS; pentlandite, (Fe,Ni)S; garnierite, $(Ni,Mg)SiO_3.xH_2O$
Potassium	carnallite, $KCl.MgCl_2.6H_2O$; saltpetre, KNO_3
Silver	silver glance (argentite), AgS_2; horn silver, AgCl
Sodium	rock salt, NaCl; Chile saltpetre, $NaNO_3$
Strontium	strontianite, $SrCO_3$; celestine, $SrSO_4$
Tin	tinstone (cassiterite), SnO_2
Titanium	rutile, TiO_2; ilmenite, $FeO.TiO_2$
Uranium	pitchblende (uraninite), UO_2
Zinc	zinc blende (sphalerite), ZnS; calamine, $ZnCO_3$

NB: Gold and platinum occur in the earth as elements. Cadmium compounds are found in zinc ores.

ELECTROCHEMICAL SERIES

element	electrode potential (volts)
Lithium	−3.04
Potassium	−2.92
Barium	−2.90
Calcium	−2.87
Sodium	−2.71
Magnesium	−2.37
Aluminium	−1.66
Manganese	−1.18
Zinc	−0.76
Chromium	−0.74
Iron	−0.44
Cobalt	−0.28
Nickel	−0.25
Tin	−0.14
Lead	−0.13
Hydrogen	0.00
Copper	+0.34
Mercury	+0.78
Silver	+0.80
Gold	+1.50

MOH'S HARDNESS SCALE*

mineral	simple hardness test	Moh's hardness
Talc	Crushed by finger nail	1.0
Gypsum	Scratched by finger nail	2.0
Calcite	Scratched by copper coin	3.0
Fluorspar	Scratched by glass	4.0
Apatite	Scratched by a penknife	5.0
Feldspar	Scratched by quartz	6.0
Quartz	Scratched by a steel file	7.0
Topaz	Scratched by corundum	8.0
Corundum	Scratched by diamond	9.0
Diamond		10.0

* Used for testing hardness of materials, by comparing them with the 10 standard minerals.

Quartz crystals are formed gradually by a slow build-up of atoms and molecules.

Geology (contd.)

GEMSTONES

mineral	colour	Moh's hardness
Agate	brown, red, blue, green, yellow	7.0
Amethyst	violet	7.0
Aquamarine	sky blue, greenish blue	7.5
Beryl	green, blue, pink	7.5
Bloodstone	green with red spots	7.0
Chalcedony	all colours	7.0
Citrine	yellow	7.0
Diamond	colourless, tints of various colours	10.0
Emerald	green	7.5
Garnet	red and other colours	6.5–7.25
Jade	green, whitish, mauve, brown	7.0
Lapis lazuli	deep blue	5.5
Malachite	dark green banded	3.5
Moonstone	whitish with blue shimmer	6.0
Onyx	various colours with straight coloured bands	7.0
Opal	black, white, orange-red, rainbow coloured	6.0
Ruby	red	9.0
Sapphire	blue, and other colours	9.0
Serpentine	red and green	3.0
Soapstone	white, may be stained with impurities	2.0
Sunstone	whitish-red-brown flecked with golden particles	6.0
Topaz	blue, green, pink, yellow, colourless	8.0
Tourmaline	brown-black, blue, pink, red, violet-red, yellow, green	7.5
Turquoise	greenish-grey, sky blue	6.0
Zircon	All colours	7.5

ALLOYS

name	composition
copper	
Aluminium bronze	90% Cu, 10% Al
Manganese bronze	95% Cu, 5% Mn
Gun metal bronze	90% Cu, 10% Sn
Red brass	90% Cu, 10% Zn
Naval brass	70% Cu, 29% Zn, 1% Sn
Yellow brass	67% Cu, 33% Zn
Nickel silver	55% Cu, 18% Ni, 27% Zn
gold	
18-carat gold	75% Au, 25% Ag & Cu
Palladium, or white, gold	90% Au, 10% Pd
iron	
Steel	99% Fe, 1% C
Stainless steel	Fe with 0.1–2.0% C, up to 27% Cr or 20% W or 15% Ni and lesser amounts of other elements
silver	
Sterling silver	92.5% Ag, 7.5% Cu
US silver	90% Ag, 10% Cu
miscellaneous	
Britannia metal	90% Sn, 10% Sb
Dentist's amalgam	70% Hg, 30% Cu
Type metal	82% Pb, 15% Sb, 3% Sn

Opals are cut and polished to show their magnificent play of colour to the greatest advantage.

Right: Crystals of amethyst, a gem variety of quartz.

Below: There are many varieties of the silicate mineral beryl. This picture shows an emerald crystal in a lump of rock, and a huge crystal of blue-green aquamarine. In the foreground are cut stones from these and other varieties of beryl.

World production

MINERALS

	total	leading country
Bauxite	79,600*	Australia (29%)
Copper	8,000*	USA (17%)
Iron ore	482,000*	USSR (27%)
Nickel ore	800,600†	Canada (29%)
Silver	10,240†	Mexico (14%)
Tin ore	185,000†	Malaysia (32%)
Gold	988,000‡	South Africa (71%)
Diamonds	40,366**	Zaire (28%)

Figures are from UN statistics for 1977 including estimates.
*World production in 1,000 metric tons
†World production in metric tons
‡World production in kilograms
**World production in 1,000 metric carats of both industrial and gem diamonds. South Africa is the leading country in the production of gem stones with 38% of the world total of 10,210 thousand metric carats.

FUEL AND ENERGY

	total	leading country
Crude petroleum	2,985,879*	USSR (18.3%)
Coal	2,475,948*	USA (24.4%)
Natural gas	11,820,600†	USA (42%)
Electric energy	7,209,682‡	USA (30.5%)
Nuclear energy	508,951‡	USA (49%)

Figures are based on latest available UN statistics
*World production in 1,000 metric tons
†World production in teracalories
‡World production in 1,000,000 kWh

FOOD AND LIVESTOCK

product	total*	leading country
Bananas	36,892	Brazil (16.7%)
Barley	196,123	USSR (31.7%)
Cassava	119,374	Brazil (21.2%)
Grapes	56,030	France (16%)
Maize	362,971	USA (50%)
Millet	37,699	China (34.5%)
Oats	50,463	USSR (36.7%)
Potatoes	272,975	USSR (31.5%)
Pulses	62,008	China (40%)
Rice	376,448	China (35%)
Rye	32,389	USSR (50%)
Sorghum	69,117	USA (27.5%)
Soya beans	80,832	USA (62.5%)
Sugar beet	289,080	USSR (32.4%)
Sugar cane	781,291	India (23.2%)
Sweet potatoes	99,780	China (78.7%)
Tomatoes	47,087	USA (14.4%)
Wheat	441,474	USSR (27.4%)

animals	total†	leading country
Asses	42,313	China (27.1%)
Buffaloes	132,425	India (46%)
Camels	16,991	Somalia (31.8%)
Chickens	6,467,758	China (21.2%)
Cattle	1,213,092	India (15%)
Ducks	132,887	Vietnam (27%)
Goats	435,352	India (16.2%)
Horses	61,639	USA (15.5%)
Mules	11,725	Mexico (27.7%)
Pigs	731,799	China (39.4%)
Sheep	1,055,697	USSR (13.4%)
Turkeys	90,529	USSR (39.7%)

Figures are based on latest available FAO statistics, including estimates.
*World production (1,000 metric tons).
†World population (1,000 head of stock).

Crude petroleum production	(metric tons)
USSR	545,799,000
Saudi Arabia	458,460,000
USA	402,489,000
Iran	282,608,000
Iraq	122,390,000
Venezuela	117,007,000
Nigeria	102,970,000
Libya	99,503,000
Kuwait	98,744,000
Indonesia	82,998,000

Iron ore production	(metric tons)
USSR	131,418
Australia	60,164
Brazil	56,600
USA	35,042
China	32,500
Canada	31,828
India	26,520
South Africa	16,576
Sweden	16,116
Liberia	11,960

A North Sea oil production platform is towed out to its site. Once in position it will form a stable base for the oil-pumping equipment.

Wheat production (metric tons)

USSR	120,800,000
USA	49,954,000
China	44,008,000
India	31,328,000
Canada	21,146,000
France	21,057,000
Australia	18,300,000
Turkey	16,500,000

Rice production (metric tons)

China	131,775,000
India	79,010,000
Indonesia	25,739,000
Bangladesh	18,898,000
Thailand	17,000,000
Japan	16,000,000
Burma	10,500,000
Vietnam	9,880,000

Potato production (metric tons)

USSR	85,900,000
Poland	46,600,000
USA	16,356,000
China	12,048,000
W. Germany	10,510,000
E. Germany	10,100,000

Cattle stock

India	181,651,000
USA	116,265,000
USSR	112,690,000
Brazil	89,000,000
China	65,630,000
Argentina	61,280,000
Australia	29,379,000
Mexico	29,333,000

Sheep stock

USSR	141,025,000
Australia	131,510,000
China	88,000,000
New Zealand	60,300,000
Turkey	42,708,000
India	40,432,000
Argentina	34,000,000
Iran	33,600,000

Pig stock

China	288,321,000
USSR	70,511,000
USA	56,584,000
Brazil	37,600,000
Poland	21,717,000
W. Germany	21,386,000

Coal production (metric tons)

USA	603,772,000
USSR	499,768,000
China	490,000,000
Poland	186,112,000
UK	122,150,000
India	100,110,000
W. Germany	91,310,000
South Africa	85,570,000

Electric energy production (1,000,000 kWh)

USA	2,211,031
USSR	1,150,074
Japan	532,609
W. Germany	335,320
Canada	316,549
UK	283,280
France	210,845
Italy	166,545

Natural gas production (teracalories)

USA	4,932,118
USSR	2,889,335
Netherlands	732,594
Canada	685,899
UK	376,701

Nuclear energy production (1,000,000 kWh)

USA	508,951
UK	40,021
W. Germany	36,059
USSR	34,826
Japan	31,659
Canada	24,850
Sweden	19,913
France	17,986

Pigs are comparatively cheap and easy to rear, whether in the open or in huge enclosed rearing units.

Science & Technology

Telescope 1608

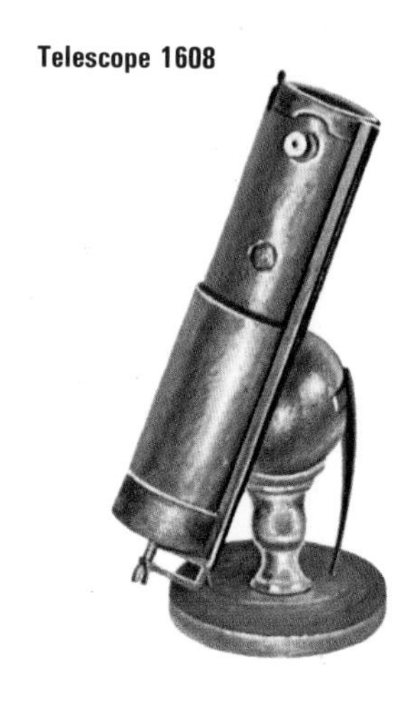

Invention

4000–3000 BC Bricks—in Egypt and Assyria
c.3000 BC Wheel—in Asia
c.3000 BC Plough—in Egypt and Mesopotamia
c.500 BC Abacus—the Chinese
c.300 BC Geometry—Euclid (Gk.)
200s BC Screw (for raising water)—Archimedes (Gk.)
AD 105 Paper (from pulp)—Ts'ai Lun (Chin.)
AD 250 Algebra—Diophantus (Gk.)
c.1000 Gunpowder—the Chinese
c.1100 Magnetic compass—the Chinese
c.1100 Rocket—the Chinese
c.1440 Printing press (movable type)—Johannes Gutenberg (Ger.)
1520 Rifle—Joseph Kotter (Ger.)
1589 Knitting machine—William Lee (Eng.)
c.1590 Compound microscope—Zacharias Janssen (Neth.)
1593 Thermometer—Galileo (It.)
1608 Telescope—Hans Lippershey (Neth.)
1614 Logarithms—John Napier (Scot.)
1636 Micrometer—William Gascoigne (Eng.)
1637 Co-ordinate geometry—René Descartes (Fr.)
1640 Theory of numbers—Pierre de Fermat (Fr.)
1642 Calculating machine—Blaise Pascal (Fr.)
1643 Barometer—Evangelista Torricelli (It.)
1650 Air pump—Otto von Guericke (Ger.)
1656 Pendulum clock—Christian Huygens (Neth.)
1665–75 Calculus—Sir Isaac Newton (Eng.) & Gottfried Leibniz (Ger.) independently
1675 Pressure cooker—Denis Papin (Fr.)
1698 Steam pump—Thomas Savery (Eng.)
1712 Steam engine—Thomas Newcomen (Eng.)

Pressure cooker 1675

1714 Mercury thermometer—Gabriel Fahrenheit (Ger.)
1725 Stereotyping—William Ged (Scot.)
1733 Flying shuttle—John Kay (Eng.)
1735 Chronometer—John Harrison (Eng.)
1752 Lightning conductor—Benjamin Franklin (US)
1764 Spinning jenny—James Hargreaves (Eng.)
1765 Condensing steam engine—James Watt (Scot.)
1768 Hydrometer—Antoine Baumé (Fr.)
1783 Parachute—Louis Lenormand (Fr.)
1785 Power loom—Edmund Cartwright (Eng.)
1790 Sewing machine—Thomas Saint (Eng.)
1793 Cotton gin—Eli Whitney (US)
1796 Lithography—Aloys Senefelder (Ger.)
1800 Electric battery—Count Alessandro Volta (It.)
1800 Lathe—Henry Maudslay (Eng.)
1804 Steam locomotive—Richard Trevithick (Eng.)
1815 Miner's safety lamp—Sir Humphry Davy (Eng.)
1816 Metronome—Johann Mälzel (Ger.)
1816 Bicycle—Karl von Sauerbronn (Ger.)
1817 Kaleidoscope—David Brewster (Scot.)
1822 Camera—Joseph Niepce (Fr.)
1823 Digital calculating machine—Charles Babbage (Eng.)
1824 Portland cement—Joseph Aspdin (Eng.)
1825 Electromagnet—William Sturgeon (Eng.)
1826 Photograph (permanent)—Joseph Niepce (Fr.)
1827 Match—John Walker (Eng.)
1828 Blast furnace—James Neilson (Scot.)
1831 Dynamo—Michael Faraday (Eng.)
1834 Reaping machine—Cyrus McCormick (US)
1836 Revolver—Samuel Colt (US)
1837 Telegraph—Samuel F. B. Morse (US)
1839 Vulcanized rubber—Charles Goodyear (US)
1844 Safety match—Gustave Pasch (Swed.)
1846 Sewing machine—Elias Howe (US)
1849 Safety pin—Walter Hunt (US)
1852 Gyroscope—Léon Foucault (Fr.)
1853 Passenger lift—Elisha Otis (US)
1855 Celluloid—Alexander Parkes (Eng.)
1855 Bessemer converter—Henry Bessemer (Eng.)
1855 Bunsen burner—Robert Bunsen (Ger.)
1858 Refrigerator—Ferdinand Carré (Fr.)
1858 Washing machine—Hamilton Smith (US)

Bicycle 1816

Revolver 1836

Safety match 1844

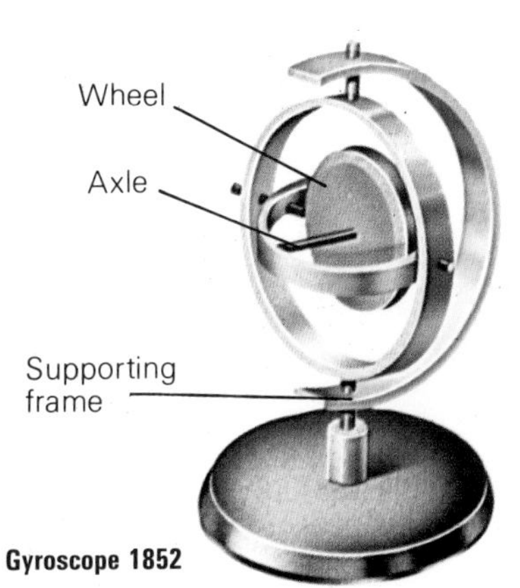

Gyroscope 1852

Invention (contd.)

1859 Internal combustion engine—Etienne Lenoir (Fr.)

1861 Linoleum—Frederick Walton (Eng.)

1862 Rapid-fire gun—Richard Gatling (US)

1865 Cylinder lock—Linus Yale, Jr. (US)

1866 Dynamite—Alfred Nobel (Swed.)

1867 Typewriter—Christopher Sholes (US)

1868 Lawn mower—Amariah Hills (US)

1870 Margarine—Hippolyte Mège-Mouriés (Fr.)

1873 Barbed wire—Joseph Glidden (US)

1876 Telephone—Alexander Graham Bell (Scot.)

1876 Carpet sweeper—Melville Bissell (US)

1877 Phonograph—Thomas Edison (US)

1878 Microphone—David Edward Hughes (Eng./US)

1879 Incandescent lamp—Thomas Edison (US)

1879 Cash register—James Ritty (US)

1884 Fountain pen—Lewis Waterman (US)

1884 Linotype—Ottmar Mergenthaler (US)

1885 Motorcycle—Edward Butler (Eng.)

1885 Vacuum flask—James Dewar (Scot.)

1885 Electric transformer—William Stanley (US)

1886 Electric fan—Schuyler Wheeler (US)

1886 Halftone engraving—Frederick Ives (US)

1887 Gramophone—Emile Berliner (Ger./US)

1887 Monotype—Tolbert Lanston (US)

1887 Motor-car engine—Gottlieb Daimler & Karl Benz (Ger.), independently

1888 Pneumatic tyre—John Boyd Dunlop (Scot.)

1888 Kodak camera—George Eastman (US)

1890 Rotogravure—Karl Klic (Czech.)

1892 Zip fastener—Whitcomb Judson (US)

1895 Wireless—Guglielmo Marconi (It.)

1895 Photoelectric cell—Julius Elster & Hans Geitel (Ger.)

1895 Safety razor—King C. Gillette (US)

1897 Diesel engine—Rudolf Diesel (Ger.)

1898 Submarine—John P. Holland (Ire./US)

1899 Tape recorder—Valdemar Poulsen (Den.)

1901 Vacuum cleaner—Cecil Booth (Eng.)

1902 Radio-telephone—Reginald Fessenden (US)

1903 Aeroplane—Wilbur & Orville Wright (US)

1904 Diode—John Fleming (Eng.)

Telephone 1876

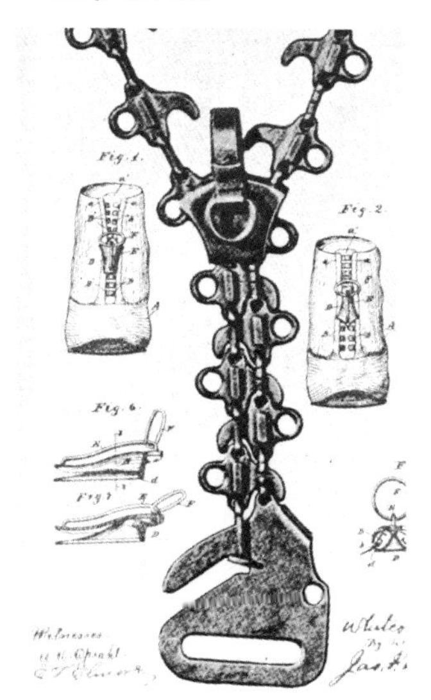

Zip fastener 1892

Aeroplane 1903—the Wright Brothers

1906 Triode—Lee De Forest (US)
1908 Bakelite—Leo Baekeland (Belg./US)
1908 Cellophane—Jacques Brandenberger (Switz.)
1911 Combine harvester—Benjamin Holt (US)
1913 Geiger counter—Hans Geiger (Eng.)
1914 Tank—Ernest Swinton (Eng.)
1915 Tungsten filament lamp—Irving Langmuir (US)
1918 Automatic rifle—John Browning (US)
1925 Television (working system)—John Logie Baird (Scot.) & others
1925 Frozen food process—Clarence Birdseye (US)
1926 Rocket (liquid fuel)— Robert H. Goddard (US)
1928 Electric shaver—Jacob Schick (US)
1930 Jet engine—Frank Whittle (Eng.)
1931 Cyclotron—Ernest Lawrence (US)
1935 Nylon—Wallace Carothers (US)
1935 Parking meter—Carlton Magee (US)
1939 Electron microscope—Vladimir Zworykin and others (US)
1939 Betatron—Donald Kerst (US)
1944 Automatic digital computer—Howard Aiken (US)
1946 Electronic computer—J. Presper Eckert & John W. Mauchly (US)
1947 Polaroid camera—Edwin Land (US)
1948 Transistor—John Bardeen, Walter Brattain & William Shockley (US)
1948 Xerography—Chester Carlson (US)
1948 Long-playing record—Peter Goldmark (US)
1954 Maser—Charles H. Townes (US)
1960 Laser—Theodore Maiman (US)
1965 Holography (on idea conceived in 1947 and subsequently developed using laser)—T. Gabor (B)
1971 EMI-Scanner—Godfrey Hounsfield (Eng.) (developed from his invention of computed tomography in 1967)

Television 1920s

Radio 1895

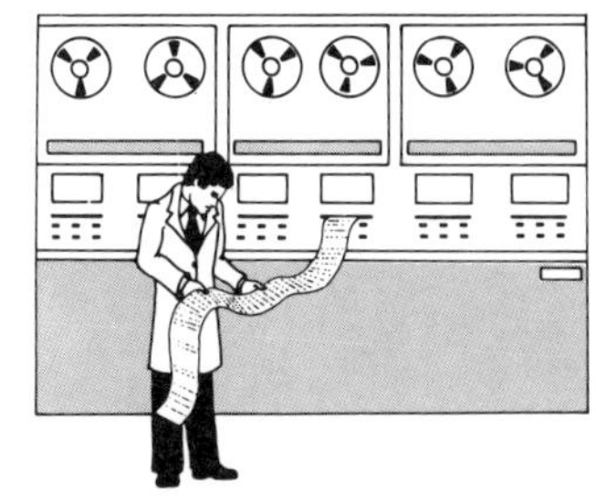

Electronic computer 1946

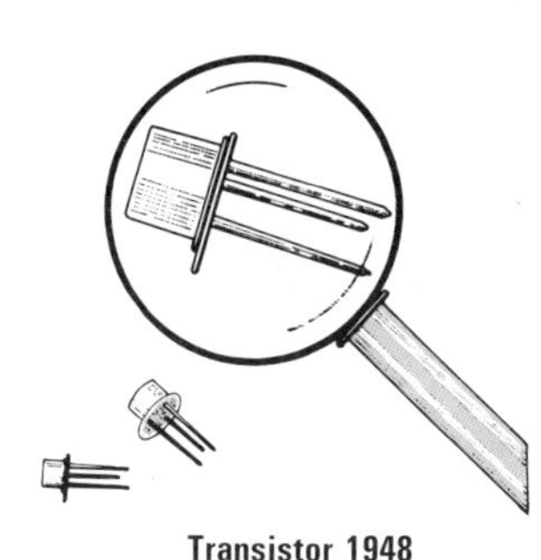

Transistor 1948

Discovery

1543 Sun as centre of solar system—Copernicus (Pol.)
1590 Law of falling bodies—Galileo (It.)
1609–19 Laws of planetary motion—Johannes Kepler (Ger.)

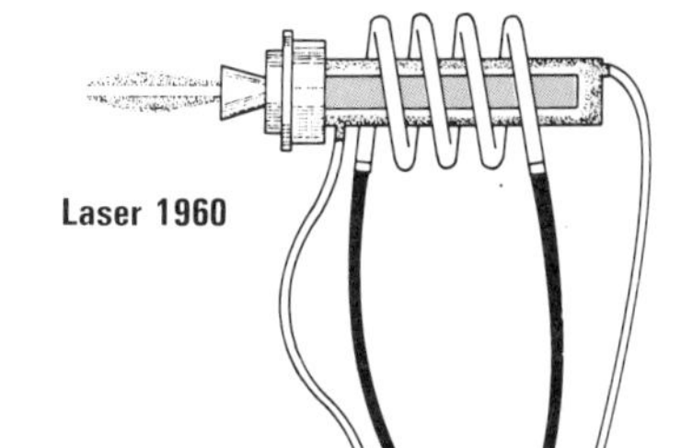

Laser 1960

Discovery (contd.)

1662 Relation between gas pressure and volume—Robert Boyle (Eng./Ire.)
1669 Phosphorus—Hennig Brand (Ger.)
1675 Measurement of speed of light—Olaus Römer (Dan.)
1678 Wave theory of light—Christian Huygens (Dut.)
1687 Laws of gravitation and motion—Isaac Newton (Eng.)
1751 Nickel—Axel Cronstedt (Swe.)
1755 Magnesium—Sir Humphry Davy (GB)
1766 Hydrogen—Henry Cavendish (GB)
1772 Nitrogen—Daniel Rutherford (GB)
1774 Oxygen—Joseph Priestly (GB); Karl Scheele (Swe.)
1774 Chlorine—Karl Scheele (Swe.)
1781 Uranus (planet)—William Herschel (GB)
1783 Tungsten—Fausto & Juan José de Elhuyar (Sp.)
1789 True nature of combustion—Antoine Lavoisier (Fr.)
1797 Chromium—Louis Vauquelin (Fr.)
1803 Atomic structure of matter—John Dalton (GB)
1811 Molecular hypothesis—Amadeo Avogadro (It.)
1817 Cadmium—Friedrich Stromeyer (Ger.)
1820 Electromagnetism—Hans Christian Oersted (Dan.)
1824 Silicon—Jöns Berzelius (Swe.)
1826 Bromine—Antoine Balard (Fr.)
1826 Laws of electromagnetism—André Ampère (Fr.)
1827 Law of electric conduction—Georg Ohm (Ger.)
1827 Aluminium—Hans Christian Oersted (Dan.)
1831 Electromagnetic induction—Michael Faraday (GB); discovered previously, but not published, by Joseph Henry (US)
1839 Ozone—Christian Schönbein (Ger.)
1841 Uranium—Martin Klaproth (Ger.)
1846 Neptune (Planet)—Johann Galle (Ger.), from predictions of others
1864 Electromagnetic theory of light—James Clerk Maxwell (GB)
1868 Helium—Sir William Ramsay (GB)
1869 Periodic arrangement of elements—Dmitri Mendeleev (Russ.)
1886 Electromagnetic waves—Heinrich Hertz (Ger.)

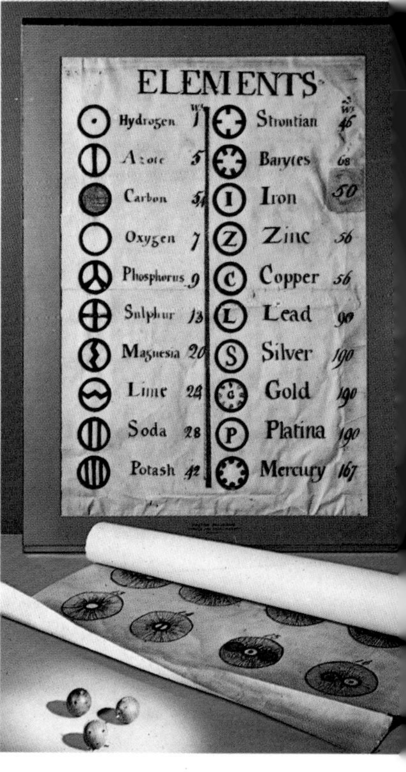

Atomic structure and weights 1803

Nitrogen 1772

1886	Fluorine—Henri Moissan (Fr.)
1894	Argon—Sir William Ramsay & Baron Rayleigh (GB)
1895	X-rays—Wilhelm Roentgen (Ger.)
1896	Radioactivity—Antoine Becquerel (Fr.)
1897	Electron—Sir Joseph Thomson (GB)
1898	Radium—Pierre & Marie Curie (Fr.)
1900	Quantum theory—Max Planck (Ger.)
1905	Special theory of relativity—Albert Einstein (Swi.)
1910	Russell-Hertzsprung diagram (star pattern)—Henry Russell & Eijnar Hertzsprung (US)
1913	Atomic number—Henry Moseley (GB)
1915	General theory of relativity—Albert Einstein (Swi.)
1919	Proton—Ernest Rutherford (GB)
1924	Wave nature of electron—Louis de Broglie (Fr.)
1926	Wave mechanics—Erwin Schrödinger (Aus.)
1927	Uncertainty principle—Werner Heisenberg (Ger.)
1930	Pluto (planet)—Clyde Tombaugh (US), from prediction by Percival Lowell (US) in 1905
1931	Existence of neutrino (atomic particle)—Wolfgang Pauli (Ger.)
1931	Deuterium (heavy hydrogen)—Harold Urey (US)
1932	Neutron—James Chadwick (GB)
1932	Positron—Carl Anderson (US)
1935	Existence of meson (atomic particle)—Hideki Yukawa (Jap.)
1940	Plutonium—G.T. Seaborg *et al.* (US)
1950	Unified field theory—Albert Einstein (Swi./US)
1950	Theory of continuous creation of matter—Fred Hoyle (GB)
1955	Antiproton—Emilio Segré & Owen Chamberlain (US)
1958	Radiation belts surrounding earth—James Van Allen (US)
1963	Quasars—Thomas Matthews & Allan Sandage (US)
1964	Omega particle—Brookhaven Laboratory, New York (US)
1967	Pulsars—Radio Astronomy Group, University of Cambridge (GB)
1974	Psi Particle—discovered independently by two US laboratories
1977	Chiron: distant asteroid orbiting between Saturn and Uranus—Charles Kowal (USA)

Relativity 1915—Einstein

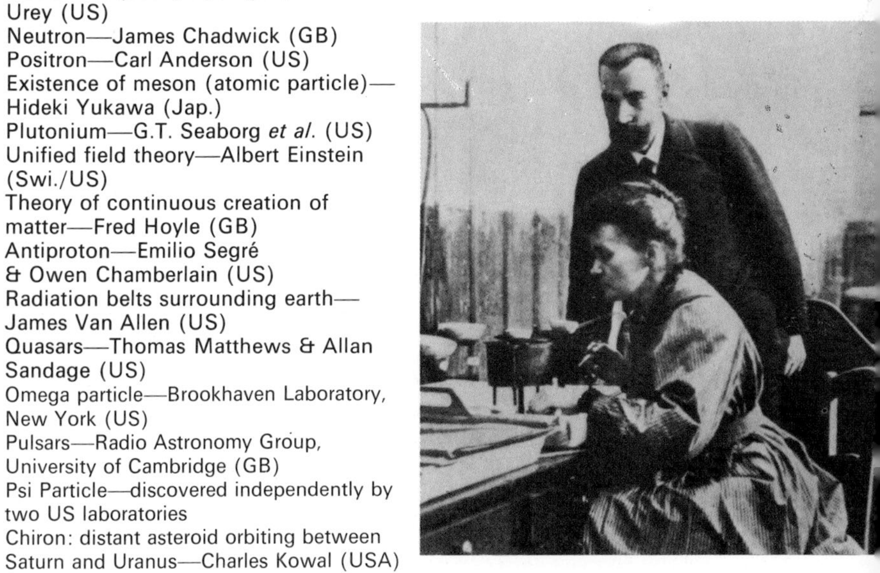

Radium 1898—The Curies

Science A-Z

aberration Distortion of image due to imperfections in construction of lens or mirror; *chromatic aberration* distorts colours; *spherical aberration* distorts shapes.
absolute temperature Temperature related to *absolute zero*. See *kelvin*.
absolute zero Lowest temperature possible in theory; zero on absolute scale is −273.15 °C. See also *kelvin*.
absorption Penetration of substance into body of another, e.g. a gas dissolving in liquid. See also *adsorption*.
acceleration Rate of change of *velocity*.
acid Chemical substance that produces free hydrogen ions in solution. Reacts with *base* to form *salt*.
acoustics Science that deals with sounds.
adhesion Attractive force between molecules of a substance that makes them stick together.
adiabatic process Physical or chemical process that takes place with no gain or loss in heat.

Ethyl alcohol, the product of sugar fermentation by yeast, is distilled in huge copper containers and blended to produce whisky.

adsorption Phenomenon by which a gas or liquid becomes concentrated on surface of a solid. See also *absorption*.
aerodynamics Branch of *mechanics* that deals with forces acting on objects moving through air.
affinity Chemical attraction between *elements* or *compounds*.
alcohols Class of organic compounds having characteristic hydroxyl group, –OH. Names end in -ol, e.g. ethanol (ethyl alcohol)
aldehydes Class of organic compounds having characteristic group –CHO.
algebra Branch of mathematics in which letters are used to stand for unknown quantities.
alkali *Base* consisting of a soluble metal hydroxide. Alkali metals, such as sodium and potassium, form *caustic alkalis*.
alkaline earths Group of metallic elements that form weakly basic (alkaline) oxides; Group II of the Periodic Table; includes magnesium, calcium, strontium, and barium.
alkaloid Varied group of naturally occurring organic compounds derived from plants; includes morphine and nicotine.
allotropy Property of an element of existing in more than one physical form, called *allotropes*.
alloy Metal composed of more than one element.
alpha-rays (α-rays) Streams of helium nuclei emitted by some radioactive elements.
alternating current Electric current flow that rapidly decreases from maximum in one direction, through zero, to maximum in other direction.
alum Double salt of a trivalent metal sulphate (such as aluminium, chromium, or ferric iron sulphates) and the sulphate of an alkali metal or ammonium; crystalizes with 24 molecules of water. Common 'alum' is potassium aluminium sulphate.
amalgam Alloy of mercury.
ammeter Electrical instrument for measuring current.
amorphous Non-crystalline.
ampere (A) Unit of electric current; defined as current that, in *electrolysis* of silver nitrate, deposits 0.001118 g of silver per second on cathode; equivalent to flow of 6×10^{18} electrons per sec.

analytical geometry Same as *co-ordinate geometry*.
anhydride Compound that reacts chemically with water to form its parent substance, a *hydrate*.
anode Positive electrode through which electric current enters electrolysis cell or vacuum tube.
aqua regia Mixture of hydrochloric and nitric acids able to dissolve noble metals, such as gold.
Arab numerals Number characters (digits) normally used in western countries; e.g. 1, 2, 3.
Archimedes' principle When a body is immersed or partly immersed in a liquid, apparent loss in weight is equal to weight of liquid displaced.
armature Rotating part of electric motor or dynamo, consisting of coils of wire.
assaying Chemical analysis of ores and minerals, generally for their metal content.
atom Smallest fragment of an element that can take part in a chemical reaction. Consists of central *nucleus* (made up of *protons* and *neutrons*) surrounded by orbiting *electrons*. Number of protons (equal to number of electrons) is called *atomic number*. Total mass of all subatomic particles is called *atomic mass*. See also *isotope*.
atom smasher General name for any machine, such as *cyclotron*, that accelerates particles to sufficiently high speeds to split atoms.
atomic number See *atom*.
atomic weight Alternative name for atomic mass. See *atom*.

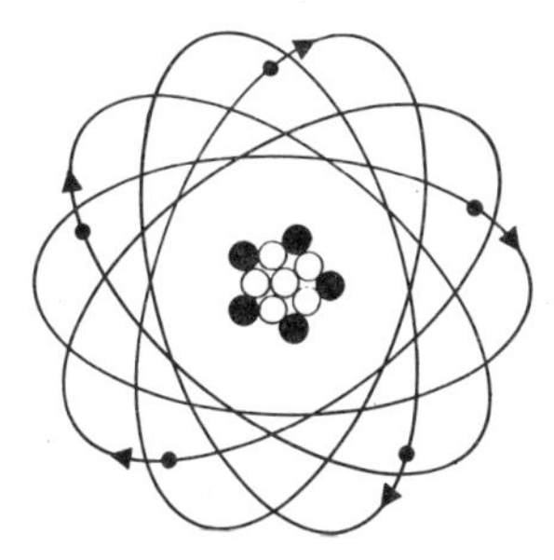

An atom of boron has five protons (dark) and six neutrons (light) in its nucleus, with five electrons orbiting the nucleus.

Magnets attract metal. Here an electromagnet is used to lift scrap metals.

attraction Any force that tends to pull objects closer together. Forces of attraction include electrostatic, gravitational, magnetic, and inter-molecular forces.
Avogadro's hypothesis Equal volumes of all gases contain equal numbers of molecules.
Avogadro's number Number of atoms in gramme-atom, or molecules in gramme-molecule (*mol*); approx 6×10^{23}.
avoirdupois System of weights, formerly used in English-speaking countries, based on units ounce, pound, stone, ton.
Bakelite Thermosetting plastic originally made from phenol and formaldehyde.
ballistics Study of paths taken by projectiles, such as bullets and rockets.
barometer Instrument for measuring pressure of atmosphere.
base Substance that reacts chemically with an *acid* to form a *salt* and water.

Science A–Z (contd.)

battery Device that converts chemical energy into electrical energy; an electric cell, a source of *direct current*.
bel Ten *decibels*.
Bernoulli's principle When a fluid flows through a tube, at any point the sum of the potential, kinetic, and pressure energies is constant.
Bessemer process Method of making steel quickly in fairly small batches, involving blowing air through molten iron to oxidize excess carbon and other impurities.
beta-rays (β-rays) Stream of electrons emitted by some radioactive elements.
betatron Machine that accelerates *electrons* in circular magnetic field to produce continuous beam of high-energy particles.
bevatron Machine that accelerates *protons* in circular magnetic field.
bicarbonate of soda Sodium bicarbonate.
binary system Number system with only two digits, 0 and 1.

Each molecule of water consists of two hydrogen atoms (blue) and one oxygen atom (yellow) bonded together. Hence, the chemical name for water is hydrogen oxide or H_2O.

binomial theorem General expansion of the polynomial $(x + y)^n$, given by

$$x^n + nx^{n-1}y + \frac{n(n-1)}{2!}x^{n-2}y^2 + \ldots + y^n$$

biochemistry Chemistry of processes that take place in living things.
bleaching Removing colour or making white; generally achieved with sunlight or a chemical oxidizing agent, such as chlorine, sulphur dioxide, or hydrogen peroxide.
block and tackle A pulley (or pulleys) and the rope or chain that works it.
boiling point Temperature at which liquid freely turns into vapour; vapour pressure of liquid then equals external pressure on it.
bond Chemical link between two atoms in a *molecule*.
Boolean algebra Type of logic, which uses symbols of algebra, applied to computer programs and operations.
Boyle's law At constant temperature the volume of a gas is inversely proportional to its pressure.
British thermal unit (BTU) Quantity of heat needed to raise temperature of 1 pound of water through 1 degree F. 1 BTU = 252 calories = 1,055 joules. See also *calorie*.
bubble chamber Apparatus in which paths of charged atomic particles are revealed as row of tiny bubbles in chamber of liquid.
calculus Branch of mathematics that deals with rates of change of variable quantities; divided into *differential calculus* and *integral calculus*.
calorie Unit of heat equal to amount needed to raise temperature of 1 gram water through 1 degree C; 1 calorie = 4.2 joules; *kilocalorie* (= 1,000 calories) written *Calorie* (capital C), used for food values.
candela (cd) Unit of luminous intensity, replacing *candle*.
candlepower Luminous intensity of light source in given direction, expressed in *candelas*.
capacitance Property of *condenser* that enables it to store electric charge; numerical value of charge, measured in *Farads*.
capacitor See *condenser*.
capillarity Phenomenon that makes *liquid* rise up narrow space, as in fine-bore tube or between two sheets of glass; caused by forces of attraction between *molecules* in

Above: **Nine different types of catalyst. Catalysis is very important to the chemical industry as it often produces reactions under less severe heat or pressure than would otherwise be necessary.**

Below: **A cathode ray tube is used by a television camera to transform an image of the scene into a signal which can be displayed on a television tube.**

surface of liquid. See also *surface tension*.

carbide Chemical compound of carbon and another element, such as calcium.

carbonate Salt of carbonic acid.

catalyst Substance that markedly alters the speed of a chemical reaction, without appearing to take part in it.

cathode Negative *electrode* through which electric current leaves an electrolysis cell or vacuum tube.

cathode rays Electrons flowing from cathode of discharge tube or valve.

cellophane Transparent plastic, generally film or thin sheet, made from cellulose.

celluloid Early *thermoplastic* material made from cellulose nitrate and camphor.

Celsius See *Centigrade*.

centigrade Temperature scale on which 0 °C is the melting point of ice and 100 °C is boiling point of water; same as Celsius.

centrifugal force Force that acts outwards on an object moving in circular path.

centrifuge Machine that rotates at high speeds and makes use of *centrifugal force* to separate solids from liquids or to separate liquids of different densities.

centripetal force Force that acts inwards as reaction to *centrifugal force*.

Science A–Z (contd.)

cgs system Metric system of units based on centimetre, gram, and second; now replaced by *SI units*.
Charles' law At constant pressure, the volume of a gas is proportional to its *absolute temperature*.
chemical change Change in type, number, or arrangement of atoms in substance, resulting in change in its chemical composition.
chemical equivalent Weight of an element that will combine with or replace 1 gram of hydrogen or 8 grams of oxygen. Of an acid, the weight containing 1 gram of replaceable hydrogen.
chloride Salt of hydrochloric acid.
chromatography Method of chemical analysis in which mixture of liquids is separated according to extent each component is adsorbed into paper or a column of chalky material.

This huge complex is the part of an oil refinery where catalytic cracking takes place. Compounds are broken down to produce fuels and by-products.

coal gas Fuel gas produced by destructive distillation of coal; consists mainly of carbon monoxide, methane, and hydrogen with various impurities.
cohesion Force of attraction between molecules that holds liquid or solid together.
colloid Substance in solution in colloidal state – a system of particles in a medium with different properties from true solution because of larger size of particles.
combination Set of specified number of different objects from larger group; arrangement of objects within set does not matter.
combustion (burning) Chemical reaction in which a substance combines with oxygen and gives off heat and light.
compound Substance consisting of two or more *elements* in chemical combination.
concentration Amount of a substance expressed as mass in a given volume; concentrations of chemical solutions generally expressed in moles/m^3.
condensation Change of *vapour* into *liquid* that takes place when pressure is applied to it or temperature is lowered.
condenser Circuit element, consisting of arrangement of conductors and insulators, that can store electric charge when voltage is applied across it; also called *capacitor*.
conductor Substance that offers little resistance to flow of electricity.
co-ordinate geometry Branch of mathematics that deals with lines, curves, and geometrical figures in terms of algebraic expressions that stand for them; also called *analytical geometry*.
corrosion Slow chemical breakdown, often *oxidation* of metals, by action of water, air, or chemicals.
cosine Trigonometrical ratio, given (for an angle) in right-angled triangle by length of the side adjacent to the angle divided by the length of the hypotenuse.
cosmic rays High-energy radiation, mainly charged particles, striking the Earth from outer space.
cosmotron Machine that accelerates *protons* in the field of a large ring magnet.
coulomb (C) Unit of quantity of electricity, defined as quantity transferred by 1 ampere in 1 second.
cracking Process in petroleum industry,

using a *catalyst*, in which heavy products are split to form lighter ones, such as petrol.
critical temperature Temperature above which a gas cannot be liquefied, no matter how great the pressure.
cryotron Switch using *superconductivity*, consisting of superconducting coil of wire wound round another superconducting wire kept at temperature close to *absolute zero*; current passed through the coil controls conductivity and hence resistance of wire.
crystallization Process in which a regular solid substance (crystal) forms from molten mass or solution. See also *hydrate*.
curie Measure of *radioactivity*, defined as the amount of a radioisotope that decays at rate of 3.7×10^{10} disintegrations per second.
current, electric Flow of electrons along a conductor. Measured in *amperes*.
cyclotron Machine for accelerating atomic particles to high speeds; particles follow spiral path in magnetic field between two D-shaped electrodes.
Dalton's law of partial pressures In a mixture of gases, the pressure of a component gas is the same as if it alone occupied the total volume. See *partial pressure*.
decay Natural breakdown of radioactive element. See *radioactivity*.
decibel Unit for comparing power levels or sound intensities; tenth of a *bel*.
decimal system Number system using the base 10, i.e. using the digits 1 to 9 and zero.
delta rays (δ-rays) Electrons knocked out of atoms by high-energy charged particles.
density Mass of unit volume of a substance. See *specific gravity*.
desiccation Drying.
diffraction Splitting of white light into spectrum of colours by passing it through narrow slit or past edge of obstacle.
diffusion Phenomenon by which gases mix together. See *Graham's law*.
dimensions Power to which fundamental unit (length, mass, or time) is raised to describe a physical quantity; e.g. area ($length^2$) has 2 dimensions of length.
dimorphism Property of substance existing in two different crystal forms. See *polymorphism*.
direct current Electric current that always flows in the same direction.
dissociation Temporary decomposition of chemical compound, into component molecules or groupings, that reverses when conditions causing it are removed.

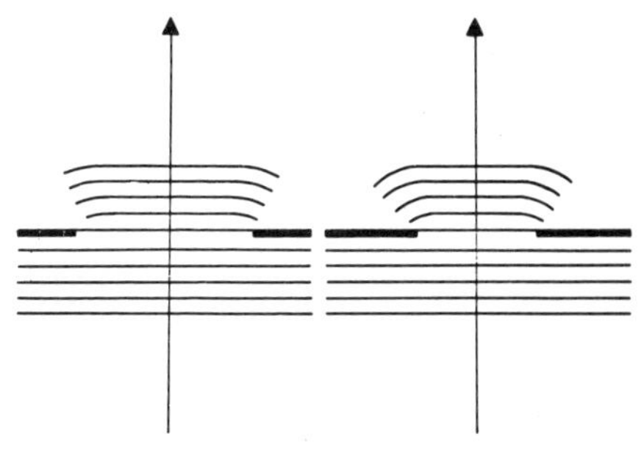

Diffraction: Waves flowing through an aperture spread out behind it; appreciable bending occurs only if the aperture is small enough compared with the wavelength.

distillation Technique of purifying or separating liquids by heating to boiling point and condensing vapour produced back to liquid.
Doppler effect Apparent change in frequency of sound or light caused by movement of source with respect to observer. Frequency rises for approaching sources, falls for receding ones.
double decomposition Chemical reaction between two compounds in which reactants form two new compounds; e.g. AB reacts with CD to form AD and CB
dry ice Solid carbon dioxide.
ductility Property of a metal that allows it to be drawn out into wire
dynamics Branch of *mechanics* that deals with action of forces on objects in motion. See also *statics*.
dynamo Device for converting mechanical energy into electrical energy; in simple form, consists of armature rotating between poles of powerful electromagnet.
dyne Unit of *force*; imparts acceleration of 1 cm/sec/sec to mass of 1 gram; equivalent to 10^{-5} newton.
earth In electric circuits, connection to piece of metal connected to the Earth.
efficiency Of a machine, ratio of energy output to energy input, generally expressed as percentage.
effusion Movement of gas under pressure through small hole.
elasticity Property of a material that makes it readopt its original shape after a force

Science A–Z (contd.)

deforming it is removed; if stressed beyond *elastic limit*, material does not return to its original shape. See also *Hooke's law*.

electric field Region surrounding electric charge in which a charged particle is subjected to a force.

electrical energy See *energy*.

electrochemical series List of metals in order of their electrode potentials. Each metal will displace from their salts those metals lower down in series; the most noble, unreactive metals, such as gold, appear at bottom of list. Also called *electromotive series*.

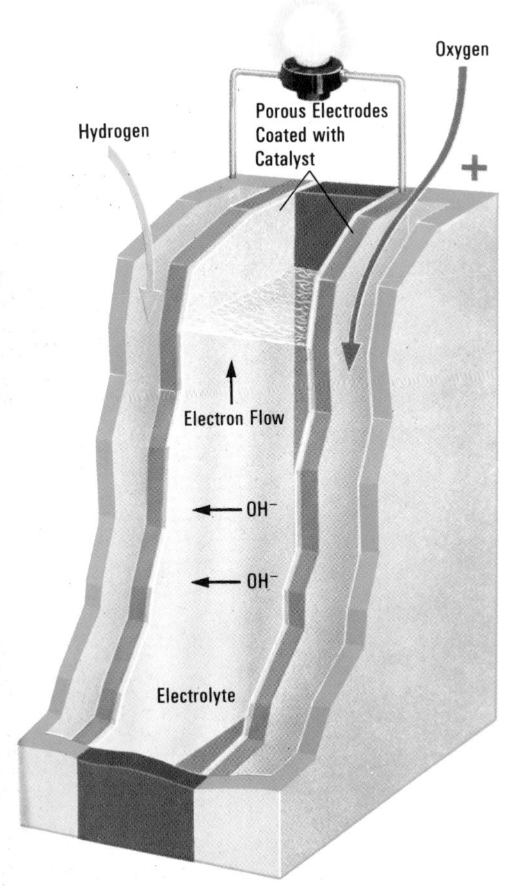

electrode Metal plate through which electric current enters or leaves electrolysis cell, battery, or vacuum tube.

electrolysis Conduction of electricity between two electrodes, through solution or molten mass (electrolyte) containing ions accompanied by chemical changes at electrodes.

electromagnet Magnet consisting of iron core surrounded by coil of wire carrying electric current.

electromagnetic units (emu) System based on unit magnetic pole.

electromagnetism Magnetism produced by flowing electric current; science that studies this phenomenon.

electromotive force (emf) Force that drives electric current along a conductor; measured in *volts*. See also *potential difference*.

electron Small, negatively charged subatomic particle; every atom has as many orbiting electrons as *protons* in nucleus. See also *current, electric*.

electron microscope Instrument that uses beam of electrons to produce magnified images of extremely small objects, beyond range of optical (light) microscope.

electron-volt (eV) Small unit of energy equal to work done on electron when it passes through potential of 1 volt; 1ev = 1.6×10^{-19} joule.

electroplating Production of thin adherent coating of one metal on another using *electrolysis*.

electrostatic units (esu) System based on force exerted between two electric charges.

element Substance made up of exactly similar *atoms* (all with same atomic number).

ellipse Plane figure formed by slicing through circular cone at angle to base.

emulsion Colloidal suspension of minute droplets of one liquid dispersed in another. See *colloid*.

In the simplest type of fuel cell, hydrogen and oxygen diffuse through the porous electrodes into the electrolyte. Hydrogen ions (OH-) form at the oxygen electrode and are attracted to the hydrogen electrode, giving the oxygen electrode a positive charge and the hydrogen a negative charge. As a result electrons flow round the circuit.

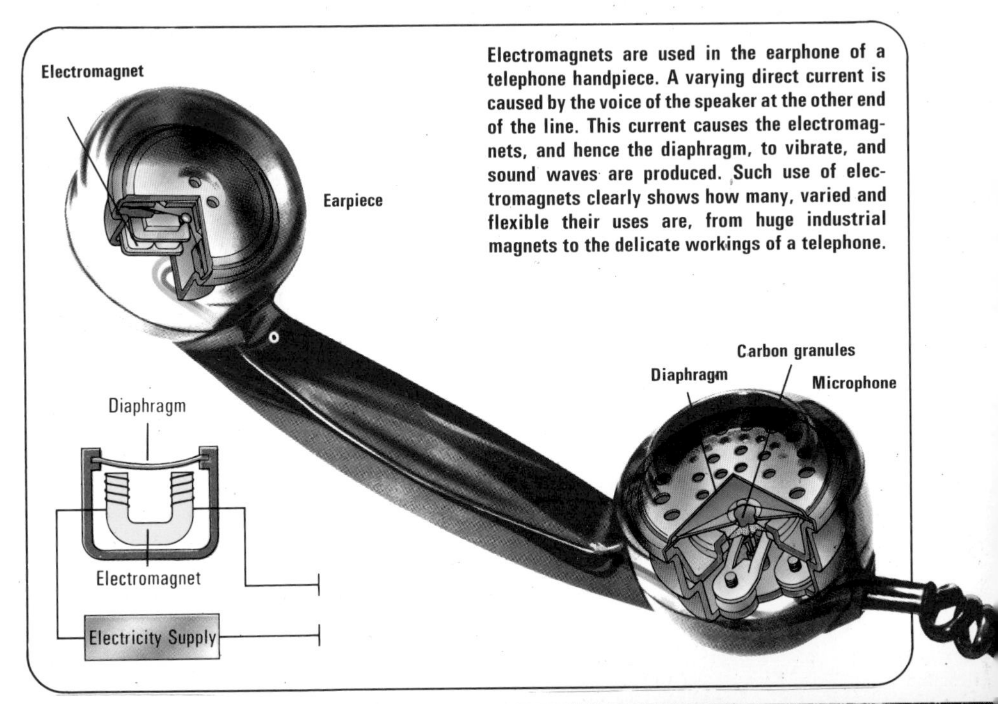

Electromagnets are used in the earphone of a telephone handpiece. A varying direct current is caused by the voice of the speaker at the other end of the line. This current causes the electromagnets, and hence the diaphragm, to vibrate, and sound waves are produced. Such use of electromagnets clearly shows how many, varied and flexible their uses are, from huge industrial magnets to the delicate workings of a telephone.

energy Capacity for doing work; examples include: *chemical energy* (possessed by substance in its atoms or molecules, and released in chemical reaction), *electrical energy* (associated with electric charges), *heat* (possessed by body because of motion of its atoms or molecules – form of kinetic energy), *kinetic energy* (possessed by body because of its motion), and *potential energy* (possessed by body because of its position). In presence of matter, any one form of energy can be converted into another.
entropy Quantity in *thermodynamics* equal to amount of heat absorbed in reversible process divided by absolute temperature at which it is taken up.
epsom salts Magnesium sulphate.
erg Absolute unit of work in *cgs system*, defined as work done by force of 1 dyne acting through 1 cm; 1 erg = 10^{-7} joule.

The turbine hall of a coal-fired power station that produces 2000 million watts. The heat energy obtained by burning the coal is converted into electrical energy by the generators.

Science A–Z (contd.)

esters Class of organic compounds formed by chemical reaction between acids and alcohols.

evaporation Phenomenon in which liquid turns into vapour, without necessarily boiling. Occurs because fast-moving molecules escape from surface of liquid. See also *boiling point*.

Fahrenheit Temperature scale on which melting point of ice is 32 °F and the boiling point of water is 212 °F.

falling bodies, laws of Distance an object falls under gravity given by $s = \frac{1}{2}gt^2$, where s is distance, g is acceleration due to gravity, and t is time taken. Its final velocity is given by $v = u + gt$, where u is initial velocity.

fallout General term for radioactive fragments and isotopes that fall to Earth from atmosphere after nuclear explosion.

farad (F) Unit of electrical *capacitance*, defined as that which requires a charge of 1 coulomb to raise its potential by 1 volt.

The froth on top of this vat of fermenting beer is caused by the action of yeast on the sugar present.

Faraday's law In an electrical circuit, any induced electromotive force is proportional to rate at which magnetic lines of force cut circuit.

fermentation Chemical reaction of organic substances brought about by bacteria, yeasts, or other fungi.

filtration Process for separating solids from suspension in liquid by straining them off, using special paper or other filter medium; pure liquid that drips through is *filtrate*.

fission (splitting) In atomic or nuclear fission, nuclei of heavy atoms split and release vast quantities of energy; this is energy-generating process of atomic bombs and nuclear reactors.

flame test Technique in chemical analysis in which element is identified by characteristic colour it imparts to gas flame.

flexibility Property of substance, such as rubber or plastic, that allows it to bend easily without breaking.

flotation Method of separating solids in which one solid is made to float on detergent-produced froth in tank of liquid.

fluid State of matter (liquid or gas) that can flow, and takes on shape of part or all of containing vessel.

fluorescence Emission of light of one wavelength (colour) after absorption of another wavelength; ceases when light source is removed (unlike *phosphorescence*).

flux Substance added to help melting, or in soldering, to clean metal surfaces to be joined.

foot-candle Unit of illumination equal to 1 lumen/ft^2. See *phot*.

foot-pound Unit of work, defined as work done by force of 1 lb acting through 1 ft.

force Agency that can make stationary body move, or moving body change speed or direction.

freezing point Temperature at which liquid changes to solid. Same as *melting point* of solid.

frequency Of a wave motion, number of vibrations or waves per second, equal to 1 divided by period (time taken for one vibration). See *wavelength*.

friction Force that resists sliding or rolling of one surface on another.

fusion (joining) In nuclear fusion (also known as a thermonuclear reaction), nuclei of light atoms join together, with the release

of vast amounts of energy; this is process that occurs in hydrogen bombs and in stars, such as Sun.
gamma-rays (γ-rays) Penetrating electromagnetic radiation of shorter wavelength than X-rays.
gas Fluid that, no matter how little there is, always takes up whole of vessel containing it. See also *vapour*.
gas constant (R) in fundamental gas equation $pV = RT$, where p = pressure, V = volume, T = absolute temperature, R = 8.31 joules/kelvin/mole. See also *Van der Waals' equation*.
gauss (G) Unit (cgs system) of magnetic induction, defined as induction produced in substance with unit magnetic permeability placed in magnetic field of 1 oersted.
Gay-Lussac's law When gases react, they combine in volumes that bear simple numerical ratio to each other and to volume of product.
Geiger counter Instrument for detecting and measuring radioactivity.
Geissler tube Electric discharge tube that glows when high voltage current flows between metal plates sealed into it.
Glauber's salt Crystalline sodium sulphate.
Graham's law Velocity of diffusion of a gas is inversely proportional to square root of its density.
gram-molecular weight See *mol*.
gravimetric analysis Chemical analysis made ultimately by weighing substances.
gravitation Force of attraction between any two objects because of their masses.
gravity, centre of Point at which all of an object's weight appears to act.

The American scientist Joseph Weber claims to have detected gravity waves coming from the centre of the Galaxy with this apparatus, shown above.

The fluorescent screen of the oscilloscope displays electrical signals in graph form. Varying electric fields deflect the fine electron beam emitted by the heated cathode, so that its bright spot traces a visible pattern on the screen.

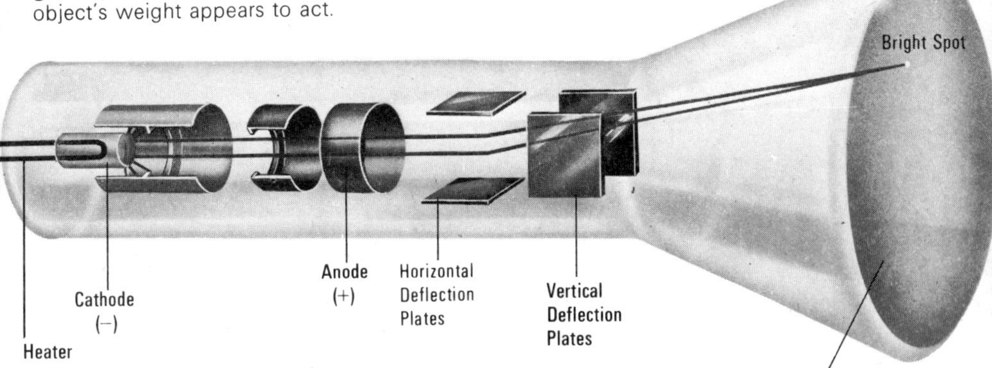

Science A–Z (contd.)

Haber process Industrial method of making ammonia from nitrogen and hydrogen in presence of catalyst.
halogens Elements of Group VII of Periodic Table; fluorine, chlorine, bromine, iodine, and astatine.
heat A form of *energy*.
heavy water Deuterium oxide, D_2O; the oxide of deuterium or 'heavy hydrogen', isotope of hydrogen having atomic mass of 2
henry (H) Unit of electrical *inductance*, defined as that producing induced electromotive force of 1 volt for a current change of 1 ampere per second.
Henry's law Weight of gas dissolved by liquid is proportional to gas pressure.
Hess's law Sum of quantities of heat evolved in each stage of multistage chemical reaction is equal to total amount of heat evolved if overall reaction proceeds in one stage.
homogenation Process for making mixture uniform (homogeneous).
homologue Member of homologous series of chemicals, such as alkanes (paraffin hydrocarbons).
Hooke's law Within elastic limit, extension (stress) is proportional to force (strain) producing it. See *elasticity*.
horsepower (hp) Unit of power, equal to work performed at rate of 550 ft-lb per sec; 1 hp = 745.7 watts. See also *watt*.
hydraulics Science that studies flow of fluids.
hydrate Compound containing chemically combined water molecules; many *salts* are hydrated by water of crystallization.
hydrocarbon Chemical compound of hydrogen and carbon.
hydrogenation Making substance combine chemically with hydrogen.
hydrolysis Decomposing substance chemically by making it react with water.
hydrostatics Branch of mechanics that deals with fluids at rest.
hydroxide Chemical compound containing the hydroxyl group –OH.
hygrometer Instrument for measuring relative humidity of the air.
hyperbola Curve traced by moving point whose distance from fixed point (*focus*) is always in same ratio, greater than 1, to its distance from fixed straight line (*directrix*). See also *parabola*.
ignition point Temperature above which substance will burn.
imaginary number Square root of a negative number; square root of −1 is imaginary number *i*.
impact (collision) See *momentum*.
incandescence Giving off light at high temperatures.
inclined plane Simple machine consisting of smooth plane sloping upwards at angle to horizontal.
indicator Substance that changes colour to indicate end of a chemical reaction or to

This aerial photograph was taken with an infra-red camera. Vegetation reflects infra-red which is why it shows up as red rather than green.

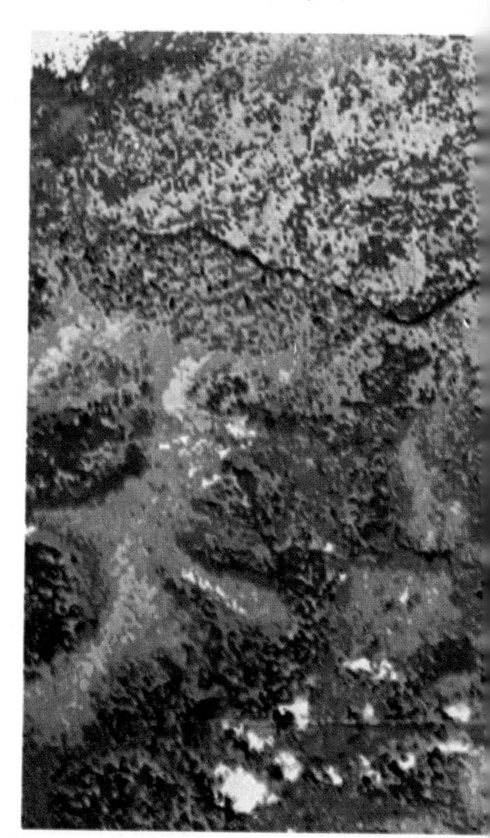

indicate the pH (acidity or alkalinity) of a solution. See *pH*.

inductance Property of electrical circuit to resist change in rate or direction of current; in single circuit called *self-inductance*, between two circuits *mutual inductance*; symbol of inductance, *L*; unit, henry.

induction, electric In *electromagnetic induction*, a moving or changing magnetic field induces an electric current in a conductor. In *electrostatic induction*, a charge on a conductor induces an opposite charge on a nearby uncharged conductor.

induction coil High voltage generator that makes use of electromagnetic induction between a coil of wire with few turns (primary) and a secondary coil with thousands of turns.

inertia Property of object that makes it resist being moved or change in its motion.

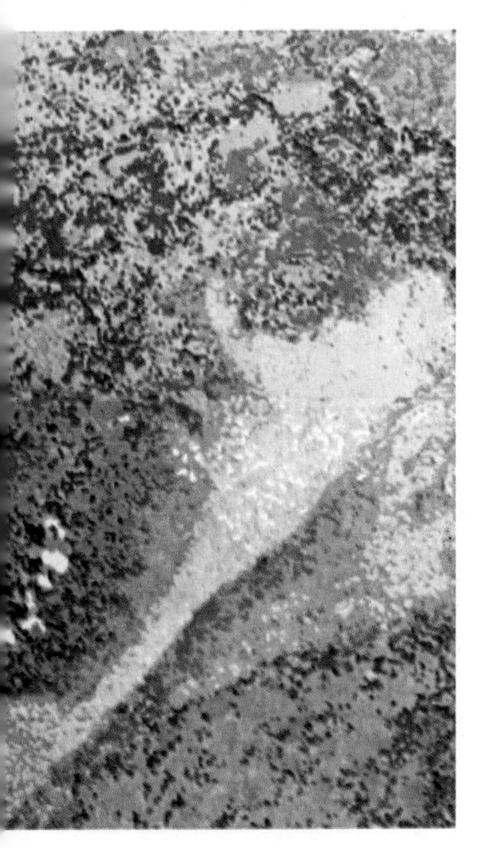

infra-red rays Electromagnetic radiation of wavelengths just longer than those of visible light; invisible heat rays.

inorganic chemistry Branch of chemistry that deals with all compounds other than those of carbon; a few carbon compounds, such as carbides, carbonates, carbon dioxide, and metallic cyanides, are also studied in inorganic chemistry. See also *organic chemistry*.

insulation Use of an insulator, a substance that is a poor conductor of heat, sound, or electricity, to prevent their passage.

insulator, electric Substance that does not conduct electricity; a non-conductor.

interference Phenomenon caused by combination of waves; spectral colours produced in thin films and by *diffraction* are examples.

interferometer Instrument that produces *interference* using two halves of a split, single light beam.

ionization Production of charged *ions* from electrically neutral *atoms* or molecular fragments; generally achieved by electrical or chemical processes.

ions Atom or group of atoms carrying an electrical charge; positively charged ions are called *cations*, negatively charged ions *anions*. During electrolysis, anions migrate towards the *anode* (positive electrode) and cations migrate towards the *cathode* (negative electrode).

isomerism Phenomenon in which two or more compounds exist with same chemical formula, but with different structures (arrangements of atoms in space).

isomorphous Having similar crystalline forms, and often similar chemical composition.

isotope One of two or more forms of an element with same atomic number (i.e. number of protons in nucleus), but different atomic masses (due to different numbers of neutrons in nucleus). See also *atom*.

joule (J) Unit of work or energy; defined as work done in 1 sec by current of 1 ampere flowing through resistance of 1 ohm; 1 J = 10^7 ergs.

kelvin (K) Unit of temperature interval; Kelvin or absolute temperature scale based on absolute zero as 0°K; on this scale, the melting point of ice is 273.15°K. To convert from Kelvin to centigrade (or Celsius), subtract 273.15 from temperature.

PHYSICS: NOBEL PRIZEWINNERS

1901	Wilhelm Roentgen (German)
1902	Hendrik Lorentz & Pieter Zeeman (Dutch)
1903	Pierre and Marie Curie & Henri Becquerel (French)
1904	Lord Rayleigh (British)
1905	Philipp Lenard (German)
1906	Sir Joseph Thomson (British)
1907	Albert Michelson (American)
1908	Gabriel Lippmann (French)
1909	Guglielmo Marconi (Italian) & Ferdinand Braun (German)
1910	Johannes van der Waals (Dutch)
1911	Wilhelm Wien (German)
1912	Nils Gustav Dalén (Swedish)
1913	Heike Kamerlingh-Onnes (Dutch)
1914	Max von Laue (German)
1915	Sir William H. Bragg & William L. Bragg (British)
1916	*No award*
1917	Charles Barkla (British)
1918	Max Planck (German)
1919	Johannes Stark (German)
1920	Charles Guillaume (Swiss)
1921	Albert Einstein (German/Swiss)
1922	Niels Bohr (Danish)
1923	Robert Millikan (American)
1924	Karl Siegbahn (Swedish)
1925	James Franck & Gustav Hertz (German)
1926	Jean Perrin (French)
1927	Arthur Compton (American) & Charles T. R. Wilson (British)
1928	Owen Richardson (British)
1929	Prince Louis Victor de Broglie (French)
1930	Sir Chandrasekhara Raman (Indian)
1931	*No award*
1932	Werner Heisenberg (German)
1933	Erwin Schrödinger (Austrian) & Paul Dirac (British)
1934	*No award*
1935	James Chadwick (British)
1936	Victor Hess (Austrian) & Carl Anderson (American)
1937	Clinton Davisson (American) & George Thomson (British)
1938	Enrico Fermi (Italian)
1939	Ernest O. Lawrence (American)
1940–42	*No award*
1943	Otto Stern (American)
1944	Isidor Isaac Rabi (American)
1945	Wolfgang Pauli (Austrian)
1946	Percy Bridgman (American)
1947	Sir Edward Appleton (British)
1948	Patrick M. S. Blackett (British)
1949	Hideki Yukawa (Japanese)
1950	Cecil Frank Powell (British)
1951	Sir John Cockroft (British) & Ernest Walton (Irish)
1952	Edward Purcell & Felix Bloch (American)
1953	Frits Zernike (Dutch)
1954	Max Born (German/British) & Walther Bothe (German)
1955	Polykarp Kusch & Willis Lamb Jr (American)
1956	William Shockley, Walter Brattain & John Bardeen (American)
1957	Tsung Dao Lee & Chen Ning Yang (Chinese/American)
1958	Pavel Cherenkov, Ilya Frank, & Igor Tamm (Russian)
1959	Emilio Segrè & Owen Chamberlain (American)
1960	Donald Glaser (American)
1961	Robert Hofstadter (American) & Rudolf Mössbauer (German)
1962	Lev Landau (Russian)
1963	Eugene Wigner (American), Maria Goeppert-Mayer (German/American), & Hans Jensen (German)
1964	Charles Townes (American) & Nikolai Basov & Alexandr Prokhorov (Russian)
1965	Richard Feynman & Julian Schwinger (American) & Shinichiro Tomonaga (Japanese)
1966	Alfred Kastler (French)
1967	Hans Bethe (American)
1968	Luis Alvarez (American)
1969	Murray Gell-Mann (American)
1970	Hannes Alfvén (Swedish) & Louis Néel (French)
1971	Dennis Gabor (British)
1972	John Bardeen, Leon Cooper, & John Schrieffer (American)
1973	Ivar Giaever (American), Leo Esaki (Japanese), & Brian Josephson (British)
1974	Sir Martin Ryle & Antony Hewish (GB)
1975	James Rainwater (US), Aage Bohr & Benjamin Mottelson (Danish)
1976	B. Richter (American) & G. Ting (American)
1977	Sir Nevill Mott (British), J. Van Vleck (American), & P. Anderson (American)
1978	P. J. Kapitsa (Russian), A. A. Penzias (American), & R. W. Wilson (American)
1979	Sheldon Glashow (American), Abdus Salam (Pakistan), & Stephen Weinberg (American)

Science A–Z (contd.)

ketones Class of organic compound containing the characteristic group =CO. See also *aldehydes*.
kilowatt A thousand *watts*.
kinematics Branch of mechanics that deals with movement independent of forces or masses.
kinetic energy See *energy*.
laser Type of *maser* that produces intense beam of light that is monochromatic (single colour) and coherent (all its waves are in step); abbreviation for *l*ight *a*mplification by *s*timulated *e*mission of *r*adiation.
latent heat Heat absorbed without temperature rise to change substance from solid to liquid or liquid to gas.
Lenz's law When a wire moves in a magnetic field, the electric current induced in the wire generates a magnetic field that tends to oppose the movement. See *induction*.
lever Simple machine consisting of rigid beam pivoted at one point, called the *fulcrum*; effort applied at one point on beam can lift load at another point.
linear equation Algebraic equation of first power; in co-ordinate geometry, it represents straight line.
liquid Fluid that, without changing its volume, takes up shape of all or lower part of vessel containing it.
litmus Chemical *indicator*, vegetable dye that is red in acid solutions and blue in alkaline solutions.
logarithm Of a number, power to which the base must be raised to equal the number; if $A = B^n$, n is the logarithm of A expressed to the base B.
lumen (lm) Unit of luminous flux equal to amount of light emitted by source of 1 candela/sec through unit solid angle.
luminescence Emission of light at low temperatures; *fluorescence* and *phosphorescence* are examples.
luminosity Brightness.
lux (lx) Unit of illumination equal to 1 lumen/m^2.
magneto High-voltage electric generator in which permanent magnet is spun inside coil; gives only short pulses of current; used for starting petrol engines. See also *dynamo*.
malleability Property of a metal that allows it to be beaten into thin sheet.
maser Microwave amplifier that uses energy changes within atoms or molecules; abbreviation for *m*icrowave *a*mplification by *s*timulated *e*mission of *r*adiation.
mass Amount of matter in an object; SI unit, kg. See also *weight*.
mass action, law of Speed of chemical reaction is proportional to active masses (concentrations) of reactants.
mass spectroscopy Technique of identifying or analysing mixture of elements by measuring masses of their atoms.
maxwell Unit of magnetic flux (cgs system), defined as flux through each square centimetre at rightangles to magnetic field of 1 gauss intensity; 1 maxwell = 10^{-8} weber.
mean Mathematical average of group of numbers, given by their sum divided by the number of them.
mechanics Branch of science that deals with behaviour of matter under action of force.
median Line from vertex (point) of triangle to mid-point of opposite side.
melting point Temperature at which solid turns to liquid; equal to *freezing point* of the liquid.
meson One of a group of unstable subatomic particles with masses between those of *electron* and *proton*.
metal Element or alloy that is a good conductor of heat and electricity, has a high density, often has characteristic lustre, and can generally be worked' by beating or drawing into wire.
metalloid Element with properties of both metals and non-metals.
micron (μm) Unit of length equal to 10^{-6} metre.
microwaves Short-wavelength radio waves (electromagnetic radiation) having wavelengths of approximately 0.1 to 30 cm.
mixture More than one element or compound together, but not in chemical combination; components can be separated by physical means.
mks system Metric system of units based on metre, kilogram, second; superseded by *SI units* based on mks.
mole (mol) Basic unit of amount of substance; weight of substance equal to its molecular weight in grams (e.g. 1 mole H_2O has mass 18.015 g); *molar solution*

Science A–Z (contd.)

contains 1 mol in 1 litre of solution.

molecular weight Sum of the *atomic weights* of the elements in one molecule of a compound.

molecule Smallest particle of a chemical substance that can exist alone; made up of one or more atoms.

momentum Of moving object, product of mass and velocity. According to principle of conservation of momentum, when two or more objects collide, total momentum before impact equals total momentum after impact.

monomer Type of chemical compound, having small molecules, capable of undergoing *polymerization*.

motion (movement) See *Newton's laws of motion*.

neutralization Combining acid and alkali so that resulting solution is neutral (neither acid nor alkaline). See also *indicator*.

neutron Uncharged subatomic particle found in the nuclei of all atoms except hydrogen.

newton (N) Unit of force, defined as that imparting acceleration of 1 m/sec/sec to mass of 1 kg.

Newton's laws of motion (1) A stationary object remains still or a moving object continues to move in a straight line unless acted on by an external force. (2) Force producing acceleration in an object is proportional to the product of the object's mass and its acceleration. (3) Every action has an equal and opposite reaction.

Newton's rings *Interference* bands produced in thin film of air, as between convex lens and plane mirror.

noble metals Chemically unreactive metals such as gold, silver, and platinum.

nylon Plastic material of polyamide type.

oersted Unit of magnetic field strength, defined as force in dynes experienced by unit magnetic pole in the field.

ohm (Ω) Unit of electrical resistance, given by potential difference across conductor in volts divided by current in amperes flowing through conductor.

Ohm's law Voltage (*V*) in volts between ends of a conductor equals product of current (*I*) in amps flowing through it and its resistance (*R*) in ohms, i.e. $V = IR$.

organic chemistry Branch of chemistry that deals with the many compounds of carbon; a few carbon compounds are studied under *inorganic chemistry*.

oscillograph *Oscilloscope* fitted with camera for photographing the 'trace'.

oscilloscope Electronic instrument in which electric signal, or anything that can be reduced to an electric signal, is displayed as 'trace' by spot of light moving on cathode ray tube screen.

osmosis In solutions, flow of water or other solvent through *semipermeable mem-*

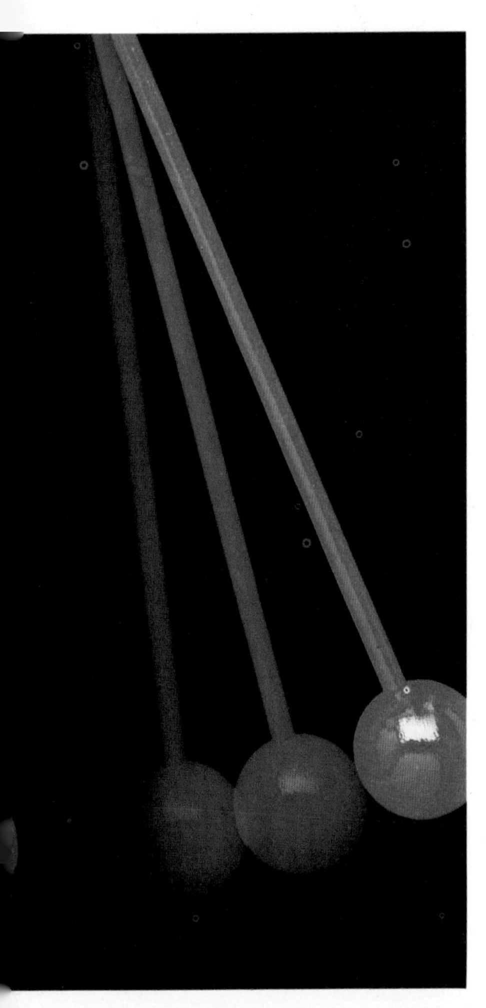

This line of balls demonstrates the principle of momentum. Momentum is transferred from a moving object to a stationary object if the two collide. Here, the swinging ball hits a line of stationary balls, and its momentum is transferred along the line to the last ball, which swings outwards.

brane because of different concentrations on each side of membrane.

osmotic pressure Pressure to which solution must be subjected in order to stop solvent flowing through *semipermeable membrane* between solution and solvent by process of *osmosis*.

oxidation Making substance combine with oxygen; removing hydrogen from substance; or raising oxidation number of an element (i.e. making it lose electrons). See *reduction*.

oxide Chemical compound of oxygen and another element.

oxidizing agent Substance that causes *oxidation*.

ozone Allotrope of oxygen containing three atoms in each molecule; O_3.

parabola Curve formed by slicing circular cone parallel to one of its sloping sides; may be traced by point that is always equidistant from fixed point F (*focus*) and fixed straight line AB (*directrix*). See also *hyperbola*.

parity (Mirror symmetry) According to principle of conservation of parity, there is no basic difference between left and right, principle does not apply to some reactions of atomic particles.

partial pressure Fraction of total pressure of mixture of gasses exerted by one of component gases. See *Dalton's Law of partial pressures*.

pascal (Pa) Unit of pressure; 1 Pa = 1 newton/m^2.

Pascal's law In a fluid, pressure applied at any point is transmitted equally throughout it.

passivity of metals Chemical unreactivity caused by oxidation of the surface of the metal.

pasteurization Prolonged heating of a liquid, such as wine or milk, to temperature sufficient to kill the bacteria in it; partial sterilization.

pendulum Device consisting of weight (bob) swinging at end of rigid or flexible support; *period* (time of one swing) of simple pendulum, which has flexible support such as length of cord, is independent of weight of bob, depending only on length of cord.

Periodic Table Organized arrangement of the chemical elements, in order of increasing atomic number; elements with similar chemical properties fall in vertical columns called Groups.

permutation Arrangement of set of specified number of different objects;

CHEMISTRY: NOBEL PRIZEWINNERS

Year	Winner(s)
1901	Jacobus van't Hoff (Dutch)
1902	Emil Fischer (German)
1903	Svante Arrhenius (Swedish)
1904	Sir William Ramsay (British)
1905	Adolf von Baeyer (German)
1906	Henri Moissan (French)
1907	Eduard Buchner (German)
1908	Ernest Rutherford (New Zealand/ British)
1909	Wilhelm Ostwald (German)
1910	Otto Wallach (German)
1911	Marie Curie (French)
1912	Victor Grignard & Paul Sabatier (French)
1913	Alfred Werner (Swiss)
1914	Theodore Richards (American)
1915	Richard Willstätter (German)
1916–17	*No award*
1918	Fritz Haber (German)
1919	*No award*
1920	Walther Nernst (German)
1921	Frederick Soddy (British)
1922	Francis Aston (British)
1923	Fritz Pregl (Austrian)
1924	*No award*
1925	Richard Zsigmondy (German)
1926	Theodor Svedberg (Swedish)
1927	Heinrich Wieland (German)
1928	Adolf Windaus (German)
1929	Arthur Harden (British) & Hans von Euler-Chelpin (German/ Swedish)
1930	Hans Fischer (German)
1931	Carl Bosch & Friedrich Bergius (German)
1932	Irving Langmuir (American)
1933	*No award*
1934	Harold Urey (American)
1935	Frédéric and Irène Joliot-Curie (French)
1936	Peter Debye (Dutch)
1937	Walter Haworth (British) & Paul Karrer (Swiss)
1938	Richard Kuhn (German)
1939	Adolf Butenandt (German) & Leopold Ružička (Swiss)
1940–42	*No award*
1943	Georg von Hevesy (Hungarian/ Swedish)
1944	Otto Hahn (German)
1945	Artturi Virtanen (Finnish)
1946	James Sumner, John Northrop, & Wendell Stanley (American)
1947	Sir Robert Robinson (British)
1948	Arne Tiselius (Swedish)
1949	William Giauque (American)
1950	Otto Diels & Kurt Alder (German)
1951	Glenn Seaborg & Edwin McMillan (American)
1952	Archer Martin & Richard Synge (British)
1953	Hermann Staudinger (German)
1954	Linus Pauling (American)
1955	Vincent du Vigneaud (American)
1956	Sir Cyril Hinshelwood (British) & Nikolai Semenov (Russian)
1957	Sir Alexander Todd (British)
1958	Frederick Sanger (British)
1959	Jaroslav Heyrovsky (Czechoslovakian)
1960	Willard Libby (American)
1961	Melvin Calvin (American)
1962	Max Perutz & John Kendrew (British)
1963	Karl Ziegler (German) & Giulio Natta (Italian)
1964	Dorothy Crowfoot Hodgkin (British)
1965	Robert Woodward (American)
1966	Robert Mulliken (American)
1967	Ronald Norrish & George Porter (British) & Manfred Eigen (German)
1968	Lars Onsager (American)
1969	Derek Barton (British) & Odd Hassel (Norwegian)
1970	Luis Leloir (Argentinian)
1971	Gerhard Herzberg (Canadian)
1972	Christian Anfinsen, Stanford Moore, & William Stein (American)
1973	Ernst Otto Fischer (West German) & Geoffrey Wilkinson (British)
1974	Paul Flory (American)
1975	John Cornforth (Australian) & Vladmir Prelog (Swiss)
1976	W. N. Lipscomb (American)
1977	L. Prigogine (Belgian)
1978	Peter Mitchell (British)
1979	Herbert C. Brown (American) & Georg Wittig (German)

number of permutations of three objects *a, b, c* is 6; *abc, acb, bac, bca, cab, cba*. 'Permutations' used in football pools are *combinations*, not permutations.

petrochemicals Range of chemicals derived from petroleum (natural gas and crude oil).

pH Measure of acidity or alkalinity of a liquid; pH of 7 is neutral, lower numbers are acidic, higher numbers alkaline; pH number is the negative logarithm of the hydrogen ion concentration.

Science A–Z (contd.)

pharmacology Science that deals with drugs and their action on animals and man.
phon Unit of loudness.
phosphate Salt of phosphoric acid.
phosphorescence Re-emission of absorbed light even after light source is removed. See *fluorescence*.
phot Unit of illumination equal to 1 lumen/cm². See *foot-candle*.
photon Quantum (packet of energy) of electromagnetic radiation, such as light.
physical change Change of form, as in melting, as opposed to chemical change.
physical chemistry Branch of chemistry that deals with physical changes accompanying chemical reactions, and the way chemical composition affects physical properties.
Planck's constant (h) Constant relating frequency (υ) of radiation with energy (E): $E = h\upsilon$; $h = 6.62 \times 10^{-34}$ joule second.
pneumatic Operated by air pressure.
polarized light Light in which electric and magnetic vibrations are restricted to two planes at right-angles, instead of being possible in all planes.
polymer High-molecular-weight chemical compound obtained by *polymerization*; most plastics are polymers. See also *monomer*.
polymerization Chemical process in which many molecules of *monomer* join together to give a *polymer*.
polymorphism Phenomenon in which chemical substance occurs in more than two crystalline forms. See *dimorphism*.
porosity Property of substance that allows gases or liquids to pass through it.
potential difference Exists between two points of differing electric potential; if connected, current flows between them; measured by work done moving unit charge between them; unit, *volt*. See also *electromotive force*.
potential energy See *energy*.
power Rate of doing work, generally expressed in watts or horsepower.
precipitation Formation and throwing out of solution of insoluble compound as *precipitate*, often achieved by *double decomposition*.
pressure Force per unit area, measured in newtons/m² or dynes/cm².
probability (likelihood) In mathematics, if an event can happen in a ways and not happen in b ways, the probability that it will happen is $a/(a+b)$ and that it will not happen is $b/(a+b)$; the sum of the various probabilities is always 1.
progression Mathematical series of terms; in *arithmetical progressions*, each term bears common difference to preceding term; in *geometrical progressions*, each term is larger than preceding term by constant factor.
proton Positively charged subatomic particle found in nuclei of all atoms.
pulley Grooved wheel round which rope or chain runs.

This giant crane in Harland and Wolff Ltd's shipyards in Belfast uses pulleys to lift immensely heavy loads.

Pythagorean theorem In a right-angled triangle, the square on the hypotenuse (longest side) is equal to the sum of the squares on the other two sides.
quadratic equation Algebraic expression of the second (square) power, which has two possible values (roots) of the unknown.
quantum theory Theory that light and other forms of energy are given off as separate packets (quanta) of energy.
rad Unit of absorbed dose of ionizing radiation, equal to energy absorption of 100 ergs/gram of substance irradiated. See *rem*.
radical Any characteristic group of atoms (e.g. the ammonium ion, NH_4^+).

Science A–Z (contd.)

radioactivity Emission of radiation, such as *alpha-rays, beta-rays,* and *gamma-rays*, from unstable elements by spontaneous splitting of their atomic nuclei.
rare earths Series of metallic elements, beginning with lanthanum, of atomic numbers 57 to 71, and having very similar chemical properties; also called *lanthanides*.
reaction Chemical process involving two or more substances (*reactants*) in which chemical change takes place.
reagent Chemical compound or solution used in carrying out chemical reactions.
reducing agent Substance that reacts chemically to remove oxygen or add hydrogen to another substance. See *reduction; oxidizing agent*.
reduction Making a substance react with hydrogen, removing oxygen from a substance, or lowering an element's oxidation number (i.e. making it accept electrons). See *oxidation*.
reflection Return or bouncing back of sound wave or electromagnetic radiation, such as a light ray, after it strikes a surface.
refraction Bending of a light ray as it crosses boundary between two media of different optical density.

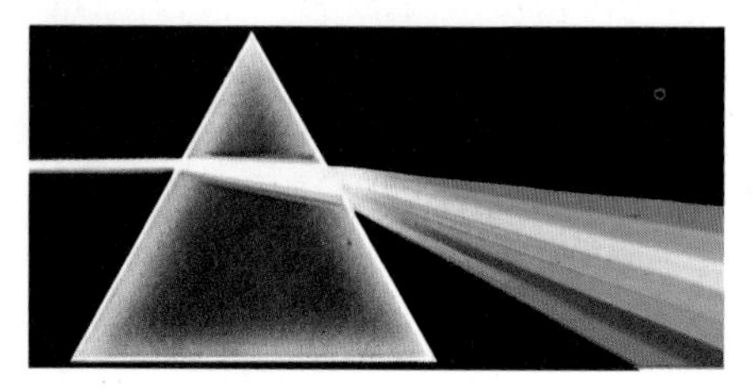

Splitting of white light into its components by refraction through a prism.

relativity Einstein's theory that it is impossible to measure motion absolutely, but only within a given frame of reference.
reluctance In a magnetic circuit, the magnetomotive force divided by the flux that generates it.
rem Abbreviation for *Roentgen equivalent mean*, dose of ionizing radiation that has same effect as 1 roentgen of X-rays. See *rad; roentgen*.
resistance Property of electrical conductor that makes it oppose flow of current through it. See *Ohm's law*.
reversible reaction Chemical reaction that can go in either direction. See also *dissociation*.
rheostat Variable resistance.
roentgen Quantity of X-rays that produce ions carrying 1 electrostatic unit of electricity in 1 cm^3 of air.
salt Chemical compound formed, with water, when a *base* reacts with an *acid*; a salt is also formed, often with production of hydrogen, when a metal reacts with an acid. *Common salt* is sodium chloride.
saturated solution Solution that will take up no more solute (dissolved substance).
semiconductor Substance, such as germanium and gallium arsenide, in which electrical resistance falls as its temperature rises. Used for making diodes and transistors.
semi-permeable membrane Membrane that allows some substances to pass through it but not others; see *osmosis*.
set theory Branch of mathematics that deals with objects as collections, called *sets*, and their interrelationships.
SI units (Système International d'Unités) Internationally agreed system built round seven basic units and replacing cgs and mks systems for scientific purposes:
silicones Group of synthetic rubbery substances made from derivatives of siloxane.
sine Trigonometrical ratio given (for an angle) in right-angled triangle by length of the side opposite the angle divided by the hypotenuse (longest side).
soda *Washing soda* is sodium carbonate; *baking soda* is sodium bicarbonate; *caustic soda* is sodium hydroxide.
solder Alloy, generally of tin and lead, having low melting point, used for joining metals.
solenoid Coil consisting of many turns of wire wound on hollow tube; behaves as magnet when carrying electric current.
solid State of matter that has definite shape and resists having it changed; crystalline solid melts to a liquid on heating above its melting point.
solid state physics Branch of physics that deals with matter in the solid state, particularly *semiconductors*.
solubility Quantity of substance (solute) that will dissolve in solvent to form solution.

solvent Liquid component of a solution.
specific gravity Ratio of density of a substance to that of water at 4°C; equals density when density is expressed in g/cm^3.
specific heat Quantity of heat needed to raise temperature of unit mass of a substance by 1 degree; in SI units, joules/kg/kelvin.
spectrograph Instrument for producing and photographing spectra.
spectroscope Instrument for splitting the various wavelengths (colours) from a single light source into a spectrum, using glass prism or diffraction grating.
spectrum analysis Method of identifying elements by means of their spectra, produced when the element is heated to incandescence.
speed Distance travelled by moving object divided by time taken. Speed in a particular direction is *velocity*.

A balloon can be used to demonstrate the effects of static electricity. When rubbed up and down against a fabric such as wool it becomes charged with static electricity. It will then cling for a time to a surface such as a ceiling.

standard temperature and pressure (STP) Temperature of 0°C and pressure of 760 mm of mercury, under which volumes of gases are compared; also called *normal temperature and pressure* (NTP).
static electricity Electricity involving charges at rest.
statics Branch of mechanics that deals with the action of forces on stationary objects.
sublimation Phenomenon in which a substance, on heating, changes directly from solid to gas or vapour without first melting to liquid.

Science A–Z (contd.)

sulphate Salt of sulphuric acid.
sulphide Chemical compound of sulphur and another element.
superconductivity Phenomenon, occurring at very low temperatures (approaching *absolute zero*), in which a metal continues to conduct an electric current without application of external electromotive force; the metal's resistance is effectively zero.
supersaturation Ability of some undisturbed solutions of being able to hold more dissolved substance (solute) than normal *saturated solution*.
surface tension Property of the surface of a liquid that makes it behave as though it were covered with a thin elastic skin; caused by forces of attraction between molecules in the surface. See also *capillarity*.
suspension System consisting of very fine solid particles evenly dispersed in liquid.
synchrocyclotron Cyclotron in which accelerating electric field is pulsed to give particles of very high energies.
synchrotron Cyclotron with pulsed magnetic field, but constant-frequency electric field.

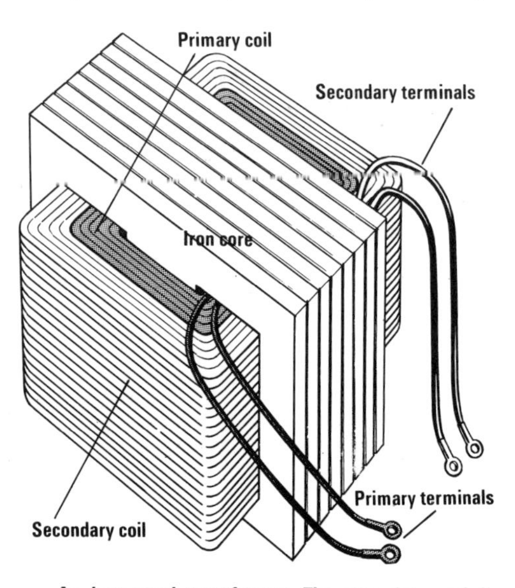

An iron-cored transformer. The secondary coil is wrapped round the primary. Voltage of current fed into the primary coil can be increased or reduced in the secondary coil by varying the number of turns in the coils.

tangent (1) Straight line touching curve at a point. (2) Trigonometrical ratio given (for an angle) in right-angled triangle by length of the side opposite the angle divided by length of the side adjacent to the angle.
temperature Degree of heat of an object referred to an arbitrary zero (see *centigrade, Fahrenheit*) or to absolute zero (see *Kelvin*).
thermocouple Device consisting of two dissimilar metals joined together, that generates small electric current when junction is heated; used for measuring temperature.
thermodynamics Branch of physics that deals with processes in which energy is conserved but heat changes take place.
thermoelectricity Electricity generated by means of heat, generally at junction between two dissimilar metals. See *thermocouple*.
thermostat Control device, sensitive to changes in temperature, that maintains temperature in an enclosure within narrow, predetermined range.
torque Turning moment produced about an axis by force acting at right-angles to a radius from the axis.
transformer Electrical machine for converting alternating-current voltage to higher or lower voltage.
transistor Semiconductor device that can amplify electric current.
transmutation of elements Changing of one element into another; impossible by ordinary chemical processes, but can be achieved using atom-smashing machines, such as *cyclotron*.
trigonometry Branch of mathematics based on properties of the triangle, particularly various relationships between lengths of sides and size of angles.
UHF Ultra-high frequency radio waves.
ultrasonic waves 'Sound' waves beyond range of human hearing.
ultraviolet rays Electromagnetic radiation of wavelengths just shorter than those of visible light.
vacuum Ideally, region in which gas pressure is zero; in practice, region in which pressure is considerably less than atmospheric pressure.
valency Number of hydrogen atoms (or their equivalent) with which an atom can combine.

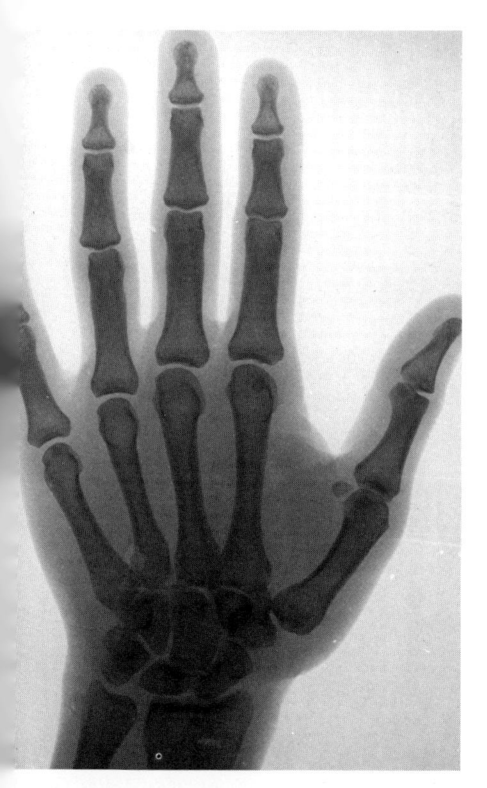

Doctors make extensive use of X-ray photography in the treatment of patients. X-rays are more greatly absorbed by bones than flesh, so on an X-ray photograph the two are easily distinguished, and any break in a bone will be clearly seen. This picture shows that the patient's hand is undamaged.

Van der Waals' equation Equation of state for gases taking into account mutual attraction of molecules: $(p + a/v^2)\ (v - b)$ $+ RT$, where a and b are constants for particular gas, and R is gas constant. See *gas constant*.
vapour Gas that can be turned into liquid by compressing it without cooling.
vapour density Density of gas or vapour, generally with respect to that of hydrogen; equal numerically to half molecular weight of gas.
vector Physical quantity that needs direction as well as magnitude to define it (e.g. velocity).
velocity Rate of change of position, equal to *speed* in a particular direction.
VHF Very high frequency radio waves.
vinyl Organic radical, $H_2C = CH$, derived from ethylene.
viscosity Property of fluid (liquid or gas) that makes it resist internal movement; sticky or thick liquids are highly viscous.
volt (V) Unit of electromotive force and potential difference, defined as potential difference between two points on conductor with current of 1 ampere when power dissipated between points is 1 watt.
volumetric analysis Method of chemical analysis using only liquids and their volumes.
water of crystallization One or more molecules of water included in crystals of substances called *hydrates*.
watt (W) Unit of electrical power, defined as the rate of work done in *joules* per second; equal to product of current (A) in amperes and potential difference in volts (V), W = AV.
wavelength Of a wave motion, distance between crests (or troughs) of two consecutive waves; equal to velocity of wave divided by its frequency.
waves Regular disturbances that carry energy. Particles of a medium may vibrate; e.g. air molecules vibrate when sound waves pass, and water molecules vibrate when ripples cross water; or electromagnetic vectors may be displaced, as when light waves pass.
weber (Wb) Unit of magnetic flux, equal to 10^8 *maxwells*.
weight Force of attraction (due to gravity) between an object and Earth; in gravitational units, weight is numerically equal to *mass*.
Wheatstone bridge Electrical circuit for measuring resistance, consisting of battery, galvanometer, three known resistances, and resistance to be measured.
Wilson cloud chamber Apparatus in which charged particles leave miniature vapour trails that reveal their paths.
work Done by a moving force; equal to the product of the force and distance it moves along its line of action; measured in *joules*, *ergs*, etc.
X-rays Very short wavelength electromagnetic waves produced when stream of high-energy electrons bombards matter.
Young's modulus For stretched wire, ratio of cross-sectional stress to longitudinal strain.

Weights and measures

Length

Metric units
millimetre (mm)
10 mm=1 centimetre (cm)
100 cm=1 metre (m)
1,000 m=1 kilometre (km)

1 micron (μ)=10^{-6}m (i.e. 1 micrometre)
1 millimicron (mμ)=10^{-9}m (i.e. 1 nanometre)
1 angstrom (Å)=10^{-10}m (i.e. 100 picometres)

Imperial units
inch (in)
12 in=1 foot (ft)
3 ft=1 yard (yd)
1,760 yd=1 mile=5,280 ft

1 mil=$\frac{1}{1000}$ in
12 lines=1 in
1 link=7.92 in
100 links=1 chain=22 yd
1 rod, pole, or perch=$5\frac{1}{2}$ yd
4 rods=1 chain
10 chains=1 furlong=220 yd
8 furlongs=1 mile
3 miles=1 league (statute)

Area

Metric units
square millimetre (mm²)
100 mm²=1 square centimetre (cm²)
10,000 cm²=1 square metre (m²)
100 m²=1 are (a)=1 square decametre
100 a=1 hectare (ha)=1 square hectometre
100 ha=1 square kilometre (km²)

Imperial units
square inch (in²)
144 in²=1 square foot (ft²)
9 ft²=1 square yard (yd²)
4,840 yd²=1 acre
640 acres=1 square mile (mile²)

625 square links=1 square rod
16 square rods=1 square chain
10 square chains=1 acre
36 square miles=1 township (US)

Human beings are unable to lift extremely heavy weights. The world record is about 250 kilograms.

Angle

second (″)
60″ = 1 minute (′)
60′ = 1 degree (°)
90° = 1 quadrant, or right-angle
4 quadrants = 1 circle = 360°
1 radian = 57.2958° = 57°17′44.8″
2π radians = 1 circle = 360°
1° = 0.017453 radian

Volume

Metric units
cubic millimetre (mm³)
1,000 mm³=1 cubic centimetre (cm³)
1,000 cm³=1 cubic decimetre (dm³)=1 litre
1,000 dm³=1 cubic metre (m³)
1,000,000,000 m³=1 cubic kilometre (km³)

Imperial units
cubic inch (in³)
1,728 in³=1 cubic foot (ft³)
27 ft³=1 cubic yard (yd³)
5,451,776,000 yd³=1 cubic mile (mile³)

Capacity

Metric units
millilitre (ml)
1,000 ml=1 litre (l)
100 l=1 hectolitre (hl)

Imperial units
gill
4 gills=1 pint
2 pints=1 quart
4 quarts=1 gallon=277.274 in^3

(dry)
2 gallons=1 peck
4 pecks=1 bushel
8 bushels=1 quarter
36 bushels=1 chaldron

(Apothecaries' fluid)
minim (min)
60 min=1 fluid drachm (fl dr.)
8 fl. dr.=1 fluid ounce (fl. oz)
5 fl. oz=1 gill
20 fl. oz=1 pint
US units
60 minims (US)=1 fluid dram (US)
8 fluid drams (US)=1 fluid ounce (US)
1 US gallon (liquid)=0.8327 gallon (imp.)
1 US gallon (dry)=0.9689 gallon (imp.)
1 fluid oz (US)=1.0408 fl. oz (apoth.)

Weight

Metric units
milligram (mg)
1,000 mg=1 gram (g)
1,000 g=1 kilogram (kg)
100 kg=1 quintal (q)
1,000 kg=1 metric ton, or tonne (t)

Imperial units (Avoirdupois)
grain (gr); dram (dr)
7,000 gr=1 pound (lb)
16 dr=1 ounce (oz)
16 oz=1 lb
14 lb=1 stone
28 lb=1 quarter
112 lb=1 hundredweight (cwt)
20 cwt=1 (long) ton=2,240 lb
2,000 lb=1 short ton (US)
(Troy)
24 gr=1 pennyweight (dwt)
20 dwt=1 (Troy) ounce=480 gr
12 (Troy) oz=1 (Troy) lb (US)=5,760 gr
(Apothecaries')
20 gr=1 scruple
3 scruples=1 drachm
8 drachms=1 (apoth.) ounce=480 gr
12 (apoth.) oz=1 (apoth.) pound=0.82 lb

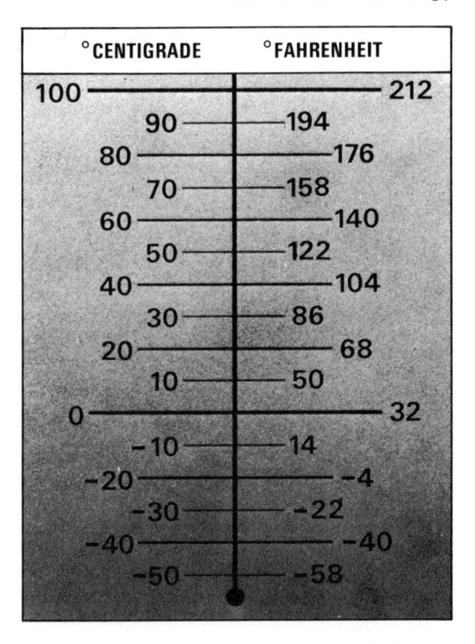

USEFUL FORMULAE*

Circumference	
Circle	$2\pi r$
Area	
Circle	πr^2
Surface of sphere	$4\pi r^2$
Ellipse, semi-axes *a, b*	πab
Triangle, base *b*	$\frac{1}{2}bh$
Rectangle, sides *a, b*	ab
Trapezium, parallel sides *a, c*	$\frac{1}{2}h(a+c)$
Regular pentagon, side *a*	$1.721a^2$
Regular hexagon, side *a*	$2.598a^2$
Regular octagon, side *a*	$4.828a^2$
Volume	
Sphere	$\frac{4}{3}\pi r^3$
Cylinder	$h\pi r^2$
Cone	$\frac{1}{3}h\pi r^2$
Rectangular prism, sides *a, b, c*	abc
Pyramid, base area *b*	$\frac{1}{3}hb$

Algebraic
$a^2-b^2 = (a+b)(a-b)$
$a^2+2ab+b^2 = (a+b)^2$
$a^2-2ab+b^2 = (a-b)^2$
For quadratic equation $ax^2+bx+c=0$,

$$x = \frac{-b \pm \sqrt{b^2-4ac}}{2a}$$

*r=radius, h=height

Weights and measures (contd.)

Miscellaneous measures

Nautical
1 span = 9 in
8 spans = 1 fathom = 6 ft
1 cable's length = $\frac{1}{10}$ nautical mile
1 nautical mile (old) = 6,080 ft
1 nautical mile (international) = 6,076.1 ft
= 1.151 statute miles (= 1,852 metres)
60 nautical miles = 1 degree
3 nautical miles = 1 league (nautical)
1 knot = 1 nautical mile per hour
1 ton (shipping, UK) = 42 cubic feet
1 ton (displacement) = 35 cubic feet
1 ton (register) = 100 cubic feet

Crude oil (petroleum)
1 barrel = 35 imperial gallons
= 42 US gallons

Timber
1,000 millisteres = 1 stere = 1 m^3
1 board foot = 144 in^3 (12×12×1 in)
1 cord foot = 16 ft^3
1 cord = 8 cord feet
1 hoppus foot = $4/\pi$ ft^3 (round timber)
1 Petrograd standard = 165 ft^3

Paper (writing)
24 sheets = 1 quire
20 quires = 1 ream = 480 sheets

Printing
1 point = $\frac{1}{72}$ in
1 pica = $\frac{1}{6}$ in = 12 points

Cloth
1 ell = 45 in
1 bolt = 120 ft = 32 ells

Brewing
9 gallons = 1 firkin
4 firkins = 1 barrel = 36 gallons
6 firkins = 1 hogshead = 54 gallons
4 hogsheads = 1 tun

HISTORICAL UNITS

where used	current equivalent
Cubit (elbow to fingertip)	
Egypt (2650 B.C.)	52.4 cm 20.6 in
Babylon (1500 B.C.)	53.0 cm 20.9 in
Assyrian (700 B.C.)	54.9 cm 21.6 in
Jerusalem (A.D. 1)	52.3 cm 20.6 in
Druid England (A.D. 1)	51.8 cm 20.4 in
Black Cubit (Arabia A.D. 800s)	54.1 cm 21.3 in
Mexico (Aztec)	52.5 cm 20.7 in
Ancient China	53.2 cm 20.9 in
Ancient Greece	46.3 cm 18.2 in
England	45.7 cm 18.0 in
Northern Cubit (c. 3000 B.C. – A.D. 1800s)	67.6 cm 26.6 in
Foot (length of foot)	
Athens	31.6 cm 12.44 in
Aegina	31.4 cm 12.36 in
Miletus	31.8 cm 12.52 in
Olympia	32.1 cm 12.64 in
Etruria	31.6 cm 12.44 in
Rome	29.6 cm 11.66 in
Northern	33.5 cm 13.19 in
England (Medieval)	33.5 cm 13.19 in
France	32.5 cm 12.79 in
Moscow	33.4 cm 13.17 in

Ancient Greece
1 digit (= 1.84 cm = 0.72 in)
100 digits = 1 orguia (about 6 ft)
10 orguias = 1 amma (about 20 yd)
10 ammas = 1 stadion (= 184 m = about 200 yd)

Ancient Rome
1 digitus (= 1.85 cm = 0.73 in)
4 digiti = 1 palmus (= 7.4 cm = 2.9 in)
4 palmi = 1 pes (= 29.6 cm = 11.7 in)
5 pes = 1 passus (= 1.48 m = 4.86 ft)
125 passus = 1 stadium (= 185 m = 202.3 yd)
8 stadia = 1 milliar (= 1,480 m = 0.92 mile)

Time

second (s, or sec)
60 s = 1 minute (min)
60 min = 1 hour (h, or hr)
24 h = 1 day (d)
7 days = 1 week
365¼ days = 1 year
10 years = 1 decade
100 years = 1 century
1,000 years = 1 millennium
1 mean solar day = 24 h 3 min 56.555 s
1 sidereal day = 23 h 56 min 4.091 s
1 solar, tropical, or equinoctial year = 365.2422 d (365 d 5 h 48 min 46 s)
1 siderial year = 365.2564 d (365 d 6 h 9 min 9.5 s)
1 synodic (lunar) month = 29.5306 d
1 siderial month = 27.3217 d
1 lunar year = 354 d = 12 synodic months

CONVERSION FACTORS

1 acre = 0.4047 hectares
1 bushel (imp.) = 36.369 litres
1 centimetre = 0.3937 inch
1 chain = 20.1168 metres
1 cord = 3.62456 cubic metres
1 cubic centimetre = 0.0610 cubic inch
1 cubic decimetre = 61.024 cubic inches
1 cubic foot = 0.0283 cubic metre
1 cubic inch = 16.387 cubic centimetres
1 cubic metre = 35.3146 cubic feet
= 1.3079 cubic yards
1 cubic yard = 0.7646 cubic metre
1 fathom = 1.8288 metres
1 fluid oz (apoth.) = 28.4131 millilitres
1 fluid oz (US) = 29.5735 millilitres
1 foot = 0.3048 metre = 30.48 centimetres
1 foot per second = 0.6818 mph = 1.097 km/h
1 gallon (imperial) = 4.5461 litres
1 gallon (US liquid) = 3.7854 litres
1 gill = 0.142 litre
1 gram = 0.0353 ounce = 0.002205 pound
= 15.43 grains = 0.0321 ounce (Troy)
1 hectare = 2.4710 acres
1 hundredweight = 50.80 kilograms
1 inch = 2.54 centimetres
1 kilogram = 2.2046 pounds
1 kilometre = 0.6214 mile = 1,093.6 yards
1 knot (international) = 0.5144 metres/sec
= 1.852 km/h
1 litre = 0.220 gallon (imperial) = 0.2642 gallon (US) = 1.7598 pints (imperial)
= 0.8799 quarts
1 metre = 39.3701 in = 3.2808 ft
= 1.0936 yd
1 metric ton = 0.9842 long ton = 1.1023 short ton
1 mile (statute) = 1.6093 kilometres
1 mile (nautical) = 1.852 kilometres
1 millimetre = 0.03937 inch
1 ounce = 28.350 grams
1 peck (imperial) = 9.0922 litres
1 pennyweight = 1.555 grams
1 pica (printer's) = 4.2175 millimetres
1 pint (imperial) = 0.5683 litre
1 pound = 0.4536 kilogram
1 quart (imperial) = 1.1365 litres
1 square centimetre = 0.1550 square inch
1 square foot = 0.0929 square metre
1 square inch = 6.4516 square centimetres
1 square kilometre = 0.3860 square mile
1 square metre = 10.7639 square feet
= 1.1960 square yards
1 square mile = 2.5900 square kilometres
1 square yard = 0.8361 square metre
1 ton (long) = 1.0160 metric tons (tonnes)
1 ton (short) = 0.9072 metric ton (tonne)
1 yard = 0.9144 metre

SI UNITS

	symbol	measurement
Basic units		
metre	m	length
kilogram	kg	mass
second	s	time
ampere	A	electric current
kelvin	K	thermodynamic temperature
mole	mol	amount of substance
candela	cd	luminous intensity
Derived units*		
hertz	Hz	frequency
newton	N	force
pascal	Pa	pressure, stress
joule	J	energy, work, quantity of heat
watt	W	power, radiant flux
coulomb	C	electric charge, quantity of electricity
volt	V	electric potential, potential difference, emf
farad	F	capacitance
ohm	Ω	electric resistance
siemens	S	conductance
weber	Wb	magnetic flux
tesla	T	magnetic flux density
henry	H	inductance
lumen	lm	luminous flux
lux	lx	illuminance
Supplementary units		
radian	rad	plane angle
steradian	sr	solid angle

*These have special names; there are other derived units, such as m^2 (area), mol/m^3 (concentration), m^3/kg (specific volume), etc.

DECIMAL MULTIPLES

prefix	symbol		multiplication factor
tera	T	10^{12}	1,000,000,000,000
giga	G	10^{9}	1,000,000,000
mega	M	10^{6}	1,000,000
kilo	k	10^{3}	1,000
hecto	h	10^{2}	100
deca	da	10	10
deci	d	10^{-1}	0.1
centi	c	10^{-2}	0.01
milli	m	10^{-3}	0.001
micro	μ	10^{-6}	0.000001
nano	n	10^{-9}	0.000000001
pico	p	10^{-12}	0.000000000001
femto	f	10^{-15}	0.000000000000001
atto	a	10^{-18}	0.000000000000000001

PERIODIC TABLE OF ELEMENTS

The elements, listed with their symbols and atomic numbers, lie horizontally in order of their atomic numbers. Those with chemically similar properties fall under one another in the columns. Elements with atomic numbers of 93 and over are man-made. Elements below and to the left of the heavy line are metals. Those above and to the right of it are non-metals.

Hydrogen H 1											
Lithium Li 3	Beryllium Be 4										
Sodium Na 11	Magnesium Mg 12										
Potassium K 19	Calcium Ca 20	Scandium Sc 21	Titanium Ti 22	Vanadium V 23	Chromium Cr 24	Manganese Mn 25	Iron Fe 26	Cobalt Co 27	Nickel Ni 28	Copper Cu 29	Zinc Zn 30
Rubidium Rb 37	Strontium Sr 38	Yttrium Y 39	Zirconium Zr 40	Niobium Nb 41	Molybdenum Mo 42	Technetium Tc 43	Ruthenium Ru 44	Rhodium Rh 45	Palladium Pd 46	Silver Ag 47	Cadmiu Cd 48
Caesium Cs 55	Barium Ba 56	Lanthanum La 57	Hafnium Hf 72	Tantalum Ta 73	Tungsten W 74	Rhenium Re 75	Osmium Os 76	Iridium Ir 77	Platinum Pt 78	Gold Au 79	Mercu Hg 80
Francium Fr 87	Radium Ra 88	Actinium Ac 89									

CHEMICAL ELEMENTS

name	symbol	at. no.	at. wt.	name	symbol	at. no.	at. wt.
Actinium	Ac	89	(227)	Erbium	Er	68	167.26
Aluminium	Al	13	26.08154	Europium	Eu	63	151.96
Americium	Am	95	(243)	Fermium	Fm	100	(257)
Antimony	Sb	51	121.75	Fluorine	F	9	18.99840
Argon	Ar	18	39.948	Francium	Fr	87	(223)
Arsenic	As	33	74.9216	Gadolinium	Gd	64	157.25
Astatine	At	85	(210)	Gallium	Ga	31	69.72
Barium	Ba	56	137.34	Germanium	Ge	32	72.59
Berkelium	Bk	97	(247)	Gold	Au	79	196.9665
Beryllium	Be	4	9.01218	Hafnium	Hf	72	178.49
Bismuth	Bi	83	208.9804	Helium	He	2	4.00260
Boron	B	5	10.81	Holmium	Ho	67	164.9304
Bromine	Br	35	79.904	Hydrogen	H	1	1.0079
Cadmium	Cd	48	112.40	Indium	In	49	114.82
Caesium	Cs	55	132.9054	Iodine	I	53	126.9045
Calcium	Ca	20	40.08	Iridium	Ir	77	192.22
Californium	Cf	98	(251)	Iron	Fe	26	55.847
Carbon	C	6	12.011	Krypton	Kr	36	83.80
Cerium	Ce	58	140.12	Lanthanum	La	57	138.9055
Chlorine	Cl	17	35.453	Lawrencium	Lr	103	(260)
Chromium	Cr	24	51.996	Lead	Pb	82	207.2
Cobalt	Co	27	58.9332	Lithium	Li	3	6.941
Copper	Cu	29	63.546	Lutetium	Lu	71	174.97
Curium	Cm	96	(247)	Magnesium	Mg	12	24.305
Dysprosium	Dy	66	162.50	Manganese	Mn	25	54.9380
Einsteinium	Es	99	(254)	Mendelevium	Md	101	(258)

				Hydrogen H 1	Helium He 2
Boron B 5	Carbon C 6	Nitrogen N 7	Oxygen O 8	Fluorine F 9	Neon Ne 10
uminium Al 13	Silicon Si 14	Phosphorus P 15	Sulfur S 16	Chlorine Cl 17	Argon Ar 18
Gallium Ga 31	Germanium Ge 32	Arsenic As 33	Selenium Se 34	Bromine Br 35	Krypton Kr 36
Indium In 49	Tin Sn 50	Antimony Sb 51	Tellurium Te 52	Iodine I 53	Xenon Xe 54
Thallium Tl 81	Lead Pb 82	Bismuth Bi 83	Polonium Po 84	Astatine At 85	Radon Rn 86

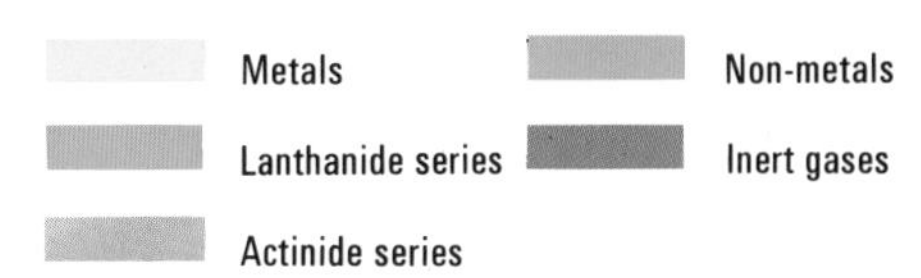

Notes on the table below

The atomic weights (at. wt.) are based on the exact number 12 as assigned to the atomic mass of the principal isotope of carbon, carbon-12, and are provided through the courtesy of the International Union of Pure and Applied Chemistry (IUPAC) and Butterworths Scientific Publications.

Values in parentheses are for certain radioactive elements whose atomic weights cannot be quoted precisely without knowledge of origin; the value given in each case is the atomic mass no. of the isotope of longest known half-life.

CHEMICAL ELEMENTS

name	symbol	at. no.	at. wt.	name	symbol	at. no.	at. wt.
Mercury	Hg	80	200.59	Samarium	Sm	62	105.4
Molybdenum	Mo	42	95.94	Scandium	Sc	21	44.9559
Neodymium	Nd	60	144.24	Selenium	Se	34	78.96
Neon	Ne	10	20.179	Silicon	Si	14	28.086
Neptunium	Np	93	237.0482	Silver	Ag	47	107.868
Nickel	Ni	28	58.70	Sodium	Na	11	22.98977
Niobium	Nb	41	92.9064	Strontium	Sr	38	87.62
Nitrogen	N	7	14.0067	Sulfur	S	16	32.06
Nobelium	No	102	(255)	Tantalum	Ta	73	180.9479
Osmium	Os	76	190.2	Technetium	Tc	43	(97)
Oxygen	O	8	15.9994	Tellurium	Te	52	127.60
Palladium	Pd	46	106.4	Terbium	Tb	65	158.9254
Phosphorus	P	15	30.97376	Thallium	Tl	81	204.37
Platinum	Pt	78	195.09	Thorium	Th	90	232.0381
Plutonium	Pu	94	(244)	Thulium	Tm	69	168.9342
Polonium	Po	84	(209)	Tin	Sn	50	118.69
Potassium	K	19	39.098	Titanium	Ti	22	47.90
Praseodymium	Pr	59	140.9077	Tungsten (Wolfram)	W	74	183.85
Promethium	Pm	61	(145)	Uranium	U	92	238.029
Protactinium	Pa	91	231.0359	Vanadium	V	23	50.9414
Radium	Ra	88	226.0254	Xenon	Xe	54	131.30
Radon	Rn	86	(222)	Ytterbium	Yb	70	173.04
Rhenium	Re	75	186.207	Yttrium	Y	39	88.9059
Rhodium	Rh	45	102.9055	Zinc	Zn	30	65.38
Rubidium	Rb	37	85.4678	Zirconium	Zr	40	91.22
Ruthenium	Ru	44	101.07				

Astronomy

Glossary of Terms

aerolite See *meteorite.*
albedo Percentage of light reflected from a surface.
aphelion Point in planet's orbit farthest from sun.
apogee Point in orbit (moon/satellite) farthest from earth.
asteroids Thousands of small bodies that orbit the sun; largest Ceres, 480 miles (772 km) diam; origin unknown.
astrobiology Study of life on other worlds.
astronomical unit (AU) Mean distance between earth and sun, 93,000,000 miles (150,000,000 km).
astrophysics Branch of astronomy concerned with physical nature of heavenly bodies.
aurora Phenomenon of the atmosphere seen around the polar regions, in form of colourful displays of light, attributed to sunspot activity. Northern Lights – Aurora Borealis; Southern Lights – Aurora Australis.

Aurorae are displays of light which occur in the extreme northern and southern skies.

azimuth Co-ordinate of a star.
big-bang theory See *Universe.*
black holes Supposed regions of space of intense gravitational force caused by collapse of star.
celestial sphere Imaginary sphere in which heavenly bodies seem to be projected from point of observation.
chromosphere Layer of crimson gas round the sun.
comet Heavenly body consisting of relatively small, star-like nucleus, surrounded by *coma*, or head (sometimes 100,000 miles diam), with, usually, a *tail* some 100 million miles long made up of dust and gas. Comets, visible near the sun, orbit it with periods of a few to thousands of years.
constellation Apparent grouping of stars together within definite region of the sky; 88 officially recognized and designated.
corona Sun's pearly-white outer layer of gas, extending more than a million miles, visible only during eclipse.
cosmogony Any theory of formation of universe.
cosmology Study of universe as a whole.
eclipse Obscuration of one heavenly body by another.
equinox Instant when sun is directly over equator, making equal day and night; occurs about 21 March (*vernal*) and 23 September (*autumnal*).
evening star Planet seen in western sky after sunset, especially Venus.
galaxy Vast system of stars (thousands of millions). Millions of galaxies exist, regular ones having spiral or elliptical forms.
halo (1) Luminous ring seen round moon or sun, caused by light refraction through high clouds. (2) Stars surrounding Milky Way in halo fashion.
helioscope Instrument for observing the sun.
interstellar space Beyond the Solar System, among the stars.
Kepler's Laws Laws of planetary motion: (1) describes planet's orbit round sun as ellipse; (2) explains planet's varying speed of motion; (3) relates size of orbits to period of revolution.
light-year Distance travelled by light in 1 year, 5·88 million million miles (9·46 million million km).
meridian Imaginary line in sky passing through poles of celestial sphere and

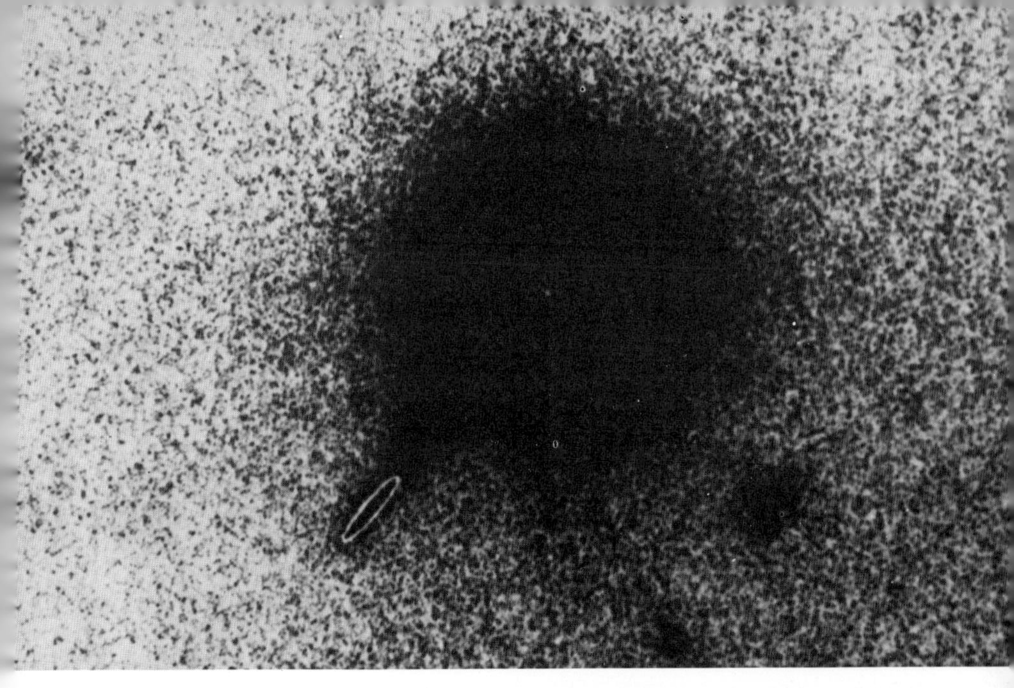

This negative photograph shows the quasar known as 3C-273. It is probably about 2400 light-years from Earth and appears only faintly in photographs, but the radio waves which it emits are very powerful.

directly over observer.
meteor Phenomenon caused by small body entering earth's atmosphere and emitting light; estimated 100 million per day.
meteorite Meteor reaching earth before burning up; lumps of stone (*aerolites*) or iron (*siderites*) up to 50-ton (51,000 kg) specimen near Grootfontein, SW Africa.
Milky Way Our galaxy; contains estimated 200,000 million stars; spiral type, about 800,000 million million miles across.
moon Any natural satellite of planet. Earth's moon has diam. 2;160 miles (3,476 km), has 1/81 mass and 1/6 gravity of earth and is mean distance of 239,000 miles (385,000 km) from earth.
morning star Planet seen in eastern sky before sunrise, especially Venus.
nebula (Lat. *mist*) Hazy mass of gases/ particles in space.
Northern Lights See *aurora*.
occultation Eclipse of star or planet.
orbit Path of one celestial body round another.
parallax Apparent change in position of heavenly body observed from two directions.
parsec Unit of distance equal to 3·258 light-years.
perigee Point in orbit (moon/satellite) nearest earth.
perihelion Point in planet's orbit nearest sun.
period Time taken to complete regular cycle, such as planet's orbit round sun, or earth's complete rotation on axis.
photosphere Visible surface of sun.
planetarium Projection instrument that demonstrates motions of heavenly bodies.
planets The nine major bodies moving in orbit around sun.
precession Slow circling of earth's axis of rotation about poles of sun's apparent annual path.
quasar Quasi-stellar radio sources – mysterious distant objects in the universe, powerful sources of radio waves and light.
radio astronomy Branch concerned with study of radio energy emitted by stars or regions in space.
radio source Discrete source of radio emission in space.
radio star Now called *radio source*.

Astronomy: glossary of terms (contd.)

radio telescope Instrument that collects radio waves from space.
red shift Spectra of galaxies shift towards the red, indicating receding of galaxies.
satellite A body, natural or man-made (artificial), that orbits a celestial body.
shooting star Common type of meteor, caused by objects as small as 1 mm diam.
siderite See *meteorite.*
solar flare Eruption of radiation on the sun.
Solar System The sun and its satellites.
solar wind Permanent particle radiation from the sun.
solstice Instant when sun is farthest from equator, making longest or shortest day; occurs about 21 June and 22 December.
Southern Lights See *aurora.*
spectroheliograph Instrument for photographing the sun.
star Heavenly body generating its own heat and light; nearest, after sun, is Proxima Centauri (4·3 light-years); 5,000 stars visible to naked eye. Brightness measured in terms of *star magnitude.*
steady-state theory See *universe.*
sun Our star, centre of Solar System, glowing ball of gases, mainly hydrogen and helium; diam 865,000 miles (1,392,000 km), surface temp 5500°C (See *corona, chromosphere, photosphere*).
sunspots Dark patches on the sun, 2000°C cooler than normal; maximum activity in 11-year cycles; origin unknown.
tektite Bead of natural glass, possibly meteoric in origin.
transit Passage of Mercury or Venus across sun's disk.
universe Everything that exists – matter, space, energy. Most astronomers set age at 20,000 million years; universe seems to be expanding, like inflating balloon. *Big-bang theory* suggests explosion of 'primeval atom' 100 million light-years in diam – hence expanding universe; *steady-state theory* suggests infinite universe, no beginning or end, matter continuously being created, changing, and 'aging'.
zenith Point in heavens directly overhead.

The Sun seems dim at sunset because its rays pass through a greater amount of atmosphere at this angle.

Above: **The Solar System (not to scale); the main diagram shows the outer planets, Neptune, Pluto, Uranus, Saturn and Jupiter; the inset shows Jupiter, Earth, Venus and Mercury (nearest to the Sun). The orbit shown in yellow is that of a typical comet that has been captured by Jupiter.**

Below: **The track of an artificial satellite is seen as a bright streak against the background of our region of the Milky Way.**

CONSTELLATIONS

Latin name	English name
Andromeda	Andromeda
Antlia	Air Pump
Apus	Bird of Paradise
Aquarius	Water Bearer
Aquila	Eagle
Ara	Altar
Aries	Ram
Auriga	Charioteer
Bootes	Herdsman
Caelum	Chisel
Camelopardus	Giraffe
Cancer	Crab
Canes Venatici	Hunting Dogs
Canis Major	Great Dog
Canis Minor	Little Dog
Capricornus	Sea-Goat
Carina	Keel (of Argo)
Cassiopeia	Cassiopeia
Centaurus	Centaur
Cepheus	Cepheus
Cetus	Whale
Chamaeleon	Chameleon
Circinus	Pair of Compasses
Columba	Dove
Coma Berenices	Berenice's Hair
Corona Australis	Southern Crown
Corona Borealis	Northern Crown
Corvus	Crow
Crater	Cup
Crux	Southern Cross
Cygnus	Swan
Delphinus	Dolphin
Dorado	Swordfish
Draco	Dragon
Equuleus	Little Horse
Eridanus	River Eridanus
Fornax	Furnace
Gemini	Twins
Grus	Crane
Hercules	Hercules
Horologium	Clock
Hydra	Sea-Serpent
Hydrus	Watersnake
Indus	Indian
Lacerta	Lizard
Leo	Lion
Leo Minor	Little Lion
Lepus	Hare
Libra	Scales
Lupus	Wolf
Lynx	Lynx
Lyra	Lyre
Mensa	Table
Microscopium	Microscope
Monoceros	Unicorn
Musca	Fly
Norma	Rule (straight-edge)
Octans	Octant
Orion	Orion (hunter)
Pavo	Peacock
Pegasus	Pegasus (winged horse)
Perseus	Perseus
Phoenix	Phoenix
Pictor	Painter (or Easel)
Pisces	Fishes
Piscis Austrinus	Southern Fish
Puppis	Poop (of Argo)
Pyxis	Mariner's Compass
Reticulum	Net
Sagitta	Arrow
Sagittarius	Archer
Scorpius	Scorpion
Sculptor	Sculptor
Scutum	Shield
Serpens	Serpent
Sextans	Sextant
Taurus	Bull
Telescopium	Telescope
Triangulum	Triangle
Triangulum Australe	Southern Triangle
Tucana	Toucan
Ursa Major	Great Bear (or Plough)
Ursa Minor	Little Bear
Vela	Sails (of Argo)
Virgo	Virgin
Volans	Flying Fish
Vulpecula	Fox

PLANETS OF THE SOLAR SYSTEM

Planet	Mean distance from sun million miles (million km)	Period years	Equatorial diameter miles (km)	Mass earth = 1
Mercury	36 (58)	0·24	3,007 (4,840)	0·04
Venus	67 (108)	0·62	7,643 (12,300)	0·83
Earth	93 (150)	1·00	7,926 (12,756)	1·00
Mars	142 (228)	1·88	4,219 (6,790)	0·11
Jupiter	484 (778)	11·86	88,980 (143,200)	318
Saturn	887 (1,427)	29·46	74,130 (119,300)	95
Uranus	1,783 (2,870)	84·01	29,300 (47,100)	15
Neptune	2,794 (4,497)	164·79	31,700 (51,000)	17
Pluto	3,697 (5,950)	247·7	3,700 (5,950)	0·1

NEAREST STARS

star	distance (light-years)
Proxima Centauri	4.2
Alpha Centauri	4.3
Barnard's Star	5.9
Wolf 359	7.6
Lalande 21185	8.1
Sirius	8.7

BRIGHTEST STARS

star	constellation	apparent magnitude	distance (light-years)
Sirius	Canis Major	−1.6	8.7
Canopus	Carina	−0.9	100+
Alpha Centauri	Centaurus	+0.1	4.3
Vega	Lyra	+0.1	26
Capella	Auriga	+0.2	45
Arcturus	Bootes	+0.2	36

FAMOUS COMETS

	First seen	Orbital period (years)
Halley's Comet	240 BC	76
Encke's Comet	1786	3·3
Biela's Comet	1806	6·7
Great Comet of 1811	1811	3,000
Pons-Winnecke Comet	1819	6·0
Great Comet of 1843	1843	512·4
Donati's Comet	1858	2,040
Schwassmann-Wachmann Comet	1925	16·2
Arend-Roland Comet	1957	10,000
Humason Comet	1961	2,900
Ikeya-Seki Comet	1965	880
Kouhouteks Comet*	1975	

*observed from Skylab and Soyuz spacecraft

Right: **Southern Hemisphere Looking north January**

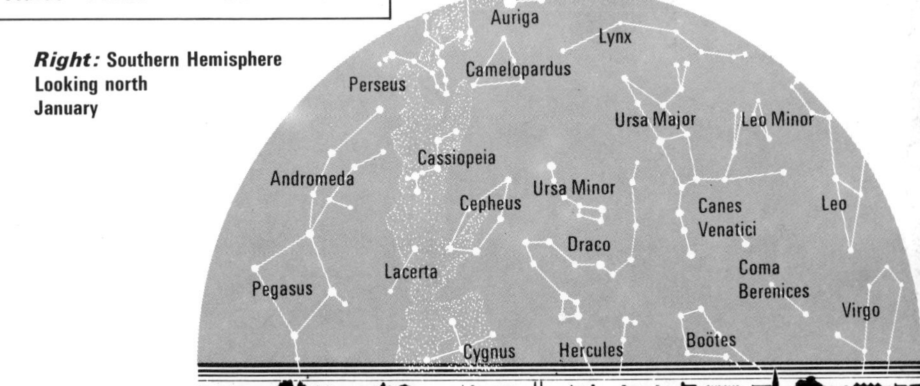

Left: **Northern Hemisphere Looking north January**

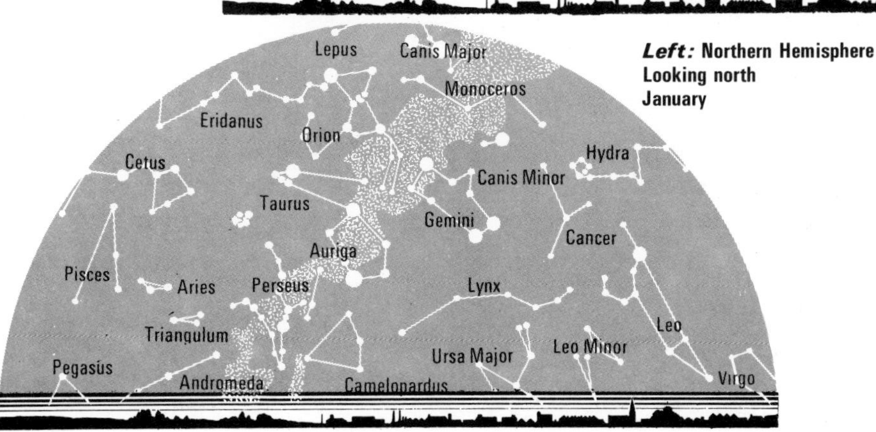

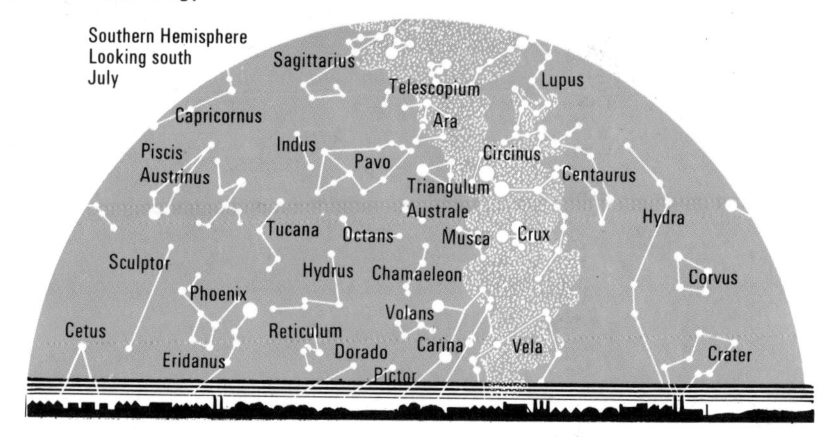
Southern Hemisphere
Looking south
July
Sagittarius
Telescopium
Lupus
Capricornus
Ara
Piscis
Austrinus
Indus
Pavo
Circinus
Centaurus
Triangulum
Australe
Hydra
Tucana
Octans
Musca
Crux
Sculptor
Hydrus
Chamaeleon
Corvus
Phoenix
Volans
Cetus
Reticulum
Carina
Vela
Crater
Eridanus
Dorado
Pictor

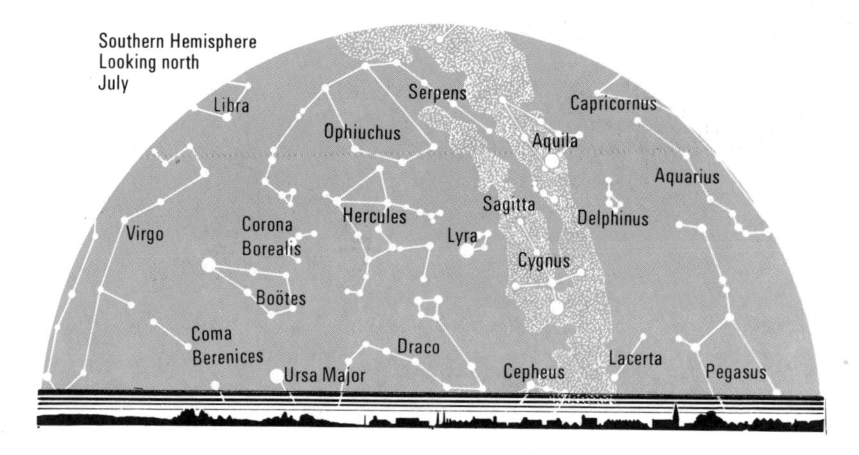
Southern Hemisphere
Looking north
July
Serpens
Libra
Capricornus
Ophiuchus
Aquila
Aquarius
Sagitta
Hercules
Delphinus
Virgo
Corona
Borealis
Lyra
Cygnus
Boötes
Coma
Berenices
Draco
Lacerta
Cepheus
Pegasus
Ursa Major

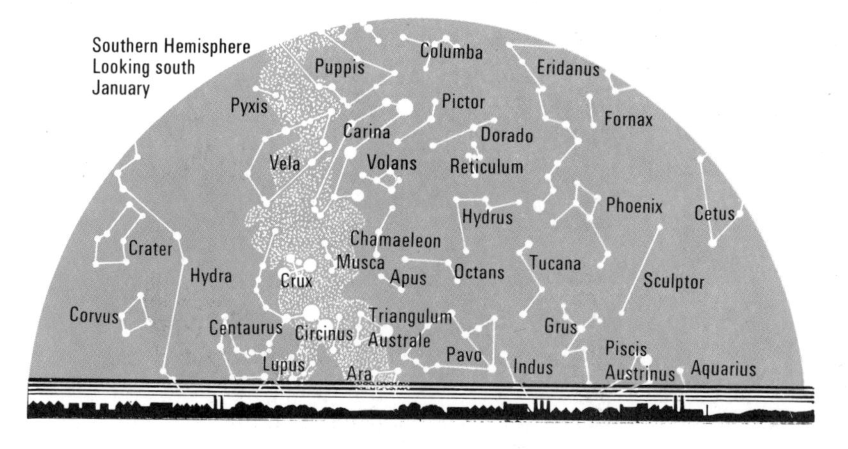
Southern Hemisphere
Looking south
January
Columba
Puppis
Eridanus
Pyxis
Pictor
Fornax
Carina
Dorado
Vela
Volans
Reticulum
Phoenix
Cetus
Hydrus
Chamaeleon
Crater
Musca
Tucana
Hydra
Crux
Apus
Octans
Sculptor
Corvus
Triangulum
Centaurus
Circinus
Australe
Grus
Pavo
Piscis
Lupus
Indus
Austrinus
Aquarius
Ara

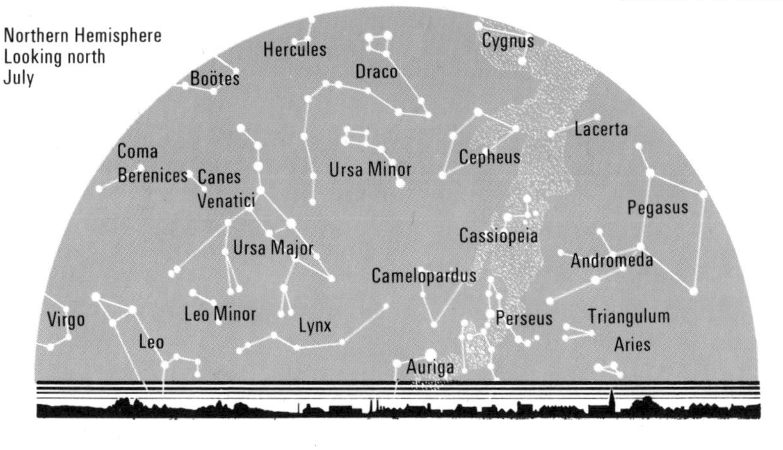
Northern Hemisphere
Looking north
July
Hercules
Cygnus
Boötes
Draco
Lacerta
Coma
Berenices
Canes
Venatici
Ursa Minor
Cepheus
Pegasus
Cassiopeia
Ursa Major
Andromeda
Camelopardus
Virgo
Leo Minor
Lynx
Perseus
Triangulum
Leo
Aries
Auriga

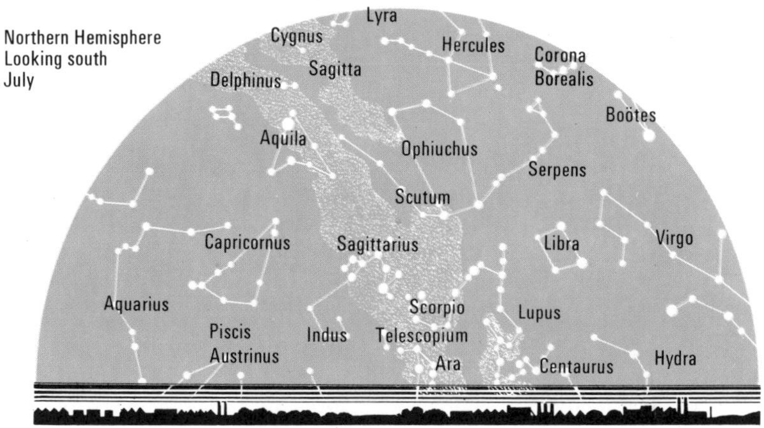
Northern Hemisphere
Looking south
July
Lyra
Cygnus
Hercules
Corona
Borealis
Delphinus
Sagitta
Boötes
Aquila
Ophiuchus
Serpens
Scutum
Capricornus
Sagittarius
Libra
Virgo
Aquarius
Scorpio
Lupus
Piscis
Austrinus
Indus
Telescopium
Ara
Centaurus
Hydra

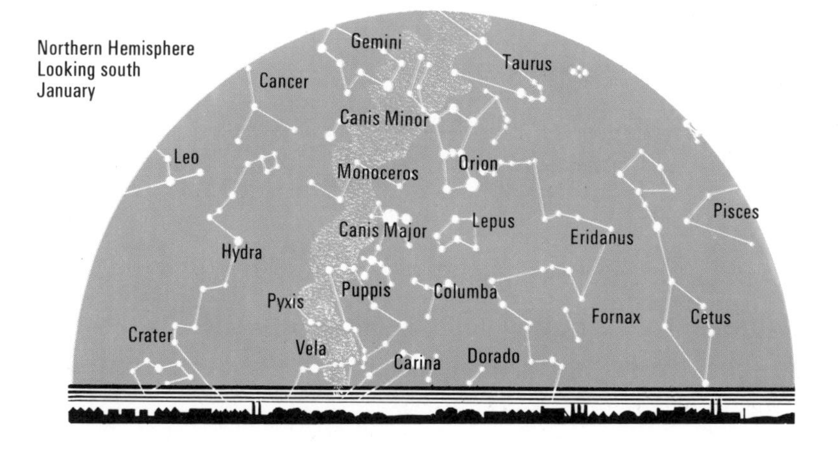
Northern Hemisphere
Looking south
January
Gemini
Taurus
Cancer
Canis Minor
Leo
Orion
Monoceros
Pisces
Lepus
Canis Major
Eridanus
Hydra
Puppis
Columba
Pyxis
Fornax
Cetus
Crater
Vela
Carina
Dorado

Space

Milestones in space travel

1232 Chinese use rockets against Mongols at battle of K'ai-fung-fu.
1609 Johannes Kepler publishes his first laws of planetary motion.
1865 Publication of Jules Verne's novel *From the Earth to the Moon* inspires serious thought about space travel.
1898 Konstantin Tsiolkovsky, a Russian schoolmaster, first to suggest use of liquid-fuelled rockets for interplanetary travel.
1924 Publication of Hermann Oberth's *The Rocket into Interplanetary Space*, first serious technical study of rocket principles.
1926 Robert H. Goddard (US) launches first (small) liquid-fuelled rocket; it travels 184 ft (56 m) in 2.5 sec.
1927 Formation in Germany of VfR, Society of Space Travel, for rocket research.
1943 German V-2 rocket, launched at Peenemünde, in the Baltic, travels 122 miles (196 km).

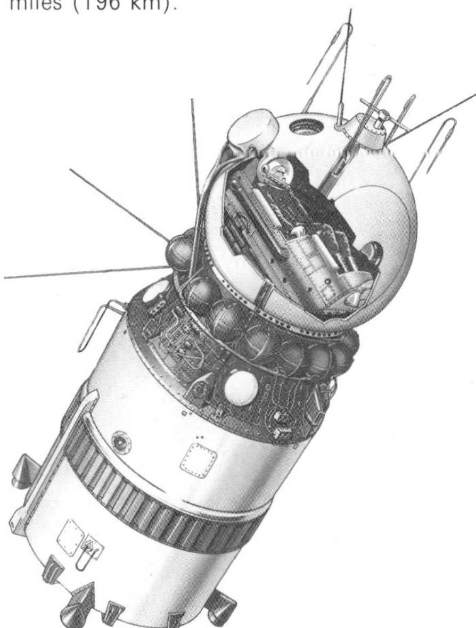

The first Soviet manned space missions used *Vostok* single-person space capsules like this one.

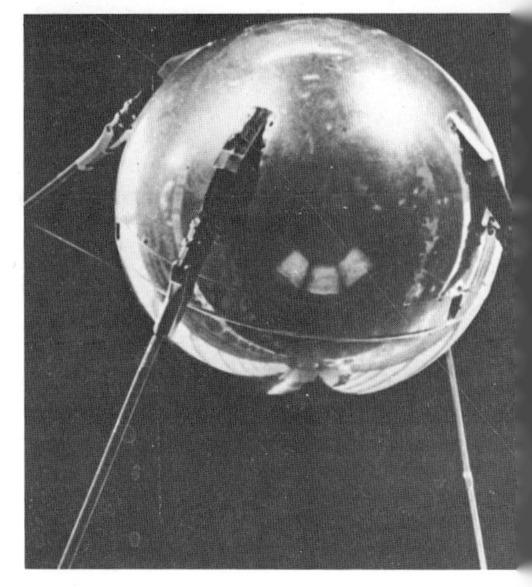

The Soviet satellite *Sputnik 1*, launched on 4 October 1957, was only 60 centimetres across yet it began the 'space race' which would end with men on the Moon.

1945 Americans establish White Sands Proving Ground in New Mexico.
1946 First successful launching of German V-2's from White Sands, reaching record altitude of 114 miles (183 km).
1949 Americans establish Cape Canaveral (later Cape Kennedy) launching site in Florida.
1957 First artificial Earth satellite: Russians launch *Sputnik 1* on 4 October, heralding Space Age; weighing 184 lb (83 kg) and transmitting for 21 days, it remains in orbit until 4 January 1958. On 3 November, Russians launch *Sputnik 2*, containing dog Laika, first mammal in space; Laika dies long before craft is destroyed on re-entry (14.4.58).
1958 On 31 January, Americans launch their first satellite, *Explorer 1*, from Cape Canaveral.
1959 Russians launch *Lunik 1* (first probe to go near Moon), *Lunik 2* (first to crash-land on Moon), and *Lunik 3* (first photographs of hidden side of Moon).
1960 *Lunik 1* becomes first artificial satellite of Sun, having missed Moon. On 1 April, US launch *Tiros 1*, first weather satellite (clear photographs of Earth's cloud

cover). US satellite *Discoverer 13* ejects capsule on 17th orbit, first object recovered from orbit (Pacific Ocean). US launch 100-ft (30-m) diameter balloon *Echo 1* into orbit (passive communications satellite). Russian dogs Belka and Strelka become first animals recovered from orbit (from returned capsule of *Sputnik 5*).

1961 First man in space: Russian cosmonaut Yuri Gagarin makes one orbit in *Vostok 1* on 12 April. First American astronaut Alan Shepard makes sub-orbital flight on 5 May to height of 116 miles (187 km). On 6 August, second Russian spaceman, Gherman Titov, begins 17-orbit, 24-hour flight in *Vostok 2*.

1962 First American in orbit, John Glenn makes 3 orbits on 20 February in *Friendship 7* (Mercury craft). On 26 April, *Ranger 4* becomes first US craft to reach Moon. First commercial communications satellite, *Telstar 1*, launched on 10 July; begins relaying TV programmes across Atlantic. *Vostok 3* (launched 11 Aug) and *Vostok 4* (12 Aug) come within 4 miles ($6\frac{1}{2}$ km) of each other, piloted by Andriyan Nikolayev and Pavel Popovich, respectively. Russians launch first Mars probe, but contact lost. US probe *Mariner 2* (launched 26 Aug) returns close-range information of Venus.

1963 First woman in space: Russian cosmonaut Valentina Tereshkova, on 16 June.

1964 Russians launch *Voshkod 1* (12 Oct) with Vladimir Komarov, Boris Yegorov, and Konstantin Feoktistov aboard, first craft with more than one spaceman (made 16 orbits)

1965 First space walk: Alexei Leonov 'walked' for 10 min (18 March) from *Voskhod 2*. First manned Gemini test flight, astronauts Gus Grissom and John Young making 3 orbits in *Gemini 3*. Ed White makes first American space walk (3 June), from *Gemini 4*. **First space rendezvous**: Wally Schirra and Tom Stafford in *Gemini 6* come within 1 ft (30 cm) of *Gemini 7* on 16 December.

1966 Russia's *Luna 9* makes soft landing on Moon and returns TV pictures from Ocean of Storms (31 Jan). Russian probe *Venera 3* (launched 16.11.65) impacts on Venus (1 March), failing to soft-land. **First 'docking' in space**: Neil Armstrong and Dave Scott,

Valentina Tereshkova made space history on 16 June 1963 by becoming the only woman so far to orbit the Earth. Formerly a Soviet textile worker, she later married a fellow cosmonaut, Nikolayev.

'That's one small step for man, one giant leap for mankind' were Neil Armstrong's words as he became the first man to walk on the Moon, on 21 July 1969. He was the first of 12 astronauts to do so.

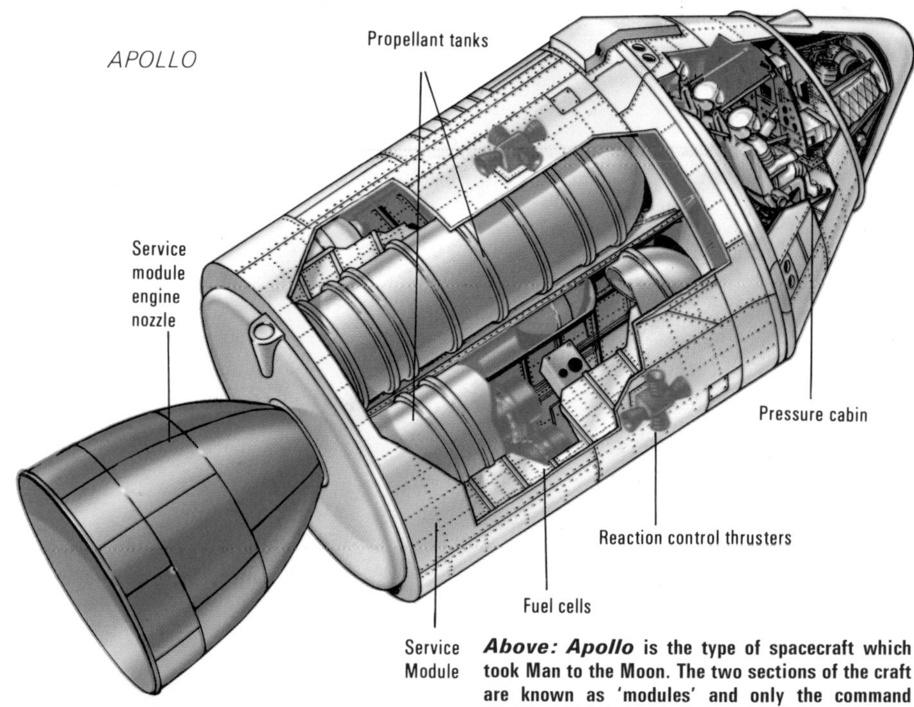

Above: Apollo **is the type of spacecraft which took Man to the Moon. The two sections of the craft are known as 'modules' and only the command module which holds the crew will return to Earth.**

Left: **The lunar module from the** ***Apollo 11*** **mission moves away from the command module towards the lunar surface. The Earth is visible above the horizon.**

Milestones in space travel (contd.)

in *Gemini 8*, dock with unmanned Agena rocket (16 March). First American soft landing on Moon (30 May) by *Surveyor 1* highly successful, over 11,000 pictures returned.
1967 First space disasters: on 27 January, three American astronauts (Ed White, Gus Grissom, Roger Chaffee) are killed in *Apollo 1* launch-pad fire; on 24 April, Vladimir Komarov is killed when *Soyuz 1* crashes on Earth after parachute failure. Russian Venus probe *Venera 4* (launched 12 June) reaches planet 17 October and transmits information.
1968 First recovery of unmanned lunar probe, Russian *Zond 5*, from Indian Ocean

on 21 September. First manned lunar flight: *Apollo 8* (Frank Borman, James Lovell, William Anders) completes 10 orbits
1969 First docking of two manned spacecraft (15 Jan), with exchange of cosmonauts by space walk (*Soyuz 4* and *5*). In March, Americans make first manned flight of lunar module, James McDivitt, David Scott, and Russell Schweickart in *Apollo 9*; and in May *Apollo 10* (Thomas Stafford, Eugene Cernan, John Young) descends to within 6 miles (10 km) of Moon's surface. Russian probes *Venera 5* and *6* (launched Jan) land on Venus 16 and 17 May, returning data. **First man on Moon**: on 21 July, American astronaut Neil Armstrong becomes first man to walk on Moon; *Apollo 11* (launched 16 July) sends Armstrong and Edwin 'Buzz' Aldrin in lunar module to Moon, while Michael Collins remains in orbiting command module; astronauts stay 21 hr 36 min 21 sec on Moon, collecting 48.5 lb (22 kg) of soil and rock samples and leaving experiments on Moon's surface during their 'moonwalks'; on 21 July, lunar module '*Eagle*' blasts off and docks with command and service module *Columbia*, which makes successful splash-down (24 July) in Pacific; astronauts go into 21-day quarantine. In October, Russians make first triple launching: *Soyuz 6*, *7*, and *8* complete rendezvous but do not dock; Valery Kubasov (in *Soyuz 6*) makes first welding of metals in space. Second Moon landing made on 14 November: Charles Conrad, Alan Bean, and Richard Gordon in *Apollo 12*, module with Conrad and Bean landing in Ocean of Storms; they make moonwalks.
1970 Russians soft-land unmanned *Luna 17* on Moon's Sea of Rains (17 Nov) and use 8-wheeled Lunokhod 1, first propelled vehicle on Moon (operated, with 3-sec delay, from Earth), for exploration and experiments. Russian probe *Venera 7* lands on Venus (15 Dec) and transmits data back.
1971 *Apollo 14* (Alan Shepard, Stuart Roosa, Edgar Mitchell) launched, Shepard and Mitchell making 3rd Moon landing (Jan/Feb). Russians launch *Salyut* space station and three *Soyuz 10* cosmonauts dock with it, but abort mission after 5½ hr (24 April). Three cosmonauts (Georgi Dobrovolsky, Vladislav Volkov, Viktor Patsayev) make longest space flight to date (23 days 17 hr 40 min), docking with *Salyut* space station (orbiting Earth for 23 days); crew die in *Soyuz 11* on re-entry, due to loss of pressurization. On 26 July, *Apollo 15* launched, with David Scott, James Irwin, and Alfred Worden aboard; Scott and Irwin make 4th lunar landing, use first

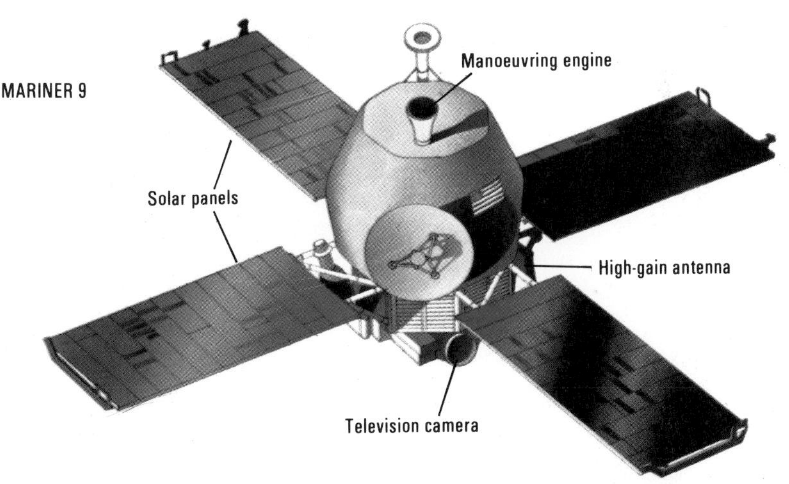

On 14 November 1971, the space probe *Mariner 9* went into orbit around the planet Mars. Its function was to photograph the surface of the planet, which it did for almost a year taking more than 7000 photographs.

Milestones in space travel (contd.)

lunar rover; first live pictures of lunar module lift-off, and longest exploration (18 hr) of Moon's surface. On 14 November, US probe *Mariner 9* becomes first artificial satellite of Mars. On 21 November, first man-made object lands on surface of Mars, when capsule from Russian probe *Mars 2* crashes.
1972 Americans launch *Pioneer 10* (3 March) on 21-month mission to Jupiter; 620-million-mile (1,000-million-km) flight path passes through asteroid belt and passes Jupiter (3 Dec), transmitting pictures and other information; scheduled to cross orbits of Saturn, Uranus, Neptune, and Pluto, and eventually become first man-made object to escape Solar System (1986). *Apollo 16* completes 5th lunar landing mission in April, Charles Duke and John Young landing and exploring Moon for 20 hr 14 min; Thomas Mattingly makes space walk of 1 hr 23 min on mission. Sixth and last Apollo mission to Moon: *Apollo 17* (Eugene Cernan, Ronald Evans, Harrison Schmitt) launched on 7 December, Cernan and Schmitt landing and making record 75-hr stay and collecting 243 lb (110 kg) of lunar samples (returned to Earth 19 Dec).
1973 *Pioneer 11* launched (6 April) towards Jupiter, scheduled to pass three times nearer than *Pioneer 10*, i.e. about 25,000 miles (40,000 km). On 14 May, Americans launch *Skylab 1*, unmanned portion of their first manned orbiting space station, including workshop and telescope mount. *Skylab 2, 3*, and *4* missions (launched 25 May, 28 July, 16 Nov), each with three astronauts.
1974 *Skylab 4* returns (8 Feb) to Earth after 84 days 1 hr 16 min 30 sec. *Mariner 10* (launched by US 3.11.73) passes Venus (5 Feb) and then within 451 miles (726 km) of Mercury (29 March) for man's first close-up look; first time gravity of one planet (Venus) used to send craft towards another; craft scheduled to take further looks at Mercury. Russians launch another Salyut space station (25 June) and follow up with two-man visit from *Soyuz 14*, but *Soyuz 15* fails to dock and has to return, Gennady Sarafanov and Lev Demin making first night landing.
1975 First joint Russian-American mission in space: *Soyuz 19* (launched 15 July) and *Apollo 18* (launched 7½ hr

Above: Pioneer 10 **sent back this photograph of Jupiter, the largest planet in our Solar System. It took** ***Pioneer*** **two years to reach Jupiter but it sent back much useful information.**

Below: **The** ***Mariner*** **space probe took this photograph of Mars in 1972. The surface is heavily marked with craters, which were probably caused by meteors and asteroids colliding with the planet.**

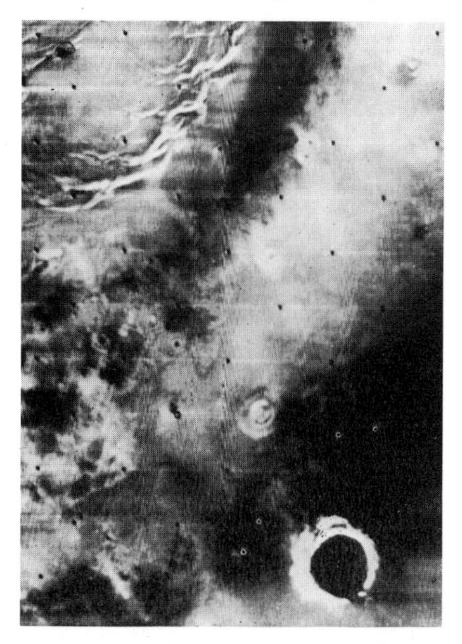

later) dock while orbiting Earth at about 140 miles (225 km) on 17 July. Astronauts Thomas Stafford, Donald Clayton (aged 51), and Vance Brand and cosmonauts Alexei Leonov and Valeri Kubasov carry out exchange visits and experiments. The Russian probes *Venera 9* and *Venera 10* soft-land on Venus (22 and 25 Oct) providing further data of importance in the study of Venusian geology. Pictures sent back suggest volcanic activity.

1976 On 16 April, *Helios B*, a research spacecraft carrying American and German instrumentation, comes within 27 million miles (43.4 million km) of the Sun. In June, data and pictures from the US spacecraft *Viking I* on Mars produce a wealth of new geological information, but no trace of organic compounds; yet the evidence of one of the instruments still seems to favour the existence of life and new investigations are planned to test these strange results. *Viking II* goes into orbit around Mars. The Soviet spacecraft *Luna 24* makes a soft landing on the surface of the Moon (18 Aug) near the south-east part of the Sea of Crises, to take soil samples with automatic scoop.

1977 The Soviet craft *Soyuz 24* docks successfully with orbiting *Salyut 5* space laboratory one day after launch (8 Feb). The US launch two *Voyager* spacecraft to fly to Jupiter (arriving 1979) and Saturn (arriving 1980), in order to investigate their satellites and interplanetary gas.

1978 Two Soviet spacecraft dock with the orbiting *Salyut* space laboratory (11 Jan) thus achieving the first triple link-up in space. On 24 January, a Soviet surveillance satellite, *Cosmos 954*, disintegrates in the atmosphere and falls to Earth in the New Territories of Canada. Russian cosmonauts Yuri Romanenko and Georgy Grechko return to Earth on 3 March after spending 84 days in *Salyut 6*. The Russians launch *Soyuz 29* on 15 June carrying cosmonauts Vladimir Kovalyonok and Aleksandr Ivanchenko to the *Salyut 6* space laboratory. *Soyuz 30* launched on 27 June also links with *Salyut 6*. Kovalyonok and Ivanchenko subsequently spent more than 139 days in space, having travelled more than 56 million miles (90 million km). It is reported that they experienced some difficulties adjusting back to the Earth's gravity from 'weightlessness', and had to relearn how to walk and pick up a cup of tea.

1979 Soviet spacecraft is launched on 25 February with two cosmonauts on board—Valery Ryumin and Vladimir Lyakhov—who go on to spend a record 175 days in space aboard the *Salyut-Soyuz* orbital research station, returning to Earth on 19 August. The American *Skylab I* falls to Earth on its 34,981st orbit on 11 July, strewing pieces over the Western Australian desert and coast. The Americans proceed with their plan for a reusable space shuttle to be launched in 1980.

US and Soviet cosmonauts meet in space when *Apollo 18* and *Soyuz 19* dock while orbiting Earth in 1975.

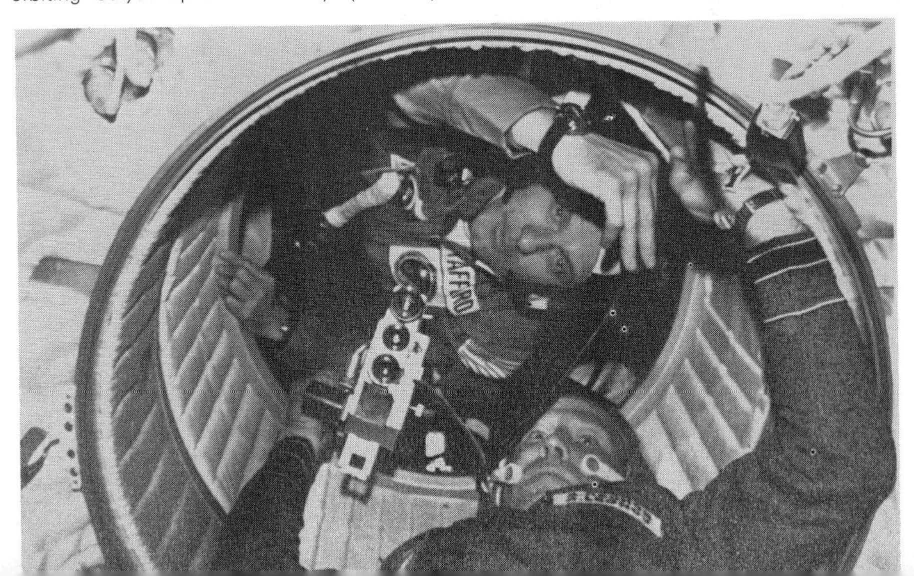

Engineering

Engineering terms

abutment Thick, upright support.
adit Almost horizontal access tunnel leading to main tunnel (often used in excavation).
aggregate Loose material used in making concrete. See *concrete*.
aqueduct Bridge or conduit for carrying water over distances.
asphalt Viscous, black material (from petroleum) used for road-surfacing, etc.
bearing walls Load-supporting walls.
bent Trestle unit consisting of two uprights and crossbar.
brace Angled support, usually beam or girder.
caisson Open-ended chamber used for digging sea or river bed, usually left as part of structure.
cantilever Beam weighted at one end, with other end supporting structure.
causeway Road carried by *embankment* or *retaining wall* over water or marsh.
compaction Packing down of material to increase density.
concrete Mixture of water, *aggregate* (sand, gravel, crushed rock, etc.), and binding material such as cement; *reinforced concrete* has steel rods embedded in it for strength, *prestressed concrete* has steel bars or wires embedded in it and is compressed, and *precast concrete* is hardened into the required shape before use.

The aqueduct known as the Pont du Gard, near Nîmes in France, was built by the Romans.

curtain walls Enclosing walls that do not bear weight.
embankment Hard, raised ridge of earth, stone, etc., used to carry road or railroad at higher level; protective bank.
fill Heavy, loose material (gravel, earth, etc.) used for filling up excavations, strengthening soft ground, etc.
foundation Underground part of structure that takes its weight, or earth or rock on which structure is built; in *piled foundation*, structure rests on deep-driven piles; in *raft foundation*, it rests on flat bed of concrete.
gantry Platform or framework used for transporting heavy loads or for travelling crane.
hardcore Hard, bulky *fill* of broken bricks, concrete, rocks, cinders, etc.
joist Term used mostly for beams supporting floor of building.
macadam Hard road-surface made by embedding small, uniform stones in cement and rolling flat.
member Any single element of a structure.
overfall Opening in dam through which water can pour.
pier Thick supporting column; wall built out into sea.
pile Long timber, steel, or concrete post driven into ground to support weight or form *retaining wall*. See *foundation*.
portal Access tunnel, or *adit*; structural frame consisting of two uprights and crossbar.
Portland cement Commonest building cement, made from ground limestone by burning it with materials such as shale or clay.

precast concrete See *concrete*.
prestressed concrete See *concrete*.
reinforced concrete See *concrete*.
retaining wall Wall built to hold back earth or water.
sluice-gate Gate that is raised or lowered to control flow of water.
span Distance between supports of bridge.
spillway Channel in dam through which water is allowed to overflow.
stanchion Vertical, load-bearing support, usually of steel.
strut Column or *stanchion*.
subsidence Sinking of ground due to weakening.
tachometer See *theodolite*.
tarmacadam Road-surface material made by coating small stones with tar and then compacting.
theodolite Surveyor's instrument fitted with special telescope (*tachometer*) for measuring angles; also called *transit*.
transit See *theodolite*.
truss Rigid, triangulated steel framework used as support for bridges, etc.
viaduct Bridge (road or rail) carried on series of closely spaced piers.

Types of bridges

arch Any bridge that uses the arch as the load-bearing element, either as the simple hump-backed bridge or as support for a flat deck.
Bailey Light, easily constructed temporary bridge, made of steel lattice girders supporting deck of prefabricated steel panels.
bascule Movable bridge with arm or arms that are raised or lowered like a hinge by means of counterweights.
beam Bridge consisting of beam or beams supported at both ends.
cantilever Bridge with cantilever arms from each side, either meeting in the middle or supporting centre span.
girder Same as *beam*.
pile Bridge resting on piles.
pontoon Bridge built on flat-bottomed boats or floating piers. The *pontoons*, as they are called, are moored to the riverbed.
suspension Bridge whose deck is hung from cables suspended between towers on each bank.
swing Movable bridge that turns on a pier in the middle of the waterway to allow passage of traffic.
traverser Movable bridge with section that may be drawn back onto one shore.
trestle Bridge supported by a series of connected sections in the form of uprights and crossbar with strong bracing.
truss Bridge supported by rigid framework of triangulated steel girders.

The famous Golden Gate suspension bridge, which spans the entrance to San Francisco Bay, USA.

Types of dams

arch Dam built with arch that curves into water.
barrage Any low dam used for raising level of river.
buttress Dam with face held up by supporting walls (buttresses).
coffer Easily erected temporary dam used for diverting flow of river.
crib Dam built of interlocking beams (timber or precast concrete), the spaces being filled with earth or rock.
earth-fill Dam built of layers of earth material compressed into watertight mass.
flat-slab Dam with flat slab placed across buttress supports at 45° angle; weight of water holds slab in place.
gravity Dam that depends primarily on weight of materials for stability.
hollow Dam with single wall braced by buttresses.
rock-fill Dam built of coarse rock and boulders, with watertight covering (steel, concrete, asphalt, etc.) facing water.

LONGEST BRIDGE SPANS

	location	longest span (ft)	longest span (m)	opened
Suspension				
Akashi-Kaikyo	Japan	5,840	1,750	*
Humber Estuary	England	4,626	1,410	1980
Verrazano Narrows	NY, USA	4,260	1,298	1964
Golden Gate	Calif., USA	4,200	1,280	1937
Cantilever				
Quebec Railway	Canada	1,800	549	1917
Forth Rail	Scotland	1,700	518	1890
Steel Arch				
New River Gorge	W. Va., USA	1,700	518	1977
Bayonne	NJ, USA	1,652	504	1931
Sydney Harbour	Australia	1,650	503	1932
Cable-Stayed				
Second Houghly	Calcutta, India	1,500	457	*
St-Nazaire	Loire, France	1,325	404	1975
Duisburg-Neuenkamp	W. Germany	1,148	350	1970
Continuous Truss				
Astoria	Oregon, USA	1,232	376	1966
Concrete Arch				
Gladesville	Australia	1,000	305	1964
Longest bridge (total length)				
Pontchartrain Causeway	Louisiana, USA	23.9 mi	38.4 km	1969

* Under construction.

The Humber Estuary bridge in north-eastern England under construction.

LONGEST TUNNELS

Railway*	miles:yards	km	opened
Seikan (Japan)	33:862	53.9	**
Oshimizu (Japan)	13:1397	22.2	**
Simplon II (Switz./It.)	12:559	19.823	1922
Road			
Arlberg (Austria)	8:1232	14.0	1978
Mont Blanc (France/Italy)	7:350	11.585	1965
Underwater			
Seikan (Japan)†	14:880	23.3	**
Shin Kanmon	11:1073	18.7	1974

**under construction

†length of the sub-aqueous section of the Seikan Railway Tunnel

*Longest continuous vehicular tunnel is the Morden-East Finchley stretch of the London underground (completed 1939): 17 mi 528 yd (27.842 km).

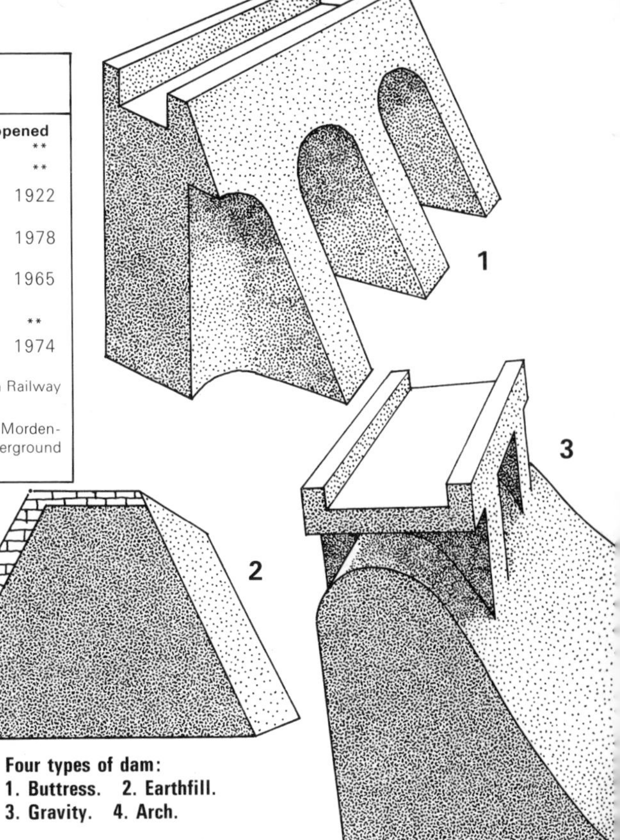

Four types of dam:
1. Buttress. 2. Earthfill.
3. Gravity. 4. Arch.

DAMS: HIGHEST & LARGEST

Highest	location	type	(ft)	(m)	completed
Nurek	USSR	earthfill	1,040	317	1980
Grande Dixence	Switzerland	gravity	932	284	1962
Inguri	USSR	arch	892	272	*
Vaiont	Italy	multi-arch	858	262	1961
Mica	Canada	rockfill	794	242	1973
Mauvoisin	Switzerland	arch	777	237	1958

Largest†	location	(cub. yd)	(cub. m)	completed
New Cornelia Tailings	Arizona, USA	274,026,000	209,506,000	1973
Tarbela	Pakistan	186,000,000	142,000,000	1979
Fort Peck	Montana, USA	125,600,000	96,000,000	1940
Oahe	S. Dakota, USA	92,000,000	70,000,000	1963
Mangla	Pakistan	85,870,000	65,650,000	1967
Gardiner	Canada	85,740,000	65,550,000	1968
Oroville	California, USA	78,000,000	60,000,000	1968

* Under construction.

† All earthfill except Tarbela (earth- and rock-fill).

The Living World

Prehistoric life

The pictures on this page and the next one show how living things have developed from their primitive beginnings in the sea until recent time. Geologists divide the millions of years of pre-history into Eras, each made up of a number of Periods. Below is the Palaeozoic ('Old Life') Era, which lasted until 225 million years ago. During this time, life evolved from simple marine creatures and plants to include amphibians and insects which could live on land among coniferous trees. Towards the end of this time the reptiles became the dominant species of life.

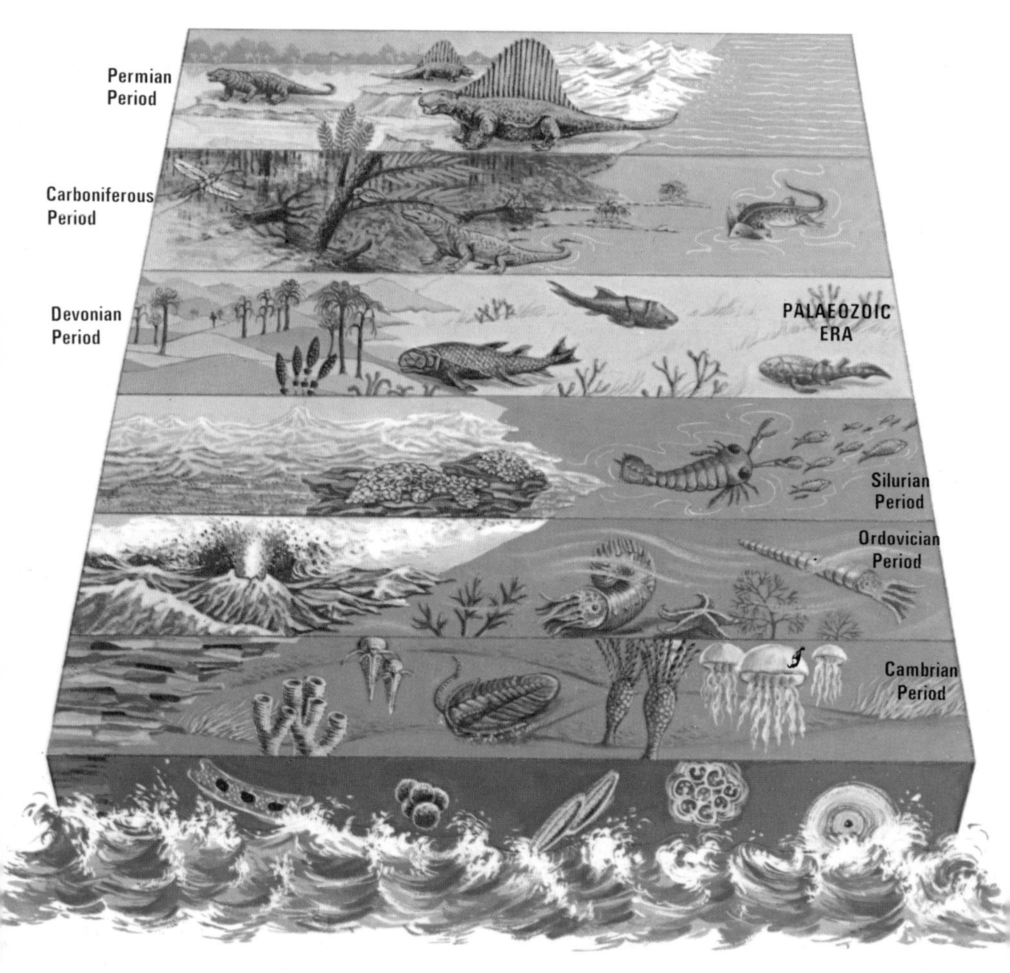

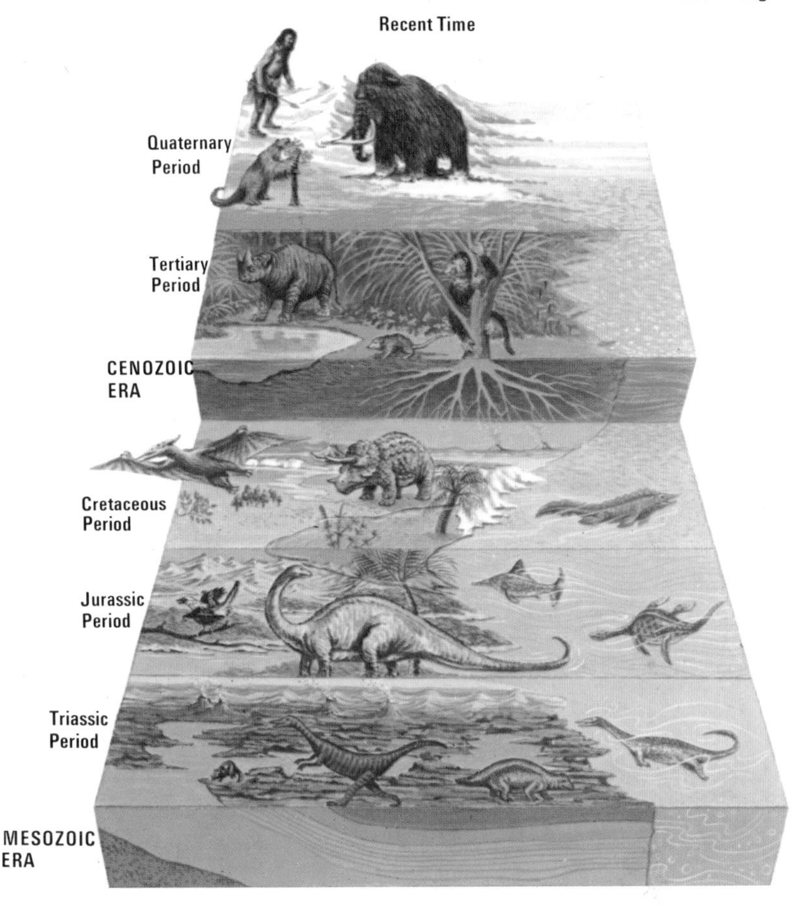

This diagram shows the Mesozoic ('Middle Life') and Cenozoic ('Recent Life') Eras. During the Mesozoic Era the reptiles were dominant; huge dinosaurs, whose name means 'terrible lizards', developed. The ancestors of the birds appeared. The mammals only became important in the Cenozoic Era. They developed from little shrew-like creatures. The great dinosaurs died out, no one is really certain why. The ancestors of Man split off from the ancestors of the apes. About 1 million years ago the Earth entered an Ice Age. Mammoths, giant sloths, wooly rhinoceroses, and sabre-toothed tigers lived then; all of them have long since become extinct. When the ice sheets retreated about 30,000 years ago modern Man, Homo sapiens, was becoming established. About 10,000 years ago men began to settle and farm. They were becoming civilized.

Biological terms

adaptation Process by which animal or plant becomes better fitted to survive in particular circumstances.
aestivation Period of sleep undergone by many animals in dry parts of world during summer.
albinism Lack of pigment in the skin that produces pure white animals with pink eyes.
amino-acid Organic acid containing the amino group, made up of 1 nitrogen and 2 hydrogen atoms (NH_2).
annual Plant that completes entire life-cycle within I year.
bacteria (singular, *bacterium*) Minute, single-celled organisms, many of which break down organic materials.
biennial Plant that completes entire life-cycle within 2 years.
cell Unit of protoplasm usually with a nucleus, and surrounded by either a membrane or a cell wall.
cellulose Carbohydrate that makes up cell wall of plants.
chlorophyll Green colouring matter in plants that absorbs light energy for photosynthesis.
chromosomes Threadlike bodies that carry the genes in nuclei of cells.
classification Scientific way in which animals and plants are grouped together and defined.
cotyledon First leaf or pair of leaves of embryo, which stores food in seed of flowering plant.

Hormone imbalance can have drastic effects. Growth hormone is produced by the pituitary gland, and too much or too little can produce giants or midgets. This man grew to 9 feet 5 inches (2870 centimetres) tall.

Colonies of Streptomyces, a group of soil bacteria.

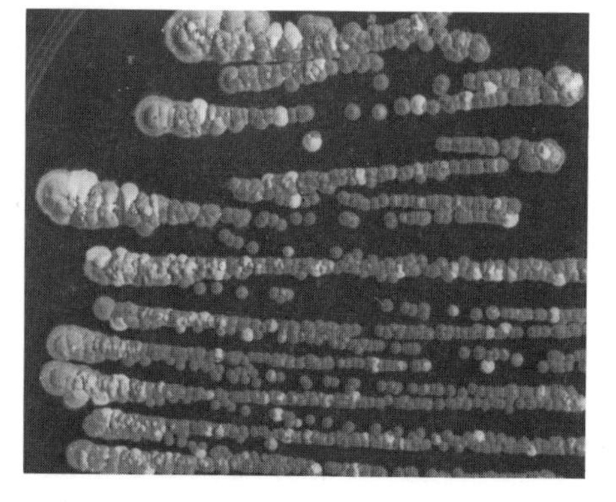

deciduous plant Tree or shrub that sheds all its leaves at certain season of year.
ecology Study of living things in relation to their natural environment.
embryo Young animal or plant before it is able to lead self-supporting life.
enzyme Catalyst (substance that quickens or slows chemical changes without being used up in them), made up of protein, occurring only in living organisms.
epiphyte Plant that grows on another for support only, not for food.
evolution Process by which higher forms of life are believed to have developed gradually from more primitive forms.

fauna Animal life of place or period.
fermentation Breakdown of organic substances by micro-organisms.
fertilization Union of male gamete with female gamete.
flora Plant life of place or period.
fossil Remains of animal or plant preserved in rocks.
gamete Sex-cell that joins with another cell to produce new organism.
gene Hereditary unit in chromosome that produces particular effect in animals or plants as it passes on from generation to generation.
gland Organ that manufactures substances in body.
hibernation Period of deep sleep undergone by certain animals throughout winter.
hormone Chemical, produced in small quantities in animals and plants, that affects body's growth or function.
hybrid Offspring of two different species; usually sterile.
inheritance Transmission of characteristics from one generation to another.
instinct Natural tendency to act in certain ways under given circumstances; inborn in almost all animals.
larva Free-living, self-supporting young form of certain animals that is quite different from adult into which it eventually changes.
metabolism Whole of the chemical changes taking place in plants or animals.
mutation Sudden change in gene or chromosome of animal or plant that produces characteristic in offspring not found in parents.
natural selection Process of evolution by survival of fittest.
nucleic acid Complex chemical substance found in chromosomes and in cytoplasm of cell; DNA is a nucleic acid that forms genes.
nucleus Round or oval part of almost all cells that contains chromosomes bearing genes.
ovary Organ of female animal that produces eggs; part of flowering plant that contains ovules.
parasite Animal or plant that lives on another animal or plant and depends on it for food without giving anything in return.
photosynthesis Process by which green plants manufacture food from inorganic materials with help of light.
pollen Powdery reproductive spores found in anthers of stamens in flowering plants.
pollination Transfer of pollen from anthers to stigmas in flowering plants.
protein Chemical compound produced by living things; contains at least carbon, hydrogen, oxygen, and nitrogen; is built up of amino-acids.
protoplasm Substance of all living plant and animal cells.
regeneration Ability possessed by some plants and animals to replace lost or damaged parts by growing new ones.
reproduction Process by which plant or animal is created by one or two parents of same kind.
respiration Process by which oxygen is absorbed and carbon dioxide and water vapour given out in order to provide energy for all living things.
symbiosis Partnership in which animals or plants of different kinds live together to their mutual benefit.
transpiration Loss of water vapour from surface of plants by evaporation.
tropism Response of plant or sedentary animal to stimulus, such as light or gravity.
virus Minute organism that reproduces only in living cells and causes disease.
vitamins Food substances required by body in very small doses to keep it healthy.
zygote Fertilized egg before it begins to divide.

Edward Cope found many spectacular fossils.

Trees

Some common trees are shown, with detailed illustrations of their leaves and fruits.

Lombardy Poplar
Whitebeam
Holly
Wych Elm
Alder
Field Maple
Rowan
Norway Spruce
Sessile Oak

THE PLANT KINGDOM

This tree shows the main branches of the plant kingdom with examples. It is difficult to know whether to class bacteria as plants or animals.

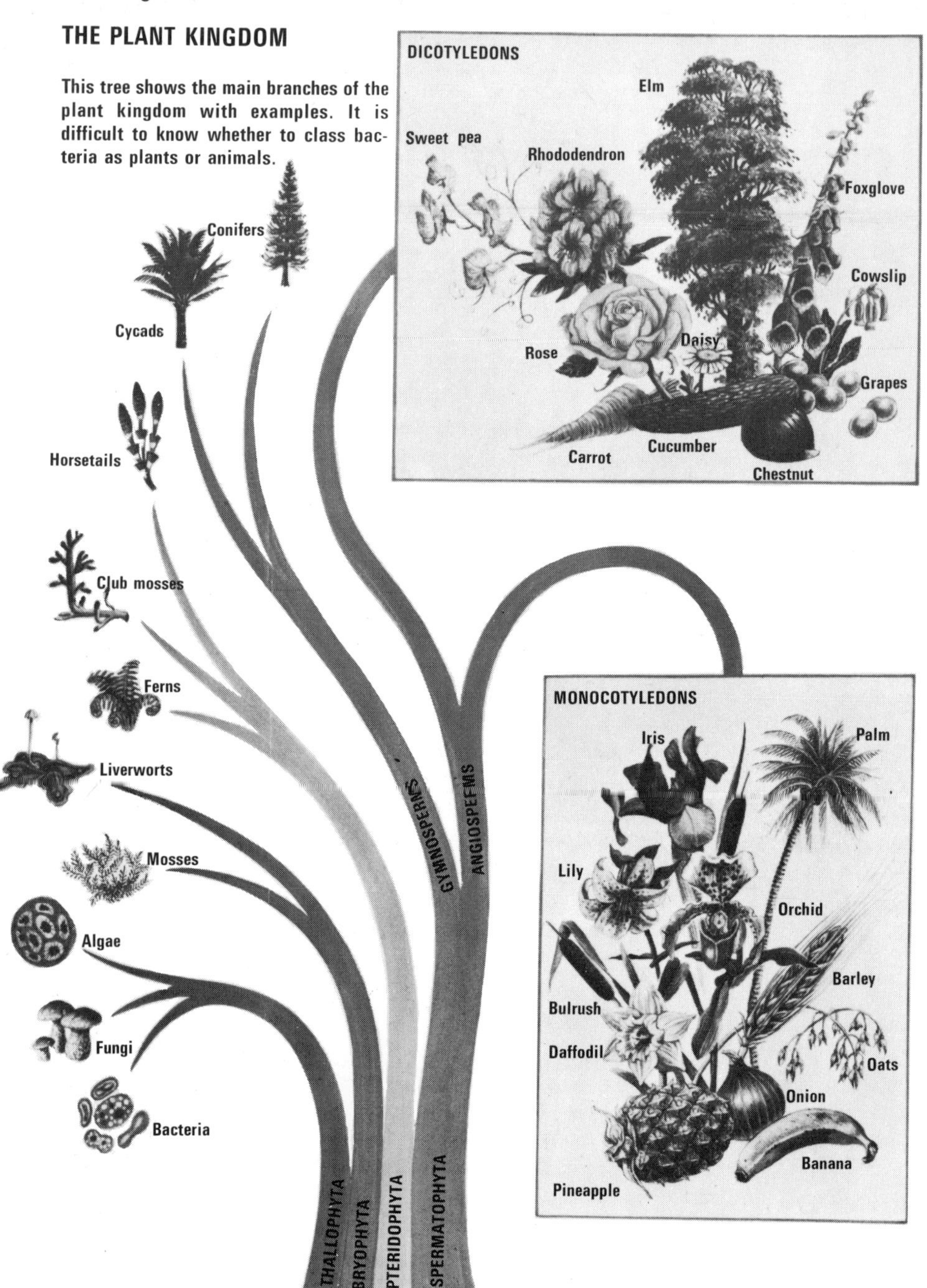

THE ANIMAL KINGDOM

The main groups of the animal kingdom. The smallest division shown is the class. The table is simplified; some of the many classes of worms have been omitted.

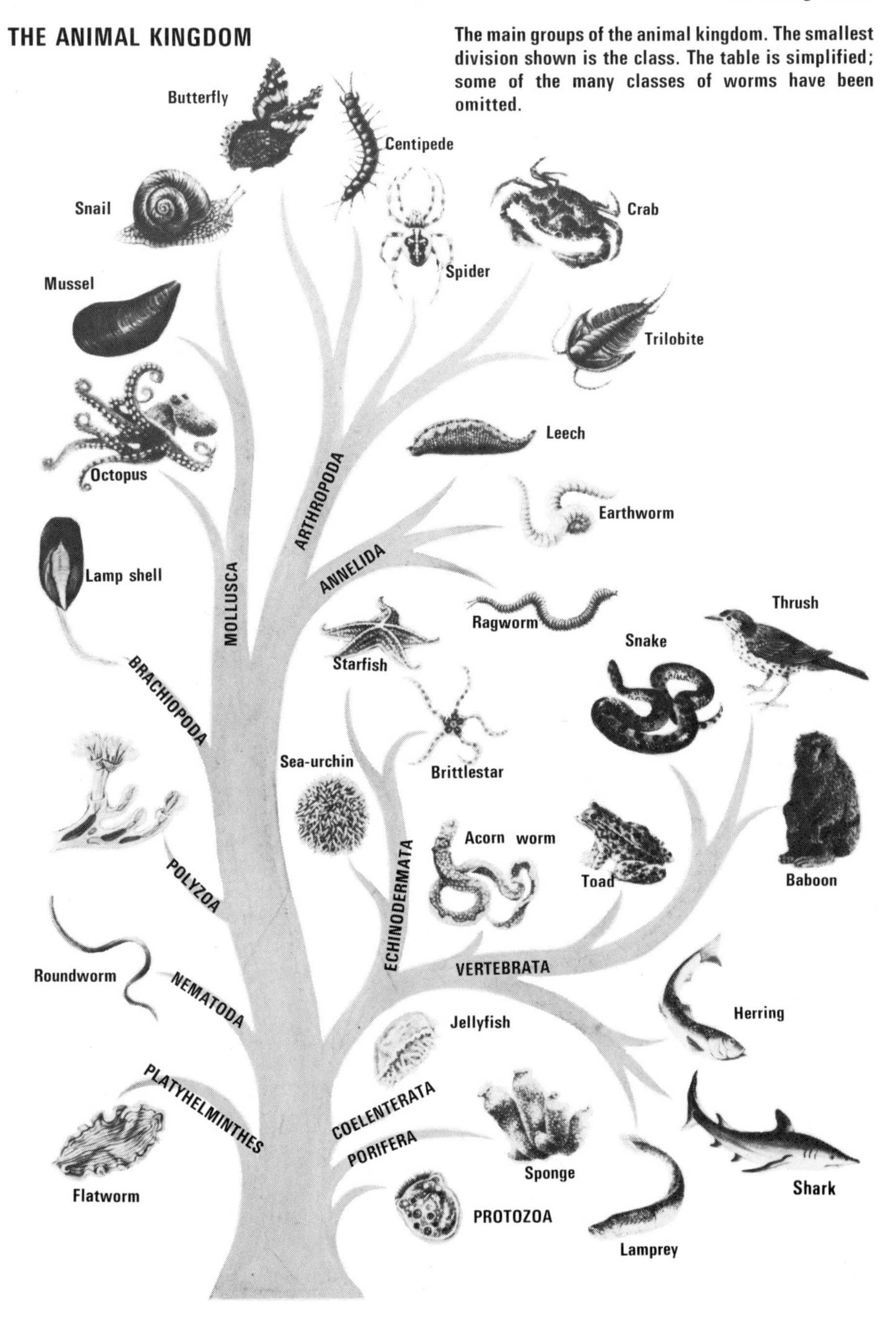

Birds

Where the male and female of a species are markedly different, they are both illustrated and are denoted as follows:

Male: ♂
Female: ♀

♀
Whitethroat
♂
Dunnock or Hedge Sparrow
Blackcap
♂
♂
♀
Greenfinch
♀
Bullfinch
Chaffinch
Redwing
Song Thrush
Yellowhammer
Collared Dove
Turtle Dove
Wood Pigeon

PHYSIOLOGY AND MEDICINE: NOBEL PRIZEWINNERS

Year	Prizewinner(s)
1901	Emil von Behring (German)
1902	Sir Ronald Ross (British)
1903	Niels Finsen (Danish)
1904	Ivan Pavlov (Russian)
1905	Robert Koch (German)
1906	Camillo Golgi (Italian) & Santiago Ramón y Cajal (Spanish)
1907	Charles Laveran (French)
1908	Paul Ehrlich (German) & Elie Metchnikoff (Russian/French)
1909	Emil Theodor Kocher (Swiss)
1910	Albrecht Kossel (German)
1911	Allvar Gullstrand (Swedish)
1912	Alexis Carrel (French)
1913	Charles Richet (French)
1914	Robert Bárány (Austrian)
1915–18	*No award*
1919	Jules Bordet (Belgian)
1920	August Krogh (Danish)
1921	*No award*
1922	Archibald Hill (British) & Otto Meyerhof (German)
1923	Sir Frederick Banting (Canadian) & John Macleod (British)
1924	Willem Einthoven (Dutch)
1925	*No award*
1926	Johannes Fibiger (Danish)
1927	Julius Wagner-Jauregg (Austrian)
1928	Charles Nicolle (French)
1929	Christiaan Eijkman (Dutch) & Sir Frederick Hopkins (British)
1930	Karl Landsteiner (American)
1931	Otto Warburg (German)
1932	Edgar Adrian & Sir Charles Sherrington (British)
1933	Thomas H. Morgan (American)
1934	George Minot, William P. Murphy, & George Whipple (American)
1935	Hans Spemann (German)
1936	Sir Henry Dale (British) & Otto Loewi (German/Austrian)
1937	Albert Szent-Györgyi (Hungarian)
1938	Corneille Heymans (Belgian)
1939	Gerhard Domagk (German) – declined
1943	Henrik Dam (Danish) & Edward Doisy (American)
1944	Joseph Erlanger & Herbert Gasser (Amer.)
1945	Sir Alexander Fleming, Howard Florey, & Ernst Chain (British)
1946	Hermann Muller (American)
1947	Carl and Gerty Cori (American) & Bernardo Houssay (Argentinian)
1948	Paul Müller (Swiss)
1949	Walter Hess (Swiss) & Antonio Moniz (Portuguese)
1950	Philip Hench & Edward Kendall (American), Tadeus Reichstein (Swiss)
1951	Max Theiler (S. African/American)
1952	Selman Waksman (American)
1953	Fritz Lipmann (German/American) & Hans Krebs (German/British)
1954	John Enders, Thomas Weller, & Frederick Robbins (American)
1955	Hugo Theorell (Swedish)
1956	André Cournand & Dickinson Richards Jr (American) and Werner Forssmann (German)
1957	Daniel Bovet (Italian)
1958	George Beadle, Edward Tatum, & Joshua Lederberg (American)
1959	Severo Ochoa & Arthur Kornberg (American)
1960	Sir Macfarlane Burnet (Australian) & Peter Medawar (British)
1961	Georg von Békésy (Hungarian/American)
1962	Francis Crick & Maurice Wilkins (British) & James Watson (American)
1963	Alan Hodgkin & Andrew Huxley (British) & Sir John Eccles (Australian)
1964	Konrad Bloch (German/American) & Feodor Lynen (German)
1965	François Jacob, André Lwoff, & Jacques Monod (French)
1966	Charles Huggins & Francis Peyton Rous (American)
1967	Ragnar Granit (Swedish) & Haldan Hartline & George Wald (American)
1968	Robert Holley, Har Gobind Khorana, & Marshall Nirenberg (American)
1969	Max Delbrück, Alfred Hershey, & Salvador Luria (American)
1970	Sir Bernard Katz (British), Ulf von Euler (Swedish), & Julius Axelrod (American)
1971	Earl Sutherland Jr (American)
1972	Rodney Porter (British) & Gerald Edelman (American)
1973	Karl von Frisch & Konrad Lorenz (Austrian) & Nikolaas Tinbergen (Dutch)
1974	Albert Claude & Christian de Duve (Belgian) & George Palade (Romanian-American)
1975	David Baltimore & Howard Temin (American), Renato Dulbecco (Italian)
1976	B. S. Blumberg & D. G. Gajdusek (American)
1977	Rosalyn Yalow, R. Guillemin & A. Schally (American)
1978	W. Arber (Swiss), D. Nathans & H. Smith (American)
1979	Godfrey Newbold Hounsfield (British) & Allan McLeod Cormack (American)

Medical dictionary

abrasion Area where skin has been scraped away, allowing blood or clear plasma to ooze out.
abscess Infected area where pus collects.
acne Infection of sebaceous glands of skin by bacteria, causing inflammation.
allergy Reaction, such as sneezing, to external substances, such as pollen.
alopecia Baldness; loss of hair from scalp.
amnesia Loss of memory.
amoebic dysentery See *dysentery*.
amphetamine Addictive stimulant, such as benzedrine or dexedrine.
anaemia Weakness of blood caused by lack of haemoglobin or too few red blood cells.
anaesthetic Substance producing loss of sensation in one part of the body (*local anaesthetic*) or total unconsciousness (*general anaesthetic*).
analgesic Pain-killing drug that does not produce unconsciousness.
angina Spasmodic pain as in chest (*angina pectoris*), due to diseased heart arteries.
antacid Alkali, such as sodium bicarbonate, taken internally to neutralize excess stomach acid.
anthrax Bacterial disease of cattle and sheep that can be passed on to man; symptoms include fever, swelling of lymph nodes, and pneumonia.
antibiotic Drug obtained from fungus, used to combat bacteria.

Francis Crick *(left)* and Maurice Wilkins shared the 1962 Nobel prize for work on DNA.

antihistamine Drug used to reduce symptoms of colds and allergies. See *allergy; histamine*.
antitussive Drug used to suppress part of brain that causes coughing.
appendicitis Inflammation of appendix.
arteriosclerosis Hardening and thickening of artery walls due to fatty and mineral deposits.
arthritis Inflammation of joints.
aspirin Analgesic and fever-reducing drug; chemical name, *acetylsalicylic acid*.
asthma Disorder of bronchial tubes due to either infection or allergy.
astringent Substance causing contraction of blood vessels and tissues; used to stop bleeding and body secretions.
atherosclerosis Formation of fatty deposit that obstructs blood flow in arteries.
athlete's foot Fungus infection of skin between toes.
autopsy Post-mortem (after death) examination.
barbiturate Sedative used in sleeping pills, e.g. amytal, nebutal, pentothal, phenobarbitone, seconal.
BCG vaccine Bacille Calmette Guèrin, used in vaccination against tuberculosis.
benign See *tumour*.
benzedrine Dangerous amphetamine with no medical uses; use results in wakefulness and feeling of elation.
beri-beri Disease resulting in swelling of body and numbness and weakness of legs; caused by lack of thiamine (vitamin B_1).
bile Fluid produced by liver that aids digestion of fats.
bilharzia (schistosomiasis) Group of tropical diseases caused by parasitic worms.
bilious Connected with nausea or vomiting.
biopsy Removal of small piece of tissue for examination under a microscope.
blackwater fever Advanced complication of malaria in which black or brown urine is produced.
blood groups Four types of blood that differ in presence or absence of factors in red blood cells (A and B) and serum (anti-A and anti-B).
boil Pus-filled infection of hair follicle or sweat gland caused by bacterium.
bone Hard compact tissue which forms skeleton; human body contains 212 bones.
botulism Rare food poisoning caused by bacterium in food.

Medical dictionary (contd.)

bronchitis Inflammation of bronchial tubes caused by bacterium or virus.
brucellosis Disease caused by bacterium; symptoms include fever, weakness, aches.
bubonic plague Disease caused by bacterium; symptoms include vomiting, delirium, swelling of lymph nodes (buboes); also called *Black Death* from dark spots due to bleeding under skin.
bunion Bony deposit in big toe; develops due to irritation caused by deformity in which toe is rotated sideways.
cancer Abnormal growth of cells, resulting in malignant tumour. See also *leukaemia*.
carbuncle Deep skin infection, filled with pus and having hard covering; can spread round body. See also *boil*.
carcinogen Irritant substance that helps cancer develop.
carcinoma Malignant tumour that arises in epithelium, tissue that lines skin, mucous membranes, and glands.
carrier Person who harbours infection without suffering from it or showing symptoms.
cartilage Hard flexible tissue that lines joints; found in other parts of body.
cataract Cloudy condition of eye lens, causing blurring of vision and eventual blindness.
catarrh Discharge from inflamed mucous membrane.
catheter Thin tube, used for injecting or removing fluid; it is passed up body tube, such as a vein.
cerebral palsy Muscular disability caused by damage to brain in unborn or young infant.
chicken pox Infectious disease caused by virus; symptoms, which appear 10–18 days after exposure, are marks on skin, which develop into blisters and erupt.
chilblain Localized red swelling, usually caused by exposure to extreme cold.
chlorpromazine Tranquillizer often used in treatment of mental illness.
cholesterol Steroid substance present in body.
cholera Disease caused by bacterium in food and water; can become epidemic in unsanitary conditions.
circumcision Surgical removal of part of foreskin of penis.
cirrhosis Liver disease; cells are destroyed and replaced by fatty or fibrous tissue.
codeine Analgesic derived from morphine.
colic Abdominal pain; often caused in infants by swallowing air during feeding; in adults there are a variety of causes.
congenital defect Disorder arising before birth.
conjunctivitis Inflammation of conjunctiva, membrane covering eye.
contagious disease One that can be transmitted by contact with someone who has it.
contusion Bruise.
coronary thrombosis See *heart attack*.
cortisone Steroid hormone produced by adrenal glands; can be manufactured for medical use.
cretinism Stunted growth, together with mental retardation, resulting from underactivity of thyroid gland.
croup Respiratory infection caused by virus or, sometimes, bacterium.
deficiency disease Caused by lack of vitamins or minerals.
depressant Drug that slows down a mental or physical activity of body.
dermatitis Inflammation of skin.
dexedrine Amphetamine drug that inhibits appetite.
diabetes mellitis Disorder in which body cannot control amount of sugar in blood; due to lack of hormone *insulin*.
digitalis Several poisonous compounds obtained from foxglove plant; used in treatment of heart disease.
dilatation Expansion of an opening or cavity; (widening of eye pupil is called *dilation*).
diphtheria Contagious disease due to bacterium; grey membrane forms in throat; patient very ill.
dysentery Infection of intestine causing diarrhoea and bleeding; due to bacterium or an amoeba.
dyspepsia Indigestion caused by overeating or improper diet.
eczema Skin disorder characterized by patches of red scaly skin.
electrocardiograph Machine used to record pulses of heart beat on graph (*electrocardiogram*).
electroencephalograph Machine used to record electrical activity of brain on graph (*electroencephalogram*).

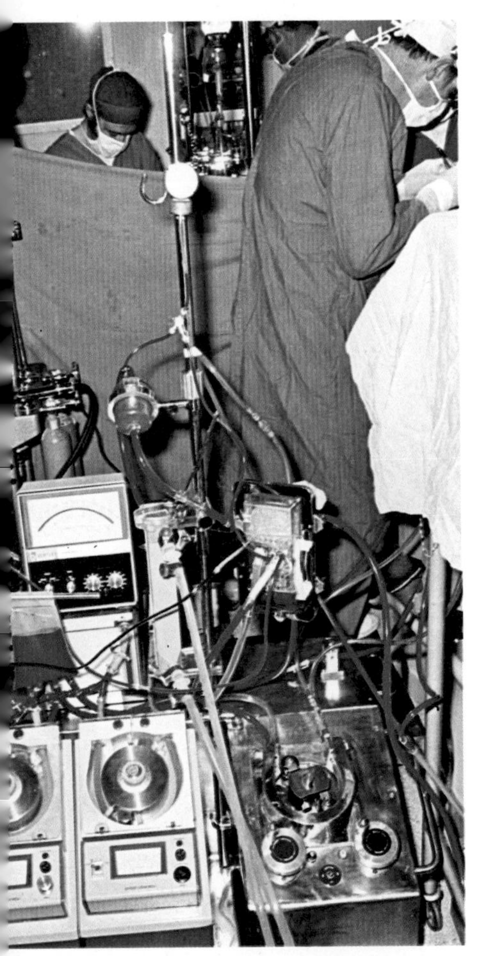

The heart-lung machine takes over functions of heart and lungs during major heart surgery, maintaining circulation and balance of oxygen and CO_2 in blood.

emetic Substance that promotes vomiting.
endemic Disease that persists in particular place among certain group of people.
enema Liquid injection into rectum and colon, e.g. as purgative.
enteritis Inflammation of intestine or stomach membrane, due to bacterium or virus infection, food poisoning, or too much alcohol or food; chief symptom is diarrhoea.
epilepsy Disorder of nervous system; periodic loss of consciousness, perhaps with convulsions.
expectorant Drug that aids coughing up of sputum.
flukes Small parasitic flatworms that infect man and animals; e.g. liver fluke, bilharzia.
gallstones Stones that form in gall bladder; composed of substances such as cholesterol and calcium.
gastrectomy Surgical removal of part or all of stomach.
gastritis Inflammation of stomach.
German measles (rubella) Contagious virus disease; pink rash on body, perhaps with tenderness of lymph nodes, appears 2 – 3 weeks after exposure; in pregnant woman can cause defects in infant.
glandular fever (mononucleosis) Disease in which blood contains unusually large amount of white blood cells; symptoms include fever, headache, swollen lymph glands.
glaucoma Eye disorder due to increased pressure of eyeball fluid; can lead to blindness.
goitre Disease caused by iodine deficiency; enlarged thyroid gland.
gonorrhoea See *venereal disease*.
gout Inflammation of various joints due to disorder of chemical processes and increased amount of uric acid in blood.
haemophilia Inherited disease in which blood clots very slowly when exposed to air.
haemorrhage Severe bleeding.
haemorrhoids (piles) Enlarged veins in wall of rectum near anus.
hallucinogen Drug causing abnormal mental states – hallucinations.
heart attack Occurs when blood supply to heart muscle stopped by clot (*coronary thrombosis*) or other blockage (*cardiac infarction*).
heartburn Chest pain, symptom of indigestion.
heart-lung machine Mechanically performs functions of heart and lungs – pumping and supplying oxygen to blood.
heart murmur Abnormal sound produced by heart; usually heard through stethoscope.
hemiplegia Paralysis of one side of body.
hepatitis Inflammation of liver due to virus infection.
hernia Weakening of muscle tissue round organ resulting in bulging through muscle.

Medical dictionary (contd.)

hexachlorophane Antiseptic used in, or in place of, soap to kill germs on skin.
histamine Substance produced by breakdown of histidine, an amino-acid, in all parts of body, normally in small amounts with irritating effects. See also *allergy; antihistamine.*
hydrophobia See *rabies.*
hypothermia Lowering of body temperature; can be medically achieved or may occur in old people living in cold conditions.
hysterectomy (uterectomy) Surgical removal of womb.
immunity Resistance to infection by particular disease.
immunization Artificial production of immunity, usually by injection.
industrial disease Any disorder that results from a person's occupation.
infarction Death of tissue due to stoppage of blood supply.
infectious disease One caused by infection by microscopic organism.
inflammation Reaction of tissues to infection or injury; symptoms include swelling, redness, warmth, pain.
influenza Infectious disease due to virus; symptoms include chills, fever.
inoculation Introduction of germs into body to produce immunity.
jaundice Condition shown by yellowish skin as result of too much bilirubin (constituent of bile) in blood; several causes, including hepatitis and gallstones.
laryngitis Inflammation of larynx (voice box).
laudanum Alcoholic solution of opium, once used as pain-killing drug.
leprosy Disease of skin, nerves, muscles, and bones; caused by bacterium.
lesion Wound or sore.
leukaemia Type of cancer in which blood contains abnormally large numbers of white blood cells.
ligament Band of fibrous tissue that binds bones together.
ligature Thread of material used to constrict part of body, such as blood vessel.
lobotomy Operation in which nerve fibres in lobe of brain are cut.
lumbago Persistent pain in lower part of back.
lumbar puncture Insertion of needle into small of back to remove fluid from spinal canal.
malaria Disease characterized by chills and fever; caused by protozoan parasite, *Plasmodium*, transmitted by mosquitoes.
malignant See *tumour.*
malnutrition Badly nourished condition of body.
mastectomy Surgical removal of breast.
mastitis Inflammation of breast due to infection or incorrect hormone balance.
measles Contagious disease due to virus, characterized by red rash on body, which appears about 10 days after exposure.

Inoculation for smallpox was pioneered by Edward Jenner in 1796. He saved thousands of lives.

meningitis Inflammation of membranes that surround brain and spinal cord.
metabolism All the chemical changes that occur in the body – the building-up (*anabolic*) and breaking-down (*catabolic*) processes.
metastasis Spread of disease round body by blood or lymphatic system.
migraine Disorder in which patient has severe headaches, perhaps with vision and speech disturbances or with nausea.
mongolism Congenital disorder in which child has short, broad face, slant eyes, weak muscles, and some mental retardation.
mononucleosis See *glandular fever*.
morphine Addictive analgesic derived from opium.
mucous membrane Smooth tissue that lines most cavities and passages of body and produces mucus.
multiple sclerosis Disease in which certain nerve linings are attacked and possibly destroyed, leading to weakness or non-function of parts of body.
mumps Contagious disease due to virus causing swelling of parotid gland in neck; symptoms 2 – 3 weeks after exposure.
muscle Connective tissue used for control and movement throughout body; human body has about 650 muscles of three types: *skeletal* (voluntary or striped); *visceral* (smooth); *cardiac*.
myxoedema See *goitre*.
narcotic Analgesic drug that produces stupor and sleep.
nephritis Inflammation of kidney.
nerve Body tissue that passes electrical impulses.
neuralgia Severe pain along nerve due to injury or irritation.
neuritis Inflammation of nerve.
neurosis Mental condition, often emotional, in which patient shows obsessional behaviour.
osteoarthritis Wearing away of cartilages of joints, often with bony outgrowths.
osteomyelitis Inflammation of bone marrow due to infection by bacterium.
osteoporosis Brittleness of bones due to loss of part of protein structure.
otosclerosis Deafness due to thickening and hardening of part of middle ear.
ovariectomy Surgical removal of one or both ovaries.

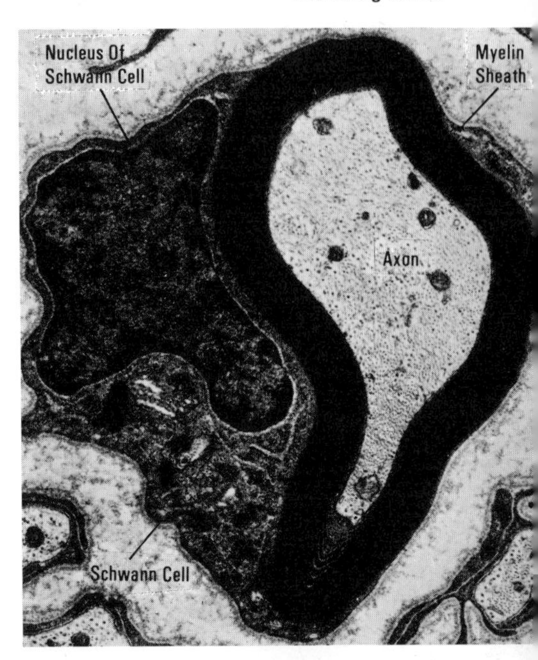

A section through a nerve cell, highly magnified. The axon carries the impulses, and the fatty sheath acts as an insulator.

pandemic Epidemic disease that spreads to many countries.
paracetamol Mild analgesic used in place of aspirin.
paraplegia Paralysis of lower part of body and legs.
Parkinson's disease Brain disorder in which voluntary movement becomes uncontrollable; may result from carbon monoxide poisoning or arteriosclerosis in brain.
penicillin Antibiotic obtained from *Penicillium*, a fungus mould.
peritonitis Inflammation of lining of abdominal cavity.
pessary Device worn inside vagina; may be contraceptive device or designed to correct displacement of womb.
pharyngitis Inflammation of pharynx, passage between mouth and gullet.
phenobarbitone Barbiturate used as mild sedative.
pleurisy Inflammation of membranes that cover lungs and line chest cavity.

Medical dictionary (contd.)

pneumoconiosis Inflammation of lungs due to dust, resulting in formation of fibrous tissue.
pneumonia Inflammation of lungs, which become filled with fluid; caused by bacterium, virus, or other foreign matter.
prosthesis Artificial replacement of part of body, such as limb.
pus Yellowish fluid produced by body against bacterial infection; consists of blood serum, white blood cells, bacteria, and damaged body tissue.
pyloric stenosis Obstruction of outlet of stomach into intestine.
quinine Antimalarial drug obtained from bark of cinchona tree.
rabies Virus disease transmitted in saliva of infected animals; symptoms include convulsions and extreme rage.
radiotherapy Treatment using X-rays, radium, or other radioactive substances.
resection Surgical removal of part of organ.
rheumatic fever Inflammation of inner lining and valves of heart; characterized by fever and swollen joints.
rheumatism Several disorders involving pain in joints and bones.
rheumatoid arthritis Inflammation of joint linings, leading to stiffness, swollen joints, deformity.
rickets Disease of children in which bones do not develop properly; due to Vitamin D deficiency.
ringworm (tinea) Fungus infection of skin.
roundworm Several types of worm, parasites of intestine.
sarcoma Malignant tumour that originates in connective tissue, such as muscle.
scarlet fever Disease occurring in people susceptible to poison released by bacterium; characterized by fever, sore throat, bright red rash.
sciatica Severe pain in sciatic nerve, which runs from lower back into legs.
sclerosis Hardening of tissues.
seborrhoea Excessive production of sebum, oily substance produced by sebaceous glands of skin; often associated with acne, eczema, and dandruff.
sedative Drug acting on nervous system to reduce tension and excitement.
septicaemia Blood poisoning due to infection and multiplication of bacteria.
shingles Inflammation along sensory nerve from spinal cord; characterized by blisters and great pain.
silicosis Inflammation of lung due to rock dust.
sinusitis Inflammation of mucous membranes of sinuses, head cavities linked to nose.
sleeping sickness Disease due to trypanosome, a protozoan, spread by tsetse fly; symptoms include fever and blood poisoning.
slipped disc Condition when cartilage disc of spine develops crack and piece of disc presses against nerve, causing pain.
smallpox Contagious virus disease characterized by rash of spots that leave scars; symptoms appear 10–14 days after exposure.
soporific Drug used to induce sleep.

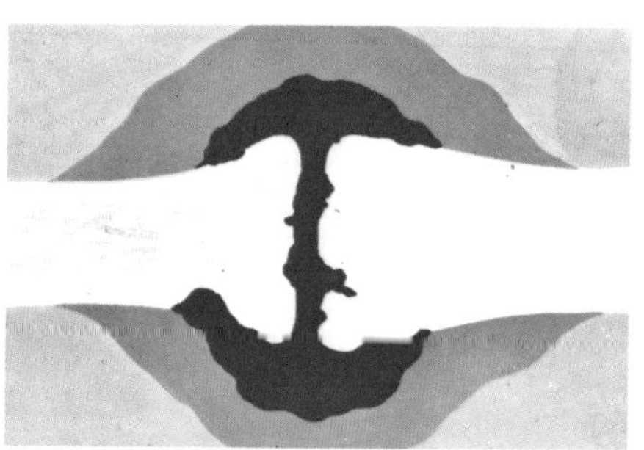

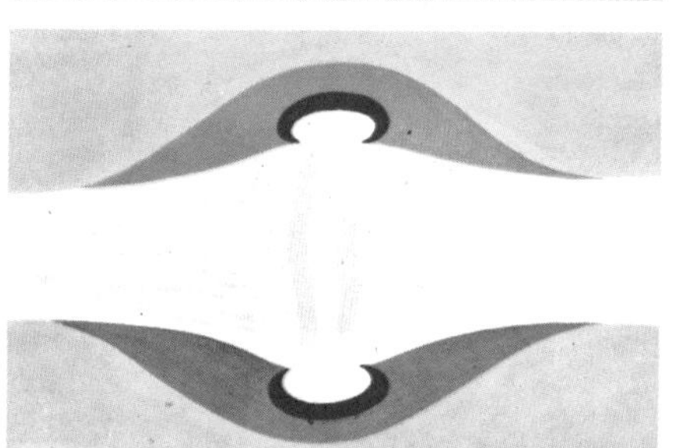

A normal joint in the finger (top) and a joint with arthritis (bottom). Cells that secrete lubricating fluids have reproduced too fast and filled the joint, wearing away tissue and causing swelling.

sphygmomanometer Instrument used to measure blood pressure.
spina bifida Congenital disorder due to improper formation of spine and spinal cord; affects muscles and bladder.
steroids Large group of natural and synthetic compounds, including many hormones; often used to act against inflammation.
stimulant Drug that stimulates rate of mental or physical body process.
strabismus (squint) Condition in which person cannot focus both eyes on one spot at same time.
stroke Brain damage resulting from lack of blood, and hence oxygen, due to blockage or rupture of artery.
sulfa drug Sulphonamide drug used against bacteria in various diseases.
suppository Small cone of glycerin inserted into rectum or vagina, containing antiseptic or other medication.
syphilis See *venereal disease*.
tapeworms Several intestinal parasitic worms that attach themselves by hooks on the head and produce reproductive segments which break off; can be caught from uncooked beef, pork, or fish.
tendon Strong band of connective tissue that connects muscle to bone.
tetanus Disease caught by bacterium, results in spasms of voluntary muscles.
threadworm Small roundworm that infects large intestine.
thrombosis Blockage of blood vessel by clot.
tinea See *ringworm*.
tonsillitis Inflammation of the tonsils, two pieces of tissue that protect throat from invading germs.
tracheotomy Surgical operation in which opening is made through neck into trachea, the wind-pipe.
tranquillizer Drug that calms mental agitation without causing much drowsiness.
trephining (trepanning) Operation making hole in skull by removing piece of bone.
tuberculosis Disease of lungs that may also affect pharynx, bones, joints, or skin; caused by bacterium; symptoms include coughing, blood-streaked sputum, enlargement of lymph glands, general ill-health.
tumour Swelling resulting from abnormal growth of tissue; *benign tumours* are harmless; *malignant tumours* (cancer) may spread.
typhoid Disease caused by salmonella bacteria, transmitted in food or water; symptoms include fever, chills, red spots on chest.
typhus Group of diseases caused by organisms intermediate between bacteria and viruses.
ulcer Inflamed open sore on skin or membrane lining body cavity.
uraemia Blood poisoning due to non-removal by kidneys of toxic waste products.
urethritis Inflammation of urethra, the bladder tube.
uterectomy See *hysterectomy*.
vaccination Technique of producing immunity by injecting a vaccine.
vaccine Preparation containing germs, live, weakened or dead.
venereal disease Disease of the genitals – *chancroid*, *gonorrhoea*, and *syphilis* – transmitted through sexual contact.
whooping cough Contagious disease of bronchial tubes; symptoms, which appear 7–14 days after exposure, are feverish cold and cough, which develops into 'whoop'.
yellow fever Tropical virus disease transmitted by mosquito; affects liver and kidneys, causing jaundice.

Tumours can now be detected with radiation, and strong doses can even cure them.

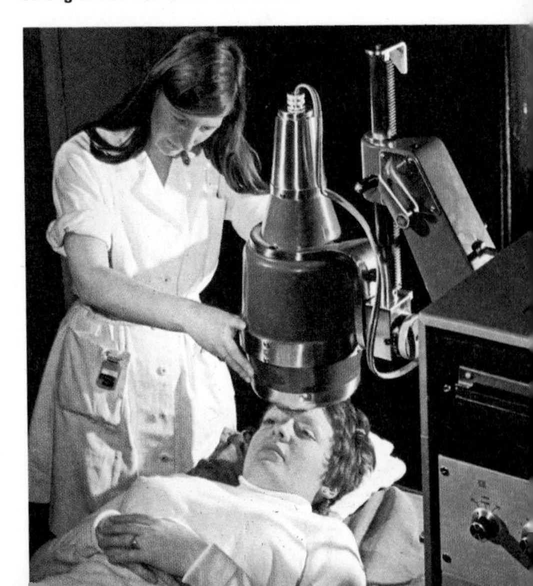

The Arts

Painting

abstract art Art form that represents ideas (by means of geometric and other designs) instead of natural forms; pioneered by Kandinsky (early 1900s), and taken up by Miró and de Kooning.

abstract expressionism A combination of abstract art and expressionism; consists mainly of dripping and smearing paint at random. It was pioneered in US by Jackson Pollock after World War II.

action painting Type of abstract expressionism.

airbrush Device used by artist to spray paint, varnish, or fixative; worked by compressed air.

aquarelle A water-colour painting.

Barbizon School Group of mid-19th-century French landscape painters (including Corot, Millet, and Rousseau) who worked in village of Barbizon (Forest of Fontainbleu). They tried to paint nature as it is.

baroque Style that flourished from late 1500s to early 1700s. Characterized by exaggerated shapes, with rich, flowing curves (Tintoretto, El Greco, Rubens).

Blaue Reiter ('blue rider') Group of Munich artists (1911) who highlighted various modern art forms; started by Kandinsky and Marc; joined later by Klee.

Byzantine Style practised in Eastern Roman Empire (400s–1453); figures are stiff and formal, with rich colours.

Camden Town Group Splinter group of English painters who came out of New English Art Club in early 1900s; possibly introduced post-impressionism into English art. Group led by Sickert and included Gilman.

cave paintings Pictures (mostly animals) painted by prehistoric artists on the walls of caves; best known are in Lascaux (France) and Altamira (Spain).

This painting *Guernica* by Picasso was produced after the bombing of the Basque town in 1937. It is painted in shades of grey and black.

chiaroscuro ('light-dark') Balance of light and shade in a picture and the artist's skill in handling this.

conversation piece Type of portrait painting that included two or more people (usually of the same family) informally or casually posed; popular in Netherlands (1600s) and England (1700s); often painted by Hogarth, Zoffany, Devis.

cubism Important movement in modern French painting started by Picasso and Braque in 1907. Cubists aimed to reduce objects to basic shapes of cubes, spheres, cylinders, and cones.

dadaism (derived from *dada*, French for 'hobby-horse') Outrageous and nihilistic movement started in Zurich (1916) as protest against all artistic and civilized standards. Duchamp was a leading exponent; Modigliani and Kandinsky dabbled.

diptych Picture painted on two panels, often hinged like pages of a book; popular in 15th-century Flanders.

direct painting School of American landscape painters of late 1800s; characterized by extremely bold brushwork (Redfield, Symons, etc).

distemper Cheap and impermanent method of painting in which powdered colours are mixed with glue; often used for theatrical scenery.

Dutch School Art and artists of Netherlands in 1600s; typified by precise draughtsmanship, wonderful colour, and great attention to detail. Leading exponents were Rembrandt, Hals, Van der Velde, Maes, Metsun, Hobbema, Cuyp, Huysum.

ebauche First coat, or undercoat, in oil painting; should have low oil content.

egg tempera A painting medium in which the colours are ground with pure egg yolk; one of the most permanent media available.

ethnic art Term used increasingly, particularly in America, when describing art produced by distinct groups—such as Puerto Ricans or Negroes—and reflecting the increased importance given to the rights of minority groups in society.

expressionism Movement that aims at expressing the artist's inner feelings and experiences, rejecting reality and idealism even to point of distortion. Began in late 1800s; Van Gogh, Gauguin, Matisse, Picasso, and Rouault were adherents at various times.

Fauves ('wild beasts') Group of Parisian painters of early 1900s (Dufy, Matisse, Rouault, Vlaminck, etc) who shocked the critics by their brilliant use of colour.

finger painting Chinese water-colour technique using finger instead of a brush.

French Romantic School Early 19th-century movement of French painters, led by Delacroix; artists mixed fantasy with realism and at the same time aimed at 'getting back to nature'.

fresco Method of great antiquity but perfected during Italian Renaissance; uses pigments ground in water applied to a fresh lime-plaster wall or ceiling.

Turner, with Constable, founded a great British tradition of landscape and seascape painting. This is Turner's ***Ulysses deriding Polyphemus.***

futurism Italian artistic movement (1905–15) that emphasized violence, machinery, and politics, and was anti-cultural and anti-romantic. Painters used cubist forms and strong colours.

genre painting One that shows simple scenes from everyday life; some pictures tell a story. Dutch painters of 1500s and 1600s (De Hooch, Steen, Metsu, etc) were experts.

gesso Mixture of plaster and glue used to cover wooden panels before painting.

gouache Non-transparent water-colour paint that provides easy way of obtaining oil-painting effects. Turner and Girtin pioneered the method in England.

icon Religious picture (usually painted on wood or ivory) associated with Eastern Church. Earliest surviving icons date from 500s.

impasto Thick laying on of paint on canvas or wood. Brush marks are clearly visible on oil paintings with heavy impasto.

impressionism Important movement that developed among French painters just

Below: **This Roman wall-painting dates from the 1st century AD. It was preserved by lava when the volcano Vesuvius erupted in AD 76.**

after mid-1800s. Impressionists were particularly concerned with light and its effects. They put down on canvas their immediate impressions of nature. Monet, Renoir, Pissaro, Sisley, Cézanne, and Degas were leading impressionists.

intimism Kind of impressionism technique applied to intimate and familiar interiors instead of landscape; adopted by small group of French painters led by Bonnard and Vuillard.

Kitchen Sink School Group of British painters who aimed at depicting 'realism' of the 1950s; pioneered by David Bomberg and John Bratby.

landscape painting Picture whose main subject is pure landscape without human figures; rare before 1600s. Dutch painters (van Ruisdael, Hobbema) and later British painters (Turner, Constable, Cox) made the form fashionable.

London Group Group (founded 1913) formed by union of Camden Town Group and Vorticists. Members included Gilman and Sickert. It still exhibits (including many *avant-garde* works).

mannerism Style of European art (1520–1600) that set out to break rules with strained, exaggerated figures in vivid colours. Vasari was prominent mannerist.

Mariola Painting of the Virgin Mary.

Meldrum School Australian group of painters inspired by Max Meldrum; founded 1913.

miniature Tiny painting (less than 6 in, or 15 cm, across), usually a portrait, most often in gouache or water-colour on card, parchment, ivory, or metal sheet. English artists of 1500s and 1600s (Hilliard, Oliver, Hopkins) excelled.

mural Wall-painting, usually executed in fresco, oil, or tempera.

Nabis (Hebrew, 'prophet') Small group of French painters, founded in late 1890s, who tried to convey a depth of emotion and mysticism to everyday scenes. Inspired by Maurice Denis; led by Vuillard and Bonnard.

narrative painting One that tells a story; popular in Victorian England and exploited by Landseer, Mulready, etc.

naturalism Style that portrays objects with photographic detail. Compared with realism it is often stilted and monotonous.

Nazarenes Semi-religious group of artists founded in Vienna (1809) by Overbeck and Pforr. They held that art should be subject to religious ideas.

Persians were very skilled miniature painters. This picture of a hunting party, which dates from the 15th century, illustrates a book of poems.

neo-classicism Movement, started in Rome in mid-1700s, that imitated simple art of the Greeks and Romans. In painting, mythological and anatomical subjects were popular. David, Ingres, Alma-Tadema, Lord Leyton, and Allston were leading artists.

neo-impressionism Type of painting that developed in France in late 1800s. Relied largely on formal composition and application of pure blobs of colour. Pioneered by Seurat and Signac. Also called *pointillism.*

neo-romanticism Romantic realism of the 1900s in England. Inspired by words of

Painting (contd.)

Blake and works of Palmer and Calvert; typified by paintings of Sutherland, Nash, Piper.
nimbus Halo or disc surrounding head of religious figure.
Norwich School Group of East Anglian painters of 1700s. Leading members included Crome and Cotman.
oil painting Technique of covering a slightly absorbent surface with pigment ground in oil; introduced in 1400s, perfected by Van Eyck brothers.
op art (optical art) Modern technique with which painter creates optical illusions by means of dazzling patterns.
orphism French abstract movement founded in 1912. Followers described it as 'art of painting new structures out of elements that have . . . been created entirely by the artist himself'. Delaunay was one of founders. Later called *simultaneism.*
palette Range of colours available to a painter; usually arranged on little board for easy mixing, with thumb-hole for holding.
pastel Painter's colouring medium consisting of crayon of pure pigment or pigment mixed with chalk and other materials. First used in 1500s; Chardin and Fantin La Tour became masters of pastel in 1700s.
pastiche Painting made up of motives and fragments copied from another artist.
pigments Dry paints or dyes that are mixed with oil, water, or other fluid and used to paint with.
pointillism See *neo-impressionism.*
polyptych Series of painted doors, panels, etc, with more parts than *triptych,* hinged or folded together.
pop art Movement born independently in Britain and US in 1950s and 1960s. Uses photos, strip cartoons, adverts, etc, as sources, often enlarged and painted surrealistically in garish colours. Paolozzi, Johns, and Rauschenberg were among pioneers.
portrait painting Representation in painting of a human being. First portraits were usually of kings and other leaders. Among self-portraits, those of Rembrandt are the most numerous and famous.
post-impressionism Work of French painters that followed impressionism between 1885 and 1905. Artists experimented freely with expression, form, and design instead of representing nature realistically; typified by Cézanne, Gauguin, Van Gogh, Renoir, and Degas.
Pre-Raphaelite Brotherhood Group mainly of painters who advocated return to spirit and manner of art before time of Raphael (1483–1520). Founded in England (mid-1800s) by Rossetti, Holman Hunt, and Millais; members practised truthful adherence to natural forms and effects.
realism Approach to painting that began with Courbet in France in 1800s. Its adherents tried to portray an impression of everyday life.

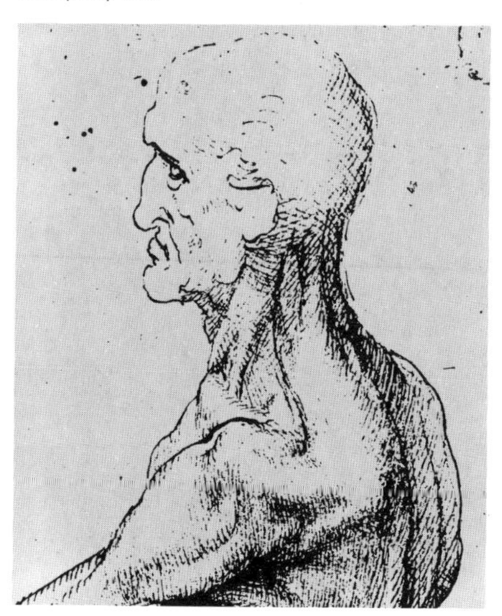

A study by Leonardo, one of the great artists of the Renaissance.

Renaissance Rebirth in arts and learning that took place in Europe (especially Italy) from 1300s to 1500s. In painting it was typified by original styles, underived from antiquity. Among the masters of this period were Leonardo da Vinci, Michelangelo, Titian, and Raphael.
representational art Type of painting that shows objects as nearly as possible as they actually are; the opposite of *abstract art.*
rococo European art style (about 1735–1765) characterized in painting by lavish decoration and extravagant ornament.

This family portrait was drawn by the French neo-classical artist Ingres (1780–1867). He used fine lines and worked in great detail, giving a slightly romantic view of his sitters.

romanticism Works in which painter allows his emotions, personal feelings, and imagination free play; the opposite of *classicism.* Géricault, Delacroix, Turner, Constable, and Blake were romanticists.
secco painting Method of wall-painting in which wall is first soaked with lime water. Pigments are mixed with solution of glue, casein, or egg yolk and applied to moist wall. Easier to use but less permanent than fresco.
simultaneism See *orphism.*
still life Art form in which subject of picture is made up of inanimate objects; favourite form of Dutch School.
stippling Type of water-colour painting in which artist applies colours in series of minute spots; Holman Hunt favoured this method.

Painting (contd.)

Sung Period Painting executed during Sung Dynasty (960–1280), characterized by magical landscapes, paintings on silk, and huge temple frescoes.
surrealism 20th-century art movement that aimed at escaping control of reason and tried to express subconscious mind pictorially. Ernst, Arp, and Dali have been leading exponents.
symbolism See *synthetism*.
synthetism A movement started by Gauguin in late 1800s as kind of post-impressionism involving the use of broad, flat tones of colour; also called *symbolism*.
tachisme (from French for 'stain' or 'blot') Freest form of action painting. Accidental patterns are produced by applying paint to any surface in any way at all. Dubuffet was a pioneer.
tempera Binding medium for powder colours, made up of egg yolk, sometimes thinned with water. Tempera mixtures last longer than oil colours.
tenebrists School of painters in 1500s who followed style of Caravaggio. Their pictures, often gloomy, made great use of light and shade.
triptych Series of three painted panels or doors that are hinged or folded.
underpainting First thin layers of colour in oil painting
Utrecht School Group of Dutch painters who worked in Utrecht in early 1600s. Among them were Terbrugghen, Honthurst, and Baburen.
Venetian School Painters who worked in Venice during High Renaissance. They included Titian, Veronese, Tintoretto, and Giorgione; work marked by masterly use of chiaroscuro and rich colouring.
vorticism English *avant-garde* art movement started by Wyndham Lewis in 1912. Adherents painted in an abstract style.
water-colour Technique of painting with colours that have been mixed with water-soluble gum; paints are applied to paper with soft, moistened brush. English painters such as Cozens, Sandby, Cotman, Girtin, and Turner were supreme at the art.

The *Consecration of St Nicholas*, by Veronese, is a fine example of the work of the Venetian School.

Surrealism let the artist create as his subconscious mind dictated; it released a new dream world of art.

This abstract bronze sculpture is by the British sculptor Henry Moore, who was born in 1898. Many of his works are on a massive scale and decorate public buildings in many parts of the world.

Sculpture

A-Z of Sculpture

armature Wood or metal framework used to support sculptor's model.
boucharde Stonemason's hammer with heavy steel head with pyramidal points; used for initial blocking out of stone.
bronze Alloy of copper and tin used by sculptors in Ancient Greece, Rome, China, and Africa; revived in modern times.
bust Sculpture of the upper part of the human body.
cast Figure made from mould of original model. See *cire perdue, plaster cast, sand cast.*
ciment fondu Fine-grade black or white aluminous cement used for delicate modelling.
chisel See *boucharde, pitcher, point, claw chisel.*
cire perdue (French, 'lost wax') Traditional method for casting bronze sculptures: Model with wax surface is enclosed in mould; wax is melted and runs out through holes at bottom; molten metal poured through holes at top, filling up space left by wax.
claw chisel Toothed chisel that gives furrow-like effect to stone; used prior to final defining of form with cutting chisel or by abrasion.
figurine Miniature figure.

The *Venus de Milo,* now in the Louvre, Paris, was found on the Greek island of Melos in 1820.

free-stone An easily worked fine-grained limestone or sandstone.
genre sculpture Style that reflects everyday or rustic life; hallmark of Etruscan art and of Biblical subjects in Middle Ages.
glyptic Carved as opposed to modelled.
heroic Any figure or group of figures carved larger than life.
intaglio Hollow relief, in which the form is cut out of surface.

A–Z of sculpture (contd.)

maquette (French, 'small model') Small wax or clay model made by sculptor in preparation for larger work.
marble Popular stone for sculpture because of its extreme durability; found in all colours from nearly pure white to nearly pure black.
mobile Movable sculpture of shapes cut out of wood or sheet metal, linked by wires or rods in order to revolve easily or move up and down; invented by American sculptor Alexander Calder (1932).
modelling Building-up of forms in three dimensions by means of plastic material such as clay or wax.
patina Greenish surface film on old bronze, generally enhancing appearance.
plaster cast Intermediate stage in bronze sculpture from which final mould is made.
pitcher Wide chisel, used after *boucharde*, for removing large quantities of material from flat surfaces.

A bronze woman and child by the French Impressionist painter Renoir (1841–1919), who turned to sculpture in his old age.

Michelangelo's marble sculpture of Lorenzo de' Medici.

point Pointed chisel used for channelling surface to near required depth; used after *pitcher*.
pointing machine Device for reproducing cast in stone.
polychromatic sculpture Sculpture painted in naturalistic colours to make it more lifelike; mostly pre-1500s.
relief Sculpture not free-standing from background; various degrees, from *bas-relief* (low relief) to *alto-relievo* (high relief).
riffler Small, curved file for intricate work in wood, stone, or metal.
sand cast Mould of special sand made from plaster model and from which bronze cast is made.
sculpture-in-the-round Sculpture that can be seen from all sides.
stabile Sculpture that does not move, as opposed to *mobile*.

Music

Glossary of Musical Terms

accelerande Gradually faster.
adagio At a slow pace.
agitato Restless or agitated.
allegretto At a fairly fast pace.
allegro At a fast pace.
alto Highest adult male voice (artificially produced).
andante At a quiet, peaceful pace.
animato Quickening, in a lively fashion.
arpeggio Notes of chord played in rapid succession, one after the other.
atonality Absence of key; used by some contemporary composers who discard traditional major and minor scales.
bar Metrical division of music bounded by vertical bar-lines.
baritone Male voice higher than bass and lower than tenor.
bass Lowest male voice.
brass instruments Metal instruments sounded by blowing through mouthpiece and altering tension of lips (French horn, trumpet, euphonium, trombone, tuba).
cadenza Solo passage in musical piece (written or improvised) for soloist to show off technique.
cantabile Expressive or songlike.
cantata Vocal work for soloists, chorus and orchestra.
chamber music Music for a room or small hall, played by two or more solo instruments.
chord Three or more notes sounded together.
choir A body of singers.
chorus Main body of singers in choir; words and music repeated after each stanza of song.
chromatic scale Scale made up of semitones.
classical music Music that aims at perfection of structure and design (period of Bach to Brahms).
clef Sign in musical notation that fixes pitch of each note written on the stave.
coda 'Rounding off' passage of music.
concerto Substantial work for one or more solo instruments and orchestra.
contralto Lowest female voice.
contrapuntal Adjectival form of *counterpoint.*
counterpoint Two or more melodies combined to form a satisfying harmony.
counter-tenor Another name for alto.
crescendo Increasing in loudness.
descant The addition of a second melody above a given melody; form of counterpoint.
diatonic scale Major or minor scale that includes whole tones and semitones.
diminuendo Gradually softer.
flat Conventional sign showing that pitch of a certain note has been lowered by a semitone.
forte Played or sung loudly.
fortissimo Very loud (loudest).

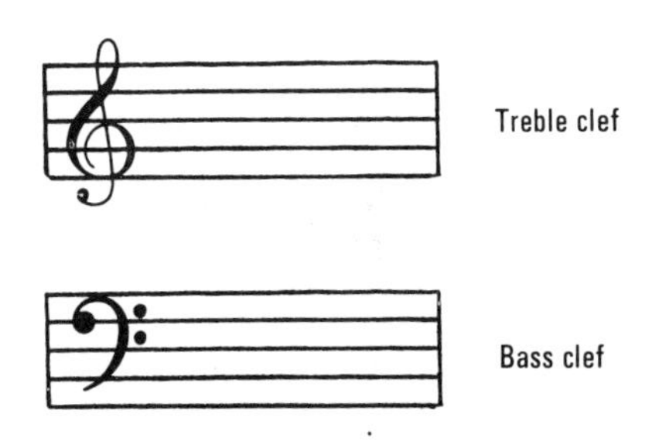

fugue Method of writing contrapuntal music for various parts or 'voices' in which one or more subjects are treated imitatively.
glissando Gliding; rapid scales (on piano or harp), played with sliding movement.
harmony Combining of chords to make musical sense.
interval Distance in pitch between notes.
key Classification of the notes of a scale.
key-note Note on which a scale is based.
key signature Indication of number of sharps or flats in piece of music; usually written at beginning of each line.
largo At a slow pace.
legato One note leading smoothly to next.
leger lines Short extra lines added above or below stave to accommodate very high or low notes.
Lied German word for 'song' (plural *Lieder*).
major One of the two main scales, with semitones between 3rd and 4th and 7th and 8th notes.
measure *Bar* (American).
melody A tune; series of musical sounds following each other, as distinct from harmony.
mezzo Half or medium.

The instruments of the orchestra. They are divided into families. Immediately below are the woodwind instruments, the piccolo, flute, oboe, clarinet, cor anglais, and bassoon. They are generally, though not always, made of wood, which gives them their name. Below are the brass wind instruments, the trumpet, trombone, horn and tuba. They have long tubes sometimes coiled round several times.

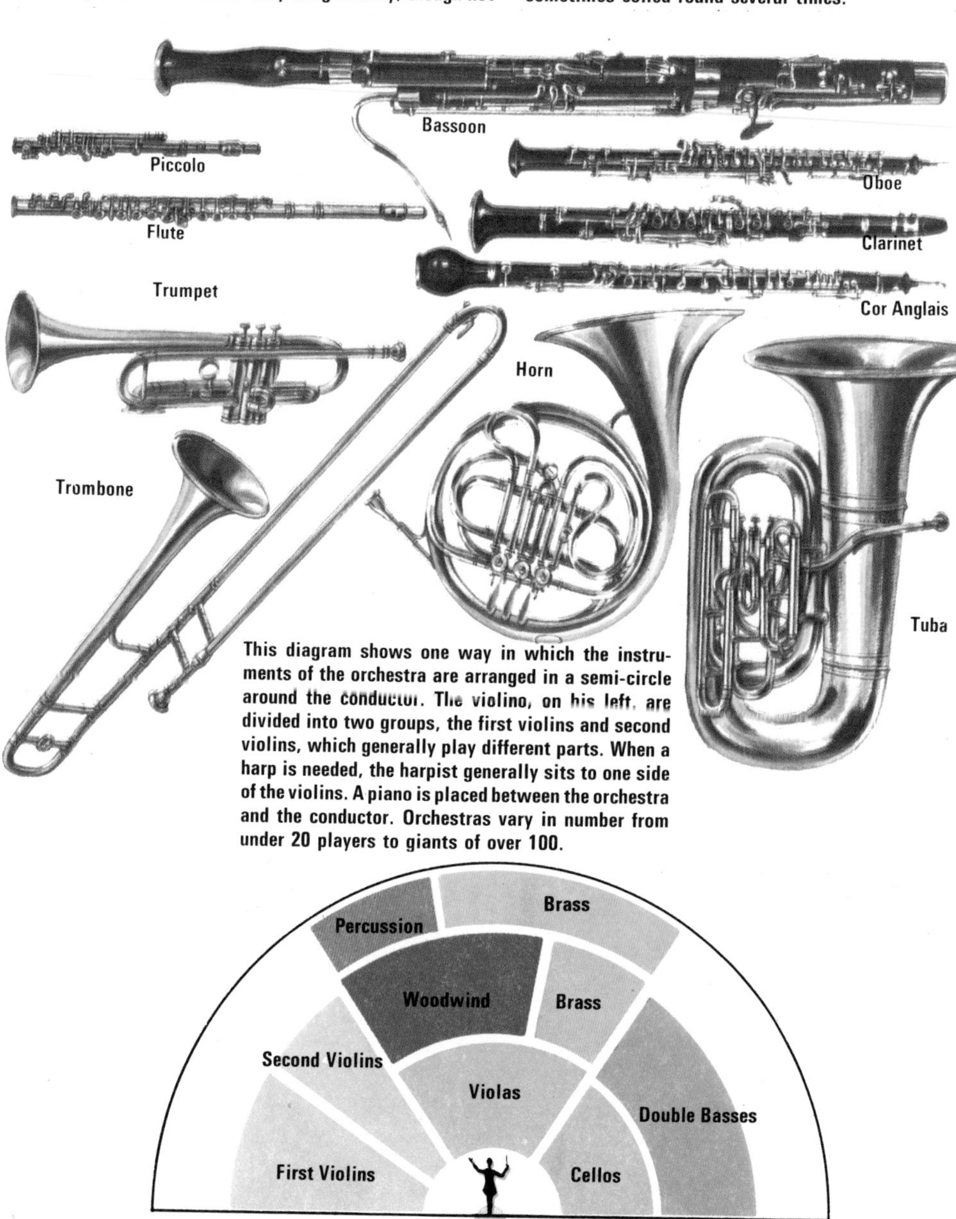

This diagram shows one way in which the instruments of the orchestra are arranged in a semi-circle around the conductor. The violins, on his left, are divided into two groups, the first violins and second violins, which generally play different parts. When a harp is needed, the harpist generally sits to one side of the violins. A piano is placed between the orchestra and the conductor. Orchestras vary in number from under 20 players to giants of over 100.

On the left are the stringed instruments, the violin, viola, cello, and double bass. They are played by drawing taut horsehairs strung on a bow across their strings. The harp, below, is only occasionally used with the orchestra. The other instruments on this page are all percussion instruments, that is they are struck to produce a sound. Shown here are tubular bells, four types of drum, cymbals and triangle.

Glossary of musical terms (contd.)

mezzo-soprano Female voice between contralto and soprano.
minor One of the two main scales. Harmonic minor scales have a semitone between 2nd and 3rd, 5th and 6th, and 7th and 8th notes. In the *melodic minor*, there are semitones between 2nd and 3rd and 7th and 8th notes ascending, and between 6th and 5th and 3rd and 2nd descending.
modulation Changing from one key to another according to rules of harmony.
movement Complete section of larger work (such as a symphony), played at different speed from its predecessor.
musique concrète Music based on sound patterns produced electronically.
natural Conventional sign that restores note to its natural pitch after it has been previously sharpened or flattened.
nocturne A 'night-piece', tuneful but sad.
octave Interval made up of 8 successive notes of scale, from one note to note of same name, above or below.
opus A work; when followed by a number indicates order of musician's compositions.
oratorio Religious musical composition for soloists, chorus, and orchestra, but without costume or scenery.
percussion instruments Instruments that are struck (drums, tambourine, cymbals, bells, glockenspiel, xylophone, vibraphone, marimba, triangle, gong, castanets, etc.),
pianissimo Very soft (softest).
piano Played or sung softly; shortened to *p*.
pitch Highness or lowness in sound of one note compared with another.
pizzicato Playing strings by plucking.
plainsong Unaccompanied vocal melody used in medieval church music.
prestissimo Extremely fast.
presto At a fast pace.
programme music Music that tells a story.
rest Conventional sign denoting silence on performer's part.
ritardando Slowing down.
romantic music Music (mainly 19th century) that plays on the emotions, as distinct from classical music.
scale Progression of successive notes ascending or descending.
scherzo A jest; hence a lively, unsentimental piece of music.

These Indian musicians do not use the Western scale.

score Written music showing all parts (vocal and instrumental) of composition on separate staves.
semitone A half-tone; smallest interval commonly used in western music.
sharp Conventional sign indicating that note referred to has been raised in pitch by semitone.
sonata Musical piece, usually for one or two players, following the *sonata-form*; made up of exposition, development, and recapitulation.
soprano Highest female voice.
sostenuto Sustained.
sotto voce Passage performed in undertone.
staccato In short, detached fashion; notes to be played thus have a dot over them.
stave or **staff** Framework of lines and spaces on which music is usually written.
stringed instruments Instruments that are played with a bow (violins, violas, cellos, double basses).
suite Orchestral piece in several movements.
symphony Large orchestral piece of music of a serious nature, usually in four movements.
syncopation Shifting of accent onto beat not normally accented.
tempo Pace or speed of piece of music.
tenor Highest natural male voice.
time signature Figures written at beginning of piece to indicate kinds of beats in a bar and their number.
toccata Instrumental piece (usually for

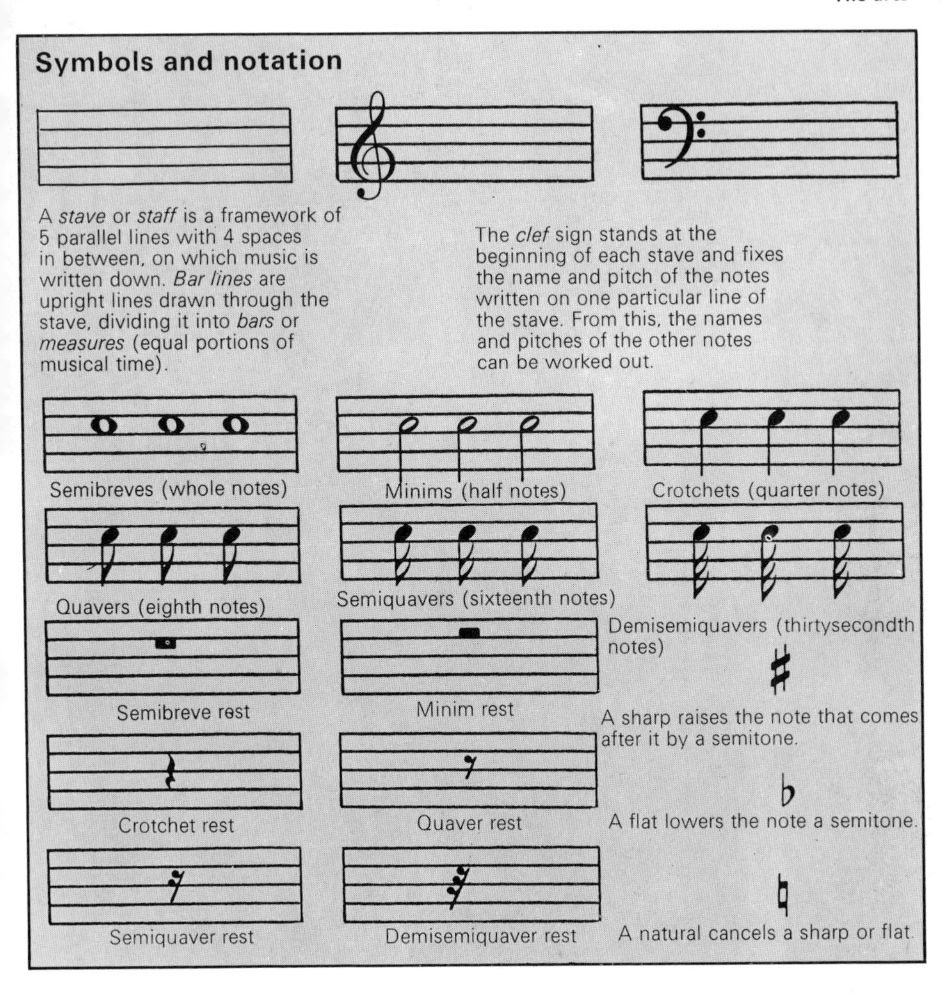

one performer) that requires a rapid and brilliant touch (e.g. for organ).
tone Quality of musical sound; an interval made up of two semitones.
treble Upper part of a composition; a high voice, usually of children.
tremolo Literally, 'trembling'; on stringed instruments, a single note repeated extremely rapidly over and over again, with an alternation in volume.
tutti All performers (not soloists) together.
twelve-note Method of composition in which all 12 notes in octave (on piano, 5 black and 7 white) have equal importance.
unison United sounding of same note by two or more instruments or voices.
vibrato Rapid regular fluctuation in pitch of note produced by string player or singer to increase emotional effect.
virtuoso Musician of outstanding technical skill.
vivace Played in a lively manner.
woodwind instruments that are blown and are traditionally, but not always, made of wood; they may be blown direct or by means of reed; they include clarinet, oboe, flute, piccolo, recorder, saxophone, bassoon, and English horn.

The Ballet

arabesque Position in which dancer stands on one leg with arms extended, body bent forward from hips, while other leg is stretched out backwards.
attitude Position in which dancer stretches one leg backwards, bending it a little at knee so that lower part of leg is parallel to floor.
ballerina Female ballet dancer.
barre Exercise bar fixed to classroom wall at hip level; dancers grasp it when exercising.
battement Beating movement made by raising and lowering leg, sideways, backwards, or forwards.
choreography Art of dance composition.
corps de ballet Main body of ballet dancers, as distinct from soloists.
entrechat Leap in which dancer rapidly strikes heels together in air.
fouetté Turn in which dancer whips free leg round.
glissade Gliding movement.
jeté Leap from one foot to another.
pas Any dance step.
pas de deux Dance for two.
pas seule Solo dance.
pirouette Movement in which dancer spins completely round on one foot.
pointes Tips of dancer's toes, on which many movements are executed.
positions Five positions of feet on which ballet is based (see illustrations).
tutu Short, stiff, spreading skirt worn in classical ballet.

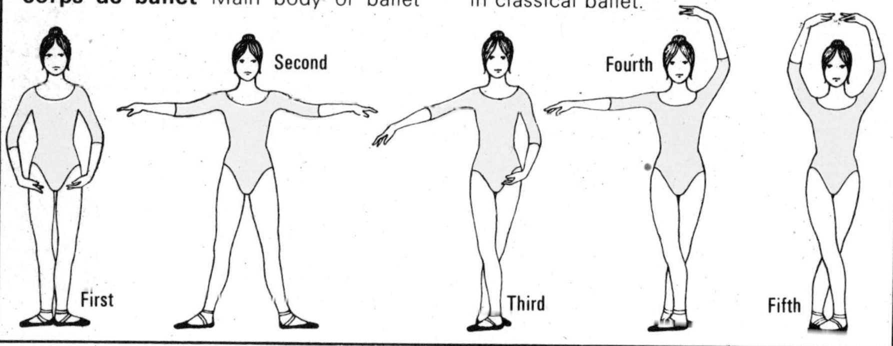

Opera Terms

aria (Italian, 'air') A solo.
ballad opera Simple kind of opera, made up of popular tunes interspersed with spoken dialogue.
bel canto (Italian, 'beautiful song') Style of singing favoured by great Italian opera singers of 1700s, in which tone was more important than emotion.
claque Group of concert-goers hired to applaud particular singer or opera.
comic opera Opera with a farcical plot.
diva Another name for *prima donna*.
finale Closing portion of act or opera; usually whole company sings together.
folk opera Opera based on folk music and folk tales.
grand opera Opera with libretto entirely set to music.
intermezzo Instrumental piece interposed between scenes or acts of opera; also called *interlude*.
Leitmotiv (German, 'leading motive') Short theme in opera that emphasizes by repetition an individual character, object, or idea.
libretto Text of opera.
light opera English term for *operetta*.
opera buffa Humorous opera, but not farcical as *comic opera*; typical is Rossini's *Barber of Seville*.
opéra-comique Opera that includes spoken dialogue; not necessarily *comic opera*.
opera seria Serious opera, as distinct from *opera buffa*.
operetta Light opera based on amusing subjects and implying some spoken dia-

logue; nowadays often synonymous with *musical comedy*.
patter song Comical song made up of string of words and sung at high speed; Gilbert and Sullivan's operas include many such.
prima donna (Italian, 'first lady') Principal female singer in cast; or, more often, most famous or most highly paid; also called *diva*.
recitative Sung dialogue or narrative.
repertory Roles an opera singer is able to perform; programme of operas put on by company during a season.
Singspiel (German, 'singplay') Opera that has spoken dialogue interspersed with songs; usually has humorous subject.

Margot Fonteyn and Rudolf Nureyev, who formed one of the most famous ballet partnerships of all time in the 1960s and early 1970s.

Popular Music

acoustic Non-electric, with reference usually to guitars.
bebop, bop Intellectual type of jazz that started in 1940s in attempt to break monotonous rhythm of earlier jazz.
big bands Dance bands of 'swing' era (late 1930s and early 1940s), featuring many musicians and one or more vocalists.
bluegrass 'Folk music with overdrive'; folk and country music played with a distinctive beat; line-up includes some or all of following: acoustic guitar, banjo, mandolin, fiddle, dobro, autoharp, string bass.
blues Form of jazz using 12-bar melodic section; essentially vocal, the music is often slow and sad.
boogie woogie A jazz barrelhouse style of piano playing, with repetitive bass in left hand and stylized melodic variations in right.
calypso Folk music of West Indies, usually sung, in 4/4 time.
combo Small group of musicians.
country and western Topical and traditional rural music, mainly vocal and American, evolved from folk, blues, and hillbilly music; now known simply as 'country'.
dixieland jazz Originally, early Negro jazz; later applied to music of white imitators.
folk music, folk song Music and ballads of the people, usually handed down from one generation to another.
gig One-night stand or engagement.
gospel See *spiritual*.

The British 'pop' group The Beatles: Ringo Starr and George Harrison (*above*), and Paul McCartney and John Lennon.

Popular music (contd.)

jitterbugging Improvised, 'all-in', athletic dancing, originating in late 1930s with development of boogie woogie.
jive A later, slightly more sober and respectable form of jitterbugging.
mainstream jazz Middle-of-the-road jazz that avoids extremes of 'trad' or progressive jazz; expertly played by experienced professionals.
pop Currently popular music or song, generally launched and performed with maximum publicity and an eye to record sales.
progressive jazz Attempt to fuse jazz with other musical elements and thus break away from more traditional aspects.
ragtime Essentially Negro piano music based on rigidly syncopated pattern; had some influence on jazz.
Reggae A gay West Indian type of rock jazz with simple 2-beat rhythm.
rhythm and blues Urban blues performed mainly by black musicians; traditional blues were hotted up with infusions of rock and roll and later developments.
riff Device used mainly in jazz, consisting of prolonged repetition of 2-bar or 4-bar phrase behind soloist.
rock and roll, rock 'n roll, rock Rhythmic development of blues and skiffle, with undisguised emphasis on the beat, and body movements of dancers.
skiffle Makeshift jazz music (in vogue mid-1950s) that included guitars, banjos, mandolins, and a number of home-made instruments such as washboard, tea-chest bass, and paper-and-comb; repertoire largely folk music with a beat.
spiritual Religious folk song, usually of Negro origin (also 'white spirituals'); generally superseded by religious country music known as 'gospel'.
swing Commercialized jazz featured by the *big bands*; period 1935–46 known as 'swing era'.
steel bands West Indian percussion bands, originating in Trinidad, that use as instruments the tops of oil drums, tuned to various pitches.
Tin Pan Alley Originally 28th Street in New York City, where most of commercial song hits were published; today, term describes any well-known area of the 'pop' publishing business.
traditional jazz, 'trad' Jazz that adheres to old traditional New Orleans highly improvised, contrapuntal sounds.

Theatre

Terms used in the Theatre

anti-masque Comic-grotesque prelude to *masque.*
apron-stage Stage projecting into audience.
arena theatre *Theatre-in-the-round.*
backdrop Painted cloth hung across rear of stage.
ballad opera Popular drama with spoken dialogue; evolved from English opera of late 1600s.
burlesque Play that mocks or parodies another; in America, vulgar kind of variety performance for male audiences.
business Player's minor actions on stage, performed when not centre of attraction.
cabaret Intimate entertainment performed while audience wines and dines.
catwalk Narrow platform above stage from which stagehands adjust scenery, etc.
chorus In Greek drama, group of actors performing role of commentators; in modern theatre, singers and dancers in musicals, etc.
closet drama Drama read rather than acted.
commedia dell'arte Italian comedy (16th-18th century) performed by travelling group of actors who improvised play with stock plot and characters.
deus ex machina (Latin, 'god from a machine') Character who appears at end of play to sort out difficulty in plot (from crane in Greek drama used to show actor 'flying').
downstage Part of stage near audience.
entr'acte Diversion between acts, usually musical.
epilogue Speech delivered at end of play, usually in verse and by member of cast.
farce Extravagant comedy based on tor-

tuous manipulation of situation rather than wit.

flats Flat piece of scenery used to build up three-dimensional set.

flies Space above *proscenium*, from which scenes are controlled.

float *Footlights*.

footlights Stage lights arranged across front of stage at stage level.

fourth wall The 'wall' removed from room through which audience sees action.

grand guignol Play built round sensational situation, with element of 'horror'.

harlequinade 18th-century play built round version of Harlequin and Columbine story, with much use of machinery and magic.

joruri Major Japanese puppet-theatre in which puppet masters operate in full view of audience.

kabuki Japanese theatre, popular version of *nō*, with far less stylization.

kitchen-sink drama Term for realistic working-class drama originating in 1950s.

legitimate theatre Straight drama, without music.

masque Spectacular entertainment (mid-1500s to 1600s) performed on special occasions, usually as tribute to monarch in form of songs, dances, and recitation.

melodrama Play with conventional, sensational plot, with hero triumphing in the end over villain; audience's emotions artificially heightened by music, etc.

method, the Acting based on 'living the part' in which actor loses himself completely in role.

mime Acting without speech, by exaggerated action and gesture; particularly popular in France.

miracle play, miracle Medieval drama in verse, based on miracles of Virgin Mary or saints; in English drama, also includes *mystery plays*.

morality play, morality Late medieval allegorical drama in verse, with personified characters used to present sermon.

musical comedy Light-hearted entertainment with songs (and dances) held together by loose plot.

music hall Entertainment popular in England (mid-1800s to early 1900s, latterly

Modern drama: *Endgame,* by Samuel Beckett, an Irish dramatist who writes in French.

Terms used in the theatre (contd.)

revived as 'old-time music hall') which includes variety of turns – singers, comic acts, acrobats, etc.
mystery play, mystery Medieval religious drama based on scenes from Bible or, in England, on lives of saints (see *miracle play*).
nō Traditional Japanese theatre in which stylized plays based on well-known historical themes are performed to music, with chanting and dancing.
open stage Stage jutting out into auditorium, with part of audience sitting round sides.
passion play Religious drama based on crucifixion of Christ (such as famous one at Oberammergau, in Bavaria, performed every 10 years by villagers).
prologue Speech, like *epilogue*, but delivered at beginning of play.
properties, props Articles required on stage apart from costume, furniture, and scenery.
proscenium theatre Usual western type of theatre in which 'wall' divides auditorium from stage, the wall having large rectangular opening, the *proscenium*, top of which is called the *proscenium arch*; also known as *picture-frame stage*.
realism Movement (late 1800s) towards natural style of acting, away from histrionics and contrived drama; pioneered by Ibsen, Shaw, etc.
repertory theatre Theatre with repertoire of plays and permanent company of actors.
revue Entertainment comprising number of short items (sketches, songs, etc.), often topical or satirical.
shadow play Theatre, popular particularly in Indonesia, in which flat leather puppets are manipulated in front of palm-oil lamp which throws shadows onto translucent screen; stories from Mahabharata and Ramayana (ancient epics of India) played out to music.
showboat Floating theatre (1800s) on American rivers, presenting vaudeville, etc.
son et lumière Open-air entertainment (in castle, cathedral, etc.) relating history of place, using special lighting and sound effects.
soubrette Coquettish maidservant in comedy; female member of company specializing in such roles.

A mystery play is performed in the market place of a medieval English town. Guilds presented these plays, which showed scenes from the Bible or from the lives of saints.

super, supernumerary Player without speaking part.
theatre-in-the-round Theatre in which stage or acting area is surrounded by audience.
theatre of the absurd Drama based on fantastic, unreal situations, abandoning all logical thought and processes; pioneered by Beckett, Ionesco, Pinter, etc.
tormentors Sides of *proscenium arch*.
toy theatre Miniature replicas in cardboard, popular in early 1800s, with cut-out actors in costume.
upstage Back of stage, away from audience; to 'upstage' another actor is to manoeuvre him into less favourable position.
vaudeville American equivalent of British music hall, popular from late 1890s to advent of 'talking pictures'.
wings Side scenery; sides of stage.

Terms such as comedy and tragedy will be found in the glossary of *Literary Forms and Terms* on pp. 124–126.

Above: The ruins of the great theatre at Delphi in Greece. Drama developed in Greece from religious rituals. By the 400s BC people were building huge amphitheatres like this, where they would see the plays by the great writers Aeschylus, Sophocles, Euripides and Aristophanes. The theatres were so carefully constructed that someone standing in the middle of the central stage and speaking quite quietly could be heard by people right up in the highest rows.

Right: The Japanese created two national forms of drama, the nō play in the 1300s and kabuki in the 1600s. In nō, every word and gesture is based on formal rules; kabuki, shown here, is livelier, with much song and dance.

Cinema

Academy Awards (Oscars)

Film

1927–28 *Wings*
1928–29 *The Broadway Melody*
1929–30 *All Quiet on the Western Front*
1930–31 *Cimarron*
1931–32 *Grand Hotel*
1932–33 *Cavalcade*
1934 *It Happened One Night*
1935 *Mutiny on the Bounty*
1936 *The Great Zigfield*
1937 *The Life of Emile Zola*
1938 *You Can't Take It With You*
1939 *Gone With the Wind*
1940 *Rebecca*
1941 *How Green Was My Valley*
1942 *Mrs Miniver*
1943 *Casablanca*
1944 *Going My Way*
1945 *The Lost Weekend*
1946 *The Best Years of Our Lives*
1947 *Gentleman's Agreement*
1948 *Hamlet*
1949 *All the King's Men*
1950 *All About Eve*
1951 *An American in Paris*
1952 *The Greatest Show on Earth*
1953 *From Here to Eternity*
1954 *On the Waterfront*
1955 *Marty*
1956 *Around the World in 80 Days*
1957 *The Bridge on the River Kwai*
1958 *Gigi*
1959 *Ben-Hur*
1960 *The Apartment*
1961 *West Side Story*
1962 *Lawrence of Arabia*
1963 *Tom Jones*
1964 *My Fair Lady*
1965 *The Sound of Music*
1966 *A Man for All Seasons*
1967 *In the Heat of the Night*
1968 *Oliver*
1969 *Midnight Cowboy*
1970 *Patton*
1971 *The French Connection*
1972 *The Godfather*
1973 *The Sting*
1974 *The Godfather Part II*
1975 *One Flew Over the Cuckoo's Nest*
1976 *Rocky*
1977 *Annie Hall*
1978 *Deer Hunter*

Actor

1927–28 Emil Jannings (*The Way of All Flesh* and *The Last Command*)
1928–29 Warner Baxter (*In Old Arizona*)
1929–30 George Arliss (*Disraeli*)
1930–31 Lionel Barrymore (*A Free Soul*)
1931–32 Frederick March (*Dr Jekyll and Mr Hyde*) Wallace Beery (*The Champ*)
1932–33 Charles Laughton (*The Private Life of Henry VIII*)
1934 Clark Gable (*It Happened One Night*)
1935 Victor Mclaglen (*The Informer*)
1936 Paul Muni (*The Story of Louis Pasteur*)
1937 Spencer Tracy (*Captains Courageous*)
1938 Spencer Tracy (*Boy's Town*)
1939 Robert Donat (*Goodbye Mr Chips*)
1940 James Stewart (*The Philadelphia Story*)
1941 Gary Cooper (*Sergeant York*)
1942 James Cagney (*Yankee Doodle Dandy*)
1943 Paul Lukas (*Watch on the Rhine*)
1944 Bing Crosby (*Going My Way*)
1945 Ray Milland (*The Lost Weekend*)
1946 Frederic March (*The Best Years of Our Lives*)
1947 Ronald Colman (*A Double Life*)
1948 Laurence Olivier (*Hamlet*)
1949 Broderick Crawford (*All the King's Men*)
1950 Jose Ferrer (*Cyrano de Bergerac*)
1951 Humphrey Bogart (*The African Queen*)
1952 Gary Cooper (*High Noon*)
1953 William Holden (*Stalag 17*)
1954 Marlon Brando (*On the Waterfront*)
1955 Ernest Borgnine (*Marty*)
1956 Yul Brynner (*The King and I*)
1957 Alec Guinness (*The Bridge on the River Kwai*)
1958 David Niven (*Separate Tables*)
1959 Charlton Heston (*Ben-Hur*)
1960 Burt Lancaster (*Elmer Gantry*)
1961 Maximilian Schell (*Judgment at Nuremberg*)
1962 Gregory Peck (*To Kill a Mockingbird*)
1963 Sidney Poitier (*Lilies of the Field*)
1964 Rex Harrison (*My Fair Lady*)
1965 Lee Marvin (*Cat Ballou*)
1966 Paul Scofield (*A Man for All Seasons*)
1967 Rod Steiger (*In the Heat of the Night*)
1968 Cliff Robertson (*Charly*)
1969 John Wayne (*True Grit*)

1970 George C. Scott (*Patton*)
1971 Gene Hackman (*The French Connection*)
1972 Marlon Brando (*The Godfather*)
1973 Jack Lemmon (*Save the Tiger*)
1974 Art Carney (*Harry and Tonto*)
1975 Jack Nicholson (*One Flew Over the Cuckoo's Nest*)
1976 Peter Finch (*Network*)
1977 Richard Dreyfus (*Goodbye Girl*)
1978 Jon Voight (*Coming Home*)

Elizabeth Taylor, the child star who has won two Oscars as an adult actress.

Actress

1927–28 Janet Gaynor (*Seventh Heaven; Street Angel;* and *Sunrise*)
1928–29 Mary Pickford (*Coquette*)
1929–30 Norma Shearer (*The Divorcee*)
1930–31 Marie Dressler (*Min and Bill*)
1931–32 Helen Hayes (*The Sin of Madelon Claudet*)
1932–33 Katharine Hepburn (*Morning Glory*)
1934 Claudette Colbert (*It Happened One Night*)
1935 Bette Davis (*Dangerous*)
1936 Luise Rainer (*The Great Zigfield*)
1937 Luise Rainer (*The Good Earth*)
1938 Bette Davis (*Jezebel*)
1939 Vivien Leigh (*Gone With the Wind*)
1940 Ginger Rogers (*Kitty Foyle*)
1941 Joan Fontaine (*Suspicion*)
1942 Greer Garson (*Mrs Miniver*)
1943 Jennifer Jones (*The Song of Bernadette*)
1944 Ingrid Bergman (*Gaslight*)
1945 Joan Crawford (*Mildred Pierce*)
1946 Olivia de Havilland (*To Each His Own*)
1947 Loretta Young (*The Farmer's Daughter*)
1948 Jane Wyman (*Johnny Belinda*)
1949 Olivia de Havilland (*The Heiress*)
1950 Judy Holliday (*Born Yesterday*)
1951 Vivien Leigh (*A Streetcar Named Desire*)
1952 Shirley Booth (*Come Back, Little Sheba*)
1953 Audrey Hepburn (*Roman Holiday*)
1954 Grace Kelly (*The Country Girl*)
1955 Anna Magnani (*The Rose Tattoo*)
1956 Ingrid Bergman (*Anastasia*)
1957 Joanne Woodward (*The Three Faces of Eve*)
1958 Susan Hayward (*I Want to Live*)
1959 Simone Signoret (*Room at the Top*)
1960 Elizabeth Taylor (*Butterfield 8*)
1961 Sophia Loren (*Two Women*)
1962 Anne Bancroft (*The Miracle Worker*)
1963 Patricia Neal (*Hud*)
1964 Julie Andrews (*Mary Poppins*)
1965 Julie Christie (*Darling*)
1966 Elizabeth Taylor (*Who's Afraid of Virginia Woolf?*)
1967 Katharine Hepburn (*Guess Who's Coming to Dinner*)
1968 Katharine Hepburn (*A Lion in Winter*)
Barbra Streisand (*Funny Girl*)
1969 Maggie Smith (*The Prime of Miss Jean Brodie*)
1970 Glenda Jackson (*Women in Love*)
1971 Jane Fonda (*Klute*)
1972 Liza Minnelli (*Cabaret*)
1973 Glenda Jackson (*A Touch of Class*)
1974 Ellen Burstyn (*Alice Doesn't Live Here Any More*)
1975 Louise Fletcher (*One Flew Over the Cuckoo's Nest*)
1976 Fay Dunaway (*Network*)
1977 Diane Keaton (*Annie Hall*)
1978 Jane Fonda (*Coming Home*)

Pottery

A-Z of Pottery

biscuit ware Pottery fired but not glazed.
body Term applied to mixture of clays for making earthenware or stoneware.
bone china Type of porcelain made in England today, for high-quality tableware.
cann Cylindrical cup, usually for coffee.
celadon A pale green kind of porcelain.
ceramics Term for anything made of baked clay; the potter's art; more widely, any product first shaped and then hardened by heat, including glass and certain plastics as well as pottery.
china (originally 'Chinaware') Chinese porcelain of 16th century; now any Chinese porcelain or western version of it.
china clay Kaolin (see *clay*).
chinoiserie Decoration on 18th-century European porcelain, depicting Chinese scenes.
clay The basic potter's material, found just beneath the topsoil, formed by decomposition of rock; *kaolin*, or *china clay*, a pure white coarse clay; *ball clay*, a highly plastic, fine pure clay; *fireclay*, a dark, rough clay, able to stand high temperatures, but not plastic; *buff*, or *stoneware*, *clay*, a smooth plastic clay hardening at high temperatures.
crackle Network of cracks (accidental or intentional) due to uneven cooling.
creamware High-quality earthenware perfected by Josiah Wedgwood in Staffordshire (18th century).
delftware Tin-enamelled earthenware, mostly blue-and-white, originally made in Delft (Holland) in 17th/18th centuries.
diapered Scalloped border decoration.
earthenware Pottery fired to relatively low temperature (about 1100°C), easy to work and having dull finish.
enamel Coloured glaze used to decorate pottery already glazed.
export porcelain Chinese and Japanese porcelain made to foreign specifications.
faience Tin-glazed earthenware originally from Faenza, Italy, now made in many parts of Europe.
firing Process of hardening shaped clay; heat melts substance (usually silica) in clay which binds other constituents.
glazing Process for producing smooth, waterproof finish to pottery; *glaze* is liquid clay-like mixture with certain compounds added depending on type of finish required; applied before or after firing (in latter case, pottery fired again).
hard-paste porcelain See *paste*.

Stages in the making of fine porcelain figures. *Below:* The separately moulded pieces are assembled; then they are dipped in glaze (*below right*). The figures are stacked on shelves in a kiln where they will be fired (*opposite left*), and then coloured by hand (*opposite right*).

jasper Fine, unglazed Wedgwood stoneware adorned in white relief on delicate colours, especially the famous 'Wedgwood blue'.
kiln Chamber in which clay is fired.
majolica (maiolica) White, tin-glazed earthenware, originally from Majorca; best examples from 16th-century Italy; term now used for modern *faience*.
onion pattern Porcelain pattern (Meissen) originating in 18th century and derived from Chinese design, but using pomegranate instead of onion.
paste Term for mixture from which porcelain is made; *hard-paste* porcelain made from kaolin and petuntse, the true porcelain originating in China and rediscovered at Meissen (Germany) in 18th century, fired at very high temperatures; *soft-paste* porcelain made from white clay and fusible silicate, more translucent than hard paste but with softer whiteness.
petuntse Feldspathic rock, a main ingredient of hard-paste porcelain.
porcelain The finest kind of pottery, white all through and translucent. See *paste*.
pottery Strictly, all baked-clay ware except stoneware and porcelain, but more widely the term encompasses those, too.
refractory Able to withstand great heat.
slip Clay in liquid form, used for casting, joining, or decoration.
soft-paste porcelain See *paste*.
stoneware Hard, strong type of pottery fired at about 1250°C and able to hold liquid without glazing, made from clay and fusible stone (e.g. feldspar); used for pots, heavy dishes, etc.
terracotta Brownish-red burnt-clay pottery, baked in moulds and used for architectural mouldings.
throwing Shaping wet clay by hand on potter's wheel.
turning Final trimming of partially dried pottery on wheel or lathe.
tyg Many-handled beaker.
vitrification Changing of silica in clay to glass, which fuses other constituents (see *firing*); porcelain is completely vitrified, earthenware only partially and thus still porous.
wedging Initial preparation of clay, cutting and banging it together to make it homogeneous and remove air bubbles.
willow pattern Romantic English interpretation of Chinese pattern in form of dark blue, engraved design incorporating popular legend; originated late 18th century.

ANCIENT GREEK VESSELS

amphora	storage jar
crater	large, open bowl
cylix	drinking cup
hydria	water pot
lecythos	oil flask
oinochoë	wine pitcher
rhyton	head-shaped cup

Literature

An illustration by Tenniel to Lewis Carroll's children's book ***Alice Through the Looking Glass.***

Literary Forms and Terms

allegory Story in which characters and events have a second, symbolic, meaning.
assonance Correspondence of vowel sounds in poetry or prose.
ballad Story in verse, a narrative song, usually treating a single event.
ballade Poetic form, originating in 14th-century France, with three stanzas of 8 or 10 lines and one with 4 or 5.
belles-lettres Term that encompasses all 'fine literature'.
blank verse Unrhymed verse (usually written in iambic pentameters).
bound verse Verse based on metrical pattern.
cadence Rhythm and phrasing of language.
caesura Pause in line of verse.
comedy Humorous dramatic piece; *high comedy* has well-drawn characterization and witty dialogue; *low comedy*, or *slapstick*, has absurd situations and boisterous action; *farce* is exaggerated comedy; *tragicomedy* is a blend of the tragic and comic; *satire* uses sarcasm and wit to ridicule people's follies and vices (originally in verse).
dénouement Final unwinding of complex plot.
dramatic irony Situation or remark that has a significance unperceived by the character involved.
eclogue Short poem, particularly pastoral dialogue between shepherds.
elegy Mournful poem, often lamenting death.
epic Long narrative poem, especially of heroic characters and deeds.
essay Short prose composition expressing author's views on a particular subject.
fable Short tale, often with animals, illustrating a moral.
farce See *comedy*.
first person Style of novel, etc., in which narrator is a character.
folk tale Story handed down by word of mouth from generation to generation.
foot In poetry, rhythmic unit of two or three syllables.
free verse (*vers libre*) Poetry free from mechanical restrictions such as metre and rhyme, cadenced according to meaningful stress.
haiku Japanese verse form composed of 17 syllables (5, 7, 5).
heroic couplet Rhymed couplet in *heroic lines* (iambic pentameters).
heroic verse That used in *epic poetry*.
high comedy See *comedy*.
Horatian ode See *ode*.
idyll Short pastoral poem conveying mood of happy innocence.
imagism School of poetry (early 1900s) concerned with precise language, direct treatment, and freedom of form.
limerick Humorous verse form of five lines rhyming *a-a-b-b-a* (*a* in trimeter, *b* in dimeter).
low comedy See *comedy*.
lyric poem Usually short, song-like poem in which poet expresses personal feelings.
metre Measurement used for rhythm of line of verse, the number of feet or number and kind of feet.

Above: **The German poet and novelist Goethe (1749–1832).** ***Left:*** **An engraving by Doré for the Spanish classic novel** ***Don Quixote.***

narrative poem Poem that tells a story, such as a *ballad* or *epic*.
neoclassicism Movement of late 17th and 18th century reviving classical values in English literature, emphasizing discipline, reason, and clarity.
New Wave (*la Nouvelle Vague*) Term applied to movement in literature and cinema originating in France in late 1950s that attempted to eschew fixed values, revealing a character by the way he experienced objects and events, which were often meticulously described.
novelette Long short story of some 15,000 words.
novella Short novel (about 30,000 words); originally, short prose narrative in Medieval and Renaissance Italy.
ode Lyric poem devoted to exaltation of subject; *Pindaric ode* (Ancient Greece) written for choral recitation in units of three stanzas (called *strophe, antistrophe, epode*);

Literary forms and terms (contd.)

Horatian ode (Ancient Rome) consisted of succession of stanzas following pattern of first one.
parable Brief story that uses everyday events to illustrate moral or doctrine.
parody Comic imitation of serious piece of writing, often satirical and exaggerated.
pastoral Term applied to literature depicting idealized rural life.
picaresque Term describing literature chronicling adventures of a rogue; originated in 16th-century Spain.
Pindaric ode See *ode*.
prose Writings not in verse.
prosody Study of the handling of language in poetry.
realism Literature that attempts to depict life objectively and faithfully.
roman à clef Novel based upon actual people under disguised names.
romance Tale of chivalry, originally written in verse (Medieval times); term applied now to any wonderful or mysterious tale far removed from reality.
romanticism Term applied to movement originating in late 18th century as revolt against *neoclassicism*, emphasizing imaginative style.
saga Prose story in old literature of Iceland and Norway.
satire See *comedy*.
scansion Determination of metrical pattern of piece of poetry.
science fiction Literature based on scientific fact or fantasy, on earth or on other worlds in space, often set in periods in the distant future.
short story Work of fiction usually revolving around single event.
slapstick See *comedy*.
sonnet 14-line poem of set rhyme-scheme; Elizabethan (Shakespearean) *ababcdcdefefgg*, Italian *abbaabba cdcdcd* (or *cdecde*).
stanza Group of lines of verse in definite pattern, usually repeated in a poem.
symbolism French poetic movement of late 19th century that developed as revolt against realism, concentrating on evoking emotions by use of indirect suggestion (symbol and metaphor); flourished in Russia at turn of century as literary movement, and later in British novel.
third person Style of novel, etc., in which narrator is outside action.
tragedy Drama in which human conflict ends in calamity.
tragi-comedy See *comedy*.
versification Study of how traditional verse is constructed.

Alfred, Lord Tennyson, the 19th-century Poet Laureate. He wrote in outstandingly rich and beautiful language.

POETS LAUREATE

Ben Johnson	1619–1637
Sir William Davenant	1638–1668
John Dryden	1668–1688
Thomas Shadwell	1689–1692
Nahum Tate	1692–1715
Nicholas Rowe	1715–1718
Laurence Eusden	1718–1730
Colley Cibber	1730–1757
William Whitehead	1757–1785
Thomas Warton	1785–1790
Henry James Pye	1790–1813
Robert Southey	1813–1843
William Wordsworth	1843–1850
Lord Tennyson	1850–1892
Alfred Austin	1896–1913
Robert Bridges	1913–1930
John Masefield	1930–1967
Cecil Day Lewis	1968–1972
Sir John Betjeman	1972–

LITERATURE: NOBEL PRIZEWINNERS

1901 René Sully Prudhomme (French)
1902 Theodor Mommsen (German)
1903 Björnstjerne Björnson (Norwegian)
1904 Frédéric Mistral (French) and José Echegaray (Spanish)
1905 Henryk Sienkiewicz (Polish)
1906 Giosuè Carducci (Italian)
1907 Rudyard Kipling (English)
1908 Rudolf Eucken (German)
1909 Selma Lagerlöf (Swedish)
1910 Paul von Heyse (German)
1911 Maurice Maeterlinck (Belgian)
1912 Gerhart Hauptmann (German)
1913 Sir Rabindranath Tagore (Indian)
1914 *No award*
1915 Romain Rolland (French)
1916 Verner von Heidenstam (Swedish)
1917 Karl Gjellerup and Henrik Pontoppidan (Danish)
1918 *No award*
1919 Carl Spitteler (Swiss)
1920 Knut Hamsun (Norwegian)
1921 Anatole France (French)
1922 Jacinto Benavente (Spanish)
1923 William Butler Yeats (Irish)
1924 Wladyslaw Reymont (Polish)
1925 George Bernard Shaw (Irish)
1926 Grazia Deledda (Italian)
1927 Henri Bergson (French)
1928 Sigrid Undset (Norwegian)
1929 Thomas Mann (German)
1930 Sinclair Lewis (American)
1931 Erik Karlfeldt (Swedish)
1932 John Galsworthy (English)
1933 Ivan Bunin (Russian)
1934 Luigi Pirandello (Italian)
1935 *No award*
1936 Eugene O'Neill (American)
1937 Roger Martin du Gard (French)
1938 Pearl S. Buck (American)
1939 Frans Eemil Sillanpää (Finnish)
1940–43 *No award*
1944 Johannes V. Jensen (Danish)
1945 Gabriela Mistral (Chilean)
1946 Hermann Hesse (Swiss)
1947 André Gide (French)
1948 Thomas Stearns Eliot (Anglo-American)
1949 William Faulkner (American)
1950 Bertrand Russell (English)
1951 Pär Lagerkvist (Swedish)
1952 François Mauriac (French)
1953 Sir Winston Churchill (English)
1954 Ernest Hemingway (American)
1955 Halldór Laxness (Icelandic)
1956 Juan Ramón Jiménez (Spanish)
1957 Albert Camus (French)
1958 Boris Pasternak (Russian) – declined
1959 Salvatore Quasimodo (Italian)
1960 Saint-John Perse (Alexis Saint-Léger Léger) (French)
1961 Ivo Andric (Yugoslavian)
1962 John Steinbeck (American)
1963 George Seferis (Giorgios Seferiades) (Greek)
1964 Jean-Paul Sartre (French) – declined
1965 Mikhail Sholokhov (USSR)
1966 Shmuel Yosef Agnon (Israeli) and Nelly Sachs (Swedish)
1967 Miguel Angel Asturias (Guatemalan)
1968 Yasunari Kawabata (Japanese)
1969 Samuel Beckett (Irish)
1970 Alexander Solzhenitsyn (Russian)
1971 Pablo Neruda (Chilean)
1972 Heinrich Böll (W. German)
1973 Patrick White (Australian)
1974 Eyvind Johnson and Harry Edmund Martinson (Swedish)
1975 Eugenio Montale (Italian)
1976 Saul Bellow (American)
1977 V. Aleixandre (Spanish)
1978 Isaac Bashevis Singer (American)
1979 Odysseus Alepoudhelis (Greek) – known as Odysseus Elytis

William Wordsworth, another 19th-century Poet Laureate, expressed his deep love of nature in poems often written in deliberately simple language.

Architecture

Terms and Styles

abacus Slab forming upper part of *capital*.
apse Semicircular (or polygonal) area with domed roof at end of aisle of church.
arcade Row of arches supported by columns and carrying roof.
arch Curved structure spanning an opening.
architrave Lowest section of *entablature*.
Art Nouveau Anti-historical style (1890–1910) characterized by use of coloured materials, moulded stonework, writhing floral motifs, tapered wrought-iron brackets, etc., as reaction against both the technological revolution and imitations of past styles.
Baroque Heavily decorated European style (1600s–1700s) involving flamboyant use of *Renaissance* forms.
barrel vault See *vault*.
basilica Huge vaulted civic hall (Roman) or early Christian church.
Brutalism Reforming movement in modern architecture that emerged in Britain in 1950s; an attempt by young architects at honest presentation of structure and materials based on the uncompromising ruthlessness of Le Corbusier and Mies van der Rohe.
buttress Projecting support (mass of masonry) built on outside of wall; in *flying-buttress*, masonry is free-standing with half-arch transferring thrust from wall.
Byzantine Style that flourished in East Roman Empire (AD 400s to 1453), characterized by ornately domed and vaulted churches.
cantilever Horizontal beam or girder supported in middle and weighted at one end, allowing it to support weight at other.
capital Broad top part of column, supporting *entablature*.
caryatid Draped female figure used as pillar in classical architecture.
cloisters Quadrangle surrounded by roofed passages connecting parts of monastery.
chevet Eastern end of Romanesque or Gothic church.
classical Style of Ancient Greece or Rome, or any style based on these; opposite to *romanticism*.
columnar and trabeate Using columns and beams for support as opposed to arches.
corbel Block of stone projecting from wall and acting as bracket.
corbel arch Opening constructed by overlapping blocks on either side until gap can be bridged at top with single slab.
Corinthian See *orders*; *Greek*.
cornice Top, projecting section of *entablature*, supporting roof.
decorated See *Gothic*.
dome Roof in shape of semi-sphere, usually built over square base by means of *pendentives* or *squinches*.
Doric See *orders*; *Greek*.
dormer Small gabled window projecting from sloping roof.
Elizabethan English style of late 1500s marking change from Gothic to Renaissance and featuring sturdy, squared buildings with large windows.
engaged column Column partly attached to wall or other structure.
entablature Part of building in classical architecture between top of columns and

PERIODS OF ARCHITECTURE

Greek	600s – 100s BC
Roman	100s BC – AD 400s
Byzantine	AD 400s – 1453
Romanesque (N. Europe)	mid-900s – late 1100s
Norman (England)	late 1000s – 1100s
Gothic (France)	mid-1100s – 1400s
Renaissance (Italy)	1400s – 1500s
French Renaissance	1500s
Baroque (Italy)	1600–1750
Georgian (England)	1725–1800
Rococo (Italy)	mid-1700s
Regency (England)	1800–1825
Art Nouveau (Europe)	1890–1910
Expressionism (Germany)	1910–1930s
Functionalism	1920s–
International Style	1920s–
Brutalism	1950s–

The Sydney Opera House was completed in 1973. Its complicated and controversial design, resembling the sails of boats, caused many construction problems.

roof; consists of *architrave, frieze,* and *cornice.*
entasis Thickening of pillar in Greek architecture.
Expressionism Style that flourished in Germany (c. 1910–1930s), part of a wider movement in the arts in which reality was distorted to express artist's inner feelings.
façade Main face of building.
fan vault See *vault.*
fenestration Arrangement of windows in a building.
fluting Longitudinal grooves in a column.
frieze Middle section of *entablature.*
Functionalism Modern principle that form of building should follow from its proposed function and that of its parts.
gable Triangular end of roof with two sloping sides.
gargoyles Projecting stone sprouts (usually grotesquely carved) acting as outlets for gutter water on medieval buildings.
geodesic dome Light, stong dome constructed on framework of triangular or other straight-line elements.
Georgian English style (1700s) based on Renaissance and influenced by Palladio; a quiet, dignified classical style.

The cathedral at Amalfi in Italy is built in the Sicilian-Norman Gothic style.

Gothic Style developed in France in 1100s, lasting until Renaissance, when the term was coined as contemptuous of anything not based on classical ideas; characterized by pointed arch, elaborate vaulting, flying-buttress, slender pillars, large stained-glass windows, and intricate tracery. English Gothic is divided into three styles: *Early English* (late 1100s to 1200s), *decorated* (late 1200s to 1300s), *perpendicular* (mid-1300s to 1500s).
Greek Beautifully proportioned classical style lasting from about 700 BC until conquest by Romans in mid-100s BC. Graceful buildings of simple column-and-lintel structure, with three *orders* of columns: *Doric* (stubby columns) and the later (from about 400 BC) *Ionic* (longer, slimmer columns on moulded bases with intricately carved capitals) and *Corinthian* (more elaborate, with foliage on capital).
groin vault See *vault*.
hall-church Gothic church (common in Germany) with nave and aisle vaults springing from same height.
helm roof Pointed roof with four diamond-shaped sides.

ARCHITECTS

Adam, Robert (1728–92), Scottish
Alberti, Leone Battista (1404–72), Italian
Bernini, Lorenzo (1598–1680), Italian
Bramante, Donato (1444–1514), Italian
Brunelleschi, Filippo (1377–1446), Italian
Gaudí, Antoni (1852–1926), Spanish
Gropius, Walter (1883–1969), German
Jones, Inigo (1573–1652), English
Le Corbusier (1887–1965), French-Swiss
Michelangelo (1475–1546), Italian
Mies van der Rohe, Ludwig (1886–1969), Ger./US
Nash, John (1752–1835), English
Nervi, Pier Luigi (1891–   ), Italian
Niemeyer, Oscar (1907–   ), Brazilian
Palladio, Andrea (1518–80), Italian
Wren, Sir Christopher (1632–1723), English
Wright, Frank Lloyd (1869–1959), American

Tallest structures

The world's tallest building is the 110-storey 1,454 ft (443 m) Sears Tower in Chicago, USA. With TV antennae, it reaches 1,800 ft (548.6 m). The world's tallest structure is the 2,120 ft (646 m) mast of Warszawa Radio at Konstantynow, near Plock, in Poland. Made of galvanized steel, it was completed in May 1974.

The highest structures of ancient times were the pyramids of Egypt. The Great Pyramid of Cheops, at el-Gizeh, built in about 2580 BC, reached a height of 480.9 ft (146.6 m). It was another 4,000 years before this was surpassed – by the central tower of Lincoln Cathedral, England, which was completed in 1548 and stood 525 ft (160 m) before it toppled in a storm.

International Style Term given to modern style of architecture that evolved in W. Europe in 1920s, spread internationally in 1930s, and flourished in United States. Basic concepts are volume rather than mass, regularity rather than axial symmetry – principles employed in buildings ranging from houses to skyscrapers.
keystone Locking stone at top of arch.
lantern Small decorative turret or tower on dome, with openings or windows to admit light to building.
lintel Horizontal piece above doorway or window, supporting wall above.
minaret Tower of mosque, with gallery for muezzin to call Muslims to prayer.
moulding Decorative edging on architectural surface.
mullion Vertical bar dividing window.
nave Main body of church, west of crossing, flanked by aisles.
Norman The Romanesque style brought to Britain by Normans in 1066.
orders The classical styles of columns and entablatures: *Doric*, *Ionic*, and *Corinthian*.
organic architecture Complete harmony of parts of buildings with whole, and integration with site and surroundings.
pagoda Tower, of Chinese origin, partitioned horizontally with balconies or cornices.

The Great Pyramid of Cheops, the highest of the pyramids of Egypt. Scholars think that a huge ramp was used to raise the stones, which were dragged to their positions on sledges. The pyramids were built not by slaves but by peasants who were unable to work on the land during the annual floods.

The Crystal Palace, London, was built in 1851. It was made of steel and glass, and was designed by a former gardener called Joseph Paxton who had earlier built conservatories.

pedestal Block used to support column.
pediment Triangular end of sloping roof in classical architecture.
pendentives Curved triangular supports for dome at each corner of building.
peristyle Row of columns round building or courtyard.
piazza Open space surrounded by buildings.
pier Free-standing vertical support for arch, beam, etc.
pilaster Flat, rectangular column attached to or built into wall.
portico Area with roof supported by rows of columns.
post-and-lintel Construction using vertical elements (posts) and horizontal beams (lintels); also called *trabeated*.
Regency English style of the early 1800s, predominantly neo-classical, showing much Greek influence and characterized by restrained simplicity.
Renaissance Movement of the arts that emerged in Italy in 1400s, based on classical style of Ancient Rome; characterized in architecture by return to austere proportions, orders, and simple line combined with many current Gothic features. Reached France and Germany in late 1500s, and later influenced English architecture (Elizabethan, Jacobean, etc.).
rib vault See *vault*.
Rococo Light, airy version of Baroque style that emerged in France in early 1700s.
romanticism Style prevalent in England and France in late 1700s in which emphasis was on picturesque design; part of general movement in arts.
rotunda Circular building, usually domed.
rustication Giving rough appearance to surface of building-blocks.
shaft Main, cylindrical part of column.
spandrel Roughly triangular wall space between arches or arch and wall.
squinches Diagonal arches or vaults across corners of building to support dome.
steel-frame Skeleton of steel girders that provides framework for buildings such as skyscrapers.

The mosque of the Dome of the Rock in Jerusalem. The Muslims adapted the styles of art and architecture in the countries they conquered for their own buildings.

string-course Horizontal brick band projecting across face of building.
trabeated See *post-and-lintel*.
transept In cruciform church, hall running north-south and crossing nave at right-angles.
tracery Elaborately patterned openwork in Gothic architecture, originally framework of light stone bars dividing large window.
transom Horizontal bar dividing window.
triforium Middle storey of medieval church.
Tudor English late-Gothic period (1500s) exhibiting effect of Renaissance thinking on English perpendicular style.
vault Brick or stone ceiling built on arch principle; *barrel*, or *tunnel*, *vault* rests on two continuous supporting walls; *groin*, or *cross*, *vault* formed by joining barrel vaults at right-angles; *rib-vault* has diagonal stone ribs projecting from surface; *fan vault* is ornamental rib vault, the ribs springing from walls in fan shapes.
volute Spiral scroll of Ionic capital.
voussoir Wedge-shaped block used in forming arches.
ziggurat Pyramid-shaped, tiered construction used in ancient Mesopotamia and Mexico for supporting temple or altar.

History

Chronology

BC

c.3500 Sumerians develop flourishing civilization along Euphrates.
c.3400 Upper and Lower Egypt united to form one nation.
c.2100 Abraham migrates from Ur.
c.2000 Bronze Age begins in north Europe.
c.1750 Hammurabi of Babylon draws up first known legal code.
1500s Shang Dynasty of China founded.
1570 Hyksos invaders of Egypt defeated.
1450 Minoan civilization flourished in Crete: begins to decline soon after.
1410 Reign of Amenhotep III of Egypt: golden age of nation at height.
1400 Beginning of Iron Age in India and Asia Minor (Turkey).
1358 Tutankhamen becomes pharaoh of Egypt. restores old religion destroyed by his predecessor Akhenaton.
1292–1225 Rameses II pharaoh of Egypt; Abu Simbel temple built.
1230–1200 Israelites leave Egypt and make their way to Canaan (Palestine).
c.1100 Assyrian empire founded in Mesopotamia.
c.1020 Saul becomes first king of Israel
c.1000 Chou dynasty founded in China.
1000–961 David king of Israel.
922 Death of Solomon: kingdom divided into Judah and Israel.
800s Homer writes the *Iliad* and the *Odyssey* in ancient Greece.
814 Phoenicians found Carthage.
776 Earliest known Olympic Games.
753 Traditional date of founding of Rome.
722 Assyrians conquer Israel.
689 Assyrians capture and destroy Babylon.
670 Assyrians ravage Egypt; destruction of Thebes and Memphis.
626 Nabopolassar liberates Babylon from Assyrian rule and becomes king.
612 Babylonians, Medes, and Scythians overthrow Assyrian empire, destroying capital, Nineveh.
586 Nebuchadnezzar of Babylon seizes Jerusalem and takes people of Judah into captivity.
563 Siddhartha Gautama, later the Buddha, born at Lumbini, Nepal.
550–530 Reign of Cyrus the Great, founder of Persian empire.
551 Birth of K'ung Fu-tzu – Confucius, great Chinese philosopher.
539 Jews allowed to return to Jerusalem; rebuilding of city begins.
535–404 Persians rule Egypt.
510 Last king of Rome, Tarquin, deposed; city becomes republic.
499–494 Ionian War: Greek revolt against Persian rule.
494 Thirty cities of Latium form Latin League against Etruscans.
492 First Persian expedition against Athens ends in disaster when storm destroys Persian fleet.
490 Athenians crush second Persian expedition at Battle of Marathon.
485 Xerxes king of Persia.
480 Persian fleet defeated by Greeks at Battle of Salamis.
479 Greek soldiers rout Persians at Battle of Plataea; end of Persian attempt to subdue Greece.
460 Pericles becomes leader of Athenians.
431–421 Great Peloponnesian War between Athens and Sparta.
415–404 Second Peloponnesian War, ending with Spartan capture of Athens.

The mask of Tutankhamen, pharaoh of Egypt in 1350s BC. His tomb was opened in 1922.

403 Thirty Tyrants seize power in Athens.
399 Philosopher Socrates put to death for teaching heresies to the young.
395–387 Corinthian War: coalition of Argos, Athens, Corinth, Thebes against Sparta; Sparta victorious.
391 Romans conquer Etruscans.
390 Gauls under Brennus sack Rome.
352–336 Philip II king of Macedon; rise of Macedon to power in Greece.
350 Persians suppress revolt of Jews.
338 Philip of Macedon conquers Greece.
336–323 Reign of Alexander III, the Great, succeeding father, Philip II.
335 Alexander destroys Thebes.
332 Alexander conquers Egypt and Jerusalem, destroys Tyre.
331 Alexander overthrows Persian empire, defeating Darius III and capturing Babylon.
326 Greeks under Alexander extend empire to River Indus, in what is now Pakistan.
323 Death of Alexander; birth of Euclid.
320 Egyptians under Ptolemy Soter capture Jerusalem.
305 Seleucus I Nicator founds Seludic dynasty in Syria, Persia, Asia Minor.
305 Romans extend their rule over southern Italy.
301 Egyptians conquer Palestine.
295–294 Demetrius captures Athens and makes himself master of Greece.
290 Romans finally defeat Samnite attempt to usurp Roman power in Italy.
280 Achaean League of 12 Greek city-states formed.
274 Pyrrhus of Epirus conquers Macedonia; killed two years later.
264–241 First Punic War between Rome and Carthage; Carthage defeated and surrenders Sicily.
221 Ch'in dynasty founded in China.
218–201 Second Punic War.
218 Carthaginians under Hannibal cross Alps to invade Italy; Romans defeated at River Trebbia.
216 Hannibal defeats Romans at Cannae.
206 Romans under Scipio drive Carthaginians out of Spain.
202 Carthaginians defeated at Zama.
202 Han dynasty founded in China.
200–197 Romans drawn into war against Macedonia; Philip V of Macedon defeated.
192 Rome defeats Sparta.
182 Suicide of Hannibal to avoid capture by Romans.
171–167 Perseus of Macedonia attacks Rome; crushingly defeated; Roman rule in Macedonia.
168 Antiochus IV Epiphanes of Syria persecutes Jews, and desecrates Temple in Jerusalem.
167 Revolt of Jews under Judas Maccabaeus against Antiochus.

SEVEN WONDERS OF THE WORLD*

Pyramids of Egypt Oldest and only surviving 'wonder'. Built in the 2000s BC as royal tombs, about 80 are still standing. The largest, the Great Pyramid of Cheops, at el-Gizeh, was 481 ft (147 m) high.

Hanging Gardens of Babylon Terraced gardens adjoining Nebuchadnezzar's palace said to rise from 75 to 300 ft (23-91 m) Supposedly built by the king about 600 BC to please his wife, a princess from the mountains, but they are also associated with the Assyrian Queen Semiramis.

Statue of Zeus at Olympia Carved by Phidias, the 40-ft (12-m) statue marked the site of the original Olympic Games in the 400s BC. It was constructed of ivory and gold, and showed Zeus (Jupiter) on his throne.

Temple of Artemis (Diana) at Ephesus Constructed of Parian marble and more than 400 ft (122 m) long with over 100 columns 60 ft (18 m) high, it was begun about 350 BC and took some 120 years to build. Destroyed by the Goths in AD 262.

Mausoleum at Halicarnassus Erected by Queen Artemisia in memory of her husband King Mausolus of Caria (in Asia Minor), who died 353 BC. It stood 140 ft (43 m) high. All that remains are a few pieces in the British Museum and the word 'mausoleum' in the English language.

Colossus of Rhodes Gigantic bronze statue of sun-god Helios (or Apollo); stood about 117 ft (36 m) high, dominating the harbour entrance at Rhodes. The sculptor Chares supposedly laboured for 12 years before he completed it in 280 BC. It was destroyed by an earthquake in 224 BC.

Pharos of Alexandria Marble lighthouse and watchtower built about 270 BC on the island of Pharos in Alexandria's harbour. Possibly standing 400 ft (122 m) high, it was destroyed by an earthquake in 1375.

*Originally compiled by Antipater of Sidon, a Greek poet, in the 100s BC.

153 Jews win independence from Syrian rule.
149–146 Third Punic War ends in destruction of Carthage.
101 Romans defeat Cimbri at Vercellae.

Augustus Caesar brought the Roman Civil Wars to an end and became the first emperor of Rome.

Chronology (contd.)

88–82 Civil war in Rome; L. Cornelius Sulla emerges victor.
87 Sulla defeats attack by Mithradates, King of Pontus, and captures Athens.
86 Civil war in China.
82 Sulla dictator of Rome.
73–71 Revolt of gladiators and slaves under Spartacus; defeated by consuls Gnaeus Pompeius (Pompey) and Licinius Crassus.
70 Birth of poet Virgil.
65 Roman armies under Pompey invade Syria and Palestine.
64 Romans occupy Jerusalem.
61 Gaius Julius Caesar becomes Roman governor of Spain.
60 Pompey, Crassus, and Caesar form First Triumvirate.
58–51 Caesar conquers Gaul and invades Britain; British pay tribute to Rome.
53 Death of Crassus in battle.
52 Pompey appointed sole consul in Rome.
49 Caesar crosses River Rubicon in Italy to challenge Pompey for power.
48 Pompey, defeated at Pharsalus, flees to Egypt and is assassinated.
47 Caesar appoints Cleopatra and her brother Ptolemy XII joint rulers of Egypt; Cleopatra disposes of Ptolemy.
45 Caesar holds supreme power in Rome.
44 Brutus, Cassius, and others murder Caesar.
43 Mark Antony, Marcus Lepidus, and Caesar's nephew Octavian form Second Triumvirate.
43 Cleopatra queen of Egypt.
36 Mark Antony marries Cleopatra; prepares to attack Octavian.
31 Battle of Actium: Octavian's fleet defeats Antony and Cleopatra, who commit suicide. Rome conquers Egypt.
27 Octavian emperor of Rome, with title of Augustus.
6 Romans seize Judaea.
4 Birth of Jesus Christ at Bethlehem;

AD

9 Battle of Teutoburg Forest: German leader Arminius wipes out three Roman legions.
14 Augustus dies; succeeded by stepson Tiberius.
26 Pontius Pilate appointed Procurator of Judaea.
27 Baptism of Jesus by John the Baptist.
30 Jesus crucified on Pilate's orders on charge of sedition.
32 Saul of Tarsus converted; baptized as Paul.
37–41 Caligula emperor of Rome; orders Romans to worship him as god.
41–54 Claudius emperor of Rome.
43–51 Roman conquest of Britain under Aulus Plautius.
54–68 Reign of Emperor Nero, following assassination of Claudius.
64 Fire destroys Rome; Christians persecuted; St Paul and St Peter put to death.
65 Gospel of St Mark probably written.
66–70 Revolt of Jews; subdued by Vespasian and his son Titus.
68 Suicide of Nero; Galba becomes Emperor of Rome.
69–79 Reign of Vespasian.
77–84 Roman conquest of northern Britain.
79 Vesuvius erupts, destroying Pompeii, Herculaneum, and Stabiae.
98–117 Reign of Trajan; Roman empire at greatest extent.
122 Emperor Hadrian (ruled 117–138) visits Britain; orders building of wall to keep out Picts and Scots.
132–135 Jewish revolt led by Simon Bar-Cochba suppressed; Romans disperse Jews from Palestine (*Diaspora*).
161–180 Marcus Aurelius emperor: Roman empire at most united.
177 Increased persecution of Christians in Rome.
205–211 Revolts and invasions in Britain suppressed by emperor Septimius Severus.
212 Emperor Caracalla (211–217) issues edict giving Roman citizenship to all free men in the empire.
220 Han dynasty in China ends.
226 Artaxerxes founds new Persian empire.
249 Emperor Decius (249–251) inaugurates first general persecution of Christians.
253–259 Franks, Goths, and Alamanni cross empire's frontiers and invade Italy.
268 Goths sack Sparta, Corinth, Athens.
284–305 Reign of Diocletian, who reorganizes empire to halt break-up.
285 Empire divided into West (based on Rome) and East (based on Nicomedia in Bythnia).
c.300 Buddhism spreading throughout China.
303–313 New persecution of Christians.
306–337 Constantine the Great emperor of Rome.

313 Edict of Milan proclaims toleration for Christians in Roman empire.
314 Council of Arles: meeting of Christian leaders at which Constantine presides.
320 Gupta empire founded in India.
324 Eastern and Western empires reunited under Constantine's rule.
325 First world council of Christian Church at Nicaea in Asia Minor.
330 Foundation of Constantinople on site of village of Byzantium, as capital of Roman Empire.
337 Constantine baptized on death-bed.
360 Huns invade Europe; Picts and Scots cross Hadrian's Wall to attack north Britain.
369 Picts and Scots driven out of Roman province of Britain.
378 Battle of Adrianople: Visigoths defeat and kill Emperor Valens, and ravage Balkans.
379–395 Reign of Theodosius the Great; on his death, empire is again split up.
407 Roman troops leave Britain to fight Barbarians in Gaul.
410 Goths under Alaric sack Rome.
425–450 Jutes, Angles, and Saxons invade Britain.
451 Battle of Châlons: Franks and allies defeat Attila the Hun.

476 Goths depose Emperor Romulus Augustus, ending western Roman empire; date generally regarded as beginning of Middle Ages.
481 Clovis king of Franks.
493 Theodoric the Ostrogoth conquers Italy.
496 Clovis converted to Christianity; increases Frankish power.
527–565 Justinian the Great, Byzantine (eastern Roman) emperor.
529–565 Justinian has Roman laws codified.
534 Franks conquer Burgundy.
534 Eastern Empire reconquers northern Africa from Vandals.
535 Byzantine troops occupy southern Italy.
550 St David introduces Christianity into Wales.
552 Buddhism introduced into Japan.
554 Byzantine armies complete conquest of Italy.
563 St Columba preaches Christianity to the Picts in Scotland.
568 Lombards conquer north and central Italy.
570 Prophet Muhammad born at Mecca.
581 Sui dynasty founded in China.
590 Gregory the Great pope.
597 St Augustine converts south-eastern England to Christianity for Rome.
611–622 Persians conquer Palestine and Egypt; Jerusalem sacked.
616 Visigoths drive Romans from Spain.
618 T'ang dynasty founded in China.

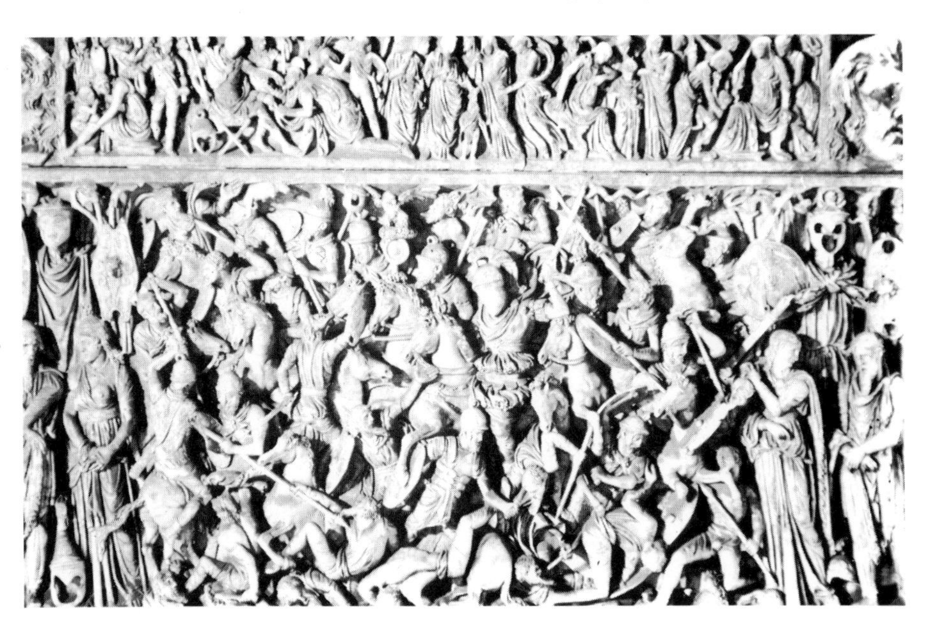

A relief carving showing a battle between Roman soldiers and Germanic barbarian invaders.

Chronology (contd.)

622 The Hegira: Muhammad flees from Mecca to Yathrib, afterwards called Medina.
624 Japan adopts Buddhism.
625 Muhammad begins dictating material later gathered into the *Koran*.
622–630 Byzantine emperor Heraclius drives Persians from Egypt and Palestine.
628 Muhammad enunciates principles of Islamic faith.
632 Death of Muhammad.
634–641 Muslim Arabs conquer Syria, Jerusalem, Mesopotamia, Egypt, and overthrow Persian empire.
634–642 Oswald, king of Northumbria, introduces Celtic Christian Church to his country.
646 Taikwa – Japanese edict of reform; Japanese begin to copy Chinese culture.
664 Synod of Whitby: Oswy, king of Northumbria, joins England to Church of Rome.
712 Islamic state set up in Sind, now part of Pakistan.
711–715 Spain conquered by Moors.
717–718 Arab siege of Constantinople fails.
720 Moors invade France.
732 Charles Martel of Franks defeats Moorish invaders at Poitiers.
752 Pepin the Short elected king of Franks.
756 Donation of Pepin: Franks agree to popes' controlling central Italy.
771–814 Reign of Charlemagne, king of Franks.
773–774 Charlemagne conquers Lombardy.
778 Moors defeat Franks at Roncesvalles; traditional date of death of Roland, Charlemagne's nephew.
781 Christian missionaries reach China.
786–809 Rule of Harun Al-Raschid as Caliph of Baghdad.
787 First attacks by the Northmen on England.
800 Pope Leo III crowns Charlemagne as Roman Emperor of the West.
814 Division of Charlemagne's empire following his death.
832 Muslims capture Sicily.
c.850 Jainism and Hinduism established as main religions of northern India.
871–899 Reign of Alfred the Great in southern England.
874 Northmen begin settling in Iceland.
885 Paris besieged by Vikings.
896 Magyar tribes conquer Hungary.
906 Magyars begin invasion of Germany.
907 End of T'ang dynasty in China; civil war breaks out.
919–936 Reign of Henry I (the Fowler) of Germany.
926 Athelstan, king of England, conquers Wales and southern Scotland.

The Ka'aba in Mecca, a building sacred to Islam. Muslim Arabs carried the faith into Asia and Europe in a rapid series of conquests.

935 Wenceslaus of Bohemia – 'good King Wenceslaus' – murdered by brother.
936–973 Reign of Otto I, the Great, of Germany.
955 Battle of the Lechfeld: Otto the Great repulses Magyars.
960 Sung dynasty founded in China.
962 Revival of Roman empire in West: Pope John XII crowns Otto of Germany as emperor.
978 Ethelred II, the Redeless, becomes king of England.
986 Eric the Red founds colonies of Osterbygd and Vesterbygd in Greenland.
987 Hugh Capet elected king of Franks; Capetian dynasty founded.
988 Foundation of Al-Azhar University in Cairo.
994 London besieged by Olaf Trygvason of Norway and Sweyn of Denmark.
c.1002 Leif Ericson of Norway discovers Vinland in North America.
1004–1013 Danish attacks on England, bought off by Ethelred II.
1014 Canute (Cnut) becomes king of Denmark and Norway.
1016 Canute also becomes king of England, deposing Ethelred.

1040 Macbeth murders Duncan, king of Scots, and becomes king.

1042–1066 Edward the Confessor, son of Ethelred, king of England.

1058 Malcolm III Canmore becomes king of Scots, having killed Macbeth.

1066 Harold II chosen king of England; invasion of England by William of Normandy, who seizes throne.

1075–1122 Struggle between popes and German emperors over right to appoint bishops.

1076 Pope Gregory VII excommunicates Emperor Henry IV.

1077 Penance at Canossa: Henry submits to the Pope.

1084 Normans under Robert Guiscard sack Rome.

1096–1099 First Crusade to free Holy Land (Palestine) from Muslim rule; capture of Jerusalem.

1100 William II (Rufus) shot while hunting; brother Henry I becomes king of England.

1106 Henry I wrests Normandy from elder brother Robert.

1113 Foundation of Order of the Knights of St John.

1119 Order of Knights Templars founded.

1122 Concordat of Worms ends disputes between emperors and popes.

1147–1149 Second Crusade: Christian armies disagree and crusade fails.

1152–1190 Frederick I (Barbarossa) king of Germany and Holy Roman Emperor.

1154–1189 Reign of Henry II of England, son of Geoffrey of Anjou; much of France under English rule.

1174–1193 Rule of Saladin as Sultan of Egypt and Syria.

1182 Expulsion of Jews from France.

1187 Saladin captures Jerusalem.

1189–1192 Third Crusade, led by Frederick Barbarossa, Philip II of France, and Richard I of England; Acre and Jaffa captured.

1192–1194 Richard of England prisoner of Leopold of Austria and Emperor Henry VI.

1197–1212 Civil war in Germany following death of Emperor Henry VI; ends with election of Frederick II (*Stupor Mundi*).

c.1200 Settlement of Mexico by Aztecs.

1200–1450 German cities form Hanseatic League to promote their trade.

1202–1204 Fourth Crusade: Crusaders, in debt to Venice, capture Constantinople for Venetians.

1206 Mongol leader Temujin proclaimed *Genghis Khan* (Emperor within the seas).

1210 Francis of Assisi founds Franciscan order of monks.

1211–1222 Mongol invasion of China.

1212 Children's Crusade: 30,000 children from France and Germany set off to free Holy Land; many die.

1215 King John of England agrees to Magna Carta, statement of the rights of his subjects.

1215 St Dominic founds Dominican order of friars.

1217–1221 Fifth Crusade fails to liberate Holy Land.

1223 Mongol invasion of Russia.

1224 Carmelite order of friars founded.

1228–1229 Sixth Crusade led by Emperor Frederick II regains Jerusalem.

1238 Mongol warriors capture Moscow.

1240 Russian hero Alexander Nevsky defeats Swedish force at River Neva.

1241 'Golden Horde' Mongol kingdom established on banks of River Volga.

1244 Muslims recapture Jerusalem.

1248 St Louis (Louis IX of France) leads Seventh Crusade; captured by Muslims and ransomed in 1254.

1256 Foundation of Augustinian order.

1260–1294 Kublai Khan becomes ruler of Mongol Empire and founds Yuan dynasty in China.

Temujin is proclaimed Genghis Khan (1206). Having united the Mongolian tribes, he established a vast empire.

The castle called Krak des Chevaliers, in modern Syria, was built by crusading knights.

Chronology (contd.)

1268 Egyptians capture Antioch, held by Christians.
1270 Eighth and last Crusade, led by St Louis, who dies during it.
1271–1295 Marco Polo visits court of Kublai Khan, travels in Asia, and returns to Venice.
1273 Rudolf I of Habsburg becomes Holy Roman Emperor, founding Habsburg dynasty.
1282 Edward I of England conquers Wales.
1290 Expulsion of Jews from England.
1295 First truly representative parliament summoned in England.
1301 Edward I of England creates his son Edward Prince of Wales.
1302 Papal Bull *Unam sanctam* proclaims papal superiority over national rulers.
1305–1378 Avignonese Papacy: seven popes based at Avignon in France because of unrest in Italy.
1306 Robert Bruce leads Scottish revolt against English rule.
1314 Scotland becomes independent after Bruce defeats English at Battle of Bannockburn.
1325 Aztecs found Tenochtitlán, now Mexico City.
1334–1351 The Black Death (bubonic plague) ravages Europe, killing one in four.
1337 Hundred Years War between England and France starts when Edward III of England takes title of king of France.
1339 English invasion of France begins.
1346 Edward III defeats French army at Battle of Crécy: long-bow proved to be the most formidable weapon.
1356 English under Edward the Black Prince capture John II of France at Battle of Poitiers.
1360 First part of Hundred Years War ended by Treaty of Bretigny.
1368 Ming Dynasty begins in China.
1369 War breaks out again between England and France.
1369–1405 Reign of Tamerlane, Mongol ruler of Samarkand, and conqueror of much of southern Asia.
1371 Robert I becomes first Stuart king of Scotland.
1374 Peace between England and France, England having lost nearly all its French possessions.
1378–1417 The Great Schism: rival lines of popes elected, splitting Church in two.
1396 Bulgaria conquered by Ottoman Turks.
1397 Union of Kalmar: Denmark, Norway, and Sweden united under one king.
1400 Welsh revolt led by Owen Glendower.
1414 Lollards (heretics) persecuted in England.
1414–1417 Council of Constance called to heal Great Schism; Martin V elected pope.
1415 Henry V of England renews claim to French throne, and defeats French at Battle of Agincourt.
1420 Treaty of Troyes: Henry V acknowledged as heir to French throne.
1422 Deaths of Henry V and of Charles VI of France; renewed struggle for French throne.
1429 Joan of Arc raises English siege of Orléans; Charles VII crowned king at Rheims.
1431 Joan of Arc burned as witch.
1437 Portuguese naval institute founded by Prince Henry the Navigator.
c. 1450 Invention of printing from moveable type by Johannes Gutenberg
1453 Hundred Years War ends, leaving England with Calais as only French possession.
1453 Ottoman Turks capture Constantinople, ending Byzantine Empire.
1455–1485 Wars of the Roses: civil wars in England between rival families of York and Lancaster.
1461–1485 House of York triumphant in England.
1475 Edward IV of England invades France; bought off by Louis XI.
1476 Charles the Bold of Burgundy killed in rebellion by Swiss.
1479 Crowns of Castile and Aragon united, making Spain one country.
1480 Ivan III, first tsar (emperor) of Russia, makes himself independent of Mongols.

1483 Boy king Edward V of England deposed and killed by uncle, Richard III.
1485 Richard III killed at Battle of Bosworth; Henry Tudor brings Lancastrians back to power as Henry VII.
1488 Bartolomeu Dias, Portuguese navigator, becomes first European to sail round Cape of Good Hope.
1492 Spaniards finally drive Moors out of Granada, last Muslim province.
1492 Christopher Columbus discovers West Indies while searching for westward route to eastern Asia.
1498 Vasco da Gama of Portugal discovers sea route to India by way of Cape of Good Hope.
1502 Columbus reaches mainland of America on fourth and last voyage.
1506 Work begins on St Peter's Basilica, Rome; Donato Bramante, chief architect.
1508–1512 Michelangelo paints ceiling of Sistine Chapel in Vatican.
1516 African slave traffic to Americas begins.
1517 Beginning of Reformation: Martin Luther publishes *95 Theses* at Wittenberg, Germany.
1519–1555 Reign of Emperor Charles V, who became king of Spain two years earlier.
1519–1521 First voyage round world; expedition led by Ferdinand Magellan, who dies during journey.
1519–1521 Conquest of Mexico by Spanish adventurer Hernando Cortés.
1520 Field of Cloth of Gold: meeting between Francis I of France and Henry VIII of England.
1521 Diet of Worms condemns doctrines of Martin Luther.

The Italian Christopher Columbus pioneered sea-routes to the New World.

Martin Luther, the German priest who challenged the authority of the Roman Catholic Church.

1524–1525 Peasants' War: revolt of German peasants defeated and punished.
1525 Battle of Pavia: Imperial forces defeat and capture Francis I of France.
1527 Sack of Rome by imperial forces; Pope Clement VII taken prisoner.
1529 Turkish armies advancing through Hungary besiege Vienna.
1530 Baber, founder of Mogul Empire in India, dies.
1533 Henry VIII of England excommunicated by pope for divorcing Catherine of Aragon.
1534 Act of Supremacy: Henry VIII assumes leadership of the Church in England, and breaks with Rome.
1534 Society of Jesus (Jesuits) founded by Ignatius Loyola.
1541 John Calvin takes Reformation movement to Geneva.
1545–1563 Council of Trent marks beginning of Counter-Reformation.
1549 Book of Common Prayer introduced in England.
1553–1558 Reign of Mary I brings England into reconciliation with Rome.
1558 French capture Calais, last English possession in France.
1558–1603 Reign of Elizabeth I in England; return to Protestantism.
1562–1598 Religious Wars in France between Roman Catholics and Huguenots.
1567 Foundation of Rio de Janeiro.
1568 Mary, Queen of Scots, driven into exile; imprisoned by Elizabeth I of England.
1571 Battle of Lepanto: allied Christian fleet defeats Turkish fleet.
1572 Massacre of St Bartholomew in France; thousands of Huguenots killed.
1572 Active rebellion of the Netherlands against Spain begins.

Chronology (contd.)

1575 Bengal conquered by Akbar the Great.
1577–1580 Sir Francis Drake sails round world.
1582 Pope Gregory XIII introduces reformed Gregorian calendar, which most Roman Catholic countries adopt.
1585–1589 War of the Three Henrys in France – Henry III, Henry of Navarre, Henry of Guise.
1587 Elizabeth I of England orders execution of Mary, Queen of Scots, found guilty of treason.
1587 Sir Francis Drake destroys Spanish fleet at Cádiz.
1588 Invincible Armada sets sail to invade England; defeated by English fleet.
1589 Assassination of Henry III of France; succeeded by Huguenot Henry of Navarre, who adopts Roman Catholicism.
1598 Edict of Nantes: French Protestants gain political rights.
1592 Conquest of Sind by Akbar the Great.
1600 English East India Company founded.
1602 Dutch East India Company founded.
1603 French East India Company founded.
1603 Death of Elizabeth I: James VI of Scotland becomes James I of England, uniting two countries under one crown.
1607 John Smith founds Colony of Virginia.
1609 Netherlands win independence from Spain.
1610 Henry IV of France assassinated; succeeded by Louis XIII, aged nine.
1610–1611 Henry Hudson discovers Hudson Bay; set adrift by his crew.
1611 English and Scottish colonists begin settlement in Ulster.
1611 Publication of Authorized (King James) Version of Bible.
1616 Dutch navigator Willem Schouten makes first voyage round Cape Horn.
1618–1648 Thirty Years War in Europe; begins with revolt by Protestants in Prague.
1620 Pilgrim Fathers sail to America in *Mayflower*.
1625–1649 Reign of Charles I in England.
1626 Dutch colony of New Amsterdam (now New York) founded.
1629 Massachusetts colony founded.
1631 First colonists settle in Maryland.
1631 Sack of Magdeburg by Tilly; defeat of Tilly by Gustavus Adolphus of Sweden at Battle of Leipzig.

Having chased the Spanish Armada (1588) into Calais harbour, the English sent in fireships. These were small craft filled with gunpowder and tar and set alight. They flushed out the Spanish fleet.

1633 Colonists settle in Connecticut.
1638 Japanese massacre Christians, and stop all foreign visitors to country.
1639 Colonists settle in New Hampshire and Maine.
1640 Financial crisis in England: Charles I summons Long Parliament.
1641 French colonize Michigan.
1642–1646 Civil War in England; Parliament in revolt against Charles I.
1642 Abel Tasman discovers New Zealand.
1643–1715 Reign of Louis XIV of France.
1643 Manchu dynasty founded in China.
1648 Peace of Westphalia: end of Thirty Years War.
1648 Second Civil War in England; crushed by Parliamentary forces.
1649 Charles I tried and executed for treason; England a republic.
1651 Charles II tries to regain throne, but is defeated by Oliver Cromwell.
1652 Dutch pioneer Jan van Riebeeck founds first European settlement in South Africa.
1652–1654 War between Dutch and English.
1653 Oliver Cromwell becomes Lord Protector of England, Scotland, Ireland.
1660 Charles II restored to thrones of England and Scotland.
1665–1667 Second Anglo-Dutch War.
1665 New Jersey colony founded.
1665 Great Plague ravages London.
1666 London destroyed by fire.
1667–1668 War of Devolution between France and Spain.
1668 Spain recognizes Portuguese independence.
1672–1674 Third Anglo-Dutch War; France allied to England.
1685 Louis XIV of France revokes Edict of Nantes; Huguenots flee from France.
1688–1689 Glorious Revolution in England: Roman Catholic James II deposed; Parliament offers throne to William III of Orange and his wife Mary II.
1689 France declares war on Spain and England.
1690 Battle of the Boyne: William III defeats James II, ending Stuart hopes.
1696–1725 Reign of Peter I, the Great, of Russia.
1698 Thomas Savery makes first effective steam engine.
1700–1721 Great Northern War: Sweden fights other Baltic states.
1701–1713 War of the Spanish Succession.
1704 Britain captures Gibraltar.
1707 Formal union of England and Scotland.
1709 Battle of Poltava: Charles XII of Sweden beaten by Peter the Great.
1714 Elector George of Hanover becomes King George I of England, ensuring Protestant succession.
1715–1774 Reign of Louis XV of France, great-grandson of Louis XIV.
1715 Jacobite rebellion in Britain fails.
1718 Quadruple Alliance of Britain, the Empire, France, and the Netherlands against Spain.
1721 Robert Walpole, world's first prime minister, becomes First Lord of the Treasury in Britain.
1733–1735 War of the Polish Succession.
1739 War of Jenkins' Ear between Britain and Spain.
1740–1786 Reign of Frederick II, the Great, of Prussia.
1740–1748 War of the Austrian Succession: dispute over Maria Theresa's right to inherit throne of Austria.
1745–1746 Second Jacobite rebellion in Britain fails.
1751 Robert Clive for Britain captures Arcot from French in India.
1755 Lisbon earthquake: 30,000 people die.
1756 Start of Seven Years War; Britain, Hanover, and Prussia against Austria, France, Russia, and Sweden.
1756 Black Hole of Calcutta.
1759 British capture Quebec from French.
1760–1820 Reign of George III of Britain.
1762 War between Britain and Spain.

Robert Clive is granted new rights for the East India Co. some 160 years after its foundation.

The American War of Independence began at Lexington, Massachusetts on 19 April 1775.

Chronology (contd.)

1763 Peace of Paris ends Seven Years War.
1764 James Hargreaves invents the spinning jenny, marking start of Industrial Revolution.
1767 British government imposes import taxes on North American colonies.
1770 James Cook discovers New South Wales.
1773 Boston Tea Party.
1775–1783 American War of Independence.
1775 Battles of Lexington, Concord, and Bunker Hill.
1776 Declaration of Independence.
1777 Battle of Saratoga: a British army surrenders to Americans.
1778–1779 War of the Bavarian Succession between Austria and Prussia.
1778 France declares war on Britain to support American colonies.
1779 Spain joins war against Britain.
1781 British forces surrender at Yorktown.
1783 Treaty of Versailles: Britain recognizes independence of United States of America.
1785 First balloon crossing of English Channel.
1788 United States adopts its constitution.
1789 George Washington first president of the United States.
1789–1799 French Revolution; begins with fall of Bastille.
1790 Washington, DC founded.
1792 France proclaimed a republic.
1793 Louis XVI of France executed; Reign of Terror.
1792–1799 War of the First Coalition: Austria, Britain, the Netherlands, Prussia, Spain against France.
1798 Napoleon Bonaparte in Egypt: cut off by Horatio Nelson's victory in Battle of the Nile.
1799 Coup d'état of Brumaire: Napoleon becomes First Consul of France.
1800 British capture Malta.
1801 Britain and Ireland united.
1799–1801 War of the Second Coalition.
1803 Louisiana Purchase: United States buys Louisiana territory from France.
1804 Napoleon crowned Emperor of France.
1805–1808 War of the Third Coalition: Austria, Britain, Naples, Russia, Sweden against France and Spain.
1805 Battle of Trafalgar: Nelson defeats French and Spanish fleets.
1805 Battle of Austerlitz: Napoleon defeats Austrians and Russians.
1806 Napoleon ends Holy Roman Empire, makes his brothers kings of Naples and Holland.
1807 Britain abolishes slave trading.
1808–1814 Peninsular War in Spain and Portugal.
1809–1825 Wars of Independence in Latin America.
1812 Napoleon invades Russia; forced to retreat, losing most of his army.
1812–1815 War between United States and Britain over searching of neutral shipping.
1813 Napoleon defeated at Battle of Leipzig; French driven from Spain.
1814 Napoleon abdicates; exiled to Elba.
1815 Napoleon tries to regain power; finally defeated at Battle of Waterloo and exiled to St Helena.
1818 Chile becomes independent.
1819 United States gains Florida from Spain.
1819 Argentina becomes independent.
1821 Mexico and Peru gain independence.
1822 Greece and Brazil declare their independence.

1823 Monroe Doctrine: United States guarantees Western Hemisphere against European interference.
1825 First passenger railway opens in England (Stockton to Darlington).
1825 Bolivia and Paraguay become independent.
1826 First photograph taken by Nicéphore Nièpce of France.
1830 July Revolution: Charles X of France deposed; Louis Philippe elected king.
1830 Belgium and Ecuador become independent.
1833 Slavery abolished in British colonies.
1836 Great Trek: Boer colonists move north from Cape Colony.
1837–1901 Reign of Queen Victoria of Britain.
1839 Guatemala becomes a republic.
1840 Prepaid postage stamps introduced in Britain.
1841 New Zealand becomes British colony.
1841 Upper and Lower Canada united.
1842 China yields Hong Kong to Britain.
1846 Great Famine in Ireland: a million people die, a million emigrate.
1848 Year of Revolutions: in France, Berlin, Budapest, Milan, Naples, Prague, Rome, Venice, and Vienna.
1848 France becomes republic, with Louis Napoleon as president.
1848 Karl Marx and Friedrich Engels publish *Communist Manifesto*.
1849 Britain annexes Punjab.
1851 Australian gold rush begins.
1852 Napoleon III proclaimed Emperor of French.
1854–1856 Crimean War: Turkey, Britain, France, Sardinia against Russia.
1857–1858 Indian Mutiny; British government takes over rule from East India Company.
1861 Unification of Italy.
1861–1865 American Civil War over slavery; southern states secede.
1863 Slavery abolished in United States; Battle of Gettysburg.
1867 Canada proclaimed Dominion.
1867 United States buys Alaska from Russia.
1867 Luxembourg becomes independent.
1869 Suez Canal opened.
1870–1871 Franco-Prussian War: fall of Napoleon III; France a republic again; Germany united under William of Prussia.
1876 Telephone invented.
1876 France and Britain take joint control of Egypt.
1877 Romania becomes independent.
1880–1881 First Boer War.
1884 Leopold II of Belgium sets up private colony in the Congo.
1887 First motor-cars built.
1896 Klondyke gold rush begins.
1898 Battle of Omdurman: British forces defeat the Mahdi and his dervishes.
1898 Spanish-American War: United States wins Guam, Puerto Rico, and Philippines; Cuba wins independence.

Below: **The remains of a Confederate mule wagon after a battle in the American Civil War of 1861 to 1865.** ***Right:*** **British troops in South Africa during the wars against the Dutch Boer settlers.**

Chronology (contd.)

1899–1902 Second Boer War.
1900 Boxer Rebellion in China.
1901 Australia becomes Commonwealth.
1901 First radio signals sent across Atlantic.
1903 First aeroplane flight.
1904–1905 Russo-Japanese War: Japan wins.
1905 Revolution in Russia: Tsar Nicholas II grants limited reforms.
1907 New Zealand becomes a Dominion.
1909 Robert Peary reaches North Pole.
1910 South Africa becomes Dominion.
1911 Agadir Crisis.
1911 Roald Amundsen reaches South Pole.
1911–1912 Italo-Turkish War: Italy gains Tripoli and Cyrenaica.
1912 China proclaimed a republic.
1912–1913 First Balkan War.
1913 Second Balkan War.
1914–1918 World War I: begun by assassination of Archduke Ferdinand of Austria at Sarajevo.
1914 Panama Canal completed.
1915 Allies fail in Dardanelles campaign against Turkey.
1916 Easter Rebellion in Ireland fails.
1916 Battle of Jutland; defence of Verdun; Battle of the Somme; first use of tanks, by the British.
1917 Revolutions in Russia: Bolsheviks under Lenin seize control; United States enters the war; Battles of Aisne, Cambrai, Passchendaele.

Soldiers in the trenches during World War I, 1914–1918.

Adolf Hitler arriving at a mass rally of members of his National Socialist Party—the Nazis.

1918 War ends after final German offensive fails; Germany becomes republic.
1920 League of Nations meets for first time; Americans refuse to join.
1920 Civil war in Ireland.
1921 Southern Ireland becomes Dominion.
1922 Fresh civil war in Ireland.
1923 Turkey becomes republic.
1924 First Labour government in Britain.
1925 Locarno Treaties.
1926 General Strike in Britain.
1927 Charles Lindbergh makes first solo flight across Atlantic Ocean.
1929 Wall Street crash: start of world depression.
1933 Adolph Hitler becomes chancellor of Germany; burning of Reichstag.
1934 Hitler becomes Führer of Germany.
1935 Germany regains Saarland.
1935–1936 Italians conquer Ethiopia.
1936–1939 Civil War in Spain.
1936 Germany reoccupies Rhineland.
1938 The Anschluss: Germany annexes Austria.
1938 Munich crisis: France, Britain, and Italy agree that Germany should take Sudetenland from Czechoslovakia.
1939 Germans occupy remainder of Czechoslovakia.
1939 Russo-German treaty.
1939–1945 World War II: Germany invades Poland; Britain and France declare war.

1940 Germans invade Denmark, Norway, Belgium, the Netherlands, and France; Britain and Empire left to carry on fight.
1940 Battle of Britain: German air attack fails.
1941 Germans invade Greece, Yugoslavia, and Russia.
1941 Japanese attack on Pearl Harbor brings United States into war.
1942 Japanese capture Malaya, Singapore, Burma, and Philippines; Battle of El Alamein in Egypt marks turning point in war.
1943 Allies invade North Africa, Sicily, and Italy; German army surrenders at Stalingrad (Volgograd).
1944 Allies land in Normandy, liberating France and Belgium; major Russian attack begins.
1945 Germany overrun from east and west; Hitler commits suicide; atomic bombs on Japan end war in East.
1946 First session of United Nations General Assembly.
1947 India, Pakistan, and Burma independent.
1948 Israel becomes independent.
1948 Russians blockade West Berlin.
1949 NATO formed.
1949 Communist rule established in China.
1950–1953 Korean War: United Nations force helps defend South Korea.
1954 French Indochina becomes independent countries of Laos, Cambodia, South Vietnam, and North Vietnam after fierce Communist attacks.
1956 Egypt becomes republic; Suez Canal nationalized.
1956 Russia crushes Hungarian uprising.
1956 Morocco, Tunisia, Sudan all independent.

Lancaster bombers of the British Royal Air Force's Bomber Command during World War II.

A World War II propaganda poster from the USSR. 20 million Soviet citizens perished during the war.

Chronology (contd.)

1957 European Common Market set up.
1957 Russia launches first spacecraft.
1957 Ghana and Malaysia independent.
1958 Guinea becomes independent.
1960 Year of Independence for Cameroon, Central African Republic, Chad, Congo (Brazzaville), Congo (now Zaïre), Cyprus, Dahomey, Gabon, Ivory Coast, Madagascar, Mali, Niger, Nigeria, Senegal, Somalia, Togo, Upper Volta.
1960 Earthquake destroys Agadir.
1961 First man in space: Yuri Gagarin of Russia.
1961 Mauretania, Mongolia, Sierra Leone, Tanzania become independent.
1962 Independence of Algeria, Burundi, Jamaica, Rwanda, Trinidad and Tobago, Uganda.
1963 Assassination of President John F. Kennedy of United States.
1963 Kenya and Kuwait independent.
1964 Malawi, Malta, and Zambia independent.
1965 Gambia, Maldive Islands, Singapore all independent; Rhodesia proclaims own independence with white minority rule.
1967 Six-Day War: Israel defeats Arab countries.
1967 Southern Yemen independent.
1968 Russian troops occupy Czechoslovakia.
1968 Independence of Nauru, Equatorial Guinea.
1969 First man on Moon.
1969 Civil disturbances in Northern Ireland begin to escalate.
1970 Bloodless coup led by Lon Nol topples Cambodia's Prince Sihanouk.
1970 Guyana, Fiji become independent.
1971 East Pakistan rebels and becomes independent as Bangladesh; Qatar, Bahrain also indpendent.
1972 Britain takes over direct rule in Northern Ireland.
1973 American forces end military intervention in Vietnam War in signing of Paris peace settlement.
1973 Independence of Bahamas.
1973 The October War: Arab states attack Israel; war halted after five weeks.
1973 Arab oil-producing states impose oil embargo, then raise prices; world economic crisis begins.
1974 President Nixon of the United States resigns because of Watergate scandal.
1974 Portugal's African colonies win independence agreement.
1974 World economic crisis deepens.
1975 Communists win decisive victories in Indochina: Khmers Rouges defeat Lon Nol's regime in Cambodia; South Vietnam surrenders to North Vietnam and the Vietnam War is over.
1975 Independence of Papua New Guinea, São Tomé and Principe, and Angola.
1975 Reopening of Suez Canal to shipping after years of closure.
1975 Military coup in Nigeria deposes General Gowon while absent in Kampala; Brigadier Murtala Mohammed new head of state.
1975 Death of General Franco; Prince Juan Carlos crowned King of Spain.
1975 Iceland unilaterally extends its fishing rights from 50 to 200 miles, and a 'Cod War' develops.
1976 North and South Vietnam reunified.
1976 Independence for the Seychelles.
1976 Two earthquakes destroy mining town of Tangshan in China; more than 700,000 die.
1976 Death of China's Chairman Mao Tse-tung.
1976 Nigeria's head of state, General Murtala Mohammed, assassinated in unsuccessful coup.
1977 Britain, together with EEC countries, agrees to extend fishing limits to 200 miles offshore.
1977 The report of International Commission of Jurists to UN tells of appalling massacres and murders in Uganda under General Amin's rule (80,000–90,000 killed 1971–1972).
1977 Historic meeting in Israel of President Sadat of Egypt and Prime Minister Begin of Israel, in attempt to gain peace for Middle East.
1977 Conflict in Ogaden desert between Ethiopia and Somalia approaches full-scale war.
1977 Army takes charge in Pakistan.
1978 Japan and China sign treaty of peace.
1978 Somalia withdraws from Ogaden.
1978 Independence of Solomon Islands, and Ellice Islands (renamed Tuvalu).
1978 President Kenyatta of Kenya dies and is succeeded by Daniel Arap Moi.
1978 Cambodia invaded by Vietnamese who support rebel forces in opposition to regime of Pol Pot.
1979 USA re-establish diplomatic relations with Communist China.
1979 Phnom Penh, Cambodian capital, captured by Vietnamese and rebel forces; serious famine develops in the country.
1979 Rhodesian referendum among whites results in 6:1 majority in favour of Ian Smith's proposals for transfer to majority rule. Bishop Abel Muzorewa's UANC take 51 of 72 African seats in subsequent election but his government is not recognized by other black leaders. A new constitution and further election proposed at a London conference in the autumn and accepted in December.
1979 Kampala captured by Tanzanian troops and Ugandan exiles; General Amin forced to flee.
1979 Adolfo Suarez becomes Spain's first elected Prime Minister for more than 40 years.
1979 Shah of Iran deposed; exiled Muslim leader, the Ayatollah Khomeini, returns to Iran which is declared an Islamic Republic.
1979 Independence for St Lucia and St Vincent.

MAJOR WARS

name	date	won by	against
American War of Independence	1775–1783	Thirteen Colonies	Britain
Austrian Succession, War of the	1740–1748	Austria, Hungary, Britain, Holland	Bavaria, France, Poland, Prussia, Sardinia, Saxony, Spain
Boer War	1899–1902	Britain	Boer Republics
Chinese-Japanese Wars	1894–1895	Japan	China
	1931–1933	Japan	China
	1937–1945	China	Japan
Civil War, American	1861–1865	11 Northern States (The Union)	11 Southern States (the Confederacy)
Civil War, English	1642–1651	Parliament	Charles I
Civil War, Spanish	1936–1939	Junta de Defensa Nacional	Republican governmen
Crimean War	1853–1856	Britain, France, Sardinia, Turkey	Russia
Franco-Prussian War	1870–1871	Prussia and other German states	France
Hundred Years War	1337–1453	France	England
Korean War	1950–1953	South Korea and United Nations forces	North Korea and Chinese forces
Mexican-American War	1846–1848	United States	Mexico
Napoleonic Wars	1792–1815	Austria, Britain, Prussia, Russia, Spain, Sweden	France
Peloponnesian War	431–404 BC	Peloponnesian League, led by Sparta, Corint!	Delian League, led by Athens
Punic Wars	264–146 BC	Rome	Carthage
Russo-Japanese War	1904–1905	Japan	Russia
Seven Years War	1756–1763	Britain, Prussia, Hanover	Austria, France, Russia, Sweden
Spanish-American War	1898	United States	Spain
Spanish Succession, War of the	1701–1714	England, Austria, Prussia, the Neth-erlands	France, Bavaria, Cologne, Mantua, Savoy
Thirty Years War	1618–1648	France, Sweden, the German Protestant states	The Holy Roman Empire, Spain
Vietnam War	1957–1975	North Vietnam	South Vietnam, United States
War of 1812	1812–1815	United States	Britain
Wars of the Roses	1455–1485	House of Lancaster	House of York
World War I	1914–1918	Belgium, Britain, France, Italy, Russia, Serbia, United States	Austria-Hungary, Bulgaria, Germany, Ottoman Empire
World War II	1939–1945	Australia, Belgium, Britain, Canada, China, Denmark, France, Netherlands, New Zealand, Norway, Poland, Russia, South Africa, United States, Yugoslavia	Bulgaria, Finland, Germany, Hungary, Italy, Japan, Romania

Major battles

Marathon 490 BC Force of 10,000 Athenians and allies defeated 50,000 Persian troops, crushing a Persian invasion attempt and boosting Greek morale.
Salamis 480 BC Greek fleet of 360 ships under Themistocles defeated Persian fleet of 1,000 ships commanded by Xerxes, and Persians had to withdraw from Greece.
Arbela 331 BC Alexander the Great's Greek army defeated a Persian force twice the size under Darius III, conquering Persia. The battle was fought at Gaugamela, 25 miles (40 km) from Arbela.
Actium 31 BC Roman fleet of 400 ships under Octavian (later Emperor Augustus) defeated 500 ships, combined fleet of Mark Antony and Cleopatra. The victory made Octavian master of Rome and its empire.
Tours AD 732 The Franks under Charles Martel defeated the Muslims, halting their advance in western Europe.
Hastings 1066 About 8,000 troops under Duke William of Normandy defeated an equal force under Saxon king Harold II. England came under Norman rule.
Crécy 1346 Invading army of 10,000 English under Edward III defeated 20,000 French men-at-arms. English archers won the day.
Poitiers 1356 Edward the Black Prince of England crushed a French army, capturing the French king, John II, and many of his nobles.
Agincourt 1415 Henry V of England with 10,000 troops defeated 30,000 Frenchmen, and recaptured Normandy.
Siege of Orléans 1428–9 English troops began siege in October 1428, but in April 1429 Joan of Arc came to aid of city, and forced the besiegers to withdraw. Victory was a turning point in French campaign to drive the English out of France.
Siege of Constantinople 1453 Ottoman Turkish army of more than 100,000 under Mohammed the Conqueror captured the city, held by 10,000 men led by the last Byzantine emperor, Constantine Paleologus. The Turks gained a foothold in Europe.
Lepanto 1571 Allied Christian fleet of 208 galleys under Don John of Austria defeated Ali Pasha's Turkish fleet of 230 galleys; last great battle with galleys.
Invincible Armada 1588 Spanish invasion fleet of 130 ships led by Duke of Medina Sidonia was defeated by 197 English ships under Lord Howard of Effingham.
Naseby 1645 Sir Thomas Fairfax with 14,000 Parliamentary troops defeated Prince Rupert with 10,000 Royalist soldiers, virtually ending Charles I's power.
Boyne 1690 William III with 35,000 mixed troops routed his rival, James II, with 21,000 men, ending Stuart hopes.
Blenheim 1704 A British-Austrian army led by Duke of Marlborough and Prince Eugène defeated the French and Bavarians under Marshal Camille de Tallard during War of the Spanish Succession.
Poltava 1709 The Russians under Peter the Great routed an invading Swedish army led by Charles XII of Sweden.
Plassey 1757 Robert Clive with an Anglo-Indian army of 3,000 defeated the Narwab of Bengal's army of 60,000, conquering Bengal and setting Britain on the road to domination in India.
Quebec 1759 British troops under James Wolfe made a night attack up the St Lawrence River, climbing the cliffs to the Heights of Abraham overlooking the city. They defeated the French forces under the Marquis de Montcalm; he and Wolfe were killed.
Saratoga 1777 British troops under John Burgoyne surrendered to American colonial forces under Horatio Gates. Defeat led France to join war against Britain.
Yorktown 1781 Charles Cornwallis with 8,000 British troops surrendered to a larger force under George Washington, ending the American War of Independence.
Valmy 1792 A French Revolutionary army defeated the Prussians in heavy fog. The victory gave new heart to the Revolutionary forces in France.
Nile 1798 Horatio Nelson commanding a British fleet of 15 ships destroyed a 17-ship French fleet under Francis Paul Brueys in Aboukir Bay, cutting off Napoleon Bonaparte's French army in Egypt.
Trafalgar 1805 British fleet of 27 ships under Horatio Nelson shattered Franco-Spanish fleet of 33 ships under Pierre de

Villeneuve, ending Napoleon's hopes of invading England. Nelson was killed.

Austerlitz 1805 Emperor Napoleon I with 65,000 French troops defeated an 83,000-strong Austro-Russian army under the Austrian and Russian emperors. The Austrians sued for peace, and the Russians withdrew.

Jena and Auerstädt 1806 French forces routed the main Prussian armies on the same day (October 14), shattering Prussian power.

Leipzig 1813 Napoleon I with 190,000 French troops was surrounded and crushed by an allied force of 300,000 Austrian, Prussian, Russian, and Swedish troops. This *Battle of the Nations* ended Napoleon's domination of Europe.

Waterloo 1815 A British, Dutch, and Belgian force of 67,000 fought off 74,000 French troops under Napoleon I until the arrival of the Prussian army of Gebhard von Blücher. It ended Napoleon's final bid for power.

Gettysburg 1863 Federal forces under George Meade defeated Robert E. Lee's Confederate army, a turning point in the American Civil War.

Sedan 1870 French army of 100,000 men defeated and surrounded by German force of more than twice the size. Emperor Napoleon III and survivors surrendered. Defeat led to Napoleon's abdication, and helped to unite Germany.

Tshushima 1905 Japanese fleet destroyed Russian fleet of equal size, bringing victory for Japan in Russo-Japanese War.

Marne 1914 French and British armies halted German forces invading France. From then on war on the Western Front became a trench-based slogging match.

Verdun 1916 In a six-month struggle French forces held a major attack by German armies commanded by Crown Prince William. French losses were 348,000 men, the German losses 328,000.

Passchendaele 1917 British forces launched eight attacks over 102 days in heavy rain and through thick mud, gaining five miles and losing 400,000 men.

Britain 1940 A German air force of 2,500 planes launched an attack lasting 114 days to try to win air supremacy over Britain. The smaller Royal Air Force defeated the attack, stopping a German invasion.

Christian and Turkish galleys clash at Lepanto.

Coral Sea 1942 American fleet drove back a Japanese invasion fleet bound for New Guinea in four-day battle in which all the fighting was done by aeroplanes.

Midway 1942 A 100-ship Japanese fleet led by Isoruku Yamamoto aiming to capture Midway Island was defeated by American fleet half the size, under Raymond Spruance.

El Alamein 1942 British Eighth Army under Bernard Montgomery drove back German Afrika Korps under Erwin Rommel, out of Egypt and deep into Libya. Battle marked a turning point in World War II.

Stalingrad 1942–3 Twenty-one German divisions tried to capture Stalingrad (now Volgograd), but siege was broken and Friedrich von Paulus had to surrender with more than 100,000 German troops.

Normandy 1944 Allied forces under Dwight D. Eisenhower invaded German-held northern France in biggest-ever sea-borne attack; after a month of heavy fighting Normandy was cleared and Germans began to retreat.

Ardennes Bulge 1944–5 Last German counter-attack in west through Ardennes Forest failed; Germans lost 100,000 casualties and 110,000 prisoners.

Dien Bien Phu 1954 French surrendered to Vietminh after 8-week siege; marked end of French influence in Indochina, and beginning of long struggle between the two separated halves of Vietnam.

Rulers

Rulers of England

Saxons	
Egbert	827–839
Ethelwulf	839–858
Ethelbald	858–860
Ethelbert	860–866
Ethelred I	866–871
Alfred the Great	871–899
Edward the Elder	899–924
Athelstan	924–939
Edmund	939–946
Edred	946–955
Edwy	955–959
Edgar	959–975
Edward the Martyr	975–978
Ethelred II the Unready	978–1016
Edmund Ironside	1016
Danes	
Canute	1016–1035
Harold I Harefoot	1035–1040
Hardicanute	1040–1042
Saxons	
Edward the Confessor	1042–1066
Harold II	1066
House of Normandy	
William I the Conqueror	1066–1087
William II	1087–1100
Henry I	1100–1135
Stephen	1135–1154
House of Plantagenet	
Henry II	1154–1189
Richard I	1189–1199
John	1199–1216
Henry III	1216–1272
Edward I	1272–1307
Edward II	1307–1327
Edward III	1327–1377
Richard II	1377–1399
House of Lancaster	
Henry IV	1399–1413
Henry V	1413–1422
Henry VI	1422–1461
House of York	
Edward IV	1461–1483
Edward V	1483
Richard III	1483–1485
House of Tudor	
Henry VII	1485–1509
Henry VIII	1509–1547
Edward VI	1547–1553
Mary I	1553–1558
Elizabeth I	1558–1603

Rulers of Scotland

Malcolm II	1005–1034
Duncan I	1034–1040
Macbeth (usurper)	1040–1057
Malcolm III Canmore	1057–1093
Donald Bane	1093–1094
Duncan II	1094
Donald Bane (restored)	1094–1097
Edgar	1097–1107
Alexander I	1107–1124
David I	1124–1153
Malcolm IV	1153–1165
William the Lion	1165–1214
Alexander II	1214–1249
Alexander III	1249–1286
Margaret of Norway	1286–1290
(*Interregnum* 1290–1292)	
John Balliol	1292–1296
(*Interregnum* 1296–1306)	
Robert I (Bruce)	1306–1329
David II	1329–1371
House of Stuart	
Robert II	1371–1390
Robert III	1390–1406
James I	1406–1437
James II	1437–1460
James III	1460–1488
James IV	1488–1513
James V	1513–1542
Mary	1542–1567
James VI*	1567–1625

*Became James I of Great Britain in 1603.

Rulers of Great Britain

House of Stuart	
James I	1603–1625
Charles I	1625–1649
(*Commonwealth* 1649–1659)	
House of Stuart (restored)	
Charles II	1660–1685
James II	1685–1688
William III } jointly	1689–1702
Mary II } jointly	1689–1694
Anne	1702–1714
House of Hanover	
George I	1714–1727
George II	1727–1760
George III	1760–1820
George IV	1820–1830
William IV	1830–1837
Victoria	1837–1901
House of Saxe-Coburg	
Edward VII	1901–1910
House of Windsor	
George V	1910–1936
Edward VIII	1936
George VI	1936–1952
Elizabeth II	1952–

British Prime Ministers

prime minister (party)	term
Sir Robert Walpole (W)	1721–42
Earl of Wilmington (W)	1742–43
Henry Pelham (W)	1743–54
Duke of Newcastle (W)	1754–56
Duke of Devonshire (W)	1756–57
Duke of Newcastle (W)	1757–62
Earl of Bute (T)	1762–63
George Grenville (W)	1763–65
Marquess of Rockingham (W)	1765–66
Earl of Chatham (W)	1766–67
Duke of Grafton (W)	1767–70
Lord North (T)	1770–82
Marquess of Rockingham (W)	1782
Earl of Shelburne (W)	1782–83
Duke of Portland (Cln)	1783
William Pitt (T)	1783–1801
Henry Addington (T)	1801–04
William Pitt (T)	1804–06
Lord Grenville (W)	1806–07
Duke of Portland (T)	1807–09
Spencer Perceval (T)	1809–12
Earl of Liverpool (T)	1812–27
George Canning (T)	1827
Viscount Goderich (T)	1827–28
Duke of Wellington (T)	1828–30
Earl Grey (W)	1830–34
Viscount Melbourne (W)	1834
Sir Robert Peel (T)	1834–35
Viscount Melbourne (W)	1835–41
Sir Robert Peel (T)	1841–46
Lord John Russell (W)	1846–52
Earl of Derby (T)	1852
Earl of Aberdeen (P)	1852–55
Viscount Palmerston (L)	1855–58
Earl of Derby (C)	1858–59
Viscount Palmerston (L)	1859–65
Earl Russell (L)	1865–66
Earl of Derby (C)	1866–68
Benjamin Disraeli (C)	1868
William Gladstone (L)	1868–74
Benjamin Disraeli (C)	1874–80
William Gladstone (L)	1880–85
Marquess of Salisbury (C)	1885–86
William Gladstone (L)	1886
Marquess of Salisbury (C)	1886–92
William Gladstone (L)	1892–94
Earl of Rosebery (L)	1894–95
Marquess of Salisbury (C)	1895–1902
Arthur Balfour (C)	1902–05
Sir Henry Campbell-Bannerman (L)	1905–08
Herbert Asquith (L)	1908–15
Herbert Asquith (Cln)	1915–16
David Lloyd-George (Cln)	1916–22
Andrew Bonar Law (C)	1922–23
Stanley Baldwin (C)	1923–24
James Ramsay MacDonald (Lab)	1924
Stanley Baldwin (C)	1924–29
James Ramsay MacDonald (Lab)	1929–31
James Ramsay MacDonald (Cln)	1931–35
Stanley Baldwin (Cln)	1935–37
Neville Chamberlain (Cln)	1937–40
Winston Churchill (Cln)	1940–45
Winston Churchill (C)	1945
Clement Atlee (Lab)	1945–51
Sir Winston Churchill (C)	1951–55
Sir Anthony Eden (C)	1955–57
Harold Macmillan (C)	1957–63
Sir Alec Douglas-Home (C)	1963–64
Harold Wilson (Lab)	1964–70
Edward Heath (C)	1970–74
Harold Wilson (Lab)	1974–76
James Callaghan (Lab)	1976–79
Margaret Thatcher (C)	1979–

W=Whig, T=Tory, Cln=Coalition, P=Peelite, L=Liberal, C=Conservative, Lab=Labour

American Presidents

	president (party)	term
1	George Washington (F)	1789–97
2	John Adams (F)	1797–1801
3	Thomas Jefferson (DR)	1801–09
4	James Madison (DR)	1809–17
5	James Monroe (DR)	1817–25
6	John Quincy Adams (DR)	1825–29
7	Andrew Jáckson (D)	1829–37
8	Martin Van Buren (D)	1837–41
9	William H. Harrison* (W)	1841
10	John Tyler (W)	1841–45
11	James K. Polk (D)	1845–49
12	Zachary Taylor* (W)	1849–50
13	Millard Fillmore (W)	1850–53
14	Franklin Pierce (D)	1853–57
15	James Buchanan (D)	1857–61
16	Abraham Lincoln † (R)	1861–65
17	Andrew Johnson (U)	1865–69
18	Ulysses S. Grant (R)	1869–77
19	Rutherford B. Hayes (R)	1877–81
20	James A. Garfield † (R)	1881
21	Chester A. Arthur (R)	1881–85
22	Grover Cleveland (D)	1885–89
23	Benjamin Harrison (R)	1889–93
24	Grover Cleveland (D)	1893–97
25	William McKinley † (R)	1897–1901
26	Theodore Roosevelt (R)	1901–09
27	William H. Taft (R)	1909–13
28	Woodrow Wilson (D)	1913–21
29	Warren G. Harding* (R)	1921–23
30	Calvin Coolidge (R)	1923–29
31	Herbert C. Hoover (R)	1929–33
32	Franklin D. Roosevelt* (D)	1933–45
33	Harry S. Truman (D)	1945–53
34	Dwight D. Eisenhower (R)	1953–61
35	John F. Kennedy † (D)	1961–63
36	Lyndon B. Johnson (D)	1963–69
37	Richard M. Nixon (R)	1969–74
38	Gerald R. Ford (R)	1974–77
39	James E. Carter (D)	1977–

*Died in office. †Assassinated in office.
F=Federalist, DR=Democratic-Republican, D=Democratic, W=Whig, R=Republican, U=Union.

Archaeology

Above: **A typical 'dig'. After the layer of topsoil has been removed, each successive layer is excavated with hand tools in order not to damage any 'finds'.**

Glossary of terms

Abbevillian culture (from Abbeville, France) 510,000–310,000 B.C. Its people used crudely chipped hand-axes.
Acheulian culture (from St Acheul, in France) 310,000–235 B.C. Its people used pointed, pear-shaped hand-axes.
amphitheatre Oval stadium for games.
amphora Large jar for wine or oil, with two handles.
artefact Any object made by Man.
Aurignacian culture (from Aurignac in southern France) 85,000–50,000 B.C. Its people were cave dwellers who made narrow-bladed flint knives.
axe (formerly called *celt*) Flint cutting tool of Stone Age cultures; hafted axes used for chopping, hand-axes for slicing.
Azilian culture (from Le Mas d'Azil, in France) 10,000–2,500 B.C. Its people used small stone scrapers and arrowheads.
bailey See *curtain wall; motte and bailey*.
barrow A burial mound; *long barrows* are Neolithic, *round barrows* Bronze Age.
bath-house Roman public baths, rather like modern Turkish baths.
Beaker folk Bronze Age people who made pottery drinking vessels; 1900–1800 B.C.
Bronze Age Period when bronze was generally used, roughly 1900–500 B.C. in Europe.
burial chamber Inner part of *barrow*.
caldarium The hot-water bath in a Roman *bath-house*.
castellum A fortified camp.
circles Ring-shaped structures of stone or wood, of *Bronze Age* period; e.g. Stonehenge, in England.
Clactonian culture (from Clacton-on-Sea, England) 510,000–310,000 B.C. Its people used thick flaked flint tools.
codex Mexican manuscript painted on strips of deerskin or bark paper pre-Spanish conquest.
comb Toothed object of bone, wood, etc., used for hair, in wearing, decorating pottery, etc.
Copper Age Period, in Europe and Asia, between *Neolithic* and *Bronze Age*, that saw origins of civilization in Asia and *Beaker* and Corded Ware folk in Europe.
counterscarp The inward-facing side of the *fossa* of an *earthwork*.
Cro-Magnon Man (from Cro-Magnon Cave, Les Eyzies, France) Stone Age Man of *Aurignacian culture*.
cromlech See *dolmen*.
curtain wall Surrounding wall of castle; ground enclosed called *bailey*.
dendrochronology A system of dating by counting tree-rings.
ditch See *fossa*.
dolmen or **cromlech** Group of standing stones, often with cap-stone over top, which once formed *burial-chamber* of *barrow*.
donjon Main tower or *keep* of castle.
dorter Monks' dormitory in a monastery.
earthwork complex of *vallum* and *fossa* forming *hill-fort*.
eolith Literally 'dawn stone'; once thought to be earliest type of stone tool made by Man; up to 2,600,000 years old so far discovered, but now accepted as naturally formed.
escarpment Side of *vallum* and *fossa* next to *hill-fort*.
fluorine dating System of dating by measuring fluorine content of bones.
Folsom points Stone spearheads found at Folsom, New Mexico; 10,000–25,000 B.C.
fossa Ditch of *hill-fort*.
frigidarium Cold bath in Roman *bath-house*.
garderobe Room within thickness of castle wall, used as a wardrobe; term often misused for *latrine*.
hill-fort Fortified encampment surrounded by a *vallum* or wall of earth protected by a *fossa* or ditch, and possibly a further bank beyond the fossa called a *revetment*.
Homo sapiens Modern man, first appearing about 35,000 B.C.
hypocaust Roman underfloor central heating system.
inhumation Burial of a whole body, not just cremated remains.
interglacials Periods between the four Ice Ages: First or Aftonian 536,000–476,000 B.C. Second or Yarmouth 320,000–230,000 B.C. Third or

Sangamon 175,000–115,000 B.C.
intervallum Roadway inside Roman fort.
Iron Age Period beginning about 1200 B.C. during which iron was used for tools and weapons.
keep See *donjon*.
kitchen midden Household refuse dump, in particular the debris left by certain food-gathering peoples (sea shells, etc.).
La Tène culture Iron Age culture that began in Switzerland; from about 300 B.C.
latrine Privy built in thickness of castle wall; often incorrectly called *garderobe*.
Levalloisian culture (from Levallois, Paris suburb); about 300,000–230,000 B.C. its people used flaked flint tools.
lynchets Terraces formed by ploughing.
Magdalenian culture (from La Madeleine, in France) 35,000–10,000 B.C. Highly developed Stone Age culture, using many stone and bone tools, and making cave paintings.
megalith Very large stone used to build temple or *circle*.
Mesolithic Middle Stone Age, from 10,000 B.C. to 2500 B.C.
Microlith Small tool, a blade or flake, usually hafted.
miliari Roman milestones.
monolith Single large stone standing by itself, perhaps as memorial.
motte and bailey Simple Norman castle; *motte* was earth mound, topped by wooden fort; *bailey* was flat area of ground surrounded by ditch and palisade.
Mousterian culture (from Le Moustier Cave, Les Eyzies, France) 235,000–85,000 B.C. Its people were *Neanderthal Men*.
Neanderthal Man (from Neanderthal, near Dusseldorf, in Germany); early form of Man, not directly related to *Homo sapiens*.
Neolithic New Stone Age, 2500–1900 B.C.
Paleolithic Old Stone Age, from at least 2,600,000 to 10,000 B.C.
Posthole Hole in the ground for an upright timber; often surviving as region of darkened soil, the remains of post.
potsherds Fragments of pottery.
pottery Good guide to dating, each culture having its own style of pottery.
quern Stone hand mill for grinding corn.
radiocarbon dating C^{14} (radioactive carbon) in organic material decays at a known rate; measuring the amount left in a specimen gives the approximate age (i.e. time elapsed since specimen – animal or vegetable – died, and stopped exchanging carbon with atmosphere, where C^{14} is produced by action of cosmic rays on nitrogen).
resistivity survey Passing electric current through ground to measure resistance, and detect buried buildings.
revetment Secondary *vallum* on outside of *fossa* in earthwork.
solar South-facing room for ladies in castle, usually near Great Hall.
Solutrean culture (from Solutré, France) 50,000–35,000 B.C. Its people were hunters and also made many cave paintings.
spear-thrower Bone device used in late Stone Age times for hurling spears further.
stratigraphy Dating and classifying finds according to strata, or layers, in which they are discovered.
Stone Age Period during which Man used tools and weapons of stone; see *Mesolithic*; *Neolithic*; *Palaeolithic*.
sudatorium Hot air sweating room of Roman *bath-house*.
tepidarium Warm moist room in Roman *bath-house*, used as recreation room.
tesserae Small cubes of stone or glass used for making mosaics.
tumulus A burial-mound.
vallum Main wall of *earthwork*.
votive deposit Offering to gods left in sacred place, often natural site (cave, lake, etc.).

Below: **An aerial photograph of a site in Oxfordshire, England, taken with infra-red film, which shows up the underlying features more clearly.**

EXPLORATION AND DISCOVERY

place	achievement	explorer or discoverer	date
World	circumnavigated	Ferdinand Magellan* (Port. for Sp.)	1519–21
Pacific Ocean	discovered	Vasco Núñez de Balboa (Sp.)	1513
Africa			
River Congo (mouth)	discovered	Diogo Cão (Port.)	c. 1483
Cape of Good Hope	sailed round	Bartolomeu Diaz (Port.)	1488
River Niger	explored	Mungo Park (Scot.)	1795
River Zambezi	discovered	David Livingstone (Scot.)	1851
Sudan	explored	Heinrich Barth (Germ. for Eng.)	1852–5
Victoria Falls	discovered	Livingstone	1855
Lake Tanganyika	discovered	Richard Burton & John Speke (GB)	1858
River Congo †	traced	Sir Henry Stanley (GB)	1877
Asia			
China	visited	Marco Polo (Ital.)	c. 1272
India (cape route)	visited	Vasco da Gama (Port.)	1498
Japan	visited	St Francis Xavier (Sp.)	1549
China	explored	Ferdinand Richthofen Germ.)	1868
North America			
North America	discovered	Leif Ericson (Norse)	c. 1000
West Indies	discovered	Christopher Columbus (Ital. for Sp.)	1492
Newfoundland	discovered	John Cabot (Ital. for Eng.)	1497
Mexico	conquered	Hernando Cortés (Sp.)	1519–21
St Lawrence River	explored	Jacques Cartier (Fr.)	1534–6
Mississippi River	discovered	Hernando de Soto (Sp.)	1541
Canadian interior	explored	Samuel de Champlain (Fr.)	1603–9
Hudson Bay	discovered	Henry Hudson (Eng.)	1610
Alaska	discovered	Vitus Bering (Dan. for Russ.)	1728
Mackenzie River	discovered	Sir Alexander Mackenzie (Scot.)	1789
South America			
South America	visited	Columbus	1498
Venezuela	explored	Alonso de Ojeda (Sp.)	1499
Brazil	discovered	Pedro Alvares Cabral (Port.)	1500
Rio de la Plata	discovered	Juan de Solis (Sp.)	1516
Tierra del Fuego	discovered	Magellan	1520
Peru	explored	Francisco Pizarro (Sp.)	1530–8
River Amazon	explored	Francisco de Orellana (Sp.)	1541
Cape Horn	discovered	Willem Schouten (Dut.)	1616

†now renamed River Zaire

*Killed in Philippines, but one ship returned to Spain.

The Portuguese capital Lisbon was the starting point for many great voyages of exploration.

place	achievement	explorer or discoverer	date
Australasia, Polar regions, etc.			
Greenland	visited	Eric the Red (Norse)	c. 982
Australia	discovered	unknown	1500s
Spitsbergen	discovered	Willem Barents (Dut.)	1596
Australia	visited	Abel Tasman (Dut.)	1642
New Zealand	sighted	Tasman	1642
New Zealand	visited	James Cook (Eng.)	1769
Antarctic Circle	crossed	Cook	1773
Antarctica	sighted	Nathaniel Palmer (US)	1820
Antarctica	circumnavigated	Fabian von Bellingshausen (Russ.)	1819–21
Australian interior	explored	Charles Sturt (GB)	1828
Antarctica	explored	Charles Wilkes (US)	1838–42
Australia	crossed(S–N)	Robert Burke (Ir.) & William Wills (Eng.)	1860–1
Greenland	explored	Fridtjof Nansen (Nor.)	1888
Arctic	explored	Abruzzi, Duke of the (Ital.)	1900
North Pole	reached	Robert Peary (US)	1909
South Pole	reached	Roald Amundsen (Nor.)	1911
Antarctica	crossed	Sir Vivian Fuchs (Eng.)	1957–8

Religion & Mythology

Glossary of religion

abbey Convent under abbot or abbess.
absolution Remission of a penitent's sins, performed officially by priest.
Adventists Protestant sects that sprang from the teachings of William Miller in mid-1800s; they believe in the 2nd and pre-millennial advent of Christ. *Seventh-day Adventists* (founded 1860) form largest group.
Agapemonites English sect that lived in 'abode of love' (founded 1859); practised 'spiritual wedlock'
agnostic One who believes that nothing can be known or is likely to be known about God or anything non-material.
Allah Arabic name for supreme being of Muslims.
Anabaptists German Protestant sect (1521) that rejected infant baptism, thus requiring members to be baptized again when adult.
ancestor worship Practice of rites to appease or commemorate dead members of a family; practised in Africa and Asia.
Anglicans Members of churches that agree with Church of England.
Anglo-Catholics Those who hold to the catholicity of the Church of England.
animism Belief that natural objects do not have life in themselves but may sometimes be animated by spirits or gods.
antipope Pope set up in opposition to one elected in accordance with canon law.
Apostles' Creed Statement of the principal Christian beliefs; the oldest of such creeds, possibly used by Christ's apostles.
archbishop A bishop of the highest rank.
Armageddon Symbolical battlefield of final struggle between good and evil.
Ascension The rising of Jesus into heaven after his burial and resurrection.
Assemblies of God Largest of the Pentecostal sects, which lay stress on 'speaking with other tongues'.
atheist One who believes there is no God.
atonement An act of repentance or sacrifice that will bring person back to God. Most Christians believe that death of Jesus atoned for sins of all. See *Yom Kippur*.
Bahá'í Persian religion founded in 1800s; members believe in unity of mankind and peace through religion and science.
baptism Christian rite of plunging person into, or sprinkling him with, water as sign of purification.
Baptists Protestant denomination, one of whose key beliefs is baptism by the total immersion of adults.
bar mitzvah Confirmation ceremony for Jewish boys at age of 13.
Bhagavad-Gita Long philosophical poem forming part of the Hindu scriptures.
Bible Collection of many holy books that forms the scriptures of Christians and Jews.
bishop Head of diocese in Anglican, Roman Catholic, Eastern Orthodox, and some Lutheran churches.
Brahma One of chief gods (creator of world) in Hindu religion.
British Israelites Religious group who believe that white English-speaking peoples are descendants of the lost 10 Tribes of Israel; hence that Anglo-Saxons are God's chosen people.
Buddha (563?–483? BC) Title meaning the 'Enlightened One' bestowed on Siddhartha Gautama, Indian prince, spiritual teacher, and founder of Buddhism.
Buddhism Major oriental religion that teaches way of salvation through ethics and discipline; founded by Buddha.
caliph Title of Muhammad's successors as civil and spiritual leaders.
Calvinists Followers of teachings of John Calvin (1509–64), who accept absolute sovereignty of God and supremacy of Bible.
cardinal Ecclesiastical title and office next in rank to that of the pope.
cathedral Chief church of diocese, containing bishop's seat.
Christ Title meaning 'Anointed', applied to Jesus of Nazareth, founder of Christianity.
Christadelphians American Protestant

sect (founded 1848) who claim to represent primitive 1st-century Christianity.
Christian Scientists Followers of religious movement founded in late 1800s by Mary Baker Eddy; stress present perfectibility of God and man, and practise spiritual healing.
Christianity Religion founded on life and teachings of Jesus; many divisions.
Church of England The established church in England, springing mainly from fusion of Celtic Church with that of St Augustine; during Reformation, royal supremacy was substituted for that of pope.
Christmas Annual festival celebrated by Christians (Dec 25) to honour birth of Jesus.
circumcision Cutting away of foreskin; practised by many religions, but particularly important to Jews.
confession Statement of religious belief; in the Roman Catholic church, the acknowledgment of sins to priest.
confirmation Ceremony associated with baptism in many Christian churches; called *bar mitzvah* in Judaism.
Congregationalists Nonconformist Christians who believe that each local congregation is responsible only to God and that all Christians are equal.
convent Religious community of men or women who live under strict vows and devote their lives to religious activity.
Copts Members of an Egyptian Christian church, branch of *Eastern Orthodox Church*; have dietary laws and practise circumcision.
diocese Church district.
Dukhobors Members of Russian sect, many of whom have settled in Canada since 1899; opposed to military service, they trust to 'inner light' for guidance.
Easter Annual Christian festival that commemorates resurrection of Jesus.
Eastern Orthodox Church Federation of Christian churches (Russian Orthodox, Greek Orthodox, etc) found in eastern Europe and Egypt; faith is expressed in Creed of Constantinople.
Episcopalians Members of church governed by bishops.
eucharist Christian sacrament that celebrates the Lord's Supper.
friar Member of one of mendicant Roman Catholic orders.
Friends, Society of Christian group founded by George Fox in 1640s; they reject creeds, rites, and organized religion in favour of spontaneous worship; popularly known as Quakers.

The Buddhist way of life aspires to serenity and inner peace—reflected in this image of the Buddha.

fundamentalists Protestant Christians who believe that Bible is literally true, without error, and wholly inspired by God.
Gnostics Members of early Christian sect who claimed to possess secret knowledge (*gnosis*) based on spiritual insight.
God Supreme Being of monotheist religions; the Creator.
Good Friday Friday before Easter, commemorating Jesus's crucifixion.
heaven Dwelling-place of God; place or state of bliss.
hegira Flight of Muhammad from Mecca to Medina in AD 622.

Glossary of religion (contd.)

hell Abode of the devil; place in afterlife where wicked are punished.
Hinduism One of the great eastern religions; the main religion of India. Hindus believe in Brahman, the supreme spirit, traditionally expressed in three forms: *Brahma, Shiva,* and *Vishnu.*
imam Islamic official who conducts prayers of mosque.
Islam Major eastern religion founded by Muhammad in AD 600s. Muhammad taught that there was one God (*Allah*) and that he was his prophet. Has many followers (called *Muslims*) in Africa and Asia.
Jainism Small Indian sect, offshoot of Hinduism in the 6th century BC; teaches that salvation depends on rigid self-effort and non-violence towards all creatures.
Jehovah Name used by Christians for the Hebrew God.
Jehovah's Witnesses Adherents of a religious movement founded by the American C. T. Russell in late 1800s; they believe that Christ returned invisibly in 1874, and that Armageddon is near.
Jesus Founder of Christianity; his followers believe him to be the Christ or Messiah.
Judaism Religion of the Jews, based on Old Testament and *Talmud.*
karma Law that says a man's deeds determine his destiny; subscribed to by Buddhists and Hindus.
Koran The sacred book of Islam.
kosher Term that means 'fit to be eaten according to Jewish ritual; Jewish law prohibits eating of certain animals, and states that those that are eaten must be slaughtered and prepared in certain ways.
lama Buddhist priest in Tibet and Mongolia.
Latter-day Saints See *Mormons.*
Lent Period from Ash Wednesday to Easter, observed by some Christians with acts of self-denial in remembrance of the passion and resurrection of Jesus.
liturgy Regular form of service at church.
Lord's Prayer The only prayer taught by Jesus to his disciples, as a model; used by Christians everywhere.
Lutherans Members of oldest and largest Protestant church, founded by Martin Luther in 1500s; Bible is only authority.
mass Celebration of eucharist in Roman Catholic churches.
Mennonites Branch of Anabaptists organized in 1525 at Zurich; several groups now in US, some opposing all ritualism.
Methodists Members of Protestant movement founded by John Wesley (1703–91); they stress evangelical Christianity and religious experience.
metropolitan Archbishop of the Eastern Orthodox Church; occasionally, a Roman Catholic archbishop.
Mohammed See *Muhammad.*
Mohammedanism *Islam.*
monk Man who takes religious vows, follows a fixed rule, and withdraws from world to live with other monks.
Moral Rearmament International movement for character reformation on Christian principles; founded by American educationist Frank Buchman in 1920s; formerly called *Oxford Group.*
Moravians Members of Protestant church founded in Bohemia and Moravia in 1457; based on teachings of John Huss.
Mormons American religious sect founded by Joseph Smith (1830); officially, Church of Jesus Christ of Latter-day Saints.
Moslem See *Muslim.*
mosque Muslim place of worship.
muezzin Muslim official who calls to prayer.
Muhammad (570–632) The prophet and founder of Islam.
Muslim (Moslem) A follower of Islam.
nun Woman who has taken religious vows and lives with other nuns in a nunnery.
Oneida Community Spiritually communistic experiment run by J. H. Noyes from 1848 to 1880 at Oneida Creek, New York; based on perfectionism and community sharing.
Passion Sufferings and death of Jesus.
Passover Jewish festival, celebrates exodus from Egypt; lasts 8 days and starts in March or April.
pentecostal sects Group of fundamentalist sects distinguished mainly by 'speaking with tongues', also called 'Holy Rollers because some devotees fall to ground in trance.
pope Title of head of Roman Catholic Church; recognized by Catholics as lawful successor to St Peter.
Plymouth Brethren Sect founded in 1827 by J. N. Darby and E. Cronin; they believe that Christianity has fallen from New

MAJOR RELIGIONS: ESTIMATED WORLD MEMBERSHIP (millions)
Christians 1,000
Roman Catholics 585
Eastern Orthodox 90
Protestants 325
Jews 15
Muslims 500
Shintoists 60
Taoists 30
Confucians 300
Buddhists 200
Hindus 500

Testament ideals and this corruption can be remedied only by direct approach to God.

Presbyterians Members of Protestant churches that follow system of government established by John Calvin during Reformation.

priest Official who officiates at worship; duties vary from one religion to another.

Protestant Any Christian outside Roman Catholic and Eastern Orthodox churches.

Quakers See *Friends, Society of.*

rabbi Teacher and expounder of Jewish law, and spiritual leader of synagogue.

resurrection Belief held by Jews, Christians, and Muslims that the dead will eventually return to life in bodily form; specifically, the return to life of Jesus Christ.

Roman Catholics Christians who accept the pope as spiritual leader on earth; they claim to belong to the one Holy and Apostolic Church.

Rosh Hashanah Festival of Jewish New Year.

Sabbath Day of week set aside for rest and religious observances; for Jews it is Saturday, for most Christians, Sunday.

Salvation Army Religious movement founded by William Booth (about 1865); aims to preach evangelical Christianity to the masses normally untouched by religion.

Seventh-day Adventists See *Adventists.*

Shakers Small American sect, members of United Society of Believers; originally offshoot of Quakers in 1700; devotees shake with religious fervour.

Shinto The religion of Japan; adherents worship many gods, including nature and ancestor worship.

Shiva One of three main Hindu deities; destroyer and reproducer; also called Siva.

Sikhs Adherents of Sikhism, India's fourth largest religion, located mainly in Punjab; founded by Guru Nanak (1469–1538), who rejected formalism of Hinduism and Islam.

spiritualism Religious philosophy which claims that there is a reality distinct from matter, and that communication is possible with spirits of the dead.

Swedenborgians Followers of the teachings of Emanuel Swedenborg (1688–1722); founded Church of the New Jerusalem, claiming that teachings were new dispensation of Christianity.

synagogue Jewish house of worship.

Talmud Encyclopedia of Jewish laws and tradition supplementing first five books of Old Testament, called the Pentateuch.

Taoism Major Chinese religion founded by Lao Tzu in 500s BC; believers yield to *Tao*, 'the way', in order to restore human harmony.

Torah The Mosaic law; the Pentateuch or first five books of the Bible.

transmigration of souls Belief that after death the soul enters the body of another living creature; held by Ancient Greeks, certain Hindus, Buddhists, and others.

transubstantiation Belief that bread and wine used in eucharist are mystically changed into body and blood of Christ; held by Roman Catholics and members of Eastern Orthodox Church.

Trinity Christian belief that there are three divine persons in God: Father, Son, and Holy Ghost.

Unitarians Believers in doctrine of unity of Godhead and divinity of God the Father only.

Vedas Four holy books of the Hindus.

Vishnu One of the Hindu trinity of deities; preserver of man in various incarnations.

voodoo Superstitious beliefs and practices accepted and carried out by certain West Indians; of African origin.

yoga System of Hindu philosophy involving union with the Absolute Being; includes progressive stages of physical and mental exercises.

Yom Kippur Jewish fast day, Day of Atonement.

Zoroastrians Believers in teachings of Persian prophet Zoroaster (600s BC); morality is greatest virtue in battle between good and evil.

A bronze head of the Greek god Apollo.

Mythical characters

When there is a Latin equivalent of a Greek name, the character is listed under the Greek version, with the Latin in parentheses. A separate table on this page lists the Roman deities alphabetically and gives their Greek equivalents.

Achilles Greek hero of Trojan War; died when Paris wounded vulnerable heel.
Adonis Beautiful youth loved by Aphrodite; killed by boar.
Aneas A Trojan, son of Venus, carried his father to safety out of Troy; married and deserted Dido, queen of Carthage.
Agamemnon King of Mycenae, Greek leader against Troy; murdered by wife Clytemnestra, avenged by son Orestes.
Ajax Greek warrior; killed himself when Achilles' arms awarded to Odysseus.
Amazons Female warriors from Asia.
Andromeda Chained to rock as prey for monster, rescued by Perseus.
Aphrodite (Venus) Goddess of beauty and love; sprang from foam in sea, but also said to be daughter of Zeus; mother of Eros.
Apollo Son of Zeus and Leto; god of poetry, music, and prophecy; ideal of manly beauty; sometimes known as *Phoebus*.
Ares (Mars) God of war, son of Zeus and Hera; Roman god *Mars*, father of Romulus and Remus, identified with Ares.
Argonauts Jason and 50 heroes who sailed on *Argo* in search of Golden Fleece.
Artemis (Diana) Twin sister of Apollo; goddess of moon and famous huntress.
Asclepius (Aesculapius) Mortal son of Apollo, later deified as god of medical art; killed by Zeus for raising dead.
Athene (Minerva) Goddess of wisdom and war, daughter of Zeus and Metis; sprang fully grown and armed from father's head.
Atlas A Titan, made war on Zeus, condemned by him to bear heavens on shoulders; later turned into mountain.
Bellerophon Corinthian hero, rode winged horse Pegasus; fell to death trying to reach Olympus.
Centaurs Race of half-horses half-men.
Cerberus Three-headed dog, guarded Hades.

ROMAN-GREEK EQUIVALENTS

Roman	Greek	Roman	Greek
Aesculapius	Asclepius	Luna	Selene
Apollo	Apollo	Mars	Ares
Aurora	Eos	Mercury	Hermes
Bacchus	Dionysus	Minerva	Athene
Ceres	Demeter	Mors	Thanatos
Cupid	Eros	Neptune	Poseidon
Cybele	Rhea	Ops	Rhea
Diana	Artemis	Pluto	Pluto
Dis	Hades	Proserpine	Persephone
Faunus	Pan	Saturn	Cronos
Hecate	Hecate	Sol	Helios
Hercules	Heracles	Somnus	Hypnos
Juno	Hera	Ulysses	Odysseus
Jupiter	Zeus	Venus	Aphrodite
Juventas	Hebe	Vesta	Hestia
Latona	Leto	Vulcan	Hephaestus

Cronos (Saturn) A Titan, god of agriculture and harvests; father of Zeus.
Cyclopes Race of one-eyed giants led by Polyphemus; (singular, *Cyclops*).
Daedalus Athenian craftsman, builder of Labyrinth in Crete; imprisoned there with son Icarus, escaped with home-made wings.
Dionysus (Bacchus) God of wine and fertile crops; son of Zeus and Semele.
Demeter (Ceres) Goddess of agriculture.
Elysium Paradise of Greek mythology to which heroes passed without dying.
Eos (Aurora) Goddess of dawn.
Eros (Cupid) God of love, son of Aphrodite.
Fates Three sisters, goddesses who determined destiny of man.
Graces Three beautiful goddesses, daughters of Zeus, personifying brilliance (Aglaia), joy (Euphrosyne), and bloom (Thalia).
Hades (Dis) Abode of dead, ruled by Pluto; name sometimes used for Pluto.
Hebe (Juventas) Goddess of youth, cup-bearer of gods; daughter of Zeus and Hera; wife of Heracles.
Hecate Goddess of witchcraft and ghosts.
Hector Eldest son of Priam; chief hero of Trojans; slain by Achilles.
Helen of Troy Fairest woman in world; daughter of Zeus and Leda; cause of Trojan War.

TWELVE LABOURS OF HERCULES

1. Killing Nemean lion
2. Killing Hydra (many-headed snake)
3. Capturing hind of Artemis
4. Capturing Erymanthian boar
5. Cleansing Augean stables in a day
6. Killing man-eating Stymphalian birds
7. Capturing Cretan wild bull
8. Capturing man-eating mares of Diomedes
9. Procuring girdle of Amazon Hippolyta
10. Killing the monster Geryon
11. Stealing apples from garden of Hesperides
12. Bringing Cerberus up from Hades

Hephaestus (Vulcan) God of destructive fire, heavenly blacksmith; husband of Aphrodite; son of Zeus and Hera or just Hera.
Hera (Juno) Queen of heaven, daughter of Cronos and Rhea, wife and sister of Zeus; guardian spirit of women and marriage.
Heracles (Hercules) Famous strong man and greatest of deified heroes, performed 12 labours to be free from bondage; son of Zeus and Alcmene.
Hermes (Mercury) Messenger of gods, son of Zeus and Maia; god of physicians, traders, and thieves.

Heracles (Hercules) battling with a fish-tailed monster.

Roman relief showing Jupiter (Zeus), his consort Juno (Hera) and the helmeted Minerva (Athene).

Mythical characters (contd.)

Hestia (Vesta) Goddess of the hearth, sister of Zeus; her temple held Sacred Fire guarded by Vestal Virgins.
Hypnos (Somnus) God of sleep.
Janus Roman god of doors and gates, represented by two faces facing opposite ways.
Jason Son of Aeson; see *Argonauts*.
Laocoön Priest of Apollo at Troy; he and two sons killed by serpents sent by Athene.
Midas King of Phrygia; touch turned everything to gold.
Muses Nine lesser divinities who presided over arts and sciences; daughters of Zeus and Mnemosyne.

THE NINE MUSES

Name	Art	Symbol
Calliope	Epic poetry	Tablet & stylus
Clio	History	Scroll
Erato	Love poetry	Lyre
Euterpe	Lyric poetry	Flute
Melpomene	Tragedy	Tragic mask, sword
Polyhymnia	Sacred song	none
Terpsichore	Dancing	Lyre
Thalia	Comedy; pastoral poetry	Comic mask, shepherd's staff
Urania	Astronomy	Globe

Narcissus Beautiful youth beloved by Echo; fell in love with own image in pool.
Odysseus (Ulysses) Greek hero of Trojan War; king of Ithaca, husband of Penelope, he roamed ten years after fall of Troy.
Oedipus King of Thebes, unwittingly murdered father (Laius) and married mother (Jocasta); tore out own eyes.
Olympus Mountain in north of Greece, abode of gods.
Orpheus Skilled musician; son of Calliope and Apollo, who gave him his famed lyre.
Pan (Faunus) God of woods and fields, flocks and shepherds; part man, part goat.
Pandora First woman on earth; opened box containing all human ills.
Persephone (Proserpine) Daughter of Zeus and Demeter; wife of Pluto and queen of infernal regions.
Perseus Son of Zeus and Danaë; killed Medusa; married Andromeda.
Phoebus see *Apollo*.
Pluto God of Hades, brother of Zeus.
Plutus Greek god of wealth.
Poseidon (Neptune) Chief god of sea, brother of Zeus.
Prometheus A Titan; stole fire from heaven; punished by being chained to mountain while vultures ate his liver.
Psyche Princess loved by Eros but punished by jealous Aphrodite; became immortal and united with Eros.
Rhea Greek nature-goddess, wife and sister of Cronos; mother of Zeus, Poseidon, Pluto, Demeter, Hera; later identified with Roman goddesses Ops and Cybele.
Romulus Founder of Rome; suckled with twin brother Remus by she-wolf; killed Remus.
Satyrs Hoofed demigods of forests, fields, and streams.
Selene (Luna) Goddess of the moon.
Thanatos (Mors) God of death.
Titans Offspring of Uranus and Ge; one, Cronos, dethroned Uranus, but his son Zeus in turn hurled Titans from heaven.
Uranus Oldest of Greek gods, personification of heaven, father of Titans.
Zeus (Jupiter) Chief of the Olympian gods, son of Cronos and Rhea; god of thunder and lightning.

Norse Mythology

Aesir Collectively, the chief Norse gods.
Asgard Home of the gods.
Balder God of summer sun; son of Odin and Frigga; killed by mistletoe twig.
Bragi God of poetry; son of Odin.
Frey God of fertility and crops.
Freya (Freyja) Beautiful goddess of love and night; sister of Frey; sometimes confused with *Frigga*.
Frigga Goddess of married love; wife of Odin.
Heimdal Guardian of Asgard; he and Loki slew one another.
Hel Goddess of the dead, queen of the underworld; daughter of Loki.
Hödur (Hoth) Blind god of night; unwitting killer of twin brother Balder.
Loki God of evil; contrives Balder's death.
Odin Supreme god, head of Aesir; god of wisdom and of the atmosphere.
Thor God of thunder; eldest son of Odin.
Valhalla Hall in Asgard where Odin welcomed souls of heroes killed in battle.
Valkyries Nine handmaidens of Odin who chose warriors to die in battle and conducted them to Valhalla.

Egyptian Mythology

Amon (Ammon, Amen) A god of Thebes, united with Ra as Amon-Ra, supreme king of the gods.
Anubis Jackel-headed son of Osiris; guided souls of the dead.
Apis Sacred bull of Memphis.
Hathor Cow-headed sky goddess of love.
Horus Hawk-headed god of light, son of Osiris and Isis.
Isis Goddess of motherhood and fertility; chief goddess of Ancient Egypt.
Osiris Supreme god, ruler of the afterlife; husband of Isis.
Ptah The creator, chief god of Memphis.
Ra Sun god; ancestor of the pharaohs.
Serapis God combining attributes of Osiris and Apis.
Set God of evil; jealous brother-son of Osiris, whom he slew and cut into pieces.
Thoth Ibis-headed god of wisdom.

The Scandinavian peoples thought of their gods as fearless warriors and seafarers like themselves. This Viking stone from Sweden depicts a world of heroes, battles and adventure.

Travel & Transport

Milestones in Transport

pre-8000 B.C. Dug-out canoe.
c. 6000 B.C. Man tames beasts of burden (ox, donkey, horse).
c. 3000 B.C. Wheel invented.
c. 3000 B.C. First ships.
c. 2900 B.C. Earliest evidence of man-made road (wooden trackway found in Somerset, England).
c. 2700 B.C. System of roads in China.
c. 2000 B.C. Horse-drawn chariots used in Mesopotamia.
A.D. 900s Horse collar and traces (of harness) invented in France.
c. 1100 Magnetic compass developed.
1400s Advent of versatile three-masted ship.
1620 First 'submarine' (leather-covered rowing boat).
1662 First omnibus (horse-drawn), invented by Blaise Pascal (France).
1769 Nicolas Cugnot (France) builds first mechanically propelled passenger vehicle, a steam tractor that reached $2\frac{1}{4}$ mph (3.6 kph)
1783 First balloon ascent.
1783 First successful experiment with steamboats.
1804 First steam railway locomotive, developed by Richard Trevithick (GB).
1807 First steamboat passenger ship.
1807 First passenger trams (Oystermouth Tramroad, Swansea, Wales).
1815 Macadam paving for roads, developed by John L. McAdam (US).
1822 First iron steamship.
1826 Samuel Brown (GB) builds first true internal-combustion vehicle (gas-fuelled).
1839 First pedal-driven bicycle, invented by Kirkpatrick Macmillan (GB).
1852 First airship (France).
1863 First underground train (London).

A reconstruction of Richard Trevithick's steam locomotive, developed in 1804.

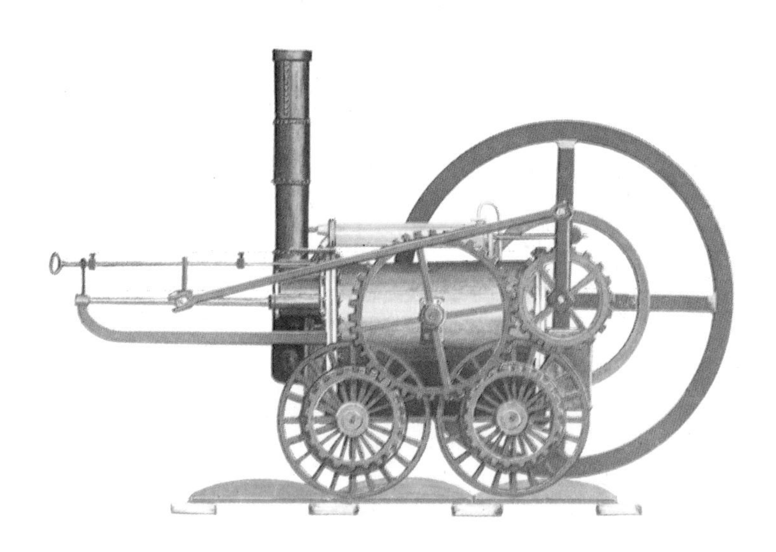

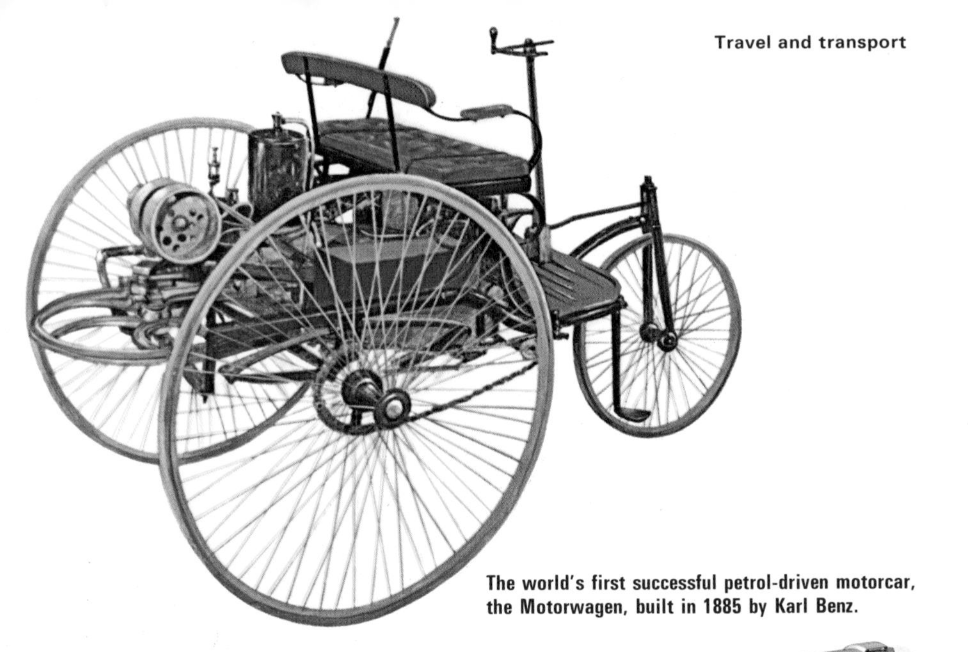

The world's first successful petrol-driven motorcar, the Motorwagen, built in 1885 by Karl Benz.

1869 Opening of Suez Canal.
1869 Rickshaws invented in Japan (by American Baptist minister).
1881 First electric train (Berlin).
1885 First petrol-driven motor-car, Motorwagen, built by Karl Benz (Germany).
1886 Gottlieb Daimler (Germany) builds first internal-combustion motorcycle, with top speed 12 mph (19 kph).
1890 First electric tube.
1894 First ships driven by steam turbine.
1897 First diesel engine built.
1903 Wright brothers (US) make first aeroplane flight.
1903 First bus service, inaugurated in England, between Eastbourne and Meads.
1908 First Model-T Ford.
1914 Completion of Panama Canal.
1925 First diesel locomotive in regular service (US).
1930 Frank Whittle (GB) patents jet engine.
1932 Beginning of age of diesel-electric trains.

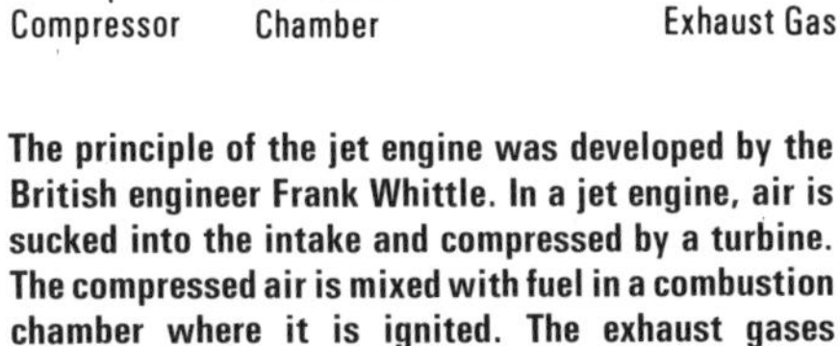

The principle of the jet engine was developed by the British engineer Frank Whittle. In a jet engine, air is sucked into the intake and compressed by a turbine. The compressed air is mixed with fuel in a combustion chamber where it is ignited. The exhaust gases produced by the combustion provide the energy, or 'thrust', of the jet engine.

1936 Prototype helicopter successfully tested.
1939 First jet aeroplane, built by Heinkel Co. of Germany.
1952 First commercial jet airliner.
1955 First nuclear-powered vessel, submarine *Nautilus* (US).
1957 First artificial satellite in space.
1959 First hovercraft.
1961 First man in space.
1962 First nuclear-powered merchant ship.
1968 First supersonic airliner.

The sea

Nautical terms

abaft Behind.
abeam About perpendicular to centre line of hull.
about To *come about* is to reverse course.
aft Towards *stern* of ship.
aloft Up masts or in *rigging*.
amidships In middle of vessel, lengthwise.
ballast Heavy material (usually water) to ensure stability when there is no cargo; *in ballast*, sailing without cargo.
beam Greatest width of ship's hull.
bell See *ship's bell*.
bilge Lowest part of hull, where sides curve in to bottom.
binnacle Housing of compass, etc.
bitts Upright fittings on deck for securing ropes.
bollard Steel or wooden post on deck or quayside for securing ropes.
bosun (bos'n) For 'boatswain', ship's 'foreman', highest rank under deck officers.
bow Front of ship.
bridge Raised platform from which ship is navigated.
bulkhead Ship's equivalent of wall in house.
bulwark Low walls or rails round ship's deck.
bunker Compartment for storing fuel.
capstan Revolving steel drum on deck for manipulating ropes or anchor chain.
catwalk Light connecting bridge.
caulk Make joints watertight.
companionway Ladder or staircase connecting decks.
crow's-nest Look-out platform on mast.
davits Curved arms or cranes for handling lifeboats.
deadweight Weight ship will carry.
displacement Weight of water displaced by ship when afloat (i.e. actual total weight), usually expressed in tons.
draught Depth of *keel* below water-line
flotsam and jetsam Goods found floating on sea or washed up ashore, from shipwreck (usually, *flotsam*) or jettisoned (*jetsam*).
forecastle (fo'c'sle) Forward part of ship usually containing crew's quarters.
fore Towards front of ship.
forward (for'd) In front of.
gangway Long stairway for boarding or disembarking.
gunwale (gunnel) Upper edge of ship's side.
hatch(way) Opening on deck with movable cover.
hawse-pipe Tube in ship's bow through which anchor cable passes.
hold Space below decks for cargo storage.
hull Body of ship without the *superstructure*.
inboard Towards centre of ship.
island Raised part of hull.
jetsam See *flotsam and jetsam*.
keel Steel 'backbone' of ship, running along bottom of hull.
knot Unit for measuring speed of ship, equal to nautical mile per hour.
lee(ward) Direction across ship towards which wind is blowing; *lee side* is sheltered side.
list Leaning over of ship to one side.
mate Ship's officer under captain.
mooring Securing a ship (e.g. to bollard).
pitching Fore-and-aft rocking of vessel at sea.
Plimsoll line 'Load line' marked on sides of hull to indicate maximum depth to which ship may be immersed.
poop Raised part of hull at stern.
port Left side of ship facing bow (front).
prow Old name for *bow*.
purser Officer responsible for paying crew and keeping other records.
quarter Ship's side at *aft* end.
quarterdeck Rear part of upper deck.
quartermaster Seaman in charge of steering.
rigging Fixed ropes or wires securing masts.
rolling Side-to-side motion of vessel at sea.
ship's bell Used for signalling time on ship; rings every half-hour. See *watches*.
starboard Right-hand side of ship facing bow (front).
stays Ropes supporting masts.
stem Extreme forward part of *bow*.
stern Rear of ship.
superstructure Part of ship built above hull (bridge, decks, etc., but not *island*, which is part of hull).
tonnage Measure of ship's volume, not its weight: 100 cubic feet equivalent to 1 ton
topside On or above main deck.
wake Foamy water left behind moving vessel.
watches Four-hour periods into which

Notable Sea Disasters

Affray (1951). British submarine, sank in English Channel; 75 died.
Andrea Doria (1956). Italian liner, collided with Swedish liner *Stockholm* off Nantucket (N.Y.) in fog; 51 died, about 1,655 rescued.
Birkenhead (1852). British troopship, ran aground off Port Elizabeth (S. Africa) and broke in two on rocks; 455 perished, 193 survived.
Curacao (1942). British cruiser, sank after collision with liner *Queen Mary*; 335 died.
Empress of Ireland (1914). Canadian steamer, sank after collision in St Lawrence River, 1,024 died.
General Slocum (1904). an excursion steamer, burned in New York harbour; 1,021 died.
Lusitania (1915). British liner, torpedoed by German submarine off Ireland; 1,198 died.
Mary Celeste (1872). American half-brig, found abandoned in Atlantic with no sign of life; great mystery of the sea.
Scorpion (1968). American nuclear submarine, sank in N. Atlantic; 99 died.
Sultana (1865). Mississippi river steamer, blew up (boiler explosion); 1,450 died.
Thetis (1939). British submarine, sank in Liverpool Bay; 99 perished.
Thresher (1963). American nuclear submarine, sank in N. Atlantic; 129 died.
Titanic (1912). British liner, struck iceberg in N. Atlantic; about 1,500 died, 705 survived.
Toya Maru (1954). Japanese ferry, sank in Tsugaru Strait; 1,172 died.
Truculent (1950). British submarine, sank in Thames Estuary after collision with tanker; 64 died.
Wilhelm Gustloff (1945). German liner, torpedoed by Russian submarine off Danzig; about 7,700 died.

ship's day is divided: *ship's bell* rung every half-hour of watch, once after half-hour, twice after hour, etc., until 'eight bells' signifies end of watch.
water-line Line on hull indicating specific condition of loading, e.g. *Plimsoll line*.
winch Machinery for hoisting or hauling.
windlass Another name for *capstan*.
windward Direction from which wind is blowing; *windward side* is unprotected side.

Chronology of the Sea

pre-8000 B.C. Old Stone Age men using form of dug-out canoe.
c. 7250 B.C. Earliest form of seafaring: trade in Mediterranean between Melos and Greek mainland.
c. 3000 B.C. First known ships: Egyptian galleys.
c. 1000 B.C. Phoenicians develop bireme, galley with two rows of oars on each side.
c. 200 B.C. Romans build huge galleys, with as many as 200 oars.
c. A.D. 1100 Sailors in the Mediterranean and in the China Seas navigating by means of magnetic compass.
1400s Portuguese develop three-masted ship; facilitates sailing against wind.
1500s Age of the galleon.
1620 Dutch scientist Cornelius van Drebbel demonstrates 'submarine', a leather-covered rowing boat, in England.
1783 Steam propulsion first achieved, by Marquis Jouffroy d'Abbans (France), with 180-ton paddle-steamer *Pyroscaphe* on the Saône, near Lyon.
1790s Sailing ships built with iron hulls.
1801 Robert Fulton (US) builds 21-ft (6.4-m) copper-covered submarine *Nautilus*.
1801 First successful power-driven vessel, the *Charlotte Dundas*, a Clyde canal tug built by William Symington (GB).

In America regular passenger steamer services began in 1807 on rivers and lakes.

Large hovercraft like this skim across the sea on a cushion of air.

Chronology of the sea (contd.)

1807 Robert Fulton (US) builds the *Clermont*, first regular passenger steamer; plies River Hudson, New York to Albany.

1822 First iron-built steamship, the *Aaron Manby*; also first prefabricated ship. Made on Thames for service in France.

1839 British steamer *Archimedes* first to use screw propeller successfully.

1845 *Rainbow* (US), first true clipper ship.

1897 Charles Parsons (GB) dramatically demonstrates first turbine-driven ship, *Turbinia*, at Spithead in front of Queen Victoria.

1912 First ocean-going diesel-driven ships.

1955 First nuclear-powered submarine, *Nautilus* (US).

1959 First hovercraft, SR-N1, invented by Christopher Cockerell (GB).

1959 First nuclear-powered surface ship, Russian ice-breaker *Lenin*.

1962 *Savannah* (US) goes into service as first nuclear-powered merchant ship.

1962 First public hovercraft service, inaugurated in Britain.

1979 First helicopter-carrying patrol vessel in operation with Danish Fisheries Protection.

British Rail's High Speed Trains can travel at 125 miles (200 kilometres) an hour.

Rail

Railway Timetable

1597 First reference to wagonway in England, linking coal-mines with River Trent; wagons drawn by pack animals.
1727 Tanfield Arch, in England, first railway viaduct.
1768 Cast-iron rails begin to replace wooden rails.
1769 First self-moving engine demonstrated, steam-carriage invented by Nicolas Cugnot (France).
1782 James Watt (GB) invents engine able to turn wheels.
1795 Invention of long brake, allowing safer descent of steep stretches by trains of wagons.
1801 Richard Trevithick (GB) makes full-size steam-carriage.
1803 First public freight railway: Surrey Iron Railway, engineered by William Jessop and James Outram (GB).
1804 Trevithick constructs locomotive to haul 10-ton load from Pen-y-darran to Glamorganshire Canal; successful, but Trevithick's locomotives prove too heavy for rails.
1810 Introduction of wrought-iron rails.
1811 John Blenkinsop (GB) designs 'rack' locomotive.
1813 William Hedley (GB) builds two smooth-wheeled engines, *Puffing Billy* and *Wylam Dilly*.
1814 George Stephenson (GB) builds *Blutcher*, first of his many engines.
1822 Opening of Hetton Colliery Company 8-mile wagonway to River Wear, constructed by Stephenson.
1825 Opening of Stockton & Darlington Railway (27 Sept.) first regularly operated steam railway in world, built by Stephenson and son Robert. Their engine *Locomotion No. I* pulled first train. Line used almost exclusively for freight.
1829 Stephensons' *Rocket* impressively wins Rainhill Trials, near Liverpool, finally establishing superiority of steam over horse.
1830 Opening of Liverpool & Manchester Railway (15 Sept.), first regular public passenger service.
South Carolina Railroad opened, first in United States.
1837 First sleeping car came into operation, in Pennsylvania (USA).
1840 Introduction of disc and crossbar signal, in England.
1844 Block signalling first adopted, by Norwich & Yarmouth line.
1846 Gauge in Britain standardized at 4 ft 8½ in (1.435 m).

Top: **John Blenkinsop's rack locomotive (1811) was the first to be commercially successful.**
Above: **The American 0–8–0 Winans locomotive of 1846. America developed locomotives with large numbers of driving wheels.**

Celebrating the completion of the first transcontinental railway across America, 10 May 1869.

Railway timetable (contd.)

1854 First military railway built, 20 miles (32 km) of double track from Balaclava to British and French front line in Crimean War – led to fall of Sebastopol.

1857 First steel rails, laid at Derby.

1859 First Pullman sleeping car, in Illinois (USA).

1863 First dining cars, between Baltimore and Philadelphia (USA).

1863 Opening of world's first underground railway, the Metropolitan, linking Paddington, Euston, St Pancras, and King's Cross, in London; mainly a cut-and-cover' line.

1867 First elevated railway, experimental overhead track in Manhattan, New York.

1869 Completion of Pacific Railroad, coast-to-coast across United States.

1879 First electric railway opened, 300-yd (274-m) electric tramway, built by Werner von Siemen (Germany) for Berlin Trade Exhibition.

1883 Orient Express (Paris–Vienna–Istanbul) comes into operation.

1885 Canadian Pacific line completed.

1890 First tube railway, City & South London, opened.

1893 World's first 100 mph run, by *Locomotive 999*, Grimesville, NY.

1893 First electric traction overhead railway, along Mersey shore, Liverpool.

1895 First main-line electrification, in tunnel under Baltimore, USA.

1897 Rudolf Diesel (Germany) builds first diesel engine.

1910 Sweden establishes main-line electrification.

1925 First diesel-electric locomotive tried out, in Canada.

1932 German State Railways introduce *Flying Hamburger*, heralding age of diesel-electric traction.

1948 First gas-turbine electric locomotive tested.

1955 World's first 200 mph run, achieved by French locomotive: 205 mph (330 kph).

1966 Japanese National Railways open New Tokaido Line: expresses cover 320 miles (515 km) Tokyo–Osaka run in 3 hr 10 min, average of 101 mph (163 kph), with two intermediate stops.

1972 Tokaido service extended from Osaka to Okayama (Sanyo Line): regular non-stop service covering 99.9 miles (160.8 km) in 58 min, i.e. 103.3 mph (166.3 kph).

1974 World rail speed record of 254.70 mph (410 kph) set up on 14 August over 6.2 miles (9.97 km) of test track in Colorado by US Federal Railroad Administration's Linear Induction Motor Research Vehicle.

1976 British Rail inaugurate their daily High Speed Train services between London–Bristol & South Wales on 4 October. On 10 April, one HST covers 94 miles (151.2 km) between Paddington/London and Chippenham, Wilts in 50 minutes 31 seconds for a start-to-stop average of 111.64 mph (179.67 kph). The peak speed is 125 mph (201 kph).

'Pendulum' suspension allows trains like this French express to travel at high speeds on existing track.

Notable Train Disasters

1876 Dec. 29: Passenger train derailed as iron bridge collapsed in snowstorm, Ashtabula River, Ohio, USA; 91 died.

1879 Dec. 28: Tay Bridge, Dundee, Scotland, blown down, taking passenger train with it; 73 drowned.

1881 June 2: Train fell into river near Cuartla, Mexico; about 200 died.

1915 May 22: Two passenger trains and troop train collided at Quintins Hill, Dumfriesshire, Scotland; 227 died.

1917 Dec. 12: Troop train derailed near mouth of Mt Cenis tunnel, Modane, France; 543 died.

1944 Jan. 16: Train wrecked inside tunnel, Leon Province, Spain; 500–800 died.

1944 Mar. 2: Train stalled in tunnel near Salerno, Italy; 521 suffocated.

1953 Dec. 24: Wellington-Auckland express plunged into stream near Waiouru, New Zealand; 155 died.

1955 Apr. 3: Train plunged into canyon near Guadalajara, Mexico; about 300 died.

1957 Sep. 1: Train plunged into ravine near Kendal, Jamaica; about 175 died.

1957 Sep. 29: Express train crashed into stationary oil train near Montgomery, W. Pakistan; nearly 300 died.

1962 May 3: Three trains collided in Tokyo; 163 died.

1963 Nov. 9: Two passenger trains hurtled into derailed freight train near Yokohama, Japan; over 160 died.

1970 Feb. 4: Express train crashed into stationary commuter train near Buenos Aires, Argentina; 236 died.

1970 Feb. 16: Train crashed in northern Nigeria; about 150 killed in crash and another 52 injured survivors killed in road crash on way to hospital.

1972 Oct. 6: Train carrying religious pilgrims derailed and caught fire near Saltillo, Mexico; 204 died, over 1,000 injured.

Aviation

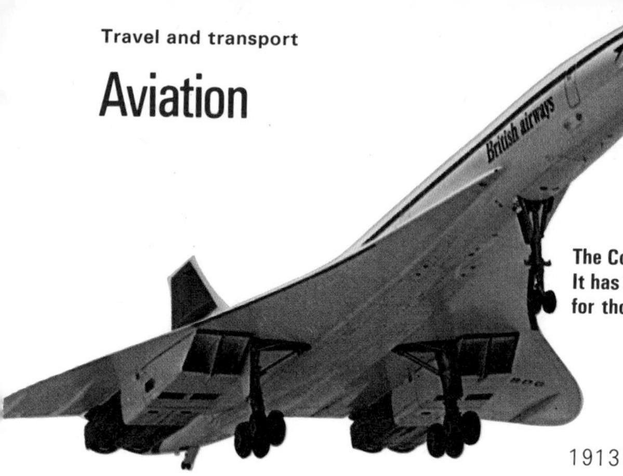

The Concorde is the world's first supersonic airliner. It has greatly reduced flying time on long journeys—for those who can afford the high fares.

Milestones in Aviation

1783 First men to achieve air travel: François Pilâtre de Rozier and Marquis d'Arlandes (France) in 49-ft (15-m) diameter Montgolfier hot-air balloon (21 Nov.), 5½-mile (8.9-km) flight.

1785 First crossing English Channel: Jean-Pierre Blanchard (France) and John Jeffries (US).

1852 First flight in airship: Henri Giffard (France) in 144-ft (43.9-m) long coal-gas airship from Paris.

1853 First heavier-than-air flight (sustained), in glider built by Sir George Cayley (GB).

1903 First controlled and sustained flight (120 ft, 36.6 m) by powered (petrol-engined) aeroplane: brothers Wilbur and Orville Wright (US) in biplane *Flyer 1* at Kill Devil Hills, Kitty Hawk, North Carolina (17 Dec.).

1905 Orville Wright completes flight of 33 min 17 sec in *Flyer III*.

1907 Louis Blériot (France) flies first monoplane, *Type VII*.

1909 Blériot makes first aeroplane flight across English Channel.

1910 First seaplane flight: Henri Fabre (France).

1911 First use of aeroplanes in warfare: Italians in Libya.

1912 Jules Védrines (France) makes first 100 mph flight.

1912 Capt. Albert Berry (US) makes first parachute descent from aeroplane, over St Louis.

1913 First Schneider Trophy (seaplane race).

1913 Igor Sikorsky (Russia) flies his 92½-ft (28.2-m) *Bolshoi*, first four-engined plane.

1914 First scheduled passenger service, between St Petersburg and Tampa, Florida (US).

1915 First specially built aircraft carrier, HMS *Ark Royal*.

1915 First all-metal aeroplane, Junkers J1 (German).

Man's first flight: the Montgolfier balloon.

The first motor-powered, heavier-than-air flight was made in 1903 by the American brothers Orville and Wilbur Wright. It took place at Kitty Hawk, North Carolina, and covered a distance of 120 feet (37 metres).

NOTABLE AIR DISASTERS

date	aircraft and nature of accident	deaths
24.8.21	ZR-2 dirigible (GB) broke in two, near Hull	62
3.9.25	*Shenandoah* dirigible (US) broke up, Caldwell, Ohio	14
4.4.33	*Akron* dirigible (US) crashed, New Jersey coast	73
6.5.37	*Hindenburg* zeppelin (Ger.) burned at mooring, Lakehurst, NJ	36
23.8.44	US Air Force B-24 hit school, Freckelton, England	76*
28.7.45	US Army B-25 hit Empire State Building, NY, in fog	19*
4.5.49	Italian airliner crashed at Superga, Turin	31†
1.11.49	DC-4 airliner (US) rammed by Bolivian P-38 fighter, Wash., DC	55
24.6.50	DC-4 airliner (US) exploded in storm over Lake Michigan	58
20.12.52	US Air Force C-124 fell and burned, Washington	87
18.6.53	US Air Force C-124 crashed and burned near Tokyo	129
30.6.56	Super-Constellation and DC-7 airliners collided over Grand Canyon	128
6.2.58	Elizabethan airliner (GB) crashed on take-off at Munich, W. Germany	23‡
27.7.60	Sikorsky S-58 helicopter crashed in Chicago suburbs	13
16.12.60	DC-8 and Super-Constellation airliners collided over New York	134*
15.2.61	Boeing 707 (Belgian) crashed near Brussels	73§
3.6.62	Boeing 707 (French) crashed on take-off, Paris	130
22.6.62	Boeing 707 (French) crashed in storm, Guadeloupe	113
20.5.65	Boeing 720B (Pak.) crashed at Cairo airport	121
24.1.66	Boeing 707 (Indian) crashed on Mont Blanc (France)	117
4.2.66	Boeing 727 (Jap.) plunged into Tokyo Bay	133
5.3.66	Boeing 707 (GB) crashed on Mt Fuji (Japan)	124
20.4.67	Britannia turboprop (Swiss) crashed at Nicosia (Cyprus)	126
16.3.69	DC-9 (Venez.) crashed on take-off, Maracaibo	155*
30.7.71	Boeing 727 (Jap.) collided with F-86 fighter, Japan	162
14.8.72	Ilyushin-62 (E. Ger.) crashed on take-off, Berlin	156
13.10.72	Ilyushin-62 (USSR) crashed near Moscow	176
4.12.72	Spanish charter jet airliner crashed on take-off, Canary Is.	155
22.1.73	Boeing 707 (chartered) crashed on landing at Kano, Nigeria	176
3.6.73	TU-144 (USSR) exploded in air, Goussainville, France	14*¶
3.3.74	DC-10 (Turk.) crashed in forest, Ermenonville, France	346
10.9.76	British Trident 3 and Yugoslavian DC-9 collided in mid-air near Zagreb (Yugoslavia)	176
27.3.77	Two Boeing 747s (American and Dutch) collided on ground at Tenerife's Los Rodeos airport (Canary Islands)	582
1.1.78	Boeing 747 (Indian) crashed into the sea off Bombay (India)	213
15.11.78	DC-8 (Iceland) crashed while attempting to land, Sri Lanka	262
14.3.79	Trident (China) crashed near Peking	200
24.5.79	DC-10 (US) crashed near Chicago	273

*Total includes deaths on ground or in buildings.
†Including the entire team of Italian football champions Torino.
‡Mostly players (8) and officials (3) of England football champions Manchester United, and 8 journalists.
§Including skaters (17) and officials of US world championships team.
¶First supersonic airliner crash.

Milestones in aviation (contd.)

1919 First non-stop Atlantic crossing: Capt. John Alcock and Lt. Arthur Whitten Brown (GB) in Vickers Vimy, from Newfoundland to Ireland.

1919 Australian brothers Capt. Ross Smith and Lt. Keith Smith make first Britain–Australia flight (Hounslow–Darwin).

1922 First King's Cup Air Race (Croydon–Glasgow–Croydon), won by Capt. Frank Barnard (GB).

1923 First flight of rotary-wing craft: Juan de la Cierva's Autogyro, in Madrid (Spain).

1927 Capt. Charles Lindbergh (US) makes first solo non-stop Atlantic crossing, in *Spirit of St Louis*.

1929 First round-the-world airship flight, by 775-ft (236-m) long *Graf Zeppelin* (German).

1933 Wiley Post (US) makes first round-the-world solo flight.

1936 First successful helicopter: prototype Focke-Wulf Fw 61V1

1939 First jet-propelled aircraft: Heinkel He 178V1 (German).

1939 Sikorsky makes first successful flight in single-rotor helicopter.

1944 First flying-bombs launched (German).

1945 First pure-jet aeroplane, Gloster Meteor (GB).

1947 Supersonic flight: first pilot to exceed speed of sound in level flight is Maj. Charles Yeager (US), in the Bell XS-1, released in mid-air by a Boeing B-29; achieved 670 mph (1,078 kph), or Mach 1.015.

1949 First non-stop round-the-world flight: Boeing B-50 Superfortress *Lucky Lady II*, flown from Texas by Capt. James Gallagher (US) with crew of 18; refuelled in air four times.

1949 First pure-jet airliner: prototype De Havilland Comet (GB), flown by Gp. Capt. John Cunningham.

1952 First pure-jet scheduled airline service established by BOAC with Comets.

1956 First 1,000 mph flight: Peter Twiss (GB) achieves 1,132 mph (1,822 kph) in Fairey Delta 2.

1968 First supersonic airliner, Tu 144 (USSR), makes maiden flight.

1969 First 'Jumbo Jet', Boeing 747 (US), 195 ft (59.4 m) long, makes maiden flight; equipped to carry over 400 passengers and crew.

1969 First prototype of Anglo-French airliner Concorde ('001') makes maiden flight.

1969 First jet aircraft with vertical take-off and landing capability, the Harrier (GB), becomes operational.

AIR RECORDS

Aircraft

Speed–2,193.167 mph (3,529.56 kph), Capt. Eldon W. Joersz & Maj. George T. Morgan Jr. (USAF) Lockheed SR-71A, Calif., USA, 28.7.76

*Altitude** – 23.39 miles (37.67 km) Alexandr Fedotov (USSR), Mikoyan E-266M (MiG-25), 31.8.77

Gliders†

Speed – 102.74 mph (165.35 kph) over triangular 100-km course, K. Briegleb (US), Arkansas, 18.7.74

Altitude – 46,267 ft (14,102 m), Paul Bikle Jr (US), Schweizer SGS 123E, Calif., 25.2.61

Distance – 907.7 miles (1,460.8 km), Hans-Werner Grosse (W. Ger.), ASW-12, Lübeck-Biarritz, 25.4.72

Balloons

Distance–3,107.61 miles (5,001.22 km), B. L. Abruzzo, M. L. Anderson, L. M. Newman (USA) Presque Isle (USA) to Miserey (France) 12–17.8.78

Duration–137 hr 5 min. 50 sec., B. L. Abruzzo, M. L. Anderson, L. M. Newman (USA) as above

*For aircraft taking off from ground under own power.
†Durations records are now discouraged.

CIVIL AIRCRAFT MARKINGS: INTERNATIONAL PREFIXES

Prefix	Country
A2–	Botswana
A40–	Oman
A7–	Qatar
AN–	Nicaragua
AP–	Pakistan
B–	Taiwan (Formosa)
C–	Canada
C2–	Nauru
CC–	Chile
CCCP–	USSR
CF–	Canada
CN–	Morocco
CP–	Bolivia
CR–	Portuguese overseas provinces
CS–	Portugal
CU–	Cuba
CX–	Uruguay
D–	West Germany
DM–	East Germany
DQ–	Fiji
EC–	Spain
EI, EJ–	Republic of Ireland
EL–	Liberia
EP–	Iran
ET–	Ethiopa
F–	France, colonies and protectorates
G–	Great Britain, Gibraltar
HA–	Hungary
HB–	Switzerland, Liechtenstein
HC–	Ecuador
HH–	Haiti
HI–	Dominican Republic
HK–	Colombia
HL–	South Korea
HP–	Panama
HR–	Honduras
HS–	Thailand
HZ–	Saudi Arabia
I–	Italy
JA–	Japan
JY–	Jordan
LN–	Norway
LQ– LV–	Argentina
LX–	Luxembourg
LZ–	Bulgaria
N–	United States
OB–	Peru
OD–	Lebanon
OE–	Austria
OH–	Finland
OK–	Czechoslovakia
OO–	Belgium
OY–	Denmark
PH–	Netherlands
PI–	Philippines
PJ–	Netherlands Antilles
PK–	Indonesia
PP– PT–	Brazil
PZ–	Surinam
S2–	Bangladesh
SE–	Sweden
SP–	Poland
ST–	Sudan
SU–	Egypt
SX–	Greece
TC–	Turkey
TF–	Iceland
TG–	Guatemala
TI–	Costa Rica
TJ–	Cameroon
TL–	Central African Empire
TN–	Congo
TR–	Gabon
TS–	Tunisia
TT–	Chad
TU–	Ivory Coast
TY–	Benin
TZ–	Mali
VH–	Australia
VP–B	Bahamas
VP–F	Falkland Islands
VP–H	Belize
VP–L	Antigua
VP–P	Western Pacific High Commission
VP–V	St Vincent
VP–X	Gambia
VP–Y, VP–W	Malawi, and Zimbabwe-Rhodesia
VQ–G	Grenada
VQ–H	St Helena
VQ–L	St Lucia
VQ–S	Seychelles
VR–B	Bermuda
VR–H	Hong Kong
VR–O	Sabah (Malaysia)
VR–U	Brunei
VR–W	Sarawak (Malaysia)
VT–	India
XA–, XB–, XC–	Mexico
XT–	Upper Volta
XU–	Kampuchea
XV–	Vietnam
XW–	Laos
XY–, XZ–	Burma
YA–	Afghanistan
YI–	Iraq
YJ–	New Hebrides
YK–	Syria
YR–	Romania
YS–	El Salvador
YU–	Yugoslavia
YV–	Venezuela
ZA–	Albania
ZK–, ZL–, ZM–	New Zealand
ZP–	Paraguay
ZS–, ZT–, ZU–	South Africa
3A–	Monaco
3B–	Mauritius
3C–	Equatorial Guinea
3D–	Swaziland
3X–	Guinea
4R–	Sri Lanka
4W–	Yemen
4X–	Israel
5A–	Libya
5B–	Cyprus
5H–	Tanzania
5N–	Nigeria
5R–	Malagasy Republic
5T–	Mauritania
5U–	Niger
5V–	Togo
5W–	Western Samoa
5X–	Uganda
5Y–	Kenya
6O–	Somalia
6V–, 6W–	Senegal
6Y–	Jamaica
7O–	Yemen PDR
7P–	Lesotho
7QY–	Malawi
7T–	Algeria
8P–	Barbados
8R–	Guyana
9G–	Ghana
9H–	Malta
9J–	Zambia
9K–	Kuwait
9L–	Sierra Leone
9M–	Malaysia
9N–	Nepal
9Q–	Zaïre
9U–	Burundi
9V–	Singapore
9XR–	Rwanda
9Y–	Trinidad and Tobago

Motoring

Below: **The layout of a typical rear-wheel-drive production saloon car.**

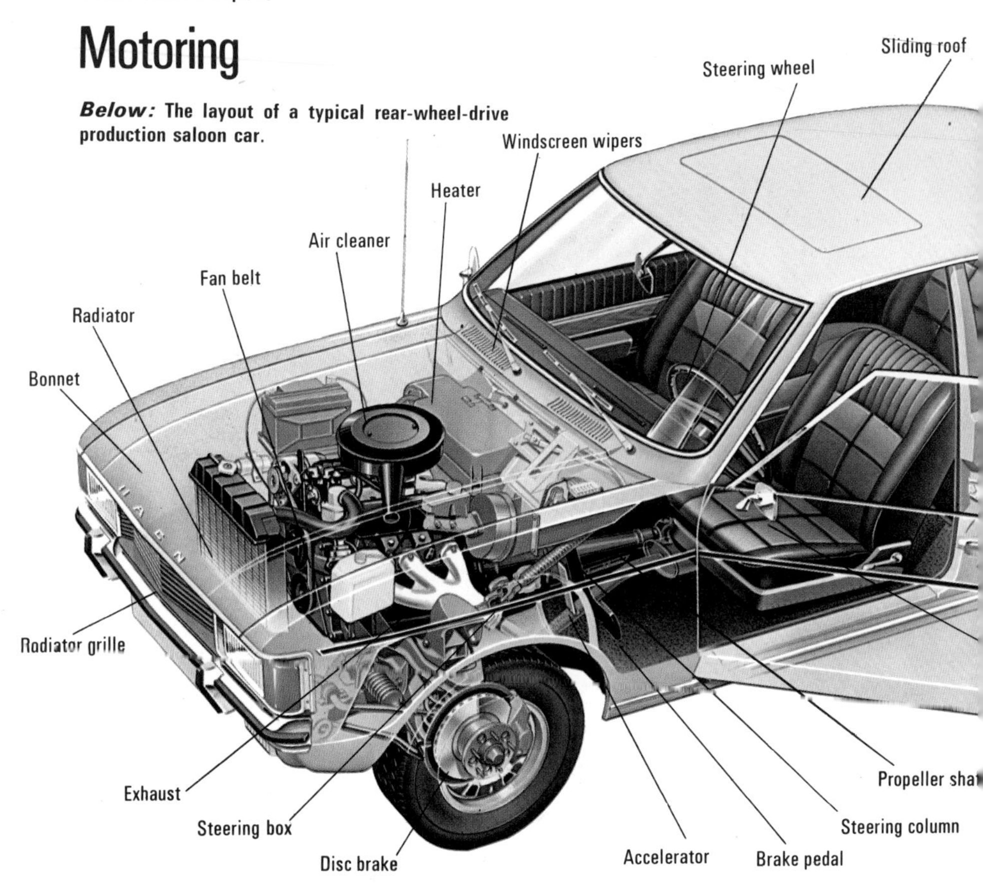

Motor-car terms

adhesion Grip between tyres and road surface.
air cleaners See *filters*.
alternator See *generator*.
automatic transmission See *transmission*.
axle Shaft carrying wheel.
battery Apparatus that provides electricity for lights, ignition, starting motor, windscreen wipers, etc. It stores electricity provided by *generator*.
big end Lower, larger end of connecting rod, attached to crankshaft.
cam Metal projection on shaft that moves another component as shaft rotates.
carburettor Apparatus that sprays mixture of petrol and air into cylinders.
c.c. Cubic centimetres, measure of capacity of cylinders.
chassis Framework 'base' of car.
choke Device for increasing petrol/air ratio of mixture; used for cold starting.
clutch Device for disconnecting engine drive from gearbox.
cooling system Method for cooling engine, with *water* (cooled in radiator and pumped through jacket round cylinder head) or *air* (fan-blown directly over cylinders).
coupé Two-door, two-seater car, sometimes with cramped rear seating.
cross-ply Tyre in which layers of fabric in carcass cross diagonally.

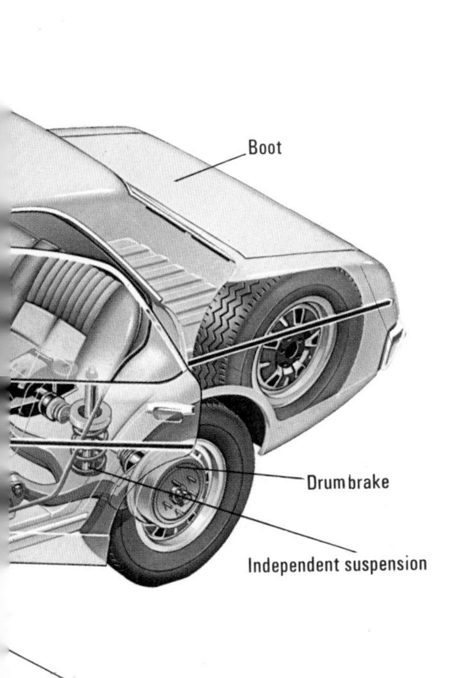

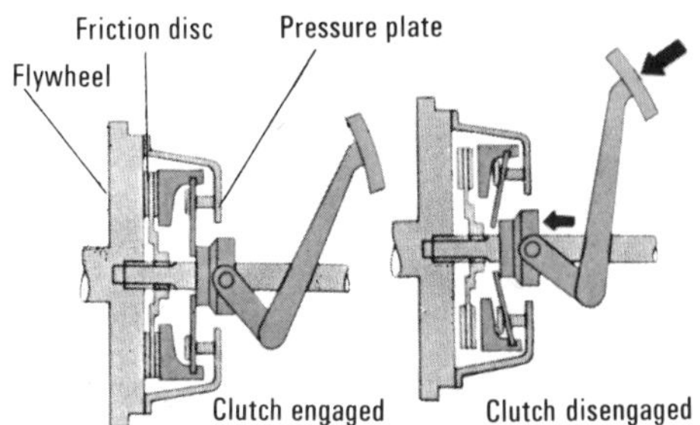

A friction clutch works by the action of a friction disc on the flywheel. A-pressure plate releases the disc when the driver depresses the clutch pedal.

crown wheel and pinion Joint that turns motion of propeller shaft through 90° to half-shafts.
cylinder Tube in which *piston* moves; *cylinder head,* bolted on top of cylinder, contains combustion chamber, where oxygen and fuel combine.
damper See *shock absorbers.*
decarbonizing ('decoke') Removal of carbon deposits from pistons and combustion chambers; necessary periodically to maintain performance.

Motor racing began as a way of improving and testing production cars. Modern racing cars, however, bear little resemblance to ordinary road cars.

Motor-car terms (contd.)

diesel engine Engine that uses heavy fuel oil under compression instead of petrol; economical without giving high performance.
differential Type of gearing in driving axles allowing wheels to move at different speeds (when turning corners).
dipstick Rod that indicates oil level.
disc brakes Brakes operated by friction pads that close hydraulically against metal disc revolving with wheel.

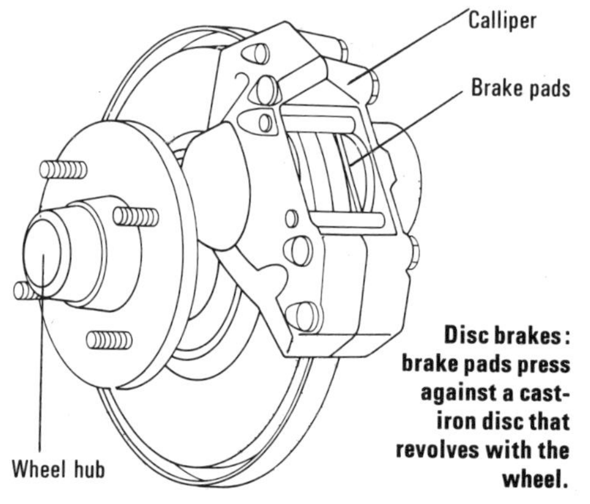

Disc brakes: brake pads press against a cast-iron disc that revolves with the wheel.

distributor Electrical equipment that sends high-voltage current to sparking plugs in rotation.
drum brakes Brakes operated by hydraulically operated brake shoes that press from inside against drum that rotates with wheel.
dynamo See *generator*.
estate car Car with large compartment at back (instead of boot) that can be loaded through rear door (*tailgate*).
exhaust system Pipes that carry burnt-out gases away from engine. See *silencer*.
fan belt Belt that connects crankshaft with cooling fan; usually drives generator too.
filters Devices for removing impurities from oil, petrol, or carburettor (*air cleaners*).
flywheel Heavy metal wheel that 'stores' power from engine and delivers steady rotation to crankshaft.
four-wheel drive System that allows all four wheels to receive drive from engine.
front-wheel drive System in which engine drives front wheels.
fuel pump Device for transferring petrol from tank to carburettor.
gaskets Washers forming gas- or liquid-tight seal; made of various materials, steel, cork, etc.
gear-box Box containing apparatus for changing gears.
generator Device for converting mechanical into electrical energy; *dynamo* produces direct current; *alternator*, alternating current.
half-shaft Either side of rear axle connecting differential to wheel.
hydraulic system System allowing control (e.g. braking) by means of pressure through a fluid.
idling Engine running by itself, without pressure on accelerator.
ignition Initial firing of fuel mixture in cylinder.
independent suspension Each wheel has own suspension.
kick-down In automatic, switch under accelerator that changes down gears when accelerator is pushed hard down.
knocking Premature ignition in combustion chamber, causing knocking noise; caused by sparking-plug fault or low-grade petrol.
limousine Large saloon built for comfort, often driven by chauffeur.
lock Full extent of turning arc of front wheels.
manifold Detachable pipe with outlets to others; *inlet manifold* channels fuel mixture from carburettor to cylinders; *exhaust manifold* channels gases and fumes out to exhaust system.
misfiring Irregularity in running caused by incorrect tuning – engine splutters.

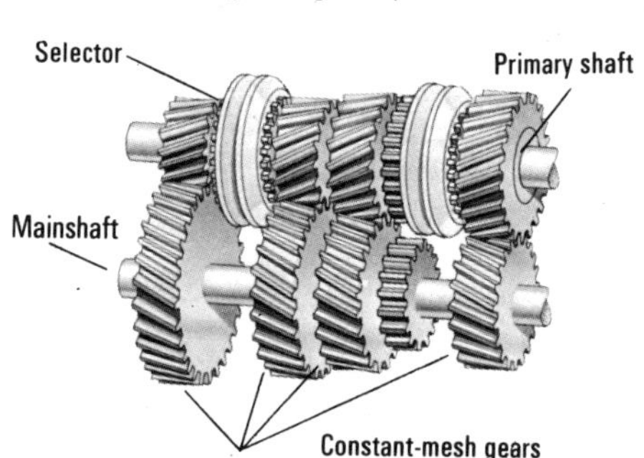

Gear-box: Power from engine enters at primary shaft and leaves at main shaft to drive wheels.

overdrive Extra top gear, cutting down petrol consumption.
overhead valve (o.h.v.) Usual positioning of valves in cylinder head.
oversteer Tendency of car to corner too sharply.
petrol injection (PI) System of supplying fuel to cylinders by injection rather than through a carburettor.
piston Component that provides pump action in cylinder, driven by ignition of fuel/air mixture.
power (assisted) steering System utilizing hydraulics to take effort out of steering.
propeller shaft Component connecting gear-box to final drive.
radial-ply Tyre in which layers of fabric in carcass are wrapped in direction radial to centre of wheel, i.e. at right-angles to direction of travel.
radiator Series of thin-walled tubes that carry water that circulates to cool engine; air rushing through radiator cools the water.
rebore Reconditioning of cylinder(s) by machining out and re-lining.
rev(olution) counter Device that measures and indicates number of engine revs per minute.
rotor arm Rotating unit in distributor that touches contacts connected to sparking plugs, distributing high-tension current to them in turn.
saloon Commonest type of family car, carrying at least 4, with permanent roof and 2 or 4 doors.
sedan Saloon.
servo system Control system that reduces effort required by driver (e.g. servo brakes).
shock absorbers Devices for damping down vibration of suspension springs.
silencer Canister-type unit in exhaust system that reduces noise of escaping gases.
sparking plug Electrical device at top of each cylinder; spark jumps across *points* of plug and ignites fuel/air mixture.
sports car Low, streamlined, light, high-powered model built for fast, zippy driving; usually two-seater.
station wagon Same as *estate car*.
stroke Distance travelled by piston between lowest and highest point.
sump Oil reservoir (at bottom of crankcase).
suspension System of springs that minimizes shocks transmitted by road irregularities to body of car.
throttle Valve in carburettor that varies supply of mixture fed to engine.
universal joint Joint coupling two shafts that turn at angle to each other.
valve Device that regulates flow of gas or liquid; cylinders have inlet and outlet *poppet-valves*; tyre valves allow air pressure to be altered.
wheelbase Distance between front and rear axles.

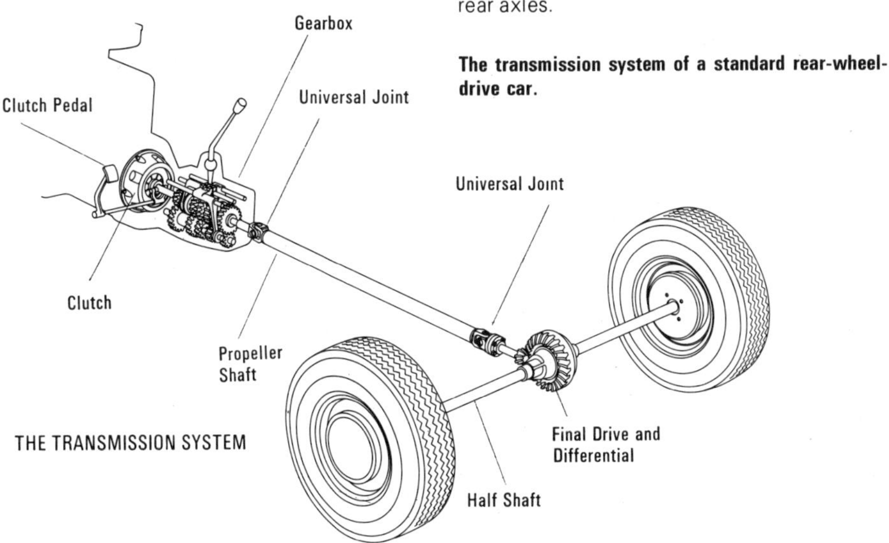

The transmission system of a standard rear-wheel-drive car.

A motor club meeting in Dorset, England, in 1905.

MOTOR-CARS: INTERNATIONAL IDENTIFICATION LETTERS

A	Austria
ADN	Yemen PDR
AFG	Afghanistan
AL	Albania
AND	Andorra
AUS	Australia
B	Belgium
BD	Bangladesh
BDS	Barbados
BG	Bulgaria
BH	Belize
BR	Brazil
BRN	Bahrain
BRU	Brunei
BS	Bahamas
BUR	Burma
C	Cuba
CDN	Canada
CH	Switzerland
CI	Ivory Coast
CL	Sri Lanka
CO	Colombia
CR	Costa Rica
CS	Czechoslovakia
CY	Cyprus
D	West Germany
DDR	East Germany
DK	Denmark
DOM	Dominican Republic
DY	Benin
DZ	Algeria
E	Spain (including provinces)
EAK	Kenya
EAT	Tanzania
EAU	Uganda
EC	Ecuador
ES	El Salvador
ET	Egypt
F	France (including overseas departments and territories)
FJI	Fiji
FL	Liechtenstein
FR	Faroe Islands
GB	Great Britain
GBA	Alderney
GBG	Guernsey Channel Islands
GBJ	Jersey
GBM	Isle of Man
GBZ	Gibraltar
GCA	Guatemala
GH	Ghana
GR	Greece
GUY	Guyana
H	Hungary
HK	Hong Kong
HKJ	Jordan
I	Italy
IL	Israel
IND	India
IR	Iran
IRL	Ireland, Republic of
IRQ	Iraq
IS	Iceland
J	Japan
JA	Jamaica
K	Kampuchea
KWT	Kuwait
L	Luxembourg
LAO	Laos
LAR	Libya
LB	Liberia
LS	Lesotho
M	Malta
MA	Morocco
MAL	Malaysia
MC	Monaco
MEX	Mexico
MS	Mauritius
MW	Malawi
N	Norway
NA	Netherlands Antilles
NIC	Nicaragua
NIG	Niger
NL	Netherlands
NZ	New Zealand
P	Portugal (including overseas territories)
PA	Panama
PAK	Pakistan
PE	Peru
PL	Poland
PNG	Papua New Guinea
PY	Paraguay
R	Romania
RA	Argentina
RB	Botswana
RC	Taiwan (Formosa)
RCA	Central African Empire
RCB	Congo
RCH	Chile
RH	Haiti
RI	Indonesia
RIM	Mauritania
RL	Lebanon
RM	Malagasy Republic
RMM	Mali
ROK	South Korea
RP	Philippines
RSM	San Marino
RSR	Zimbabwe-Rhodesia
RU	Burundi
RWA	Rwanda
S	Sweden
SD	Swaziland
SF	Finland
SGP	Singapore
SME	Surinam
SN	Senegal
SU	USSR
SY	Seychelles
SYR	Syria
T	Thailand
TG	Togo
TN	Tunisia
TR	Turkey
TT	Trinidad and Tobago
U	Uruguay
USA	United States
V	Vatican City
VN	Vietnam
WAG	Gambia
WAL	Sierra Leone
WAN	Nigeria
WD	Dominica
WG	Grenada
WL	St Lucia
WS	Western Samoa
WV	St Vincent
YU	Yugoslavia
YV	Venezuela
Z	Zambia
ZA	South Africa
ZR	Zaïre

Government

Glossary of terms

absolutism Government by one person or body having complete power.
activist Person favouring vigorous action and carrying it out.
agent provocateur Government agent who incites others to break law.
amnesty Universal pardon for people who have broken law.
anarchism Opposition to all government or rule of law.
apartheid In South Africa, a policy of segregation for whites and non-whites.
authoritarianism Government carried on by rulers without the people's consent.
autonomy Self-government.
Bolsheviks The Russian communist faction led by Lenin; later took name Communists.
brinkmanship Art, or folly, of pursuing policy to edge of, but not into, war, etc.
buffer state Neutral country between two others which might go to war.
caucus Pressure group within a political party, or meeting of such a group.
civil rights Freedoms that members of community ought to enjoy, such as right to own property, freedom from being imprisoned without cause. *Civil Rights* bill, passed by US Senate in 1964, aimed to end segregation.
Cold War The confrontation between communist and western countries since 1945.
collectivism Theory of collective ownership of land and capital.
communism In theory, society in which the people own all property in common, except for personal possessions.
condominium Joint control of a territory by two or more countries.
confederation Close alliance of several countries for a particular purpose.
congress An assembly of people; in some countries, the legislature.
conservatism Resistance to change.
corporatism Government based on system of corporations, representing workers and employers.

A political meeting in the Philippines, where feelings often run high and political rivalries are intense.

The detonator of a car bomb is shattered by a controlled explosion in Northern Ireland, where highly organized terrorism continues to resist peaceful political solutions.

Glossary (contd.)

coup d'état Sudden change of government by force, usually from within.
de facto recognition Acknowledgement that a government actually holds power.
de jure recognition Acknowledgement that a government holds power as of right.
demagogy Government by 'oratory'.
détente Easing of a political situation.
dictatorship Form of *absolutism* in which one man holds supreme power, and is answerable to no law or legislature.
disarmament Policy of reducing armed forces and weapons.
embargo Stoppage of movement of people or property; used to exert economic pressure on another country.
emerging country Country that is beginning to develop economically.
escalation Step-by-step measure and counter-measure, usually towards, and sometimes into, war.
extradition Handing an accused or convicted person over to another country for trial or imprisonment.
Fabianism Socialist movement based on evolution rather than revolution.
fascism Form of *absolutism* in which a country has only one political party, and is ruled by a dictator.
federation Union of states that retain a large measure of self-government, but yield certain powers to a central or federal government.
fellow traveller Term used in western countries to describe a Communist sympathizer who is not a party member.
franchise Right to vote.
geopolitics Science of politics in terms of land and geographical space.
gerrymander To manipulate voting districts, facts, or arguments in favour of a particular political party.
hawks and doves *Hawks* are politicians who favour military action; *doves* favour any moves to preserve peace.
home rule Self-government by the people of a country, particularly one that has been the colony of another.
imperialism Control by one country of other countries or territories, which are ruled as colonies.
intervention Interference by one country in affairs or quarrels of others.

The United Nations building in New York, where many governments are represented.

isolationism Policy that a country should keep itself to itself.
junta Council of state, or group holding power in country.
left wing Political group or party holding *radical* views; from position of radicals in French Revolutionary assembly.
liberalism Policy favouring change to suit existing conditions.
lobbying Attempting to influence members of a legislature; from the *lobby* or ante-room of a legislative chamber.
mandated territory Territory put under control of another country by League of Nations.
Maoism Type of *communism* preached by Chinese leader Mao Tse-tung, in which communist leaders may adapt *Marxism* to needs of own country.
martial law Administration of law and order in state by armed forces.
Marxism Also called Marxist-Leninism: the type of *communism* advocated by Karl Marx, as interpreted by Vladimir Lenin.
Mensheviks Moderate group in Russian Socialist party, which split from *Bolsheviks* in 1903.
Monroe Doctrine United States guarantee to all independent countries in Americas against European interference (President James Monroe, 1823).
nationalism Desire for independence and statehood by people with same language and culture; exalting one's country above all others.
nationalization State ownership of industry or business.
Nazi Short for Nationalsozialistische deutsche Arbeiterpartie, German form of *fascist* party between 1919 and 1945.

neutrality Taking neither side in war.
New Deal Reform programme introduced in United States in 1930s to combat Great Depression.
nihilism Denial of all accepted ideas.
ombudsman Independent investigator who protects citizens against maladministration by civil servants.
political science Study of government.
proletariat Body of people, with little or no property, who live by their own work, especially manual workers.
proportional representation Voting system designed to give political parties seats in proportion to total votes cast for them.
protectorate Country under control of another country.
racialism Dislike and persecution of people on account of race.
radicalism Belief in political and social change and reform.
rapprochement Reconciliation.
referendum National vote on a particular issue.
revisionism An attempt to introduce *socialist* ideas by reform rather than by revolution.
right wing Conservative, traditionalist political group. From position of conservatives in French Revolutionary assembly.
secession Withdrawal of state, party, or any large group from country or federation.
segregation Separation of people according to race.
separation of powers Division of government among executive, legislative, and judicial branches; applies especially to United States.
socialism Belief that country's people should own means of production; less extreme form of *communism*.
soviet Legislature in Russia.
suffragism Belief in right to vote.
syndicalism System in which means of production are controlled by workers.
Third World Name given to countries that do not support either of the blocs led by United States and Soviet Union.
totalitarianism System in which central government controls all aspects of people's lives and work.
Trotskyism Following teachings of Russian leader Leon Trotsky, who advocated international communism (opposed to excessive Russian nationalism).
trust territory Land administered by country on behalf of United Nations.
utilitarianism Belief that only useful actions are those that promote greatest happiness of greatest number.
Zionism Movement to set up Jewish state in Palestine (accomplished in 1948), and belief in protection of that state.

'ARCHIES & 'OCRACIES

anarchy	harmony, without law
aristocracy	a privileged order
autocracy	one man, absolutely
bureaucracy	officials
democracy	the people
despotocracy	a tyrant
diarchy	two rulers or authorities
ergatocracy	the workers
ethnocracy	race or ethnic group
gerontocracy	old men
gynocracy	women
hierocracy	priests
isocracy	all – with equal power
kakistocracy	the worst
matriarchy	a mother (or mothers)
meritocracy	those in power on ability
monarchy	hereditary head of state
monocracy	one person
ochlocracy	the mob
oligarchy	small exclusive class
patriarchy	male head of family
plutocracy	the wealthy
stratocracy	the military
technocracy	technical experts
theocracy	divine guidance

A typical Third World scene.

Laws are rules which apply to everybody in a country. Different countries make their laws in different ways. Governments follow careful procedures to make sure that laws are made as clear and effective as possible. A law begins as a proposal. It then passes through various stages of discussion until it emerges in its final form. But it can only have the force of law when it is finally approved by the highest authority in the land. In the United States this authority is the President; in the USSR, the authority is the Supreme Soviet; in the United Kingdom, it is the reigning monarch.

HOW A BILL BECOMES LAW IN CONGRESS

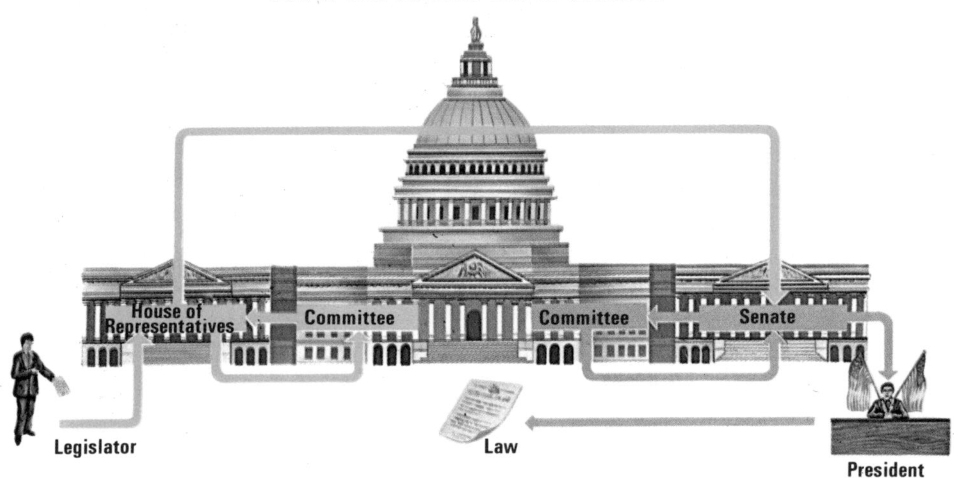

HOW LAWS ARE MADE IN THE USSR

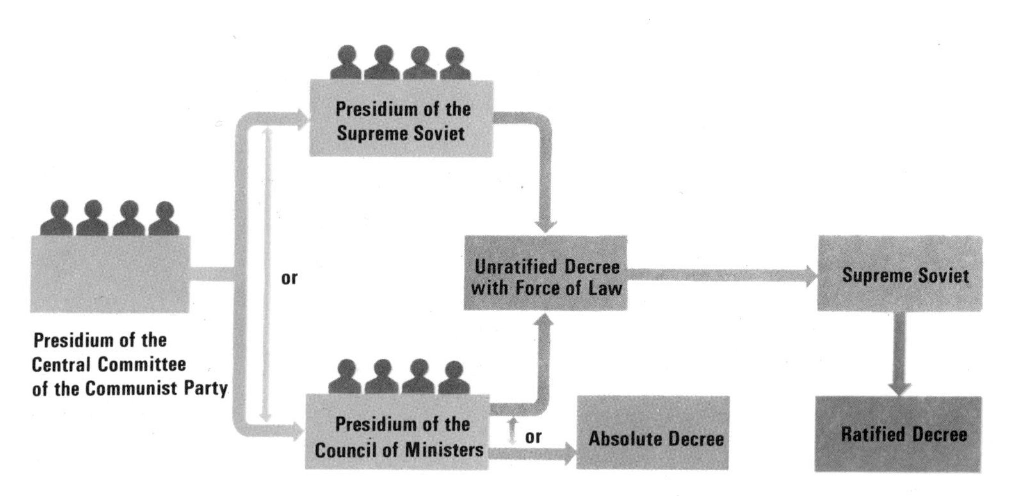

Above: **The White House in Washington D.C. is the home and office of the President of the United States.**

Above right: **The Kremlin in Moscow is the centre of government of the USSR.**

Right: **The Chamber of the British House of Commons, in Westminster, London. Here elected Members of Parliament discuss and vote on measures that will eventually become law.**

HOW A BILL BECOMES LAW IN PARLIAMENT

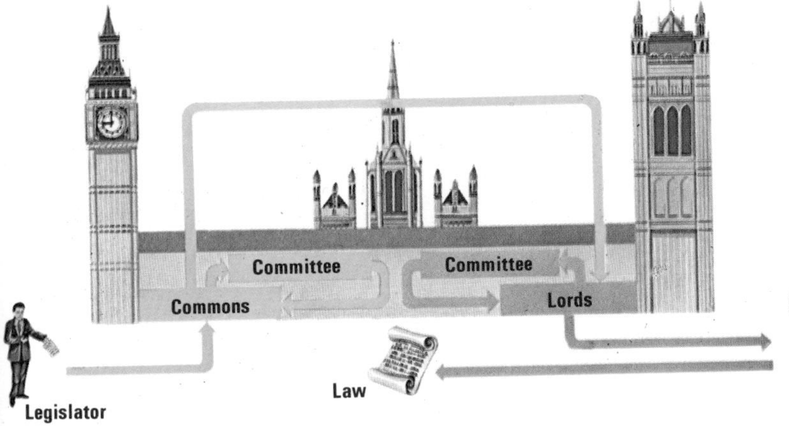

Royal Assent

UNITED NATIONS: MEMBER COUNTRIES

country	joined*	country	joined*	country	joined*
Afghanistan	1946	Ghana	1957	Oman	1971
Angola	1975	Greece	1945	Pakistan	1947
Albania	1955	Grenada	1974	Panama	1945
Algeria	1962	Guatemala	1945	Papua New Guinea	1975
Argentina	1945	Guinea	1958	Paraguay	1945
Australia	1945	Guinea-Bissau	1974	Peru	1945
Austria	1955	Guyana	1966	Philippines	1945
Bahamas	1973	Haiti	1945	Poland	1945
Bahrain	1971	Honduras	1945	Portugal	1955
Bangladesh	1974	Hungary	1955	Qatar	1971
Barbados	1966	Iceland	1946	Romania	1955
Belgium	1945	India	1945	Rwanda	1962
Benin	1960	Indonesia	1950	São Tomé & Principe	1975
Bhutan	1971	Iran	1945	Saudi Arabia	1945
Bolivia	1945	Iraq	1945	Senegal	1960
Botswana	1966	Ireland, Rep. of	1955	Seychelles	1976
Brazil	1945	Israel	1949	Sierra Leone	1961
Bulgaria	1955	Italy	1955	Singapore	1965
Burma	1948	Ivory Coast	1960	Somalia	1960
Burundi	1962	Jamaica	1962	South Africa	1945
Byelorussian SSR	1945	Japan	1956	Spain	1955
Cameroon	1960	Jordan	1955	Sri Lanka	1955
Canada	1945	Kampuchea	1955	Sudan	1956
Cape Verde	1975	Kenya	1963	Surinam	1975
Central African Empire	1960	Kuwait	1963	Swaziland	1968
Chad	1960	Laos	1955	Sweden	1946
Chile	1945	Lebanon	1945	Syria	1945
China†	1945	Lesotho	1966	Tanzania	1961
Colombia	1945	Liberia	1945	Thailand	1946
Comoros	1975	Libya	1955	Togo	1960
Congo	1960	Luxembourg	1945	Trinidad & Tobago	1962
Costa Rica	1945	Madagascar	1960	Tunisia	1956
Cuba	1945	Malawi	1964	Turkey	1945
Cyprus	1960	Malaysia	1957	Uganda	1962
Czechoslovakia	1945	Maldives, Rep. of	1965	Ukrainian SSR	1945
Denmark	1945	Mali	1960	USSR	1945
Djibouti	1977	Malta	1964	United Arab Emirates	1971
Dominican Republic	1945	Mauritania	1961	United Kingdom	1945
Ecuador	1945	Mauritius	1968	United States	1945
Egypt	1945	Mexico	1945	Upper Volta	1960
El Salvador	1945	Mongolian PR	1961	Uruguay	1945
Equatorial Guinea	1968	Morocco	1956	Venezuela	1945
Ethiopia	1945	Mozambique	1975	Vietnam	1976
Fiji	1970	Nepal	1955	Yemen	1947
Finland	1955	Netherlands	1945	Yemen PDR	1967
France	1945	New Zealand	1945	Yugoslavia	1945
Gabon	1960	Nicaragua	1945	Zaïre	1960
Gambia	1965	Niger	1960	Zambia	1964
Germany, East	1973	Nigeria	1960		
Germany, West	1973	Norway	1945		

*The UN came into existence in 1945.
†In 1971 the UN voted for the expulsion of Nationalist China and the admittance of Communist China in its place.

UNITED NATIONS AGENCIES

abbrev.	location
IAEA	Vienna
ILO	Geneva
FAO	Rome
UNESCO	Paris
WHO	Geneva
IMF	Washington DC
ICAO	Montreal
UPU	Berne
ITU	Geneva
WMO	Geneva
IFC	Washington DC
IMCO	London
GATT	Geneva
IBRD	Washington DC
IDA	Washington DC

UN: PRINCIPAL ORGANS

General Assembly Consists of all members, each having one vote. Most of work done in committees: (1) Political Security, (2) Economic & Financial, (3) Social, Humanitarian, & Cultural, (4) Decolonization (including Non-Self Governing Territories), (5) Administrative & Budgetary, (6) Legal.

Security Council consists of 15 members, each with 1 vote. There are 5 permanent members – China, France, UK, USA, and USSR – the others being elected for two-year terms. Main object: maintenance of peace and security.

Economic and Social Council is responsible under General Assembly for carrying out functions of the UN with regard to international economic, social, cultural, educational, health, and related matters.

Trusteeship Council administers Trust Territories.

International Court of Justice is composed of 15 judges (all different nationalities) elected by UN. Meets at The Hague.

The Secretariat is composed of the Secretary-General, who is chief administrative officer of the UN and is appointed by the General Assembly, and an international staff appointed by him. Secretary-Generals of the UN:

Trygve Lie (Norway)	1.2.46 to 10.4.53
Dag Hammarskjöld (Sweden)	10.4.53 to 17.9.61
U Thant (Burma)	3.11.61 to 31.12.71
Kurt Waldheim (Austria)	1.1.72 to

The General Assembly of the United Nations.

MEMBERS OF OTHER ORGANIZATIONS

COMECON: Bulgaria, Czechoslovakia, East Germany, Hungary, Mongolia, Poland, Romania, USSR.

Commonwealth: United Kingdom, Australia, Bahamas, Bangladesh, Barbados, Botswana, Canada, Cyprus, Fiji, Gambia, Ghana, Grenada, Guyana, India, Jamaica, Kenya, Lesotho, Malawi, Malaysia, Malta, Mauritius, Nauru, New Zealand, Nigeria, Papua New Guinea, Seychelles, Sierra Leone, Singapore, Solomon Islands, Sri Lanka, Swaziland, Tanzania, Tonga, Trinidad & Tobago, Tuvalu, Uganda, Western Samoa, Zambia.

European Economic Community (Common Market)**:** Belgium, Denmark, France, West Germany, Ireland, Italy, Luxembourg, Netherlands, United Kingdom,

NATO (North Atlantic Treaty Organization)**:** Belgium, Canada, Denmark, France, West Germany, Greece, Iceland, Italy, Luxembourg, Netherlands, Norway, Portugal, Turkey, United Kingdom, United States

Warsaw Pact: Albania, Bulgaria, Czechoslovakia, East Germany, Hungary, Poland, Romania, USSR.

Money Matters

Glossary of terms

account Credit allowed on commercial dealings, and on stock exchanges. See also *current account; deposit account.*
actuary Person who calculates risks and probabilities, especially in life assurance.
adjuster Person who settles insurance claims.
annuity Payment of a certain sum of money each year to a person.
assets The entire property of an individual or organization.
assurance Insurance, usually life or endowment, which is not dependent on a possibility; with *life assurance*, payment due on death of person assured. See also *endowment; insurance; term insurance; whole life.*
audit Examination of a firm's books to confirm their accuracy.
average In marine insurance, loss or damage; in fire and accident insurance, a condition under which insurers pay less for a loss if property is insured for less than its true value.
backwardation On a stock exchange, a fine imposed by a buyer on a seller who seeks to postpone delivery of stock sold ahead.
balance sheet Statement showing the financial condition of a company.
banker's order Same as *standing order.*
bankruptcy Inability of a person or business to pay its debts.
bargain Transaction on stock exchange; any agreement settling terms between buyer and seller.
bear On a stock exchange, a person who sells what he does not possess, hoping to buy it cheaply before *settling day.*
bill of exchange Written order to second person to pay sum of money to third party.
bill of sale Document transferring ownership of goods, in return for a loan.
blue chip The most reliable industrial shares on a stock exchange.
bond Written evidence of debt.
building society See *finance company.*
bull On a stock exchange, a person who buys shares hoping to sell them at a higher price.

A silver coin issued by the Greek city-state of Athens in the 5th century BC.

bullion Gold or silver, except in current coins, usually in bars of specific purity.
capital *Assets,* including ready cash.
capital gains Profit from sale of capital assets.
cash card Coded card enabling holder to draw specific sum from dispenser located on outside of bank.
cheque Written order to a bank to pay a sum of money.
collateral Security for a bank loan.
company Collection of people who have subscribed the *capital* (money) to run a business. See also *limited company.*
corporate personality A company is said to be *incorporated* – it has a legal existence or corporate personality apart from those of its owners.
corporation tax Percentage levy on profits of company.
costing Estimating the outlay needed for a particular business enterprise.
credit Allowing the purchaser of a commodity or service to pay at a later date; in book-keeping, an entry made for payment received.

credit card Document that allows its holder to buy goods on credit; it may be issued by a company or a bank.
credit rating Assessed creditworthiness of prospective customer.
creditor Party to whom money is owed.
currency Coins and bank or treasury notes.
current account At a bank, an account on which the depositor can draw at will and make payments by cheque.
customs duty Tax paid on imports or exports.
days of grace In insurance, period after premium due in which it may be paid without loss of cover.
death duty See *inheritance tax*.
debenture Document indicating that a company has borrowed money from a person; debenture holders receive interest before shareholders.
debit An entry in book-keeping for payment made or owed.
debt Money owed to a person or company.
debtor Party that owes money.
deed Written contract signed under legal seal.
deed of covenant Agreement under which party undertakes to pay set sum to organization (such as charity) for fixed period.
deposit account At a bank, an account on which depositor may be required to give notice before making withdrawal; interest is paid on it.
depreciation Fall in value of asset.
discount Sum deducted from face value of bill of exchange in consideration of early payment; any deduction from price; difference between par value of shares and lower buying price.
draft Written order to transfer money from one person to another.
endorsement Signature on back of bill of exchange, transferring it to third party; in insurance, note added to policy to modify or change certain terms.
endowment Money given for a specific purpose; in insurance, fixed sum to be paid at end of certain period.
estate duty See *inheritance tax*.

Gold bars, or bullion, are kept under maximum security at the Bank of England in London.

Money terms (contd.)

ex dividend Of shares sold without right to dividend due.
excess insurance Cover only for losses exceeding specific limit.
excise duty Tax on goods produced inside country.
finance company Firm that lends money to be repaid with interest over fixed period; *building society* is form of finance company in some countries.
gilt-edged security Safest share, usually government stock.
hire purchase British form of *instalment plan*, in which goods do not become property of buyer until final instalment is paid.
income tax Tax levied on income, including wages, interest, capital gains, etc.
indemnity In insurance, compensation paid for loss or injury.
inheritance tax Tax levied on estate of deceased person before heirs can inherit; also called *death duty*.
instalment plan Selling goods on fixed sum down, and rest of price in regular equal instalments that include interest; goods become property of buyer on payment of first instalment.
insurance Plan whereby person or company indemnifies others against loss in return for small regular payments (premiums).
in the red In debt; of an account, overdrawn.
interest Price paid for use of money; *simple interest* is paid only on *principal* (amount lent); *compound interest* paid on principal plus accumulated interest.
investment Use of money to provide income or profit.
IOU ('I owe you') Informal written promise to pay.
letter of credit Document allowing traveller (especially overseas) to draw money from banks other than his own.
limited company Company in which owners' responsibility limited to nominal value of shares held; strictly, *limited liability company*.
liquidation Winding up of company by selling assets and paying liabilities; any remaining money goes to owners.
mortgage Document giving title to property as security for loan. Mortgagor always has right to redeem.
oncosts See *overheads*.

country	currency
Afghanistan	afghani (100 puls)
Albania	lek (100 qindarka)
Algeria	dinar (100 centimes)
Andorra	franc (Fr) & peseta (Sp)
Angola	kwanza (100 lweis)
Antigua	dollar (100 cents)
Argentina	peso (100 centavos)
Australia	dollar (100 cents)
Austria	schilling (100 groschen)
Bahamas	dollar (100 cents)
Bahrain	dinar (1,000 fils)
Bangladesh	taka (100 paise)
Barbados	dollar (100 cents)
Belgium	franc (100 centimes)
Belize	dollar (100 cents)
Benin	franc
Bermuda	dollar (100 cents)
Bhutan	rupee (100 paise) (Ind)
Bolivia	peso (100 centavos)
Botswana	pula (100 thebe)
Brazil	cruzeiro (100 centavos)
Brunei	dollar (100 sen)
Bulgaria	lev (100 stotinki)
Burma	kyat (100 pyas)
Burundi	franc
Cameroon	franc
Canada	dollar (100 cents)
Central African Republic	franc
Chad	franc
Chile	new peso (100 old escudos)
China: People's Republic	yuan (10 chiao; 100 fen)
China: Taiwan	dollar (100 cents)
Colombia	peso (100 centavos)
Congo	franc
Costa Rica	colon (100 centimos)
Cuba	peso (100 centavos)
Cyprus	pound (1,000 mils)
Czechoslovakia	koruna (100 haleru)
Denmark	krone (100 öre)
Dominica	dollar (100 cents)
Dominican Republic	peso (100 centavos)
Ecuador	sucre (100 centavos)
Egypt	pound (100 piastres; 1,000 milliėmes)
El Salvador	colón (100 centavos)
Equatorial Guinea	ekpwele
Ethiopia	dollar (100 cents)
Fiji	dollar (100 cents)
Finland	markka (100 penniä)
France	franc (100 centimes)
Gabon	franc
Gambia	dalasi (100 bututs)
Germany, East	mark (100 pfennigs)
Germany, West	mark (100 pfennigs)
Ghana	cedi (100 pesewas)

CURRENCIES AROUND THE WORLD

country	currency
Gibraltar	pound (100 pence)
Greece	drachma (100 lepta)
Grenada	dollar (100 cents)
Guatemala	quetzal (100 centavos)
Guinea	syli
Guyana	dollar (100 cents)
Haiti	gourde (100 centimes)
Honduras	lempira (100 centavos)
Hungary	forint (100 fillér)
Iceland	króna (100 aurar)
India	rupee (100 paise)
Indonesia	rupiah (100 sen)
Iran	rial (100 dinars)
Iraq	dinar (1,000 fils)
Ireland, Rep. of	pound (100 pence)
Israel	pound (100 agorot)
Italy	lira
Ivory Coast	franc
Jamaica	dollar (100 cents)
Japan	yen
Jordan	dinar (1,000 fils)
Kenya	shilling (100 cents)
Kampuchea	riel (100 sen)
Korea, North	won (100 jun)
Korea, South	won (100 jun)
Kuwait	dinar (1,000 fils)
Laos	kip (100 ats)
Lebanon	pound (100 piastres)
Lesotho	rand (100 cents) (SA)
Liberia	dollar (100 cents)
Libya	dinar (1,000 dirhams)
Liechtenstein	franc (Swiss)
Luxembourg	franc (100 centimes)
Macau (Port.)	pataca (100 avos)
Madagascar	franc
Malawi	kwacha (100 tambala)
Malaysia	dollar (100 cents)
Maldives, Rep. of	rupee (100 laris)
Mali	franc
Malta	pound (100 cents; 1,000 mils)
Mauritania	ouguiya (5 khoums)
Mauritius	rupee (100 cents)
Mexico	peso (100 centavos)
Monaco	franc (French)
Mongolian People's Republic	tugrik (100 möngö)
Morocco	dirham (100 centimes)
Nauru	dollar (100 cents) ($A)
Nepal	rupee (100 pice)
Netherlands	guilder (100 cents)
New Zealand	dollar (100 cents)
Nicaragua	córdoba (100 centavos)
Niger	franc
Nigeria	naira (100 kobo)
Norway	krone (100 öre)
Oman	rial Omani (1,000 baiza)
Pakistan	rupee (100 paisas)
Panama	balboa (100 cents)
Paraguay	guaraní (100 céntimos)
Peru	sol (100 centavos)
Philippines	peso (100 centavos)
Poland	zloty (100 groszy)
Portugal	escudo (100 centavos)
Qatar	riyal (100 dirhams)
Romania	leu (100 bani)
Rwanda	franc
St Kitts-Nevis	dollar (100 cents)
St Lucia	dollar (100 cents)
St Vincent	dollar (100 cents)
San Marino	lira (Italian)
Saudi Arabia	riyal (20 qursh)
Senegal	franc
Sierra Leone	leone (100 cents)
Singapore	dollar (100 cents)
Somalia	shilling (100 cents)
South Africa	rand (100 cents)
South-West Africa	rand (100 cents) (SA)
Spain	peseta (100 céntimos)
Sri Lanka	rupee (100 cents)
Sudan	pound (100 piastres; 1,000 milliemes)
Surinam	guilder (100 cents)
Swaziland	lilangeni (pl. emalangeni) (100 cents)
Sweden	krona (100 öre)
Switzerland	franc (100 centimes)
Syria	pound (100 piastres)
Tanzania	shilling (100 cents)
Thailand	baht (100 satangs)
Togo	franc
Tonga	pa'anga (100 seniti)
Trinidad & Tobago	dollar (100 cents)
Tunisia	dinar (1,000 millimes)
Turkey	lira (100 kurus)
Uganda	shilling (100 cents)
United Arab Emirates	dirham (100 fils)
United Kingdom	pound (100 pence)
United States	dollar (100 cents)
Upper Volta	franc
Uruguay	peso (100 centésimos)
USSR	rouble (100 copecks)
Vatican City State	lira
Venezuela	bolívar (100 céntimos)
Vietnam, North	dong (100 xu)
Vietnam, South	piastre (100 cents)
Western Samoa	tala (100 sene)
Yemen	riyal (40 bogaches)
Yemen PDR	dinar (1,000 fils)
Yugoslavia	dinar (100 paras)
Zaïre	zaïre (100 makuta [sing. likuta]; 10,000 sengi)
Zimbabwe-Rhodesia	dollar (100 cents)

Money terms (contd.)

ordinary shares Shares in company which do not carry fixed rate of interest.
overdraft Type of bank loan in which account shows customer owes bank money; interest is charged on amount outstanding.
overheads Ordinary running costs of business, such as administrative or selling costs, not directly identified with product; also called *oncosts*.
paid-up policy Whole life or endowment insurance on which holder stops paying premiums, the sum insured being reduced accordingly.
partnership Simple form of business, in which each partner (two or more people) is liable for all debts of business.
portfolio Various shares, etc., held by institution or individual.
preference shares Shares of company on which interest is paid before any others, and owners have prior right to repayment of capital if company is wound up.
price-earnings ratio Ratio of market value of share capital to profit for year, used as guide to rating of stock.
profit sharing System in which employees receive share of company's profits in addition to wages.
profits tax Tax levied on total annual profits of company (superseded in Britain by *corporation tax*).
promissory note Unconditional promise in writing to pay certain sum of money; can be negotiable.
public liability insurance Policy covering businessman against claims resulting from accidents on his premises or defective products.
reserves Profits of a business set aside for policy reasons.
scrip issue Free shares issued to shareholders by capitalization of reserves; if dividend is maintained, shareholders are better off in that they do not have extra tax on profits they would have made with higher dividends.
security Anything used by borrower as safeguard for loan or debt.
settling day On stock exchange, day when all bargains are completed.
share capital Money raised by issuing shares.
share index Statistical indicator of overall share values, based on selected group.
shares Equal portions of the capital of a limited company.
specie Minted coins as opposed to notes, bills, etc.
standing order Instruction to bank to make payments at regular intervals to third party.
statement Report of condition of business, debt, or credit balance.
stock Total capital of public company; differs from shares in that it can be sold in any amount instead of in fixed units.
stock exchange Market for sale of stocks and shares.
stopped cheque Cheque on which bank has instructions not to pay.
superannuation Retirement pension.
surrender value Value of life insurance policy at any time before full term.
surtax Additional tax levied on income over certain amount.
takeover bid Offer to take over any or all of company's shares in order to acquire control.
term insurance Policy covering insured (or property) for specific period.
third party insurance Cover against claims involving damage or loss suffered by someone not involved in contract.
traveller's cheques Cheques for specific amounts issued for convenience abroad (or at home); may be cashed by bank's agents and are usually accepted at hotels, shops, etc.
trust Legal transfer of property from one person to a second, to hold and use on behalf of third party; in business, a trade combination of companies to secure monopoly.
underwriter Person or company who guarantees, in return for commission, to take up certain proportion of shares if these are not subscribed to by public; in insurance, one who guarantees cover.
unearned income Income received from investment and not as wages or profit.
unit trust Organization that invests money widely in stocks and shares on behalf of subscribers.
value added tax Form of sales tax levied at each point at which value is added to commodity or service.
wealth tax Levy on capital or property.
with profits policy Insurance in which person insured is entitled to share in profits of insurance company in form of bonuses.
without profits policy Insurance in which

person is insured for fixed sum.
whole life Insurance that matures only on death.
yield Net interest on a share or stock relative to the price at which it is bought.

Notes and coins are collectively called *specie.*

Economics terms

balance of payments Difference between country's payments to and receipts from other countries; includes *balance of trade* and 'invisible' trade such as insurance and tourism.
balance of trade Difference between value of country's exports and imports.
boom Period of increased business activity, rising stock market prices, and prosperity.
budget Financial statement showing future expenditure and income.
capital Unused wealth resulting from *labour* working on *land*; one of the *factors of production*.
capitalism Economic system based on private ownership of production, etc.
cash flow Regular cash supply for meeting current financial obligations of company.
closed economy Term used in economics for hypothetical economy that does not participate in international trade.
commodity Any tangible object satisfying human needs and limited in supply; raw materials, such as coffee, tin, and wheat, that may be graded to international standards.
common market Group of countries in economic alliance.
competition Condition in which large number of producers are able to supply consumers with similar products.
consumption Use of wealth produced; total expenditure of economy on goods and services.
controlled economy System in which government exercises extensive control. See also *planned economy*.
cost of living Amount of money needed to support certain standards of life.
crawling peg Term for devaluation or revaluation effected in small, regular steps.
customs union Alliance of two or more countries with no customs barriers between them.
deflation Reduction in business activity in economy, resulting in lower level of employment and imports, and slowing down of wage and price increases.
demand Quantity of goods or services people are prepared to pay for at given price and specific time.
depression Same as *slump*.
devaluation Lowering of currency values against currency of other countries.
direct taxation Taxes levied on wealth or income.
distribution Economic theory concerned with determination of prices of *factors of production* and resultant incomes; movement of goods from producer to consumer.
entrepreneur Person who undertakes business risks and provides jobs for others.
exchange rate Value of one country's currency in terms of another.
exports Goods or services sold to other countries.
factors of production *Labour*, *land*, and *capital*, the factors needed to make a commodity.
free (enterprise) economy System relying on supply and demand to regulate economy with minimum government intervention. See also *laissez-faire*.
galloping inflation See *inflation*.
'Gnomes of Zurich' Popular name for group of bankers thought to influence world finance.
gold standard Relating the buying power of currency to a definite value of gold.
gross national product (GNP) Total market value of goods and services produced by country over specific period, normally a year.

Economic terms (contd.)

imports Goods or services bought from other countries.
income Money and benefits accruing to individual, firm, or economy in specific period.
indirect taxation Taxes levied on expenditure rather than wealth or income, as purchase tax or value added tax.
inflation Economic situation in which speedily rising prices bring about decrease in purchasing power of money; *galloping inflation* is rapid inflation that threatens breakdown of monetary system.
interest Price paid for use of somebody else's money.
International Monetary Fund (IMF) Organization set up by Bretton Woods Agreement (1944), organized to promote international co-operation and remove foreign exchange restrictions (came into operation 1947).
investment Expenditure on capital goods.
invisible imports and exports Generally, interest on overseas investments, commission on financial transactions, payment for services, expenditure by tourists, government grants overseas, cost of membership of international bodies, etc.
labour Work of men applied to natural resources; one of the *factors of production*.
laissez-faire Economic system in which there is minimum of government intervention.
land All natural resources; one of the *factors of production*.
mercantilism A 16th-17th-century theory that a country should export more than it imports, and store its wealth in gold or other valuable metals.
middleman Man who brings buyers and sellers together, taking percentage of price for services.
money A means of exchange; any medium men agree to use to pay for goods or services.
monometallism System of currency in which one metal (usually gold) is used as standard.
monopoly When one person or group controls sufficient of the supply of a commodity or service to control its price.
national debt Money borrowed by a government from individuals and institutions to pay for expenditure that cannot be covered by ordinary revenue.

A hundred billion mark note—a grim reminder of galloping inflation in Germany in the 1920s.

nationalization The transformation from private to public (state) ownership of an industry or service.
operational research Study, using scientific principles, designed to find procedures for solving management problems.
organization and methods Application of work study to systems to achieve maximum efficiency of organization.
planned economy System of state control over allocation of resources rather than price controls.
price Amount in money that seller requests or obtains for goods or services.
production Means by which commodities are made and wealth is created. See *factors of production*.

ECONOMICS: NOBEL PRIZEWINNERS

1969	Ragnar Frisch (Norwegian) and Jan Tinbergen (Dutch)
1970	Paul Samuelson (American)
1971	Simon Kuznets (American)
1972	Kenneth Arrow (American) and Sir John Hicks (British)
1973	Wassily Leontief (American)
1974	Gunnar Myrdal (Swedish) and Friedrich von Hayek (Austrian)
1975	Leonid Kantorovich (Russian) & Tjalling Koopmans (Dutch)
1976	M. Friedman (American)
1977	J. E. Meade (British) & B. Ohlin (Swedish)
1978	H. A. Simoni (American)
1979	Theodore W. Schultz and Arthur Lewis (American)

'LAWS' OF ECONOMICS

Diminishing Returns Hypothesis that if one factor of production is increased while the others stay constant, a point is reached when the addition of one more unit of the variable quantity adds less to output than the previous unit.

Engel's Law The greater the income of a household, the lower the proportion spent on food (Ernst Engel, 1821–96).

Gresham's Law Bad money drives out good; i.e. the public tend to hoard (or even melt down) coins with greater bullion content, such as new coins (Sir Thomas Gresham, 1519–79).

Malthusian Theory Population tends to increase by geometric progression, natural resources by (slower) arithmetic progression; thus unrestricted population growth would eventually lead to universal hardship (Thomas Robert Malthus, 1766–1834).

Pareto's Law Whatever the political or tax system in a country, the distribution of income is more or less the same (Vilfredo Pareto, 1848–1923).

Parkinson's Law Work expands to fill the time available for its completion (C. Northcote Parkinson, in 1955).

Peter Principle In an organization, every employee tends to rise to his level of incompetence, so that all important work is done by those who have not reached that level (L. J. Peter, in 1969).

Say's Law Supply creates its own demand (Jean-Baptiste Say, 1767–1832; several interpretations, but taken literally it has proved to be not strictly true).

Supply and Demand, Law of Increase in supply tends to lead to a lower price for any particular product unless there is an increase in demand, and vice versa.

productivity Amount produced by *factors of production* in given time.

profit Reward of enterprise; increase in wealth resulting from operating a business or other enterprise.

protection Customs duties designed to protect home manufacturers from competition from imports.

recession Condition of economy in which decline in business activity is accompanied by short-term unemployment of men and machinery. See also *slump*.

reflation Deliberate inflation to counter serious deflation.

rent Price for use of land or goods.

revaluation Upward change in value of country's currency compared with other currencies; opposite of *devaluation*.

sanctions Withholding of goods or services as punishment or to enforce certain actions.

saving Postponement of consumption; accumulation of wealth not being immediately used.

services Non-material goods produced by *service industries* such as transport, teaching, catering, etc.

slump Period, also called *depression*, when workers and machines are persistently unemployed; the opposite of *boom*.

standard of living Degree to which people's needs and wants are satisfied.

subsidy Money or other aid given, usually by government, to industry, usually to prevent rise in prices.

supply Quantity of goods or services offered at given price.

taxation Compulsory contribution by individuals, groups, etc., to government funds.

unearned increment Increase in property value, especially land, through no effort of owner.

unemployment Shortage of work for labour available.

upmarket Of goods aimed at 'high quality' end of market.

utilitarianism Philosophy of government aimed at 'greatest happiness of the greatest number'.

utility Power of commodity or service to satisfy human wants.

value Exchange power of commodity or service in terms of other commodities or services.

wages Reward for labour.

wealth Possessions that have a market value, either tangible (such as money, shares, property, goods) or intangible (such as good-will, connections, skills).

wildcat strike Strike organized without support of union.

work study Management technique to improve production efficiency of labour.

Language & Communication

Computer terminology

accumulator Intermediate storage area where arithmetic results can be formed.
address *Characters* or *bits* identifying a specific location.
analog(ue) Representation of numerical or physical quantities by means of physical variables such as voltage or resistance.
base Number of *characters* applied to each digital position (i.e. 10 in the decimal system); also called *radix*.
binary Number system with base of two, using the *marks* 0 and 1.
bit Numeral in binary notation, i.e. 0 or 1; from *b*inary dig*it*.
block Single unit of computer instruction.
bug Error in coding causing failure of program.
call Transferring of control to *subroutine*.
card Special card on which information is stored as series of holes (12 × 80); *card-hopper* is tray that holds cards; *card-punch*, machine for punching the holes, or information, into the cards; *card-reader*, device for transcribing pattern of holes into computer data.
central processing unit (CPU) Part of system comprising memory, arithmetic, and control units.
character One of set of symbols recognized by computer, usually A–Z, 0–9, and other special symbols.
character recognition Machine-reading of characters designed for easy recognition by users; e.g. *magnetic ink character recognition* (MICR) and, for normal printing ink, *optical character recognition* (OCR).
COBOL *CO*mmon *B*usiness *O*riented *L*anguage: programming language designed for solution of commercial problems and for general use.
coding Writing programming language statements.
console Unit by which operator communicates directly with computer.
core storage Form of high-speed storage that makes use of tiny magnetic cores, each representing one of two states, symbolized by binary digits 0 and 1.
data General term for basic elements of information for processing in computer.
data processing What a computer does – receiving, processing, and producing a result from data.
debug Locate and correct errors in computer program.
digital Concerned with representation of data in numerical form.
disc storage Storage of data on magnetized surface of rotating discs.
down time Period when computer is not in use owing to mechanical defects.
field Specific set of characters treated as a whole, or recording area used for particular kind of data.
file Organized collection of records, such as payslips.
flowchart Diagram showing main steps in program.
FORTRAN *FOR*mula *TRAN*slation: programming language for scientific use based on mathematical notation.
hardware Physical working units of computer system.
housekeeping Administrational operations necessary to maintain control of process.
instruction Coded program step that defines single operation to be performed by computer.
language Defined set of characters, etc., for communication with computer.
line printer Output device that prints entire line of data at a time.
loop Repeated execution of series of instructions up to terminal condition.
mark Symbol used in number system (e.g. binary system has two, 0 and 1).
memory Storage or *core storage* in particular.
operations research Analytical study of human activities as aid to management.
overflow Production of arithmetical result greater than capacity of result field.
printout Output of *line printer*.
program Complete sequence of instructions or steps for job to be performed by computer.
radix Same as *base*.

retrieve Find and select specific record from storage.
run Complete performance of computer program.
software Library of programs available with computer to simplify programming and operations.
storage Any device – mechanical, electrical, electronic – capable of recording data and retaining it for future use.
systems analysis Examination of business procedure to determine optimum method of operation, usually with view to computerization.
translate Change information from one form to another without altering meaning.
word Set of *bits* or *characters* treated by computer as logical unit.
write Record data on output device, e.g. magnetic tape.

Thousands of tiny ferrite cores like this make up the core storage facility of a computer.

zero suppression Elimination of non-significant zeros on output.

NUMERATION

Arabic	Roman	Binary*
1	I	1
2	II	10
3	III	11
4	IV	100
5	V	101
6	VI	110
7	VII	111
8	VIII	1000
9	IX	1001
10	X	1010
11	XI	1011
12	XII	1100
13	XIII	1101
14	XIV	1110
15	XV	1111
16	XVI	10000
17	XVII	10001
18	XVIII	10010
19	XIX	10011
20	XX	10100
21	XXI	10101
29	XXIX	11101
30	XXX	11110
32	XXXII	100000
40	XL	101000
50	L	110010
60	LX	111100
64	LXIV	1000000
90	XC	1011010
99	XCIX	1100011
100	C	1100100
128	CXXVIII	10000000
200	CC	11001000
256	CCLVI	100000000
300	CCC	100101100
400	CD	110010000
500	D	111110100
512	DXII	1000000000
600	DC	1001011000
900	CM	1110000100
1,000	M	1111101000
1,024	MXXIV	10000000000
1,500	MD	10111011100
2,000	MM	11111010000
4,000	M$\overline{\text{V}}$	111110100000
5,000	$\overline{\text{V}}$	1001110001000
10,000	$\overline{\text{X}}$	10011100010000
20,000	$\overline{\text{XX}}$	100111000100000
100,000	$\overline{\text{C}}$	11000011010100000

*NB: In the binary system, there are just two symbols, 0 and 1. The base of the system is 2 (written 10), just as 10 is the base of the decimal system. And just as 10^3 (10 to the power of 3) is written in the decimal system by a one followed by three zeros, so 2^3 is written 1000 in the binary system. In other words, 8 (which is 2^3) is written 1000. To write a number in the binary system, you break it up into powers of 2. For example, 13=8+4+1, i.e. $\mathbf{1}\times 2^3$, $\mathbf{1}\times 2^2$, $\mathbf{0}\times 2^1$, $\mathbf{1}\times 2^0$; it is written 1101. If you want to double a number in the binary system (i.e. raise it to the power of 2, or the power of '10' in the binary system), just add a zero on the right.

ALPHABETS

Greek

Letter	Name	Transliteration
Α α	alpha	a
Β β	beta	b
Γ γ	gamma	g
Δ δ	delta	d
Ε ϵ	epsilon	e
Ζ ζ	zeta	z
Η η	eta	ē
Θ θ	theta	th
Ι ι	iota	i
Κ κ	kappa	k
Λ λ	lambda	l
Μ μ	mu	m
Ν ν	nu	n
Ξ ξ	xi	x (ks)
Ο ο	omicron	o
Π π	pi	p
Ρ ρ	rho	r
Σ σ, ς*	sigma	s
Τ τ	tau	t
Υ υ	upsilon	u, y
Φ ϕ	phi	ph
Χ χ	chi	kh, ch
Ψ ψ	psi	ps
Ω ω	omega	o

Hebrew

Letter	Name	Transliteration
א	aleph†	’
בּ	beth	b
ג	gimel	g
ד	daleth	d
ה	heh	h
ו	waw	w
ז	zayin	z
ח	heth	ḥ
ט	teth	ṭ
י	yod	y
כך*	kaph	k, kh
ל	lamed	l
מם*	mem	m
נן*	nun	n
ס	samekh	s
ע	ayin	‘
פּף*	peh	p, ph
צץ*	sadhe	ṣ
ק	qoph	q
ר	resh	r
שׁ	shin	sh
שׂ	sin	ś
תּ	taw	t

Russian

Letter		Transliteration
А	а	a
Б	б	b
В	в	v
Г	г	g
Д	д	d
Е	е	e, ye
Ж	ж	zh
З	з	z
И	и	i
Й	й	ĭ
К	к	k
Л	л	l
М	м	m
Н	н	n
О	о	o
П	п	p
Р	р	r
С	с	s
Т	т	t
У	у	u
Ф	ф	f
Х	х	kh
Ц	ц	ts
Ч	ч	ch
Ш	ш	sh
Щ	щ	shch
	ы	i
	ь	’
Э	э	e
Ю	ю	yu
Я	я	ya

Right: **Chinese script developed from very early forms of picture-writing. As time went on the picture-signs (ideograms) came to represent syllables.**

Below right: **In 15th-century Europe, the development of printing from movable type spread knowledge more widely than ever before.**

	宀	A ROOF (MIEN)
	豐	ABUNDANT (FENG)
	景	A SHADOW (YING)

PRINCIPAL LANGUAGES OF THE WORLD

language	speakers (millions)	where spoken
Mandarin	575	China (north and east central)
English	360	UK and Commonwealth, Ireland, South Africa, USA
Hindi	170	India (north central)
Great Russian	170	USSR
Spanish	140	Spain, Central and South America (not Brazil)
German	100	Germany, Austria, Switzerland
Japanese	100	Japan
Bengali	90	Bangladesh, India (east)
Arabic	80	Middle East, North Africa
French	80	France and French Community, Canada
Malay/Indonesian*	80	Malaysia, Indonesia
Portuguese	80	Portugal, Brazil
Urdu	80	Pakistan
Italian	60	Italy
Cantonese	50	China (south)
Min	50	China (south and east)
Wu	50	China (east)
Javanese	45	Java
Telugu	45	India (south-east)
Ukranian	41	USSR
Bihari	40	India (north-east)
Marathi	40	India (west)
Tamil	40	India (south-east), Sri Lanka
Korean	37	Korea
Punjabi	35	India (north)
Polish	33	Poland
Turkish	28	Turkey

* Officially called *Bahasa Indonesia* in Indonesia.

This first chapitre of the first tractate sheweth vnder what kyng the playe of the Chesse was founden and maad. Capitulo Primo

Amonge alle the euyl condicions & signes that may be in a man the first and the grettest is. Whan he feeth not ne dredeth to displese & make wroth god by synne & the peple by lyuyng disordonatly / Whan he retcheth not nor taketh hede vnto them that repreue hym and his vyces / But sleeth them. In suche wyse as did the emperour nero. Whiche did do slee his mayster seneque / for as moche as he myght not suffre to be repreuyd & taught of hym. in like wise was somtyme a kyng in babilon that was named

English language

Grammar glossary

ablative See *case.*
abstract noun Word standing for general idea or quality (honesty, greenness); many abstract nouns end in *-ism* (capitalism, communism).
accusitive See *case.*
active voice Form of transitive verb showing that subject of sentence or clause is the 'doer' of the action (James *ate* the cake). All intransitive verbs are active.
adjective Word describing or qualifying a noun (*fat* man, *blue* paper). Present participles of intransitive verbs are often used adjectivally (*sleeping* dog, *running* water).
adverb Word describing or qualifying a verb (I *fully* agree; he ran *fast*), adjective (*highly* satisfactory), or another adverb (*unusually* highly gifted). Many adjectives form adverbs by adding *-ly* ending (adj. *bad* becomes adv. *badly*).
antecedent Noun, clause, or sentence referred to by following adverb or pronoun, especially relative pronoun (*man* is antecedent to *who* in 'he is a man who knows what he likes').
article *The* and *a* or *an* are the *definite* and *indefinite* articles. One or the other usually precedes any noun that is not abstract or proper. *The* indicates a particular object (*the* chair I was sitting on); *a* (before a word beginning with a consonant or 'h') or *an* (before a word beginning with a vowel) refers to any object of its kind (*a* chair in *an* office).
auxiliary verb Verb used to form tenses, moods, and voices of other verbs (in future tense 'I shall go', *shall* is an auxiliary).
case Relationship between a noun, adjective, or pronoun and some other word in a sentence or clause. In *inflected* languages (e.g. Latin) different cases are shown by altered forms; in *uninflected* languages (e.g. English) case is usually shown by prepositions or position in the sentence. Case names in traditional (Latin) order are *nominative* (*subjective*), *vocative, accusitive* (*objective*), *genitive* (*possessive*), *dative,* and *ablative.* Examples of the use of each are given in this sentence: *'James* [*nom.*] ate all the *cakes* [*acc.*] made *by his mother* [*abl.*], including his sister *Jane's* [*gen.*] share, although he had promised to give some *to her* [*dat.*]. *Oh James* [*voc.*], you are awful!'

Grammar was once a fiercely taught discipline.

clause Part of sentence, separate from main sentence (or main clause), with its own subject and predicate (James, *who ate all the cakes*, is feeling ill).
collective noun Noun standing for a collection of objects, especially animals and birds (*flock* of geese, *herd* of cattle). Particular animals often have their own special collective noun (*pride* of lions).
comparison Adjectives and adverbs have three degrees of comparison: *positive, comparative,* and *superlative* (e.g. 'A is *as good as* B, and *better* than C, but D is the *best* of them all). Regular comparative and superlative adjectives add *-er* and *-est* to the positive form (*green, greener, greenest*); adjectives of three or more syllables and adverbs are preceded by *more* and *most* (more particular, most particular; more appropriately, most appropriately) or by *less* and *least.*
comparative See *comparison.*
complement Words completing the predicate of a sentence (He leaves *for the country tomorrow*); verbs requiring a complement are called verbs of *incomplete predication.*

concessive clause Subordinate clause beginning with *though* or *although* or words with similar sense.
conditional clause Clause expressing a condition (*If you insist*, I will do it).
conjugation Inflexion of a verb in voice, mood, tense, person, and number ('I am' is the active voice, indicative mood, present tense, and first person singular of 'to be').
conjunction Uninflected word connecting clauses or sentences, or co-ordinating words in a clause (*and, but,* etc.).
dative See *case*.
declension Inflexion of a noun or pronoun in case and number. In English, this amounts to giving the plural form, if irregular (mouse, mice).
demonstrative Adjective or pronoun that 'points out' (*this, that,* etc.).
double negative A second negative does not reinforce the first one, but negates it, i.e. two negatives equal an affirmative. 'I haven't got no money' is ungrammatical unless the meaning 'I have got some money' is intended.
epithet Adjective expressing quality or attribute.
finite verb Any form of verb limited by number or person, i.e. not the *infinitive* form.
fused participle Forming a compound expression by 'fusing' a participle to a noun (*James having* money is something new).
future tense Form of verb indicating a future action or intention. The *simple future* is formed with the auxiliary *shall* or *will* (I *shall go* tomorrow; so *will* he). The *future perfect* tense combines auxiliary shall/will with the *perfect tense*, indicating a completed action at some future time (by this time next year, I *shall have finished* my studies).
gender Classification of objects corresponding to either of the sexes or to sexlessness, i.e. *masculine, feminine,* or *neuter*. In English, only nouns and pronouns with definite male or female characteristics are masculine or feminine (man, woman, gander, goose); most other nouns are neuter. Certain nouns have masculine and feminine forms (actor, actress, etc.), others (ship, etc.) are sometimes personified as feminine.
genitive See *case*.
gerund Present participle of a verb used as a noun (*running* is good exercise).
grammar Study and classification of relationships between the words of a language, usually divided into *phonology* (study of vocal sounds), *accidence* (study of variable forms of words), and *syntax* (study of order and arrangement of words in sentences).
hanging participle Participle detached from noun to which it refers, producing a different meaning from the one intended (*sitting* on a gate, a bee stung him).
imperative See *mood*.
incomplete predication See *complement*.
indicative See *mood*.
infinitive Form of verb not predicated of subject (go, to go).
inflexion Variation of form of a word to show grammatical relation. See *case*.
interjection Exclamation or ejaculation grammatically unconnected with clause or sentence ('oh', 'ah', etc.).
interrogative Word used in questioning, especially interrogative pronoun (who? what? which? etc.); word order of question (Do you?).
intransitive verb Verb that does not take a direct object (sleep, walk, talk, etc.).
irregular verb Verb that does not inflect in the normal way to form past tense or past participle (e.g. regular verb: closed, closed; irregular verb: ate, eaten).
main clause Principal clause in a sentence of two or more clauses, i.e. the sentence itself when stripped of subordinate clauses (Whether you like it or not [subordinate clause], I will be there [main clause]).
mood Form of conjugation of verb showing its function, as in stating a fact, wish, etc. The *indicative mood* is used in statements of fact (He leaves tomorrow). The *subjunctive mood* is (now rarely) used in subordinate and conditional clauses to express a possibility or wish, etc. (If he were here now, he could tell us what to do). The *imperative mood* is used for second person commands (go away!).
nominative See *case*.
noun Word used as name of person or thing; also called *substantive*.
number Form of word expressing whether it refers to one thing only (*singular*) or two or more things (*plural*). Regular plural nouns are formed by addition of *-s* or *-es*. Examples of irregular plurals are *men, women, children, mice,* etc. Such plurals are survivals from the Germanic ancestors of English.

Grammar glossary (contd.)

object Noun or equivalent governed by active, transitive verb (direct object) or by preposition (indirect object). (In 'he gave some cake to John', *cake* is the direct object, and *John* the indirect object, of the verb *gave*.)

parse Grammatically describe a word or parts of a sentence ('gives' is indicative mood, present tense, third person singular of verb 'to give').

participle Adjectival form of verb. *Present participles* end in *-ing*, regular *past participles* in *-ed* (burning; burned).

passive voice Form of transitive verb showing that the action is done to the subject of the sentence (The cake *was eaten* by James).

past participle See *participle*.

past tense Form of verb indicating a past action, usually at a specified time or over a completed period (I *did* it yesterday; he *was* there for two weeks).

perfect tense Form of verb indicating completed past action at an unspecified time, or over a period leading to the present (I *have done* it; she *has been* in England since July).

personal pronoun Pronoun (I, you, he, she, we, you, they) standing for personal noun.

phrase Group of words generally not forming clause but expressing a single idea or element of a sentence, as in 'strangely enough [adverbial phrase] he came after all'.

pluperfect tense Verb tense denoting that an action happened before another past action also referred to; formed by auxiliary *had* and past participle of verb (James *had left* by the time John arrived).

possessive Form of noun indicating genitive case; singular form *-'s*, regular plural form -' (John's house; all the horses' food). *Possessive pronouns* are mine, yours, his, hers, its, theirs.

predicate Words with which something is said about the subject of a sentence, i.e. the part of a sentence that is not the subject. The predicate can consist of the verb alone (John *speaks*) or include verb and object (John *speaks German*).

preposition Word usually placed before a noun or equivalent to indicate grammatical relationship (of, from, by, with, to, etc.).

present tense Verb tense denoting a present action, a future action at a specified time, or a general rule (he is working now; he goes home tomorrow; he always has eggs for breakfast).

pronoun Word used to stand for a noun, i.e. used to indicate something without naming it.

proper noun Name of particular person or thing, place, country, etc., indicated by capital initial (James, Paris, Australia).

reflexive pronoun Form of pronoun showing that the object of a verb is the same as the subject, i.e. that the action is done to and by the same thing, formed by suffix *-self* or *-selves* (John hurt himself; they have only themselves to blame).

sentence Number of words making complete grammatical structure, i.e. containing subject and predicate at least, usually starting with capital letter and ending with a full stop.

solecism Any breach of rules of *syntax* (*Try and do it* instead of the correct *Try to do it*).

split infinitive Infinitive verb split from its 'to' by an adverb (*to* really *try* hard); often condemned as ungrammatical, but sometimes acceptable and even preferable (*to* really *enjoy* the book).

subject Part of sentence or clause denoting that about which the sentence gives information, i.e. the word or phrase governing the number and person of the verb (*James* eats cake).

subjunctive See *mood*.

subordinate clause Any clause of a sentence other than the main clause.

substantive See *noun*.

superlative See *comparison*.

syntax See *grammar*.

temporal clause Clause indicating time (*When he had finished supper*, he began his homework).

tense Form of verb indicating time of an action. See *future tense; past tense; perfect tense; pluperfect tense; present tense.*

transitive verb Verb that takes a direct object, i.e. 'transmits' an action directly from subject to object (She *caught* the train).

verb Word that indicates performance of an action, i.e. 'doing' words. See *finite verb; tense; transitive verb; intransitive verb; mood; voice; infinitive.*

vocative See *case*.

Figures of Speech

alliteration Use of words, often in verse, beginning with or containing the same letter or sound: *The weary wayworn wanderer . . .* (Poe).
anticlimax See *bathos.*
antithesis Balance of ideas: *Simplicity of character is no hindrance to subtlety of intellect.*
apostrophe Device in which writer or speaker breaks off to address someone or something present (sometimes only in imagination).
bathos Sudden descent into the ridiculous or into trivia, producing comic effect: *The explosion caused seven deaths, hundreds were injured, and typewriters were knocked off tables;* also called *anticlimax.*
climax Arrangement of ideas in ascending order of importance: *I came, I saw, I conquered.*
epigram Neat, brief, witty saying: *The vain have only one to please.*
euphemism Use of milder term for distressing idea: *South Vietnam has undergone a process of painless integration with North Vietnam.*
hypallage Emphasizing of an adjective or adverb by using it to describe, by position, a word to which it does not belong: *The waiter served an obsequious whisky and soda;* also called *transferred epithet.*
hyperbole Gross exaggeration for sake of emphasis: *Strong men have run for miles and miles when one from Cherry Hinton smiles* (Brooke).
innuendo Hint underlying surface meaning and used for insinuation: *Darkness was cheap, and Scrooge liked it* (Dickens).
irony Saying one thing but meaning the opposite: *For Brutus is an honourable man* (Shakespeare); *dramatic irony,* in the theatre or cinema, occurs when an audience is aware of something unknown to character(s).
litotes Emphasis by use of negative with word of opposite meaning: *He was no fool.* See also *meiosis.*
meiosis Expression by means of understatement: *She's a fair cook.* Opposite of *hyperbole.*
metaphor Probably the commonest figure of speech, a condensed *simile* in which one thing or person is taken to *be* another (instead of *like* another): *Some books are to be tasted.* See also *mixed metaphor.*
metonymy Reference to something by naming something associated with it: *boiling kettle; boisterous gallery; reading Shakespeare.* See also *synecdoche.*
mixed metaphor Erroneous use of metaphors inconsistent with each other: *. . . to take arms against a sea of troubles* (Shakespeare).
onomatopoeia Formation of a word in imitation of the sound of what is meant: *chortle, sizzle, quack, murmur.*
oxymoron Use of words of opposite meaning together to express an idea: *A lady's tears are silent orators.*
paradox Saying, usually epigrammatic, containing an apparent contradiction: *To die is to begin to live.*
pathetic fallacy Kind of *personification* in which human emotions are assigned to things of nature: *And daffadillies fill their cups with tears* (Milton).
personification Kind of *metaphor* in which inanimate objects or abstract ideas are credited with the qualities of living things: *Summer set lip to earth's bosom bare* (Francis Thompson).
pun Play on words, usually for humorous effect: *Some books are to be tasted, others to be swallowed, and Bacon to be chewed and digested* (deliberate misquote of a Bacon epigram in which the author's name 'Bacon' has been substituted for 'some few'), an example also of *metaphor, epigram, climax,* and *metonymy.*
rhetorical question Use of a question, not to elicit information but to emphasize a point, the answer either being obvious or delivered by the speaker (or writer) himself: *How do I love thee? . . . I love thee to the depth and breadth and height my soul can reach . . .*
simile Comparison of two things of different nature, which may be likened to each other in one or more respects: *Tall chimneys flew smoke as masts fly flags.* See also *metaphor.*
synecdoche Device for referring to something by naming part of it, or to part of it by naming whole: *A hundred head of cattle; England won the World Cup.* See also *metonymy.*
transferred epithet See *hypallage.*

People

Abelard, Peter (1079–1142); French scholar, philosopher, and theologian, taught that man's reasoning power was divine and should be used to understand God. Condemned as heretic; finally became monk. Tragic romance with Héloïse resulted in his castration by her uncle.

Abruzzi, Duke of the (Luigi Amadeo; 1873–1933); Italian naval officer, Arctic explorer, mountain climber; expedition farthest north (86°33′); mountain-climbing firsts in Alaska and Himalaya; commander Italian fleet World War I.

Adam, Robert (1728–92); Scottish architect, worked closely with his brother **James Adam** (1730–94) in designing buildings in elegant Neo-Classic style: London's Adelphi Terrace. Furniture design.

Addison, Joseph (1672–1719); English essayist and classical scholar, contributed to *Tatler* and *Spectator*. Member of Kit-Cat Club founded by leading Whigs, including STEELE and CONGREVE. MP for Malmesbury from 1708 until death.

Adenauer, Konrad (1876–1967); German statesman and lawyer; imprisoned by Nazis; chancellor of West Germany, 1949–63; led country's economic recovery.

Adler, Alfred (1870–1937); Austrian psychiatrist, disagreed with Freud's theories of infantile sexuality and proposed that power, not sex, was key. Introduced idea of inferiority complex.

Aga Khan Hereditary title carried by spiritual head of Nizari Ismaili sect of Muslims. First holder was Persian religious leader **Ali Shah Hasan** (1800–81);

Agricola, Georgius (George Bauer; 1494–1555); German mineralogist, wrote *De Re Metallica*, which summarized all practical knowledge gained by Saxon miners.

Akbar the Great (1542–1605); greatest Mughal emperor of India, succeeded father, Humayun, 1555; expanded empire.

Alexander, Harold Rupert Leofric George, 1st Earl (1891–1969); British general, directed Dunkirk and Burma evacuations; C-in-C North Africa, 1942; governor-general Canada, 1946–52; minister of defence, 1952–4.

Head of Alexander the Great, found at Pergamum, in Asia Minor (Archaeological Museum, Istanbul).

Alexander the Great (356–323 BC); King of Macedonia from 336 BC, set out to conquer world, and by 323 BC ruled empire stretching from Greece to Indus River Valley. Conquered Persia and Egypt. Died of malaria when about to invade Arabia.

Alfred the Great (849–899); became King of Wessex 871. After many defeats led Saxons to victory over Danish invaders; divided England with Danes. Revived scholarship and literature in England.

Ampère, André Marie (1775–1836); French mathematician and physicist, discovered electrodynamics and laws of electromagnetism. Found relation between magnetic field and electric current producing it. Invented solenoid.

Amundsen, Roald (1872–1928); Norwegian explorer, made first voyage through North-West Passage, 1903–6. In 1911 led first expedition to South Pole. Disappeared while searching for missing aviator in Arctic.

Anaxagoras (*c.*500–*c.*428 BC); Greek philosopher, accurately explained phases of Moon and eclipses of Sun and Moon. Proposed 'seed' theory of formation of Earth, Sun, and all heavenly bodies.

Louis 'Satchmo' Armstrong was known for his gravelly voice as well as for his fine trumpet.

Andersen, Hans Christian (1805–75); Danish author; novelist, but main claim to fame his *Fairy Tales*, including *The Ugly Duckling*, and *The Red Shoes*.

Anouilh, Jean (b. 1910); French playwright; *La Sauvage* (1935), *Le Voyageur Sans Bagages* (1936), *L'Invitation au Château* (1947; translated as *Ring Round the Moon*).

Archimedes (*c*.287–*c*.212 BC); Greek mathematician and engineer, discovered principles of buoyancy and the lever, founded science of statics. Possibly invented a 'screw pump' and planetarium. Calculated accurate value of pi. His devices prolonged Roman siege of Syracuse.

Ariosto, Ludovico (1474–1533); Italian poet and diplomat; main work, epic poem *Orlando Furioso* (1516).

Aristarchus (*c*.320–*c*.250 BC); Greek astronomer, first proposed Sun-centred idea of solar system, not accepted until after time of COPERNICUS.

Aristophanes (*c*.445–*c*.385 BC); greatest Greek comedy writer; works include *The Wasps, The Birds, The Clouds, The Frogs, Lysistrata, Plutus*.

Aristotle (384–322 BC); Greek philosopher, studied under PLATO, taught in Athens as head of Peripatetic school. Believed that happiness stems from human reason; ideal political state an enlightened monarchy. His works (*Ethics, Politics, Metaphysics*, etc.) have had a profound effect on thinkers through the ages.

Armstrong, (Daniel) Louis (1900–71); American Negro jazz trumpeter, bandleader, and vocalist, did more to popularize jazz internationally than any other single person.

Armstrong, Neil (b. 1930); American astronaut, first man to set foot on Moon, 1969. Naval pilot, he became astronaut in 1962, and made first space flight in *Gemini 8*, 1966.

Arnold, Benedict (1741–1801); colonial general in American War of Independence; went over to British, 1780.

Arnold, Matthew (1822–88); English poet and critic; inspector of schools 1851–86; professor of poetry, Oxford, 1857–67; *Essays in Criticism* (1865–88).

Arrhenius, Svante August (1859–1927); Swedish chemist, 1903 Nobel chemistry prize for theory of ionic dissociation of electrolytes in solution. Also began work on molecular biology, proposed that life began on Earth due to spores travelling in space; suggested 'greenhouse effect' of carbon dioxide in atmosphere.

Ashurbanipal (d. *c*.626 BC); last great king of Assyria. Completed Assyrian conquest of Egypt (669–662 BC) and overran Babylon (652). Empire was breaking up by time he died.

Astor, Viscountess (Nancy) (1879–1964); an American by birth, Lady Astor was the first woman MP to take her seat in the House of Commons, where she campaigned vigorously on behalf of the poor, and women in particular.

Attila (*c*.406–453); joint king of Huns with brother Bleda, 433; killed Bleda 445. Invaded Gaul 451; defeated at Châlons-sur-Marne by Romans; ravaged Italy, but forced to retreat by plague.

Auden, Wystan Hugh (1907–73); British-American poet; emigrated to US in 1939, returned to England shortly before death; poems, plays, essays; Pulitzer prizewinner. Wrote with ardent moral passion.

Audubon, John James (1785–1851); French-American ornithologist, completed large and beautiful collection of paintings of natural history studies. Initiated studies of bird migrations.

People (contd.)

Augustine, St (354–430); Numidian theologian, Bishop of Hippo in N. Africa (396–430). Author of *Confessions* (autobiography) and *City of God,* statement of idealism in Christian doctrine.

Augustus (63 BC–AD 14); first Roman emperor, named Gaius Octavianus (Octavian), great-nephew and heir of JULIUS CAESAR. Master of Roman Empire from 30 BC; Senate voted him 'Augustus' – exalted – 27 BC; finally consul for life. Made Rome strong after century of civil war.

Austen, Jane (1775–1817); English novelist. In spite of completely uneventful life, produced six great novels: *Sense and Sensibility, Pride and Prejudice, Mansfield Park, Emma, Northanger Abbey,* and *Persuasion,* published (1811–18).

Avogadro, Amedeo (1776–1856); Italian physicist, first propounded hypothesis that equal volumes of different gases contain equal numbers of particles.

Baade, Walter (1893–1960); German-American astronomer, calculated size and distance of Andromeda galaxy.

Babbage, Charles (1792–1871); English mathematician, inventor of earliest computer, a mechanical one.

Baber (1483–1530); descendant of GENGHIS KHAN, ruler of Kabul, Afghanistan, at 21; invaded India 1525–7 and set up Mughal (Mongol) Empire.

Bach, Johann Sebastian (1685–1750); German composer and organist, most famous of renowned Bach family and one of world's greatest musicians. Wrote 3 passions (including *St Matthew Passion*), 5 masses, over 200 church cantatas, 29 concerti, 48 preludes and fugues. Profoundly influenced work of almost all subsequent composers.

Bacon, Francis, Baron Verulam of Verulam, Viscount St Albans (1561–1626); English statesman (MP) and philosopher, wrote *Advancement of Learning.* Stressed importance of experiment and scientific induction to further understanding of nature. Thought by some to have written plays attributed to SHAKESPEARE.

Bacon, Roger (1220–*c.*1292); English scholar with ideas far in advance of his time. Believed Earth round; pointed out defects of Julian calendar; constructed magnifying glasses; believed in experimentation and mathematics as essentials to scientific advance.

Baden-Powell, Lord (Robert Stephenson Smyth Baden-Powell; 1857–1951); British soldier; defended Mafeking in Boer War; founded Boy Scout movement, 1908.

Baer, Karl Ernst von (1792–1896); Estonian embryologist, founded study of embryology and proposed theory of germ layer formation. Believed animal relationships to be shown by their embryos; not in favour of Darwinism.

Balboa, Vasco Núñez de (*c.*1475–1517); Spanish *conquistador,* first European to see Pacific Ocean, 1513. Executed on trumped-up charge of treason.

Balzac, Honoré de (1799–1850); French author; major work a series of novels under the title *La Comédie Humaine*; also *Les Chouans* (1829); short stories; plays.

Ludwig van Beethoven, the great German composer who developed the form of the symphony.

Banting, Sir Frederick Grant (1891–1941); Canadian physiologist, 1923 Nobel prize, with John Macleod, for isolation of insulin for treatment of diabetes.

Barbirolli, Sir John (1899–1970); English conductor and cellist, resident conductor Hallé Orchestra 1943–68.

Barnard, Christiaan Neethling (b. 1922); South African surgeon, performed first successful heart transplant.

Barrie, Sir James Matthew (1860–1937); Scottish novelist and dramatist. Works include *The Admirable Crichton* (1902), *Peter Pan* (1904), and *Dear Brutus* (1917).

Bartók, Béla (1881–1945); Hungarian composer and violinist, strongly influenced by Hungarian folk music. Original compositions sounded too 'modern' for most of contemporaries. Wrote opera *Bluebeard's Castle*, mime play *The Miraculous Mandarin*, and piano and violin concertos.

Baudelaire, Charles (1821–67); French poet, regarded in his day as 'decadent'; drug addict; *Les Fleurs du Mal* (1857) condemned as immoral in court.

Beadle, George Wells (b. 1903); American geneticist, shared 1958 Nobel prize for discovery of how genes work.

Beatles, The Britain's most successful 'pop' group; their new style of singing and playing swept world of popular music in 1960s: **John Lennon** (b. 1940), **Paul McCartney** (b. 1942), **George Harrison** (b. 1943), **Ringo Starr** (b. 1940).

Becket See THOMAS À BECKET.

Beckett, Samuel (b. 1906); Irish author, writing in French and living in France; play *Waiting for Godot* (1952); novels *Molloy* (1951), *Malone Dies* (1951), *The Unnamable* (1953); Nobel prize 1969.

Becquerel, Antoine Henri (1852–1908); French physicist, shared 1903 Nobel prize with CURIES for discovery of natural radioactivity.

Bede, the Venerable (673–735); English monk, scholar, and historian. Wrote *History of the English Church and People*, important source work later translated into Old English by ALFRED THE GREAT; many other works.

Beecham, Sir Thomas (1879–1961); English conductor, founded Royal Philharmonic Orchestra. Fervent admirer of Richard Strauss and Delius.

Beethoven, Ludwig van (1770–1827); German composer whose musical genius, especially in his 9 symphonies, has never been surpassed. Also wrote an opera, 2 masses, 16 string quartets, many songs and piano solos, and much orchestral music. In spite of increasing deafness, later works embody some of his most advanced ideas.

Bell, Alexander Graham (1847–1922); Scottish-American inventor of telephone.

Bellini, Giovanni (*c*.1430–1516); Venetian artist, profoundly influenced classical painting; pupils included TINTORETTO, TITIAN, Giorgione. Many altar-pieces and Madonnas noted for composition and original colouring.

Ben-Gurion, David (1886–1973); Polish Jew, became leading Zionist in 1919; first prime minister of Israel, 1948–1953, 1961–3; guided country through early days of war, 1948–9.

Bentham, Jeremy (1748–1832); English philosopher and legal theorist, exponent of utilitarianism; *Principles of Morals and Legislation* (1789).

Bernadotte, Count Folke (1895–1948); Swedish diplomat, nephew of Gustavus V; mediator in both world wars; assassinated while negotiating cease-fire in Israel, 1948, on behalf of UN.

Bernard, Claude (1813–78); French physiologist, discovered that main part of digestion occurs in small intestine; that body temperature controlled by dilation and constriction of blood vessels; that red blood corpuscles carry oxygen.

Bernhardt, Sarah (Henriette Rosine Bernard; 1844–1923); French actress; tragic roles, particularly Phèdre, earned her title 'Divine Sarah'; continued on stage after leg amputation 1915; silent films.

French actress Sarah Bernhardt at the age of 25.

Bernini, Giovanni Lorenzo (1598–1680); Italian baroque sculptor, architect, and painter, worked mainly in Vatican. Trevi Fountain; sculptures *Apollo and Daphne*, *David*.

Bernoulli Family of Swiss mathematicians: **Jacques Bernoulli** (1654–1705) worked

People (contd.)

on finite series, calculus, trigonometry, and theory of probability (invented Bernoulli numbers); **Jean Bernoulli** (1667–1748), Jacques' brother, worked on calculus and complex numbers; **Daniel Bernoulli** (1700–82), Jean's son, developed science of hydrodynamics and stated Bernoulli's principle (higher the velocity of fluid, lower its pressure); worked on differential equations, trigonometry, calculus, and probability.

Bernstein, Leonard (b. 1918); American conductor, composer, and pianist, became first American musical director of New York Philharmonic Orchestra; wrote score for musical *West Side Story*.

Berzelius, Jöns Jakob (1779–1848); Swedish chemist, originated modern system of chemical symbols and formulae. Responsible for discovery of cerium, selenium, and thorium, and for isolating calcium, silicon, and tantalum.

Bismarck, Prince Otto von (1815–98); Prussian statesman, prime minister from 1862. By diplomacy created united German *Reich*, 1871; German chancellor, 1871–90; dismissed by Wilhelm II; known as 'Iron Chancellor'.

Bizet, Georges (1838–75); French composer, mainly remembered for opera *Carmen*; also wrote other operas and incidental music to *l'Arlesienne*.

Björnson, Björnsterne (1832–1910); Norwegian writer; also editor and theatre director; novels include *Arne* (1859), *In God's Way* (1889); plays *Geography and Love* (1885); Nobel prize 1903.

Black, Joseph (1728–99); Scottish chemist, showed carbon dioxide could be formed by decomposition of calcium carbonate and is component of air. Discovered latent heats of melting and evaporation, and specific heats of substances.

Blackbeard (Edward Teach; d. 1718); British pirate; terrorized American shipping; killed after battle with two naval sloops from Virginia.

Blackstone, Sir William (1723–80); English judge, famous for *Commentaries on the Laws of England* (1765–9), influential legal work.

Blake, William (1757–1827); English poet, engraver, painter, and mystic. His faith in spirit of love pervades his works, which include *Songs of Innocence* (1789), *The Marriage of Heaven and Hell* (1790), and *Songs of Experience* (1794).

Blériot, Louis (1872–1936); French aviator, made first aeroplane flight across English Channel, 1909, winning £10,000.

Boadicea (Boudicca; d. AD 62); queen of Iceni tribe of Britons, led rebellion against Romans; defeated and took poison.

Bohr, Niels (1885–1962); Danish physicist, won 1922 Nobel prize for work on atomic structure. His basic theory of atom suggested 'shell' orbital structure and attributed radiation of energy to electrons 'jumping' from orbit to orbit.

Bolívar, Simón (1783–1830); South American patriot, b. Venezuela. With rebel army liberated Bolivia, Colombia, Ecuador, Peru, Venezuela from Spanish rule; president of Colombia 1819–30; known as *El Libertador*, 'the Liberator'.

Bonaparte Family name of NAPOLEON I and brothers **Joseph** (1768–1844), King of Naples and later of Spain; **Louis** (1778–1846), King of Holland; **Jerome** (1784–1860), King of Westphalia. Also of NAPOLEON III, Louis's son.

Booth, William (1829–1912); English religious leader and evangelist, founded Christian Mission (1865), renamed Salvation Army (1878); known as General Booth.

Napoleon Bonaparte, the French general and emperor.

Botticelli painted many scenes from classical mythology. *Primavera* (Spring) is an example.

Borgia Influential Italian family: **Alfonso** (1378–1458), pope as Callistus III from 1455; nephew **Rodrigo** (*c.*1431–1503), pope as Alexander VI from 1492; Alexander's children: **Cesare** (*c.*1475–1507), tried to conquer kingdom in central Italy; failed; killed in battle; **Lucrezia** (1480–1519), renowned for beauty; patroness of the arts.

Borodin, Alexander Porfirevich (1833–87); Russian composer and professor of chemistry, one of nationalist group known as 'The Five'. Remembered mainly for opera *Prince Igor*, symphonic poem *In the Steppes of Central Asia*, and *B Minor Symphony*.

Boswell, James (1740–95); Scottish writer, biographer, and libertine. Under pseudonym 'The Hypochondriak' wrote for *London Magazine*. Books include *Journal of a Tour to the Hebrides* (1785), *Life of Samuel Johnson* (1791), and *Boswell's London Journal* (pub. 1950).

Botticelli, Sandro (Alessandro dei Filipepi; *c.*1444–1510); Italian painter; delicate colouring seen at best in mythological pictures, e.g. *The Birth of Venus*.

Boult, Sir Adrian (Cedric) (b. 1889); English conductor, formed BBC Symphony Orchestra, conducting it 1930–49. Until 1957, principal conductor London Philharmonic Orchestra. Knighted 1937.

Bourbon Name of royal house of France 1589–1792, 1814–1848. First Bourbon king HENRY IV, followed by LOUIS XIII, LOUIS XIV, LOUIS XV, LOUIS XVI, LOUIS XVIII, Charles X, LOUIS PHILIPPE.

Boyle, Robert (1627–91); Irish-born scientist, noted for work on compression and expansion of gases, and Boyle's Law. Invented compressed air pump. Pioneer of fresh attitude to scientific methods.

People (contd.)

Tycho Brahe is shown here surrounded by early astronomers' instruments. He believed that the Sun circled the Earth.

Bragg English physicists, father and son. **Sir William Henry Bragg** (1862–1942) measured distance travelled by alpha-particles; 1915 Nobel prize, with son **William Laurence Bragg** (1890–1971), for work on X-ray wavelengths and crystal structure.

Brahe, Tycho (1546–1601); Danish astronomer, rejected Copernican system and corrected values of basic astronomical tables; observations provided basis for much of his assistant KEPLER'S later work.

Brahms, Johannes (1833–97); German composer and pianist, leading Romantic-Classical symphony composer of his time. Wrote more than 200 songs, 4 symphonies, piano and violin concertos, much choral and orchestral music. Close friend of SCHUMANN; also helped by Joachim and LISZT.

Brancusi, Constantin (1876–1957); Romanian sculptor, influenced 20th-century sculpture with sense of freedom evoked by simple polished shapes.

Brandt, Willy (b. 1913); German politician; mayor of West Berlin, 1957–66; chancellor of West Germany, 1969–74; resigned following spy scandal.

Braque, Georges (1882–1963); French painter, leading Fauvist; with PICASSO, founder of Cubism; specialized in still lifes.

Braun, Wernher Magnus Maximillian von (1912–1977); German rocket engineer, built first true missile, V-2 rocket, in 1942. Went to US after war and led group that put America's first satellite in orbit.

Breasted, James Henry (1865–1935); American historian and archaeologist, leading authority on history of Near East and Egypt. Founded Oriental Institute of University of Chicago. Books include *The Conquest of Civilization* (1926).

Brecht, Berthold (1898–1956); German writer and theatre producer; in US during Nazi period; plays include *The Threepenny Opera* (1928), *The Caucasian Chalk Circle* (1948).

Brezhnev, Leonid Ilyich (b. 1906); Russian Communist leader; president of USSR, 1960–4; First Secretary of Communist party from 1964.

Britten, Benjamin (1913–1976); British composer, gift for marrying words and music; operas include *Peter Grimes*, and *Billy Budd*; symphonic work *The Young Person's Guide to the Orchestra*.

Bromfield, Louis (1896–1956); American novelist; in France during 1920s, settled as farmer in Ohio, 1933; novels include *Early Autumn* (1926), *The Strange Case of Miss Annie Spragg* (1928), *The Rains Came* (1937), *Mrs Parkington* (1943).

Brontë Three English novelists and poets, sisters: **Charlotte** (Currer Bell; 1816–55) wrote *Jane Eyre*; **Emily** (Ellis Bell; 1818–48) wrote *Wuthering Heights*; Anne (Acton Bell; 1820–49) wrote *The Tenant of Wildfell Hall*. Together they produced a book of poems under their pseudonyms.

Brooke, Rupert (1887–1915); English poet; died serving in World War I; *1914 and Other Poems* (1915).

Browning English poets, husband and wife. **Elizabeth Barrett** (1806–61), was an invalid from age of 15; *Sonnets from the*

Portuguese (1850); recovered health after marriage to **Robert** (1812–89); travelled widely; dramas including *Pippa Passes*; many poems, long and short; *The Ring and the Book* (1869), his masterpiece.

Brueghel, Pieter (*c*.1525–69); Flemish painter, specialized in Flemish landscapes and peasant scenes in bright colours; *The Peasant Wedding*. Sons Pieter the Younger, Jan the Elder, and Jan's sons also painters.

Buchan, John, 1st Baron Tweedsmuir (1875–1940); Scottish author and statesman, governor-general of Canada. Wrote adventure stories and thrillers, including *Prester John* (1910), *The Thirty-nine Steps* (1915), and *Greenmantle* (1916).

Buchman, Frank Nathan Daniel (1878–1961); American evangelist, founded Oxford Group (1921), leading to Moral Rearmament movement (MRA) in 1930s. Adherents pledged to absolute honesty, purity, unselfishness, and love.

Buddha (Siddhartha Gautama; *c*.563–*c*.483 BC); founder of Buddhism, well-born Indian who renounced worldly pleasures and sat under bodhi tree until mysteries of life were unfolded to him. *Buddha* title meaning *The Enlightened One*.

Buffalo Bill (William Frederick Cody; 1846–1917); American scout for Kansas cavalry; buffalo hunter; showman from 1872.

Bunche, Ralph Johnson (1904–71); American Negro statesman; negotiated armistice between Israel and Arab neighbours, 1949; Nobel peace prize, 1950.

Bunsen, Robert Wilhelm (1811–99); German chemist, inventor of gas burner with intense flame for laboratory use.

Bunyan, John (1628–88); English nonconformist preacher; author of *Pilgrim's Progress*, an exciting moral allegory. Imprisoned several times for outspoken preaching.

Burke, Edmund (1729–97); Irish-born British statesman, orator, writer; criticized French Revolution, supported American colonists; led attack on WARREN HASTINGS; MP 1765–97.

Burke, Robert O'Hara (1821–61); Irish-Australian explorer, led first expedition to cross Australia south to north (1860–1). Let down by support party, he died on way back.

Burns, Robert (1759–96); Scottish poet; farmer, later exciseman; national poet of Scotland; many dialect poems and songs including *Auld Lang Syne, Holy Willie's Prayer, The Cotter's Saturday Night, To a Mouse*.

Burton, Sir Richard (1821–90); eccentric British traveller, explored Arabia and Africa, and with John Speke discovered Lake Tanganyika. Wrote more than 50 books.

Butler, Samuel (1612–80); English satirist; poem *Hudibras*, burlesque satire on puritanism, found great favour with Charles II.

Butler, Samuel (1835–1902); English author, painter, and musician, started working life as sheep-farmer in New Zealand, setting for satirical romance *Erewhon* (1872); works of scientific controversy against Darwinism.

Byrd, Richard Evelyn (1888–1957); American naval airman, made the first flights over both North and South poles. Led expeditions to Antarctica in 1928, 1933–5, and 1939–41. Commanded 4,000-strong party in 1946–7, mapping coast.

Buddha's childhood is depicted in this fresco.

People (contd.)

Byron, Lord (George Gordon Byron; 1788–1824); English romantic poet; born lame; left England 1816; went to help Greeks rebel against Turks, but died in Greece; poems include *Childe Harold's Pilgrimage* (1812), *The Giaour* (1813), *Manfred*, *Don Juan*.

Cabot, John (*c*.1450–*c*.1499); Italian navigator, discovered mainland of North America on behalf of Henry VII of England, in 1497.

Caesar, (Gaius) Julius (100–44 BC); Roman statesman and general, joined with Crassius and Pompey in First Triumvirate to rule Rome, 60 BC; conquered Gaul and invaded Britain. Ordered by Senate to disband army, crossed River Rubicon and invaded Italy; dictator from 49 BC; assassinated by political rivals who feared his power. Orator and writer; masterly accounts of Gallic wars and civil war.

Caligula (Gaius Julius Caesar Germanicus; AD 12–41); succeeded great-uncle Tiberius as Roman emperor, 37. Became mentally ill and ruled cruelly. Nickname 'Caligula' means 'little boots', a childhood name. Murdered by own guard.

Calvin, John (1509–64); French religious leader and theologian, a pioneer of Reformation. Established centre for preaching of his austere brand of Protestantism in Geneva. Doctrine of predestination and rejection of papal authority set forth in *Institutes of the Christian Religion*.

Camus, Albert (1913–60); Algerian-born French dramatist, novelist, philosopher; in French Resistance World War II; plays *Caligula* (1938), *Le Malentendu* (1945); novels *L'Étranger* (1942), *La Peste* (1947), *La Chute* (1956); Nobel prize 1957. Killed in car accident.

Canaletto, Antonio (1697–1768); Italian (Venetian) painter, known primarily for his views of Venice (particularly canals). In England mid-1700s, painting views of Thames and Richmond, Surrey.

Canute (Cnut; *c*.994–1035); son of Sweyn Forkbeard of Denmark. King of England from 1016; of Denmark 1018; of Norway 1028. Married Emma, widow of Saxon king Ethelred II. Restored order to England.

Čapek, Karel (1890–1938); Czech author and journalist; plays include *R.U.R.*(*Rossum's Universal Robots*, 1920), *The Insect Play* (with brother Josef, 1921), *The Makropoulos Secret* (1922); novels; short stories.

Lord Byron (portrait by T. Phillips, National Portrait Gallery, London).

Carlyle, Thomas (1795–1881); Scottish author of *The French Revolution* (1837). Translated German literature. Attacked corruptions of modern society and exerted much influence on religious, political, and ethical beliefs of time.

Carnegie, Andrew (1835–1919); Scottish-born American philanthropist, made fortune in steel; gave millions of dollars to schools, universities, and for public libraries.

Carnot, Nicolas Léonard Sadi (1796–1832); French physicist, calculated how to obtain maximum efficiency from steam engine. Founded study of thermodynamics.

Carrol, Lewis (Charles Lutwidge Dodgson; 1832–98); English writer for children, and mathematician. Wrote *Alice's Adventures in Wonderland* (1865) and *Through the Looking Glass* (1872); also *Euclid and his Modern Rivals* (1879).

Carter, James Earl (b. 1924); a Democrat peanut farmer from Georgia and former governor of that state, he became USA's 39th president in 1977.

Cartier-Bresson, Henri (b. 1908); French photographer of outstanding international events, turned photographic reportage into work of art.

Casals, Pablo (1876–1973); Spanish master cellist and conductor, renowned for playing of Bach's unaccompanied cello suites. Lived in voluntary exile in Puerto Rico when Franco came to power.

Castro, Fidel (b. 1927); Cuban Marxist, overthrew President Batista, 1959, and became prime minister.

Catherine II, the Great (1729–96); deposed her mad husband, Tsar Peter III of Russia, and became empress (1762). Strengthened power of nobility; captured Crimea, Black Sea coast, and much of Poland.

Catullus, Gaius Valerius (*c*.84–*c*.54 BC); Roman lyrical poet; bitterly attacked JULIUS CAESAR; wrote many epigrams.

Cavell, Edith (1865–1915); English nurse in Brussels in World War I; shot by Germans for helping Allied soldiers to escape.

Cavendish, Henry (1731–1810); English scientist, experimented with hydrogen, water, and air. Calculated mass and density of Earth using lead balls and Newton's Law of gravitation. Eccentric and secretive.

Caxton, William (1422–91); first English printer, set up press at Westminster (1476).

Cellini, Benvenuto (1500–71); Florentine sculptor and goldsmith; largest surviving sculpture *Nymph of Fontainebleau*, in Louvre. Sensational autobiography.

Cervantes (Saavedra), Miguel de (1547–1616); Spanish writer; fought at Lepanto, 1571; prisoner of Turks, 1575–80; many plays; eloquent short poems; novel *Don Quixote* (1605–15), and many others.

Cézanne, Paul (1839–1906); French painter, greatly influenced Impressionists; used pure colour and distorted perspectives to achieve certain effects. Painted portraits, landscapes, still lifes; *Bathers*.

Chadwick, Sir James (1891–1974); English physicist; 1955 Nobel prize for discovery of neutron.

Chagall, Marc (b. 1887); Russian painter, first of Surrealists. Left Russia after 1917 to work mainly in Europe and US. Russian Jewish influence evident in book illustrations, stage sets, mosaics, tapestries, and glass designs.

Chain, Ernst Boris (b. 1906); German-English biochemist, shared 1945 Nobel prize with FLEMING and FLOREY for work on penicillin.

Chamberlain Family of British politicians: **Joseph** (1836–1914), Liberal; colonial secretary. **Sir Austen** (1863–1937), elder son of Joseph; Conservative; foreign secretary, 1924–9; Nobel peace prize. **Neville** (1869–1940), second son of Joseph; Conservative; prime minister 1937–40; followed appeasement policy towards Nazis at Munich, 1938; forced to resign, 1940.

Chaplin, Sir Charles Spencer ('Charlie') (1889–1977); English/American film star, director, and producer. Role as baggy-trousered little tramp of silent screen endeared him to millions. Starred in *The Gold Rush*, *City Lights*, *Modern Times*, etc.

Charlemagne (Charles the Great; 742–814); King of Franks from 771, extended territory into Germany and Italy. Crowned Emperor of the West in Rome by Pope Leo III, 800; great patron of learning and subject of many legends.

Charles I (1600–49); King of England and Scotland, kept short of money by parliament, tried to rule without it. Parliament revolted against unjust taxation, and in Civil War (1642–5) defeated Charles. Executed after trial on charge of treason.

Charles I, King of England and Scotland, believed in the 'Divine Right of Kings'. His extravagance and arrogance led to civil war and his execution.

People (contd.)

Charles V (1500–58); Holy Roman Emperor from 1519; king of Spain as Charles I from 1516. Ruled over more of Europe than any other HABSBURG. Abdicated 1554.
Charles XII (1682–1718); king of Sweden from 1697. Brilliant general; led armies to victory in Northern Wars of 1700–21; but defeated by Russians at Poltava, 1709; killed in battle.
Charles, Prince (b. 1948); eldest son and heir of Queen ELIZABETH II; Duke of Cornwall; created Prince of Wales 1958; joined Royal Navy 1971.
Charles Martel (*c.*688–741); 'the hammer', Frankish ruler of Austrasia (715–41), halted Muslim advance into western Europe at Battle of Tours (732).
Chateaubriand, François René de, Vicomte (1768–1848); French author and diplomat. Went to America 1791 to escape Revolution, wrote about American Indians.
Chatham, Earl of (William Pitt the Elder, 1708–78); British statesman. As war minister, organized victory in Seven Years War. Supported American colonies in struggle for freedom.
Chaucer, Geoffrey (*c.*1340–1400); English poet, merchant, and diplomat. Translated part of *Le Roman de la Rose*, wrote *The Parlement of Foules, Troilus and Criseyde*, and *Canterbury Tales*. Buried in Westminster Abbey – first occupant of Poet's Corner.
Chekhov, Anton Pavlovich (1860–1904); Russian writer and physician; plays *The Seagull* (1896), *Uncle Vanya* (1897), *The Cherry Orchard* (1904); short stories.

Captain Cook mapped much of the South Pacific.

Chiang Kai-shek (1887–1975); Chinese statesman and general, succeeded SUN YAT-SEN as leader of Kuomintang (Nationalist) party, 1928; commander-in-chief from 1932. President 1943. Ejected from China by Communists, 1949; established government in Taiwan (Formosa).
Chippendale, Thomas (1718–79); English furniture-maker, used dark mahogany without inlays; often embodied Chinese designs in Queen Anne and Georgian styles.
Chopin, Frédéric François (1810–49); Polish composer and pianist, settled in France, and for a time lived with novelist GEORGE SAND. Wrote studies, mazurkas, polonaises, and nocturnes, almost wholly for solo piano.
Chou En-lai (1898–1976); Chinese. Communist statesman, active in Red Army from 1931; prime minister from 1949.
Christ See JESUS CHRIST.
Christie, Agatha Mary Clarissa (1891–1976); English detective-story writer, created Belgian detective Hercule Poirot. Plays include *Witness for the Prosecution* and record-breaking *The Mousetrap*.
Churchill, Sir Winston Leonard Spencer (1874–1965); British soldier, statesman, author, First Lord of Admiralty, 1911–15; Chancellor of Exchequer, 1924–9; First Lord of Admiralty, 1939–40; prime minister, 1940–5, and 1950–5; led Britain through World War II. Nobel prize for literature, 1953.
Cicero, Marcus Tullius (106–43 BC); Roman statesman, philosopher; tried to preserve the Republic; supported murder of JULIUS CAESAR; killed on orders from Octavian (AUGUSTUS).
Clausewitz, Karl von (1780–1831); Prussian general; books on art of war.

Clemenceau, Georges (1841–1929); French statesman; premier 1906–9, 1917–1920; headed Versailles Peace Conference; nicknamed 'Tiger' because of his toughness.
Cleopatra VII (69–30 BC); Macedonian queen of Egypt, joint ruler with brother, Ptolemy XII, in 51 BC; with Ptolemy XIII from 48 BC. Mistress of JULIUS CAESAR, 49–44 BC; of MARK ANTONY from 41 BC. Murdered Ptolemy XIII 44 BC. Committed suicide after defeat by Octavian (AUGUSTUS).

Clive, Robert (1725–74); British soldier. Victory at Plassey (1757) gave British control of India; governor of Bengal, 1764–7; censored for mis-government; committed suicide. Created baron, 1762.

Cockcroft, Sir John Douglas (1897–1967); English physicist; 1951 Nobel prize for devising voltage-multiplier for accelerating protons.

Cocteau, Jean (1889–1963); French dramatist, poet, critic, and film director; pioneered many literary and artistic (Cubism, surrealism) experiments, created ballets and mimes for DIAGHILEV. Wrote *Les Parents Terribles* (play 1938, film 1948), *Les Enfants Terribles* (novel 1930, film 1950).

Coleridge, Samuel Taylor (1772–1834); English poet and critic, author of *The Rime of the Ancient Mariner* (1798), *Christabel* (1816), and *Kubla Khan* (1816).

Colette (Sidonie-Gabrielle Colette; 1873–1954); French author, one-time dancer; books include *Chéri* (1920), *Gigi* (1944).

Columbus, Christopher (1451–1506); Genoese navigator, discovered New World 1492 while seeking westward route to China. Voyages were sponsored by Spain. Made four trips to west, but never realized he had found a new continent.

Compton, Arthur Holly (1892–1962); American physicist, shared 1927 Nobel physics prize with Charles Wilson for discovery of Compton effect, which led to idea of dual wave-particle nature of light. Research on nature of cosmic rays.

Columbus sailed to the New World in the ship *Santa Maria.*

Confucius (*c.*551–479 BC); Chinese philosopher and reformer, his name being Latinized form of K'ung Fu-tzu. In his *Analects* (collected sayings) he outlined man's duty to his fellow man in terms of absolute justice and moderation. Confucianism has influenced Chinese thinking more deeply than any other doctrine.

Congreve, William (1670–1729); English writer of polished comedies; *Love for Love* (1695), *The Way of the World* (1700).

Conrad, Joseph (Teodor Josef Konrad Korzeniowski, 1857–1924); Polish novelist and short-story writer who settled in England and wrote in English after seafaring career. Novels include *Lord Jim* (1900) and *Chance* (1914); short stories: *Youth, Typhoon* (1902).

Constable, John (1776–1837); English landscape painter, specialized in Suffolk scenes. Deeply influenced Delacroix, and foreshadowed Impressionists; *The Hay Wain, Salisbury Cathedral.*

Constantine I, the Great (*c.*274–337); first Christian Emperor of Rome. Defeated Emperor Maxentius and assumed power in west, 312; defeated Emperor Licinius and took power in east, 324. Founded new capital, Constantinople. Helped spread of Christianity.

Cook, James (1728–79); British navigator, was first person to sail south of Antarctic Circle. Explored Pacific, charting coasts of New Zealand and Australia and visiting many islands. Died in a scuffle in Hawaii.

Cooke, Alistair (b. 1908); British-born American journalist and broadcaster; *Letters from America* (1951).

Cooper, James Fenimore (1789–1851); American novelist of frontier life: *The Last of the Mohicans* (1826), *The Pathfinder* (1840), *The Deerslayer* (1841); travel and political works, history.

Copernicus, Nicolas (1473–1543); Polish astronomer, favoured Sun-centred idea of solar system; worked it out in mathematical detail.

Copland, Aaron (b. 1900); American composer; orchestral and chamber music shows distinct traces of jazz. *Appalachian Spring,* popular ballet music.

People (contd.)

Corbusier, Le (Charles Édouard Jeanneret; 1887–1965); Swiss architect, applied functionalism to all his designs; defined house as 'a machine for living in'; UN Building (New York), Pavillon Suisse (Paris).
Corday, Charlotte (1768–93); French patriot; killed MARAT because she was horrified at his ruthlessness; guillotined.
Corot, Jean Baptiste Camille (1796–1875); French classical landscape painter; early work distinguished by large artificial landscapes for formal exhibition; later work more subtle and natural; also figures and portraits.
Correggio, Antonio Allegri da (*c.*1494–1534); Italian painter, master of illusion by means of foreshortening. Human figures delicately modelled and painted with gentle tones. One of his masterpieces *Assumption of the Virgin*, fresco in Parma Cathedral.
Cortés, Hernando (1485–1547); greatest Spanish *conquistador*, conquered Mexico in 1519–21, with force of only 550 men. Ruled as governor until 1530.
Cousteau, Jacques-Yves (b. 1910); French oceanographer, inventor of Aqualung. Made underwater films and designed structures for underwater living.
Coverdale, Miles (1488–1568); English translator and Puritan preacher, converted Reformer; edited Great Bible (1539). Appointed Bishop of Exeter under Edward VI; fled to Switzerland when Mary I came to the throne, and worked on Geneva Bible (1557–9). Returned to England on ELIZABETH I's accession.
Coward, Sir Noël (1899–1973); British actor, director, playwright, composer; master of the sparkling dialogue; plays include *Hay Fever* (1925), *Private Lives* (1930); musicals *Bitter Sweet* (1929), *Pacific 1860* (1946); films *In Which We Serve, Brief Encounter*; 280 songs; knighted 1970.
Cranach, Lucas ('the Elder') (1472–1553); German artist celebrated for portraits and animal pictures. Designed religious woodcuts for LUTHER.
Cranmer, Thomas (1489–1556); English reformer, archbishop of Canterbury; promoted Reformation in England in reigns of HENRY VIII and Edward VI. Chief author '39 Articles' (1552); First Prayer Book (1549), etc. Imprisoned on succession of Roman Catholic Mary I (1553); burned at stake.
Crick, Francis Harry Compton (b. 1916); English biochemist, shared 1962 Nobel prize with WATSON and Wilkins for discovery of structure of DNA molecule.
Crockett, Davy (1786–1836); American scout, soldier, pioneer, politician, and folk hero. Frontiersman; Congressman from Tennessee, 1827–31, 1833–5; killed at Alamo.
Cromwell, Oliver (1599–1658); Lord Protector of England 1653–8. Country gentleman; M.P. from 1628; brilliant cavalry general in Civil War. Massacred garrisons of Drogheda and Wexford, Ireland, 1649. Dissolved parliament 1653; made Lord Protector; declined offer of crown.

Oliver Cromwell, Puritan Lord Protector of England.

Crookes, Sir William (1832–1919); English physicist, experimented with radiation and behaviour of objects in vacuum. Invented radiometer and devised improved vacuum tube, Crooke's tube.
Curie Family of scientists: **Pierre Curie** (1859–1906), French chemist, discovered piezoelectric effect in crystals; discovered critical temperature (Curie point) at which metal loses magnetism; married **Marie Sklodowska** (1867–1934), Polish chemist, who coined term *radioactivity*. They discovered polonium and radium, and shared 1903 Nobel physics prize with BECQUEREL for discovery of radioactivity. Marie Curie received 1911 Nobel chemistry prize for isolation of pure radium from

pitchblende. Daughter **Irene Joliot-Curie** (1897–1956) studied atomic structure with husband Frédéric Joliot by bombarding elements with alpha-particles. They shared 1935 Nobel chemistry prize for production of radioisotope of nitrogen.

Dante stands before a scene from his *Divine Comedy*.

Custer, George Armstrong (1839–76); US army officer, killed by Indians with 225 men at Battle of Little Big Horn ('Custer's Last Stand').

Cuvier, Georges Léopold Chrétien Frédéric Dagobert, Baron (1769–1832); French anatomist, founder of comparative anatomy; introduced phyla into classification. Studied fossils and founded palaeontology; believed in catastrophism rather than evolution.

Da Gama, Vasco (*c*.1460–1524); Portuguese navigator, made first voyage from Europe to India round Cape of Good Hope.

Daimler, Gottlieb Wilhelm (1834–1900); German inventor, first to construct high-speed engine. Built first motorcycle. Founded Daimler motor company.

Dali, Salvador (b. 1904); Spanish surrealist artist; beautifully finished and meticulously detailed works usually expression of irrational dream world and seem designed to shock.

Dalton, John (1766–1844); English chemist, proposed atomic theory and prepared table of atomic weights. This resulted from early studies of gases (Dalton's law of partial pressures).

D'Annunzio, Gabriele, Prince of Monte Nevoso (1863–1938); Italian writer and patriot; led capture of Fiume (Rijeka), 1919; novel *Il Fuoco* (1900) described his love for actress Eleonora Duse; plays; poems.

Dante Alighieri (1265–1321); Italy's greatest poet; magistrate of Florence 1300; exiled 1302; main work *Divina Commedia (Inferno, Purgatorio, Paradiso)*; *Vita Nuova*.

Danton, Georges Jacques (1759–94); French lawyer and revolutionary; helped organize Reign of Terror, but was himself guillotined by order of ROBESPIERRE.

Darwin, Charles Robert (1809–82); English naturalist, proposed theory of evolution by natural selection in *The Origin of Species* (1859) after nearly 20 years spent building up evidence; caused bitter controversy.

David, Jacques Louis (1748–1825); French painter, founder of French classical school. Court painter first to LOUIS XVI, then NAPOLEON.

Davis, William Morris (1850–1934); American geographer and geologist, 'father of geomorphology', conceived idea of cycle of erosion of land masses.

Davy, Sir Humphry (1778–1829); English chemist, inventor of miners' (Davy) lamp, and electric arc lamp. Isolated, by electrolysis, potassium, sodium, barium, strontium, and magnesium. Proved chlorine to be an element.

Debussy, Claude Achille (1862–1918); French Impressionist composer; works include orchestral music (*l'Après midi d'un faune*), piano music (*Clair de lune*), opera (*Pelléas et Mélisande*).

Defoe, Daniel (*c*.1660–1731); English author. Involved in Monmouth rebellion. Wrote political pamphlets, and novels including *Robinson Crusoe* (1719) and *Moll Flanders* (1722).

De Forest, Lee (1873–1961); American inventor of triode and tetrode valves.

An illustration from Charles Dickens's novel *Oliver Twist.*

People (contd.)

Degas, (Hilaire Germaine) Edgar (1834–1917); French Impressionist painter and sculptor, concentrated on human figure; free use of colour and composition had strong influence on GAUGUIN and PICASSO.

De Gaulle, Charles (1890–1970); French general and statesman; formed Free French movement after fall of France, 1940; president 1945–6; retired from politics; president with new constitution 1959–69; ended war in Algeria, 1962.

De la Mare, Walter (1873–1956); English novelist and poet, whose work appeals to adults and children. Wrote *Songs of Childhood* (1902), *Collected Rhymes and Verses* (1944). Anthology *Come Hither* appeared in 1923.

Delius, Frederick (1862–1934); English composer, largely self-taught; impressionistic style owed much to DEBUSSY. Operas, choral works, orchestral music; tone poem *On Hearing the First Cuckoo in Spring*.

Democritus (*c.*470–*c.*380 BC); Greek philosopher, first to propose that matter consisted of tiny indivisible particles.

Demosthenes (*c.*385–322 BC); Athenian orator; in *Philippics*, attacked Philip II of Macedon.

De Quincey, Thomas (1785–1859); English essayist; slave to opium; his *Confessions of an English Opium-Eater* (1821) won him fame; work published mostly in magazines.

Descartes, René (1596–1650); French philosopher and mathematician, invented system of plotting curves represented by algebraic equations – analytic geometry.

De Valéra, Éamon (1882–1975); Irish patriot and revolutionary; in Easter Rebellion, 1916, prime minister 1937–48, 1951–4, 1957–9; president 1959–73. Born New York City.

De Vries, Hugo Marie (1848–1935); Dutch botanist, rediscovered and publicized MENDEL'S laws of inheritance; proposed theory of mutations, thus completing DARWIN'S theory of evolution.

Diaghilev, Sergei Pavlovich (1872–1929); Russian ballet impresario; great talent lay in exploiting to full talent of others. Founded Ballets Russes, 1908; from then every great composer, painter, and dancer contributed to their success.

Dias, Bartolomeu (*c.*1450–1500); Portuguese sailor, first European to round Cape of Good Hope (1487–8).

Dickens, Charles (1812–70); English novelist, most popular of 19th century; his 15 novels include *Pickwick Papers* (1837), *A Christmas Carol* (1843), *David Copperfield* (1850), *A Tale of Two Cities* (1859), *Great Expectations* (1861); at first journalist, then theatrical manager; lecture tour of America, 1867–8.

Dickinson, Emily (1830–86); American poet; led retired life; poems published after her death, 1890–1936.

Diderot, Denis (1713–84); French philosopher, author, and encyclopedist. Chief editor of multi-volume *Encyclopédie*.

Dirac, Paul Adrien Maurice (b. 1902); English physicist; shared 1933 Nobel prize for work on wave mechanics and theory of antiparticles.

Disney, Walt (Walter Elias; 1901–66); American cartoon film maker whose characters Micky Mouse and Donald Duck are known world over; *Snow White and the Seven Dwarfs* (1938) was first ever full length animated cartoon film.

Disraeli, Benjamin, 1st Earl of Beaconsfield (1804–81); British statesman, twice prime minister (Conservative), 1868, 1874–1880; bought share in Suez Canal for Britain. Also wrote novels, including *Coningsby* (1844). Made peer 1876.

Donatello (Donato di Niccolò di Betto Bardi; *c.*1386–1466); Italian painter and sculptor; bold, original style brought new dimension to sculpture; *Gattemalata*, famous bronze equestrian statue.

Donne, John (*c.*1571–1631); English poet and clergyman; Dean of St Paul's, 1621; leader of metaphysical school; early work passionate love poems; later work religious: *Divine Poems* (1607), *Holy Sonnets* (1618), *Of the Progress of the Soul* (1633).

Dostoyevsky, Fyodor Mikhailovich (1821–81); army officer, 1841–4; sent to Siberia for conspiracy, 1849–54; founded two reviews; novels include *Crime and Punishment* (1866), *The Idiot* (1869), *The Brothers Karamazov* (1880).

Doyle, Sir Arthur Conan (1859–1930); British doctor and author, b. Edinburgh; knighted for medical services in Boer War, 1902; created Sherlock Holmes; also wrote science fiction, historical romances, and about spiritualism.

Drake, Sir Francis (*c.*1543–96); English adventurer, plundered Spanish settlements in America. Sailed round world in 1577–80. Burned a Spanish fleet at Cadiz in 1587, and helped to defeat Spanish Armada in 1588. Died in West Indies.

Dreyfus, Alfred (1859–1935); French Jewish officer falsely accused of spying and jailed for life, 1894; acquitted 1906 after two more trials and great scandal.

Dryden, John (1631–1700); English poet and dramatist; poet laureate 1668–88; political satires *Absolom and Achitophel* (1681), *The Medal* (1682); plays *The Indian Emperor* (1665), *Marriage-à-la-Mode* (1673).

Dufy, Raoul (1877–1953); French artist whose bright colours and calligraphic style of drawing make instant appeal to casual glance; much work for book illustration.

Dulles, John Foster (1888–1959); American diplomat, Secretary of State 1953–9; energetic and dedicated; inflexible in policy towards Russia.

Dumas French writers, father and son: **Alexandre the Elder** (1802–70); hundreds of novels of adventure with aid of assistants, including *The Three Musketeers* and *The Count of Monte Cristo*. **Alexandre the Younger** (1824–95); *La Dame aux Camélias* (1848) and plays.

Duns Scotus, John (*c.*1265–1308); Scottish scholastic philosopher, known as 'Subtle Doctor'. Opposed doctrines of Aquinas, teaching that God is ultimate Truth and that faith is separate from reason.

Dürer, Albrecht (1471–1528); German artist; pencil drawings, woodcuts, and copper-plate engravings; also first-rate watercolour painter. Engravings *Knight, Death, and the Devil*.

Dvořák, Antonin (1841–1904); Czech composer and violinist, much influenced by Czech folk music and Negro spirituals. Wrote operas, songs, symphonies (*From the New World*, etc.), cello concerto, and set of *Slavonic Dances*.

Earhart, Amelia (1898–1937); American aviator, first woman to fly Atlantic Ocean alone (1932); vanished on round-world flight.

Durer's skill as an engraver is seen in this detail from *Knight, Death and the Devil.*

People (contd.)

Eastman, George (1854–1932); American inventor, patented first photographic film (first made from paper, then celluloid, and finally cellulose acetate) and Kodak camera.

Eddington, Sir Arthur Stanley (1882–1944); English astronomer and physicist, made theoretical investigations into interior of stars.

Eddy, Mary Baker (1821–1910); American religious leader, founded Christian Science movement. Her doctrine, based on perfectibility of God, man, and universe as spiritual, incorporates spiritual healing; expounded in her book *Science and Health with Key to the Scriptures*.

Edinburgh, Duke of. See PHILIP, PRINCE.

Edison, Thomas Alva (1847–1931); American inventor, patented nearly 1,300 inventions, including phonograph, electric light bulb, and electricity generating station. Also invented a motion picture.

Edward, the Black Prince (1330–76); son of Edward III of England. Successful general; won Battle of Poitiers (1356).

Edward VIII (1894–1972); succeeded his father, George V, as king of Britain in January 1936. Abdicated December 1936 to marry American, Wallis Simpson, twice married previously. Made Duke of Windsor.

Ehrlich, Paul (1854–1915); German bacteriologist, shared 1908 Nobel prize for work on immunity and serum therapy.

Eijkman, Christiaan (1858–1930); Dutch physician, first discovered cause of beri beri, later established as vitamin deficiency disease.

Einstein, Albert (1879–1955); German-born theoretical physicist, made greatest scientific advances since NEWTON over 200 years earlier. In 1905 used quantum theory to explain photoelectric effect, produced famous $E = mc^2$ equation relating mass to energy, explained Browning movement thus confirming atomic theory of matter, and expounded special theory of relativity; published general theory of relativity in 1916 (superseded Newton's gravitational theory); unified field theory 1929. Became Swiss citizen 1901, American 1940 (as a Jew could not work in Germany in 1930s). Reluctantly persuaded President ROOSEVELT to begin atomic research 1939. Fought for world peace. Nobel physics prize 1921.

Eisenhower, Dwight David (1890–1969); American soldier and statesman, C-in-C, Allied forces North Africa 1942; in western Europe 1943–5. Served as 34th president, 1953–61.

Elgar, Sir Edward (1857–1934); English composer, most prolific period in early 1900s; orchestral set of *Enigma Variations*, 5 *Pomp and Circumstance Marches;* oratorio, *The Dream of Gerontius*.

Eliot, George (Mary Ann Evans; 1819–80); English author; novels include *Adam Bede* (1859), *The Mill on the Floss* (1860), *Silas Marner* (1861), *Middlemarch* (1872); poems.

Eliot, Thomas Stearns (1888–1965); American-born British poet; main poems *The Waste Land* (1922), *Ash Wednesday* (1930), *Four Quartets* (1944); plays *Murder in the Cathedral* (1935), *The Cocktail Party* (1950); Order of Merit, 1948; influenced many other writers.

Elizabeth II at the opening of Parliament.

English scientist Michael Faraday, discoverer of the principle of electromagnetic induction.

Elizabeth I (1533–1603); became queen of England 1558 at time of turmoil, and by wise statecraft made England stronger than it had ever been. Her people fought off Spanish invasion (1588) and began expansion overseas. Never married; great scholar and talented musician.
Elizabeth II (b. 1926) succeeded her father GEORGE VI as British sovereign and Head of Commonwealth in 1952. Married Lieut. Philip Mountbatten (PRINCE PHILIP) 1947.
Engels, Friedrich (1820–95); German Socialist, collaborated with MARX to write *Communist Manifesto* (1848). Revolutionary activities led him to flee to England, where he edited Marx's works.
Epstein, Sir Jacob (1880–1959); American-born British sculptor; highly individual style scandalized critics and spectators whenever statues unveiled. Most of work powerful and larger than life, carved with rugged simplicity. Busts: Maugham, Shaw, Einstein, etc.
Erasmus, Desiderius (*c.*1466–1536); Dutch Renaissance scholar, theologian, philosopher, and Augustinian monk. Sympathetic with aims of Reformation, but dislike of violence prevented his openly joining reformers. Published first Greek edition of New Testament (1516).
Eratosthenes (*c.*276–*c.*428 BC); Greek astronomer, worked out system for determining prime numbers. Made map of known world. Calculated size of Earth.
Ericson, Leif See LEIF ERICSON.
Euclid (*c.*300s BC); Greek mathematician, founder of modern geometry. Codified mathematical knowledge into *The Elements*.
Eugène of Savoy, Prince (1663–1736); Austrian general; with DUKE OF MARLBOROUGH won victories over French in War of Spanish Succession; also won victories against Turks. Born in France.
Euler, Leonhard (1707–83); Swiss mathematician, one of the most prolific mathematical writers of all time.
Euripides (*c.*480–406 BC); Greek tragic playwright; plays include *Medea, Iphigenia in Tauris, Helen, Orestes, Iphigenia in Aulis, The Trojan Women*.
Evans, Sir Arthur John (1851–1941); British archaeologist, excavated Palace of Minos at Knossos, Crete; discovered early type of Greek script.
Evelyn, John (1620–1706); English government official, author; secretary of Royal Society; books on architecture, trees, commerce, travels; his *Diary* (1640–1705), a major source book for his time.
Eyre, Edward John (1815–1901); British administrator and explorer, discovered Lakes Torrens and Eyre, S. Australia. Crossed Nullarbor Plain, 1840. Lieutenant-governor, New Zealand, 1846–53; governor, Jamaica, 1864–6.
Fahrenheit, Gabriel Daniel (1686–1736); German-Dutch physicist, made first mercury thermometer and worked out Fahrenheit scale of temperature.
Faraday, Michael (1791–1867); English scientist, founder of science of electromagnetism. Assisted and then succeeded DAVY at Royal Institution 1833. Pioneered cryogenics, discovered benzene, proposed laws of electrolysis. Devised simple electric

People (contd.)

motor, discovered induction, and invented first generator.

Faulkner, William (1897–1962); American novelist; works include *The Sound and the Fury* (1929), *As I Lay Dying* (1930); Pulitzer prizewinner; Nobel prize for literature, 1949.

Fawkes, Guy (1570–1606); English conspirator; caught trying to blow up Houses of Parliament, 5 November 1605; executed for treason.

Ferdinand II of Aragon (1452–1516); husband of ISABELLA OF CASTILE, became king of Aragon 1479, uniting almost all Spain under one rule; established Inquisition in Spain, and expelled Jews.

Fermat, Pierre de (1601–65); French mathematician, founded theory of probability (with Blaise Pascal) and theory of numbers.

Fermi, Enrico (1901–54); Italian-American physicist, won 1938 Nobel prize for work on neutron bombardment. Built first nuclear reactor, called atomic pile.

Fields, W. C. (William Claude Dukenfield; 1880–1946); American film actor; cynical, drunken, anti-sentimental roles endeared him to the discerning in such films as *David Copperfield* and *Never Give a Sucker an Even Break*.

FitzGerald, Edward (1809–83); British poet, known mainly for translation of *Rubáiyát* of OMAR KHAYYÁM (1859).

Fitzgerald, F. Scott (1896–1940); American writer; life ruined by alcohol; novels include *This Side of Paradise* (1920), *The Great Gatsby* (1925); mirrored Depression years and 'age of jazz'.

Flamsteed, John (1646–1719); English astronomer, produced first great star map.

Flaubert, Gustave (1821–80); French novelist; *Madame Bovary* (1857), *Trois Contes* (1877).

Fleming, Sir Alexander (1881–1955); Scottish bacteriologist, discovered lysosomes and penicillin. Shared Nobel prize 1945.

Florey, Sir Howard Walter (1898–1968); Australian-English pathologist, worked out chemical structure of penicillin with ERNST CHAIN. Shared Nobel prize 1945.

Foch, Ferdinand (1851–1929); French marshal; outstanding general World War I; allied C-in-C, 1918.

Fonteyn, Dame Margot (Margaret Hookham; b. 1919); English ballerina, *Prima ballerina assoluta* of Royal Ballet. Made world tours, starring especially in such roles as Giselle; partnered Nureyev in 1960s.

Ford, Gerald Rudolph (b. 1913); American statesman, nominated by RICHARD NIXON to replace Spiro Agnew as vice-president, 1973; succeeded Nixon as 38th president, 1974; withdrew US forces from Vietnam.

Ford, Henry (1863–1947); American car manufacturer; introduced mass production methods to make cheap cars.

Sir Alexander Fleming, discoverer of penicillin

Foucault, Jean Bernard Léon (1819–68); French physicist, calculated velocity of light using rotating mirror method. Demonstrated rotation of Earth using large pendulum that gradually altered its plane of oscillation.

France, Anatole (Jacques Anatole François Thibault; 1844–1924); French novelist, satirist; *Le Crime de Sylvestre Bonnard* (1881), *Thaïs* (1890), *Les Dieux Ont Soif* (1912), *L'Île des Pingouins* (1908); member of French Academy; Nobel prize for literature 1921.

Francis of Assisi, St (*c.*1182–1226); Italian friar, founded Franciscan Order of friars; love of animals proverbial.

Franco, Francisco (b. 1892); led rebellion in Spain during Civil War of 1936–9; head of state (*El Caudillo*) and dictator from 1939.

Franklin, Benjamin (1706–90); American statesman and scientist, one of founding fathers of American nation. Invented an improved stove and bifocal glasses. Experimented with static electricity and lightning; invented lightning conductor. Suggested use of positive and negative terms in electricity.

Frederick II, the Great (1712–86); king of Prussia from 1740; brilliant general; fought MARIA THERESA in War of Austrian Succession; skilled flautist.

Freud, Sigmund (1856–1939); Austrian psychiatrist, proposed idea of conscious and subconscious mind. Began psychoanalysis and interpretation of dreams. Proposed theories of infantile sexuality and their effects on adult life.

Frobisher, Sir Martin (*c.*1535–94); English explorer, made three attempts to find North-West Passage. Commanded part of fleet that defeated Spanish Armada, 1588. Fatally wounded at siege of Brest.

Fry, Elizabeth (1780–1845); a Quaker who lived in Norwich, she became an active reformer of English prisons; she was also requested by King Louis Philippe of France to inspect and report on French prisons, which led to prison reforms in France. She was involved in other fields of reform such as improving standards of nursing and education.

Gagarin, Yuri (1934–68); Russian cosmonaut, made first human space flight, in *Vostok I*, 1961. Died in plane crash.

Gainsborough, Thomas (1727–88); English painter, portraits and landscapes, strongly influenced by Rubens; much sought after by society clients; *The Blue Boy, Mrs Siddons*.

Galileo (1564–1642); Italian scientist, first to combine theory and experiment in modern scientific manner. Discovered principle of pendulum and of falling bodies. Invented telescope and made astronomical observations that finally established Copernican theory of universe, but not before he was imprisoned for his 'heretical' views.

Galsworthy, John (1867–1933); English novelist and playwright; main novels *The Forsyte Saga* and its sequels (1906–28); plays include *The Silver Box* (1906), *The Skin Game* (1920); Order of Merit 1929; Nobel prize for literature 1932.

Galton, Sir Francis (1822–1911); English scientist, cousin of DARWIN; anthropologist, studied heredity and first applied statistical methods to biology; founded eugenics. Also pioneered weather chart and devised fingerprint identification.

Galvani, Luigi (1737–98); Italian anatomist, discovered electricity produced by metals in contact, but believed it came from living tissue – 'animal electricity'.

Gandhi, Mohandas Karamchand (1869–1948); Indian lawyer, ascetic, and Hindu spiritual leader; worked for independence from Britain, largely by non-violent civil disobedience; jailed several times; assassinated by Hindu fanatic because he preached peace with Muslims. Known as *Mahatma*, 'great soul'.

Garbo, Greta (Greta Gustafsson; b. 1905); Swedish-born American film star. Cultivated well-publicized dislike of publicity. Starred in *Camille*, *Ninotchka*, etc.

Greta Garbo, who gave up acting in 1941 at the height of her career, without explaining why.

People (contd.)

Garibaldi, Giuseppe (1807–82); Italian patriot; with 1,000 men (Red-shirts) conquered Kingdom of Two Sicilies 1860; after proclamation of Kingdom of Italy, 1861, twice tried to conquer Rome (1862, 1867); fought for France, 1870–1; member of Italian parliament, 1874.

Garrick, David (1717–79); English actor-manager, managed London's Drury Lane Theatre from 1747, pioneered use of naturalistic backdrops and concealed lighting; also popular Shakespearean actor.

Gauguin, (Eugène Henri) Paul (1848–1903); French Post-Impressionist painter, abandoned 'civilization' to live and paint in Tahiti. Tremendous influence on other Post-Impressionists.

Gauss, Johann Karl Friedrich (1777–1855); German mathematician, worked out method of least squares, and theories of planetary perturbations. Did much work in all branches of mathematics including theory of numbers. Worked on terrestrial magnetism, and devised system of units.

Gay-Lussac, Joseph Louis (1778–1850); French chemist, showed different gases expand by equal amounts with increased temperature. Stated laws of combining volumes of gases. Isolated boron (jointly); showed iodine to be element.

Genghis Khan (*c*.1162–1227); tribal leader from Mongolia, named *Temujin*; conquered most of central Asia to form empire stretching from Pacific coast to River Dniepr. Took title *Genghis Khan* – 'Ruler of All Men' – 1206.

George VI (1895–1952); second son of George V of Britain, succeeded brother, EDWARD VIII, 1936. Served Royal Navy, World War I; married Lady Elizabeth Bowes-Lyon, 1923. Succeeded by ELIZABETH II.

Gershwin, George (1898–1937); American composer, originally specialized in jazz and musicals, later wrote 'serious' music with jazz flavour; *Rhapsody in Blue*, Negro opera *Porgy and Bess*.

Gibbon, Edward (1737–94); English historian, wrote *Decline and Fall of the Roman Empire* (1776–88). Became MP (1774–83);

Gauguin painted many scenes of life in Tahiti, such as this simple meal, *Le Repas*.

served as commissioner of trade and plantations.

Gide, André (1869–1951); French writer; founded magazine *La Nouvelle Revue Française* (1909); novels *Les Nourritures Terrestres* (1897), *Les Faux Monnayeurs* (1926); essays; Nobel prize for literature 1947.

Gilbert, William (1544–1603); English physician and physicist, perhaps the earliest true experimenter. Discovered magnetic dip of Earth. Made early experiments with attractive force, now known as electrostatic attraction. Had advanced ideas on structure of universe.

Giotto (di Bondone) (*c*.1266–1337); Florentine painter, first Italian artist to break with flat Byzantine tradition in favour of more naturalistic and emotional approach; magnificent religious frescoes in Florence, Padua, and Assisi.

Gladstone, William Ewart (1809–98); British Liberal statesman; four times prime minister (1868–74, 1880–5, 1886, 1892–94); tried but failed to secure home rule for Ireland.

Goddard, Robert Hutchings (1882–1945); American physicist, first to develop rocketry.

Goebbels, Joseph Paul (1897–1945); German Nazi propaganda chief; close personal friend of HITLER; committed suicide in Berlin with Hitler.

Goering, Hermann (1893–1946); German Nazi politician. Air ace, World War I; close supporter of HITLER; head of German air force, World War II; condemned for war crimes, but took poison.

Goethe, Johann Wolfgang von (1749–1832); German poet, playwright, statesman, scientist, chief minister of Weimar, 1775–88; plays *Götz von Berlichingen* (1773), *Egmont* (1788), *Torquato Tasso* (1790); *Faust* (1808–32); novels *The Sorrows of Young Werther* (1774), *Wilhelm Meister's Apprenticeship* (1796); scientific works; founder of modern German literature.

Gogol, Nikolai Vasilievich (1809–52); Russian writer; government clerk and teacher; lived in exile from 1836; comedy *The Inspector-General* (1836); novel *Dead Souls* (1842).

Goldsmith, Oliver (1728–74); Irish-born British author; worked as a book reviewer, living beyond his means; main works, poem *The Deserted Village* (1770); novel *The Vicar of Wakefield* (1766); play *She Stoops to Conquer* (1773).

Giotto's fresco of St Francis preaching to the birds.

Gordon, Charles George (1833–85); British soldier, captured Peking during Chinese rebellion, 1860; governor of Sudan, 1877–80; returned 1884 to quell Mahdi's rebellion; killed in siege of Khartoum.

Gorki, Maxim (Alexei Maximovich Peshkov; 1868–1936); Russian writer and revolutionist; in exile 1905–13, 1921–8; novels *Foma Gordeyev* (1899), *Mother* (1907); short stories; plays *The Lower Depths* (1903), *The Judge* (1924); Nizhni Novgorod now named *Gorki* for him.

Gounod Charles (1818–93); French composer and conductor, wrote *Ave Maria* based on Bach prelude; 2 operas, *Faust* and *Romeo and Juliet*.

Goya (y Lucientes), Francisco José de (1746–1828); Spanish painter and etcher; realistic style included royalty, bullfights, everyday portraits. Grim etchings, *The Disasters of War*, powerful pacifist propaganda. *La Maja Desnuda* one of most famous nudes in art.

People (contd.)

Graham, 'Billy' (William Franklin) (b. 1918); American evangelist; revivalist meetings drew huge crowds in most English-speaking countries after World War II.

Graham, Thomas (1805–69); Scottish physical chemist, studied diffusion of gases and discovered rate of diffusion inversely proportional to molecular weight. Discovered colloids, osmosis, and dialysis.

Grant, Ulysses Simpson (1822–85); American general and statesman; Union general in Civil War; Union C-in-C, 1864. Served as 18th president, 1869–77.

Graves, Robert Ranke (b. 1895); English poet, novelist, critic, son of Irish poet Alfred Percival Graves; novels include *I, Claudius* (1934), *Sergeant Lamb of the Ninth* (1940); essays; collections of poems; autobiographies; translations of Greek and Roman classics; lived in Majorca from 1929.

Gray, Thomas (1716–71); English poet; *Elegy Written in a Country Churchyard* (1751).

Greco, El (Domenicos Theotocopoulos; *c.*1541–1614); Cretan-born painter, lived and worked in Spain. Highly original style, involving vivid colours and unnatural, twisted, elongated shapes, did not always please Spanish religious hierarchy; *View of Toledo.*

Grieg, Edvard Hagerup (1843–1907); Norwegian composer, intensely nationalistic; inspired by country's folk music. Incidental music to Ibsen's *Peer Gynt, Piano Concerto in A Minor,* several songs.

Grimm, the Brothers German collectors of fairy tales (1812–15), and philologists; **Jacob** (1785–1863) and **Wilhelm** (1786–1859) began compiling the *German Dictionary* (1854); Jacob also wrote *German Grammar* (1819–37).

Gropius, Walter (1883–1969); German architect, founder and designer of Bauhaus. Industrial architecture; felt that art should subserve function. Later years in US.

Grotius, Hugo (Huig de Groot; 1583–1645); Dutch lawyer, founder of international law; jailed for opposing Calvinism; Swedish ambassador to France, 1635–45.

Gustavus II Adolphus (1594–1632); king of Sweden from 1611. Reformed government, aided by chief minister, Axel Oxenstierna; intervened in Thirty Years War, 1630; killed at Lützen.

Haber, Fritz (1868–1934); German chemist, won 1918 Nobel prize for invention of process for making ammonia cheaply by combining nitrogen and hydrogen.

Habsburg Name of family that held title of Holy Roman Emperor almost continuously 1273–1806; emperors of Austria 1806–1918. Founded by Albert, Count of Habsburg, 1153. First emperor Rudolf III. Members include CHARLES V; MARIE ANTOINETTE. Also spelt *Hapsburg*.

Hahn, Otto (1879–1968); German physical chemist, won 1914 Nobel prize for discovery of fission of uranium atoms.

Haig, Douglas, 1st Earl Haig (1861–1928), leading British general, World War I; created earl 1919.

Haile Selassie (1892–1975); king of Ethiopia 1928; emperor 1930; deposed 1974. In exile 1936–41. Original name *Ras Taffari*; regent 1916–1928.

George Frederick Handel, a prolific composer. His best known work is the oratorio *Messiah.*

Haldane, John Burdon Sanderson (1892–1964); English geneticist, estimated rate of mutation of human gene. Noted for explaining science to laymen.

Halley, Edmund (1656–1742); English astronomer, renowned for studies of comets, particularly that of 1682 (Halley's) predicting its 75-year cycle. Encouraged, financed, and published NEWTON'S *Principia* (1687). First magnetic survey of oceans; first map of global 'winds. Astronomer royal 1720–42.
Hals, Frans (*c*.1580–1666); Dutch portrait painter whose brushwork lent air of liveliness and spontaneity to faces of his sitters. *Laughing Cavalier*, one of the world's most popular paintings.
Hamilton, Alexander (1757–1804); first US treasury secretary, 1789–95; killed in duel with vice-president Aaron Burr. Trained as lawyer.
Hammarskjöld, Dag (1905–61); Swedish economist and statesman; second secretary-general of UN from 1953; killed in air crash while trying to end civil war in Congo (now Zaïre).
Hammurabi (d. 1686 BC); king of Babylon from 1728 BC; drew up code of laws, and enforced them rigidly.
Handel, George Frederick (1685–1759); German-born composer, became naturalized Briton 1726. Superb oratorios (*Messiah, Israel in Egypt*, etc.). Revered by composers such as BEETHOVEN, HAYDN, MOZART. Vast output included 27 oratorios, 41 operas, organ, orchestral (*Water Music*), and chamber music.
Hannibal (247–183 BC); Carthaginian statesman and general. In 2nd Punic War with Rome (218–201 BC) led army over Alps into Italy, winning many victories; recalled to defend Carthage; defeated at Zama, 202 BC; headed government of Carthage; exiled 196 BC; committed suicide.
Hapsburg See HABSBURG.
Hardy, Thomas (1840–1928); English novelist, poet, architect; created fictional 'Wessex'; novels include *Far from the Madding Crowd* (1874), *The Return of the Native* (1878), *Tess of the D'Urbervilles* (1891); epic play *The Dynasts* (1908).
Harvey, William (1578–1657); English physician, studied heart and blood vessels of dissected animals; discovered one-way circulation of blood.
Hastings, Warren (1732–1818); British statesman; first governor-general of India, 1773–85; impeached for cruelty and dishonesty, but acquitted after 7-year trial.
Hawthorne, Nathaniel (1804–64); American author, diplomat, customs inspector; *The Scarlet Letter* (1850); *Tanglewood Tales* (1853) for children; short stories.
Haydn, Franz Joseph (1732–1809); Austrian composer; vast output based on new symphonic form, earned him title 'Father of the Symphony'. Wrote 104 symphonies (*The Suprise, The Drum-Roll, The Clock*, etc.), 20 operas, over 80 string quartets, and sparkling oratorios.
Heath, Edward (b. 1916), first elected leader of British Conservative party, 1965; prime minister 1970–4; took Britain into European Economic Community.

Hannibal's crossing of the Alps with an entire army was an unheard of feat of courage and determination.

Heifetz, Jascha (b. 1901); Russian-born American virtuoso violinist, child prodigy during World War I. Various composers, including Walton, have written works for him.

People (contd.)

Heine, Heinrich (1797–1856); German poet and critic; poems include *The Lorelei, On Wings of Song*; *Der Salon* (art criticism, 1835–40); from 1831 in Paris; paralysed for last years of life.

Heisenberg, Werner Karl (1901-1976); German physicist, won 1932 Nobel prize for Uncertainty Principle (impossible to determine both position and momentum of any body at same time). Much work on quantum theory.

Helmholtz, Hermann Ludwig Ferdinand von (1821–94); German physicist and physiologist, invented ophthalmoscope. Proposed theory of hearing mechanism. First to measure speed of nerve impulse. Worked on theory of conservation of energy.

Hemingway, Ernest (1898–1961); American author, journalist, traveller; books based on his experiences; novels include *A Farewell to Arms* (1929), *Death in the Afternoon* (1932), *To Have and Have Not* (1937), *For Whom the Bell Tolls* (1940), *The Old Man and the Sea* (1952); short stories; Pulitzer prizewinner; Nobel prize for literature, 1954.

Henry, Joseph (1797–1878); American physicist, originally developed telegraph, discovered induction and self-induction; built electric motors.

Henry IV (1553–1610); first Bourbon King of France, leader of Huguenots and King of Navarre. Succeeded Henry III in 1589 after years of rebellion. Became Roman Catholic, but issued Edict of Nantes, giving political rights to Huguenots. Restored France's finances; assassinated.

Henry VIII (1491–1547); King of England from 1509, broke with Church of Rome in order to divorce first wife, Catherine of Aragon, and remarry so he could have son. Later marriages were to Anne Boleyn, Jane Seymour, Anne of Cleves, Catherine Howard, Catherine Parr. Ordered dissolution of monasteries.

Henry the Navigator (1394–1460); Portuguese prince, built observatory and navigation school, and pioneered study of navigation that began Age of Exploration.

Hepplewhite, George (d. 1786); English cabinet-maker; winged easy chairs with delicate, heart-shaped backs.

Hepworth, Dame Barbara (1903–75); English sculptor, work resembles HENRY MOORE's; abstract forms in wood, metal, stone.

Herodotus (*c*.484–*c*.424 BC); Greek traveller and writer, called 'the Father of History'. Recorded customs, manners, and traditions of peoples in places he visited.

Herophilus (*c*.300 BC); Greek anatomist, described sensory and motor nerves, retina of eye, liver, spleen and genital system. Named prostate gland and duodenum.

Herschel, Sir William (1792–1871); German-English astronomer, made telescopes, studied double stars, star clusters, and nebulae. Discovered Uranus.

Hertz, Heinrich Rudolph (1857–94); German physicist, confirmed usefulness of JAMES MAXWELL'S equations in electromagnetic theory. Produced electromagnetic radiation and detected its wave nature.

Hesiod (8th century BC); Greek poet; major surviving work *Works and Days*; *Theogony*; originator of didactic (instructive) verse.

Hess, (Walther Richard) Rudolf (b. 1894); German Nazi leader, close friend of ADOLF HITLER; flew to Scotland, 1941, to try to negotiate peace in World War II; jailed for life for war crimes, 1946.

Hillary, Sir Edmund (b. 1919); New Zealand explorer, one of first two men to climb Everest (1953). Reached South Pole with Commonwealth Transantarctic Expedition, 1958. Explored Himalayas 1960.

Himmler, Heinrich (1900–45); German Nazi leader; Gestapo chief from 1936; organized mass killings; captured 1945, committed suicide.

Hindenburg, Paul von (1847–1934); German general and statesman; C-in-C German armies World War I, 1916–18; president of German republic, 1925–34; made ADOLF HITLER chancellor, 1933.

Hipparchus (*c*.190–*c*.120 BC); Greek astronomer, measured size of Moon by parallax method. Made first accurate star map. First observed precession of equinoxes. Divided stars into groups according to magnitude. Devised method for calculating positions of planets.

Hippocrates (460–*c*.370 BC); Greek physician, supposed to have written 50 books, but these most likely written by members of Hippocratic school. This school believed disease to result from imbalance of vital fluids ('humours'). Hippocratic ethics are reflected in oath taken by modern doctors.

Hitler, Adolf (1889–1945); Austrian politician, became German dictator. Corporal World War I; leader National Socialist (Nazi) Party from 1920; chancellor of Germany 1933; Führer from 1934. Annexed Austria 1938. Began World War II by invading Poland, 1939. Committed suicide, 1945, in ruins of Berlin. Married Eva Braun just before death.

Hobbes, Thomas (1588–1679); English political theorist and philosopher; believed that social order should be based on human co-operation rather than ruling authority; *Leviathan* (1651).

Ho Chi Minh (1892–1969); Vietnamese statesman, original name *Nguyen Ai Quoc*; became Communist; led independence movement in Indochina; head of state of North Vietnam, 1954–69.

Hogarth, William (1699–1764); English satirical painter and engraver, specialized in 'modern moral subjects'. Exaggerated human weaknesses in series of engravings, *The Rake's Progress, Marriage à la Mode*; painting *The Shrimp Girl*.

Hohenzollern German royal family, founded in 11th century. Included kings of Prussia from 1701; Kaiser WILHELM II; kings Carol II and Michael of Romania.

Holbein, Hans ('the Younger') (*c.*1497–1543); German artist, court painter to HENRY VIII. Established reputation with illustrations for LUTHER'S Bible. Famous series of woodcuts: *Dance of Death* and *Alphabet of Death*; portrait *The Ambassadors*.

Holmes, Oliver Wendell (1809–94); American essayist and anatomist; *The Autocrat of the Breakfast-Table* (1858); other essays; novels; poems; son **Oliver Wendell Holmes Jr** (1841–1935), leading American judge.

Holst, Gustave Theodore (1874–1934); English composer, deeply influenced by English folk music. Operas include *The Perfect Fool*, and orchestral music *The Planets* suite.

Homer, legendary Greek poet; traditionally author of *The Iliad* and *The Odyssey*; lived possibly 850 BC, according to HERODOTUS.

Hood, Robin See ROBIN HOOD.

Hooke, Robert (1635–1703); English physicist, studied action of springs, and derived Hooke's law. Made microscopic observations and drawings, including those of insects, feathers, and fish scales.

Hopkins, Gerard Manley (1844–89); English poet and Jesuit priest; used compound words and 'sprung rhythm'; poems not published until 1918; had great influence.

Horace (Quintus Horatius Flaccus; 65–8 BC); Roman poet; helped by Maecenas, a rich patron; *Odes, Epodes, Epistles, Satires*; criticism.

Holbein was one of the great artists of the Northern Renaissance. This portrait is a detail from his painting *The Ambassadors.*

People (contd.)

Hounsfield, Godfrey Newbold (b. 1919); scientist and inventor of body scanner with ability to detect tumours by computer tomography; received Nobel prize for physiology and medicine for this invention in 1979.
Hoyle, Fred (b. 1915); English astronomer and writer, suggested scheme for nuclear reactions inside stars; exploding star theory of Solar System (1946). Wrote lucid *Nature of the Universe* (1952), science fiction *The Black Cloud* (1957).
Hubble, Edwin Powell (1889–1953); American astronomer, founded study of universe. Discovered that some 'nebulae', later realized to be galaxies, were outside our galaxy. Classified galaxies according to shape, calculated their real velocities. Put forward idea of expanding universe.
Hudson, Henry (d. 1611); English navigator, tried to find route to China through Arctic Ocean. Found and named Hudson River, 1609. On last voyage his mutinous crew set him and eight others adrift in Hudson Bay.
Hugo, Victor Marie (1802–85); French Romantic writer; opposed Napoleon III as emperor and spent 19 years in exile; senator 1876; plays include *Ruy Blas* (1838); novels *Notre-Dame de Paris* (1831), *Les Misérables* (1862); poems lyrical and epic; essays.
Humboldt, Friedrich Wilhelm Heinrich Alexander, Baron von (1769–1859); German naturalist and explorer, travelled in S. America, Europe, and Asia. Made important contributions to geography, meteorology, and climatology.
Hume, David (1711–76); Scottish philosopher and historian, took Berkeley's ideas (who replaced material objects with mind forms) and denied mind too. Attitude one of scepticism allowing only impressions to remain; *Treatise of Human Nature* (1739).
Huss, Jan (*c.*1370–1415); Bohemian religious reformer, foreshadowed Reformation in Europe. With followers, attacked abuses and privileges within Church; condemned for heresy and burnt at Constance.
Hutton, James (1726–97); Scottish scientist, founder of modern geology. Maintained uniformitarian principle, that there has been slow evolution of rock structure. Earlier studied medicine and chemistry, and died working on book that anticipated DARWIN's theory of evolution by 60 years.
Huxley Distinguished English family of scientists and writers: **Thomas Henry Huxley** (1825–95), zoologist, popularizer of science, spread DARWIN'S theory of evolution; invented word 'agnostic' to describe own religious beliefs. **Sir Julian Sorell Huxley** (1887–1975), biologist and writer, grandson of T.H., helped establish UNESCO (1st director-general, 1947); prominent conservationist. **Aldous Leonard Huxley** (1894–1963), author, brother of Julian, wrote witty satires of 1920s England, e.g. *Antic Hay* (1923), the brilliant science fiction satire *Brave New World* (1932), books on mysticism. **Andrew Fielding Huxley** (b. 1917), physiologist, half-brother of Julian and Aldous, shared 1963 Nobel prize for work on mechanism of nerve impulses.
Huygens, Christiaan (1629–95); Dutch physicist and astronomer, developed improved lenses for telescopes. Discovered Orion Nebula, Titan (Saturn moon), and ring round Saturn. Invented working pendulum clock.

Norwegian playright Henrik Ibsen, had a great influence as a thinker on contemporary problems.

Ibsen, Henrik (1828–1906); Norwegian dramatist; dealt with contemporary society and situations; plays include *Peer Gynt*

(1867), *A Doll's House* (1879), *The Wild Duck* (1884), *Hedda Gabler* (1890), *The Master Builder* (1892).

Thomas Jefferson, a Virginian lawyer, became the 3rd president of the United States. His 40 years of public service embodied his ideals of honesty and achievement, and he established the principle that the people, not the rulers, must decide.

Imhotep (*c.*2970 BC); Egyptian scholar, probable architect of earliest 'step pyramid'.
Ingres, Jean Auguste Dominique (1780–1867); leading French Classicist painter, pupil of DAVID. Paintings endowed with innate sensuality seen equally in nudes and historical portraits; *La Source*.
Irving, Washington (1783–1859); American author; lived in Europe, 1815–32; *Knickerbocker's History of New York* (1809); short stories, including *Rip Van Winkle* (1820).
Isabella of Castile (1451–1504); wife of FERDINAND II OF ARAGON; marriage united Spain. Financed voyage of CHRISTOPHER COLUMBUS, leading to discovery of Americas.
Ivan IV, the Terrible (1530–84); first tsar of all Russia. Became ruler 1533; assumed personal power 1546. Vicious and cruel; had many people murdered and tortured; developed religious mania; murdered eldest son, repented and became monk on deathbed.
Jackson, Glenda (b. 1936); English stage actress who took to screen and won numerous awards, including 'Oscars' for *Women in Love* (1970) and *A Touch of Class* (1973).
Jackson, 'Stonewall' Thomas Jonathan (1824–63); leading Confederate general in American Civil War. Accidentally shot by own men at Battle of Chancellorsville.
James, Henry (1843–1916); American novelist; lived in England from 1876; *The American* (1877), *What Maisie Knew* (1897), *The Turn of the Screw* (1898), *The Golden Bowl* (1904); short stories; biographies.
Jeans, Sir James Hopwood (1877–1946); English mathematician and astronomer, studied behaviour of spinning bodies, and proposed 'catastrophic' origin of Solar System.
Jefferson, Thomas (1743–1826); American lawyer, inventor, architect, and statesman. Drafted Declaration of Independence; Secretary of State 1789; president 1801–9; bought Louisiana territory from France, 1803.
Jenner, Edward (1749–1823); English physician, 'father' of immunology, developed smallpox vaccine made from cowpox germs.
Jesus Christ (*c.*4 BC–*c.*AD 29); founder of Christianity; *Jesus* Hebrew for *Saviour*, *Christ* from Greek *Christos, anointed one* or *Messiah*. Born Bethlehem, said to be miraculously conceived by mother Mary. Believed by followers to be son of God; preached Word of God and healed sick. Crucified by Pontius Pilate. Christians believe he physically rose from dead and ascended into heaven.
Jinnah, Mohammed Ali (1876–1948); led Muslim demand for independence from India, and became first governor-general of new country of Pakistan, 1947.
Joan of Arc (1412–31); French national heroine, first came to notice as peasant girl who 'heard voices'. Later led French armies and helped Dauphin to victory against English in Hundred Years War. Captured by English and burnt as witch; canonized in 1920.
John III (Jan Sobieski; 1624–96); Polish military hero, elected king 1674; defeated Turks 1683.

People (contd.)

Johnson, Lyndon Baines (1908–73); 36th president of United States. Texas schoolteacher; senator 1948; vice-president to KENNEDY 1960; succeeded as president 1963; re-elected 1964; retired 1969.

Johnson, Samuel (1709–84); English writer and lexicographer; immortalized in biography by BOSWELL; *Dictionary* (1755), *The Lives of the Poets* (1779–81); essays; poems; renowned as a wit.

Jones, Inigo (1573–1672); English architect, introduced Italian classicism into English building; banqueting house in Whitehall and Queen's House, Greenwich.

Jonson, Ben (*c*.1573–1637); English poet and dramatist; saw army service in Flanders; leader of literary circles in London; plays include *Every Man in His Humour* (1598), *Volpone* (1606), *The Alchemist* (1610).

Joule, James Prescott (1818–89); English physicist, determined accurate mechanical equivalent of heat. Discovered temperature drop of expanding gas (Joule-Thomson effect), and magnetostriction.

Joyce, James (1882–1941); Irish novelist; from 1904 lived in Zurich, Trieste, Paris; *A Portrait of the Artist as a Young Man* (1916), *Ulysses* (1922); *Finnegans Wake* (1939; full of difficult passages and invented words).

Jung, Carl Gustav (1875–1961); Swiss psychiatrist, popularized terms 'introvert' and 'extrovert'. Interpreted deeper conscious levels in terms of mythology.

Justinian I (Flavius Petrus Sabbatius Justinianus; 483–565); last great Roman emperor. Emperor of the East, 527; reconquered much of Italy from barbarians. Codified Roman law.

Juvenal (Decimus Junius Juvenalis; *c*. 60–*c*.140); Roman lawyer and satirist; attacked morals and attitudes of time.

Kafka, Franz (1883–1924); Austrian writer; three novels: *The Trial* (1925), *The Castle* (1926), *Amerika* (1927); short stories.

Kandinsky, Vassily (1866–1944); Russian painter, traditionally originator of abstract art. With Franz Marc founded *Blaue Reiter* (Blue Rider) group, Munich, pioneers of German expressionism; taught at Bauhaus school until closed by HITLER; moved to Paris.

Kant, Immanuel (1724–1804); German philosopher and author, had deep and widespread influence on 19th-century philosophy. Propounded theories in *Critique of Pure Reason* (1781), *Foundations of the Metaphysics of Ethics* (1785).

Karajan, Herbert von (b. 1908); Austrian conductor and opera producer, prominently associated with Berlin Philharmonic Orchestra, Vienna State Opera, La Scala (Milan), New York Metropolitan Opera,

Mustapha Kemal, who changed his name to Ataturk or Father of the Turks when he became president of Turkey.

Keats, John (1795–1821); English Romantic poet; studied medicine; died of tuberculosis; poems include *Endymion, Ode to a Nightingale, The Eve of St Agnes.*

Kelvin, Lord (William Thomson; 1824–1907); Scottish mathematician and physicist, developed absolute temperature scale. Worked with JOULE on Joule-Thomson effect. Invented improved electric cables and galvanometers; several navigational aids.

Kemal Atatürk (1881–1938); Turkish general and statesman; commander at Gallipoli, 1915; overthrew sultan, founded republic of Turkey, 1923; president, 1923–38; introduced sweeping reforms.

Kennedy, John Fitzgerald (1917–63); 35th and youngest president of United States, and first Roman Catholic. Took office 1961; dealt firmly with Cuban crisis 1962; assassinated.

Kepler, Johannes (1571–1630); German astronomer and mathematician, devised system of heavens based on BRAHE's observations, with planets having elliptical orbits round Sun.

Kerensky, Alexander (1881–1970); Russian revolutionary; prime minister after first revolution of 1917; overthrown by Bolsheviks; in France until 1940, then in United States.

Keynes, John Maynard, 1st Baron (1883–1946); British economist; books on money and prices have influenced all modern economists; created baron 1942.

Khrushchev, Nikita Sergeevich (1894–1971); became premier of Soviet Union 1955; denounced rule of JOSEPH STALIN. Also First Secretary of Communist party. Ousted 1964 by ALEXEI KOSYGIN and LEONID BREZHNEV.

Kierkegaard, Soren Aabye (1813–55); Danish philosopher, rejected organized religion as useless in man's personal approach to God or Truth. Works, such as *Stages on Life's Way* (1845), influenced later Existentialists.

King, Martin Luther (1929–68); American Negro clergyman and civil rights leader, advocated passive resistance in demonstrations against segregation of blacks. Nobel peace prize, 1964; assassinated Memphis, Tennessee.

Kipling, Rudyard (1865–1936); Indian-born English writer; journalist; novels *Kim* (1902), *The Light That Failed* (1891); many volumes of short stories; children's books: *The Jungle Books* (1894–5); *Just So Stories* (1901); *Stalky and Co* (1899); *Puck of Pook's Hill* (1906); much poetry.

Kissinger, Henry (b. 1923); German-born American professor of government; adviser to NIXON, 1969; Secretary of State, 1973; Nobel peace prize, 1973, for Vietnam cease-fire.

Kitchener, Horatio Herbert, 1st Earl (1850–1916); governor-general Sudan, recapturing Khartoum from Muslim fanatics; C-in-C South Africa, 1900; secretary of state for war, 1914; drowned when ship hit mine.

Knox, John (*c.*1505–72); Scottish divine, established Church of Scotland. Converted to Protestantism; exiled to Geneva and came under influence of CALVIN. After Civil War, started Presbyterianism in Scotland.

Koch, Robert (1843–1910); German bacteriologist, developed anthrax vaccine. Isolated several disease-causing bacteria, including tubercle and cholera bacilli; Nobel prize for work on tuberculosis, 1905.

Kosygin, Alexei Nikolayevich (b. 1904); premier of USSR from 1964.

Kublai Khan (1216–94); grandson of GENGHIS KHAN and greatest Mongol emperor, completed Mongol conquest of China and founded Yüan dynasty there. His empire reached to Poland and south to Vietnam.

Lafayette, Marquis de (1757–1834); French soldier and statesman, fought for colonists in American War of Independence; leader in French Revolution; joined in revolution of 1830.

Lagrange, Joseph Louis (1736–1813); Italian-French astronomer and mathematician, worked out algebraic systematization of mechanics, and laws governing motions of systems containing more than two bodies.

Lamarck, Jean Baptiste Pierre Antoine de Monet (1744–1829); French naturalist, proposed theory of evolution by inheritance of acquired characteristics.

Lamartine, Alphonse de (1790–1869); French poet, orator, and politician; *Méditations Poétiques* (1820).

People (contd.)

Lamb, Charles (1775–1834); English author; worked as a clerk; *Essays of Elia* (1823); plays; *Tales from Shakespeare* (1807), in collaboration with sister, **Mary** (1764–1847).

Langmuir, Irving (1881–1957); American chemist and inventor. Extended life of tungsten filament in electric light bulbs; developed atomic blow torch and high-vacuum tubes, later used in radios. Nobel prize for work in surface chemistry, 1932.

Lao-tze (*c.*604–531 BC); Chinese philosopher, founder of Taoism. Taught that man has lost the 'way' (*Tao*); in order to recover it and live in harmony with it, man must live simply and humbly.

Laplace, Pierre Simon (1749–1827); French astronomer and mathematician, refined work of NEWTON and LAGRANGE on motions of planetary bodies. Gave modern form to calculus.

La Salle, René Cavalier, Sieur de (1643–87); wealthy French fur trader, explored Mississippi River in 1681. Became governor of Louisiana in 1684. Shot by one of his followers after landing at remote bay in Texas.

Laue, Max Theodore Felix von (1879–1960); German physicist, Nobel prize (1914) for development of X-ray diffraction technique; enabled wavelength of X-rays to be calculated and crystal structure to be studied.

Lavoisier, Antoine Laurent (1743–94); French chemist, disproved 'phlogiston' theory, and maintained air to consist of two gases, oxygen and azote (later called nitrogen). Established law of conservation of mass. Helped devise system of chemical names.

Lawrence, David Herbert (1885–1930); English novelist and poet; influenced many other writers; novels include *The Rainbow* (1915), *Women in Love* (1920), *Lady Chatterley's Lover* (1928: banned for many years for obscenity); poems; essays; letters.

Lawrence, Ernest Orlando (1901–58); American physicist, Nobel prize for development of cyclotron, 1939.

Lawrence, Thomas Edward (1888–1935); British archaeologist, soldier, and author; helped to organize Arab revolt against Turks, World War I; sought obscurity in RAF, changing name to *T. E. Shaw*; wrote *Seven Pillars of Wisdom* (1928); *The Mint* (1955).

Anton van Leeuwenhoek, Dutch scientist who was one of the leading pioneers of microbiology.

Leakey, Louis Seymour Bazett (1903–72); British anthropologist and palaeontologist, discovered remains of early Man in East Africa, more than 1 million years older than previously believed. Also zoologist, handwriting expert.

Lear, Edward (1812–88); English book illustrator and writer of nonsense verses; specialized in bird pictures; *A Book of Nonsense* (1846) and other collections of light verse; popularized the limerick.

Le Chatelier, Henri Louis (1850–1936); French chemist, proposed principle governing changes in equilibrium. Used thermocouple to measure high temperatures; invented optical pyrometer.

Lee, Robert Edward (1807–70); American career soldier; C-in-C Confederate forces in Civil War, 1862; surrendered at Appomatox, 1865.

Leeuwenhoek, Anton van (1632–1723); Dutch biologist; observed through simple, but excellent, microscopes fine structure of many living tissues. First discovered protozoa; first described spermatozoa. Described organisms that were probably bacteria.

Leibniz, Gottfried Wilhelm, Baron von (1646–1716); German philosopher and mathematician, devised calculating mach-

David Livingstone, Scottish doctor, missionary, and explorer, died searching for source of the Nile.

ine that could add, subtract, multiply, divide. Recognized importance of binary system of numbers, and law of conservation of energy. First suggested aneroid barometer.

Leif Ericson (*c*.970–?); Viking explorer, sailed westwards in *c*.1000 and found 'Woodland' and 'Vinland', probably Newfoundland and Maryland.

Lenin, Vladimir (1870–1924); Russian revolutionary, founded Communist party (originally Bolsheviks). Exiled 1895–1917; returned to Russia to join 'February revolution'; assumed power in 'October revolution'. Became ill and lost control of government 1922. Name originally *Vladimir Ulyanov*.

Leonardo da Vinci (1452–1519); Italian artist, architect, engineer, inventor, scientist, and mathematician, epitomized 'the complete man' of Renaissance. *Mona Lisa* and *The Last Supper* fresco; advanced studies in anatomy, circulation of blood, weaponry, flying machines, submarines, meteorology, and hydraulics.

Lewis, Sinclair (1885–1951); American author and journalist; portrayed American life; novels *Main Street* (1920), *Babbitt* (1922), *Elmer Gantry* (1927); Nobel prize for literature, 1930 (first US winner).

Lie, Trygve (1896–1968); Norwegian lawyer; first secretary-general of UN, 1946–1953; resigned because of Russian opposition to his views.

Liebig, Justus von (1803–73); German chemist, helped discover organic isomers. Developed methods of organic analysis. Studied biochemistry and established that energy in living organisms is derived from fats and carbohydrates.

Lincoln, Abraham (1809–65); lawyer, became 16th president of United States, 1861; led Union through civil war; declared all slaves free, 1863; re-elected 1864; assassinated by John Wilkes Booth.

Lindberg, Charles Augustus (1902–74), American aviator; made first solo flight across Atlantic Ocean, 1927. Eldest son kidnapped and killed, 1932.

Linnaeus, Carolus (Carl von Linné; 1707–1778); Swedish botanist, established methodical classification of living things and began binomial nomenclature.

Lister, Lord Joseph (1827–1912); English surgeon, began antiseptic surgery, using carbolic acid to prevent infection.

Liszt, Franz (1811–86); Hungarian pianist and composer, arguably greatest pianist of all time. Invented tone poem; works include *Hungarian Rhapsodies*.

Livingstone, David (1813–73); Scottish missionary doctor, explored Africa. After crossing Kalahari Desert and travelling down River Zambesi, he sought sources of Congo (Zaïre) and Nile rivers. Feared lost, he was found by STANLEY (1871). Died still exploring.

Livy (Titus Livius; 59 BC–AD 17); Roman historian, spent 40 years writing history of Rome up to 9 BC, *Annals of the Roman People*. AUGUSTUS was his patron.

Lloyd George, David, 1st Earl of Dwyfor (1863–1945); British Liberal statesman. Sponsored old age pensions, 1908; coalition prime minister in World War I, 1916; resigned 1922; created peer, 1945.

Locke, John (1632–1704); English philosopher and empiricist; in *Essay Concerning Human Understanding* (1690), abjured philosophical speculation in favour of sense experience as source of knowledge.

Lockyer, Sir Joseph Norman (1836–1920); English astronomer, observed spectra of solar prominences, and shared discovery of new element with French astronomer Pierre Janssen; named it helium. Founded and edited journal *Nature*, 1869–1920.

People (contd.)

Lomonosov, Mikhail Vasilievich (1711–1765); founder of Russian science; ahead of his time with antiphlogistic and atomist views; suggested law of conservation of mass and wave theory of light; first to record freezing of mercury; first observed atmosphere of Venus (1761), some 150 years before Western scientists. Also wrote important poems, dramas, grammar (reformed Russian language); first history and first accurate map of Russia. Two centuries later, birthplace Denisovka changed name to Lomonosov; crater on Moon named after him; still largely unrecognized in West.

Longfellow, Henry Wadsworth (1807–1882); American poet; professor of modern languages, 1835–54; poems include *The Wreck of the Hesperus, The Song of Hiawatha, The Courtship of Miles Standish, Evangeline.*

A statue to the Roman emperor Marcus Aurelius.

Lorca, Federico García (1898–1936); Spanish poet and playwright; killed in Spanish Civil War; *Romancero Gitano* (1928).

Lorentz, Hendrik Antoon (1853–1928); Dutch physicist, postulated that volume of electron decreases to zero, mass increases to infinity as it reaches speed of light; 1902 Nobel prize.

Louis XIV (1638–1715); king of France from 1643, had longest reign of any European monarch. Held magnificent court at Versailles and ruled as complete autocrat. Persecution of Huguenots led 400,000 to flee country.

Louis XVI (1754–93); became king of France 1774. Country was poor and torn by class hatred. Under influence of nobility and his wife, MARIE ANTOINETTE, Louis antagonized the people. Revolution broke out 1789; Louis guillotined for treason.

Louis Philippe (1773–1850); last king of France. In 1830 rebellion placed him on throne in place of Charles X. His repressive measures led to new revolt in 1848 and he abdicated.

Lovell, Sir Alfred Charles Bernard (b. 1913); English astronomer, built 250-ft dish radio telescope at Jodrell Bank.

Lowell, Percival (1855–1916); American astronomer, studied Mars and began 'intelligent life' cult. Predicted discovery of Pluto.

Loyola, St Ignatius (*c.* 1491–1556); Basque nobleman, soldier, and theologian. After being wounded in battle, experienced religious conversion that led to his founding Society of Jesus (Jesuits).

Luther, Martin (1483–1546); German reformer, Bible scholar, and writer, initiated Protestant Reformation. Nailed 95 Theses to door of church in Wittenburg in protest at Church decadence; refused to retract at Diet of Worms and was excommunicated. Translated Bible into contemporary German; hymns and prose works.

MacArthur, Douglas (1880–1964); American general, C-in-C Allied forces, south-west Pacific, World War II; headed military government of Japan, 1945–51. C-in-C UN forces in Korea, 1950–1; dismissed for controversial statements.

Macaulay, Thomas Babington, 1st Baron Macaulay (1800–59); British his-

Mao Tse-tung united his country under Communism.

torian and statesman, wrote *History of England*, covering 1685–1702; *Lays of Ancient Rome*; essays. Barrister and MP; secretary for war, 1839–41.

MacDonald, Flora (1722–90); Scottish Jacobite; helped Prince Charles Edward to escape after Culloden, 1746.

Mach, Ernst (1838–1916); Austrian physicist, discovered sudden change in airflow over object as it nears speed of sound; speed of sound in air called Mach 1.

Machiavelli, Niccolò (1467–1527); influential Italian statesman and author, claimed in *The Prince* that all rulers should aim for welfare of state, regardless of methods. Name became byword for devious plotting.

McMillan, Edwin Mattison (b. 1907); American physicist, developed synchrocyclotron. Discovered elements neptunium and plutonium; shared Nobel chemistry prize 1951.

Macmillan, Harold (b. 1894); British Conservative statesman; prime minister 1957–63; referred to 'wind of change' in Africa, 1960.

Magellan, Ferdinand (1480–1521); Portuguese navigator, found route to Pacific Ocean round south of America. Forcing way through Magellan Strait, he entered Pacific 1520. Was killed in skirmish in Philippines. Remaining ship and 18 men completed first voyage round world.

Mahler, Gustav (1860–1911); Bohemian composer and conductor; 9 symphonies, songs. Director Vienna State Opera (1897–1907); conductor New York Philharmonic Orchestra (1908–11).

Malphighi, Marcello (1628–94); Italian physiologist, first to discover, through microscope, number of fine structures in living tissue, including blood capillaries.

Malthus, Thomas (1766–1834); British economist; believed population grew faster than food supplies.

Manet, Édouard (1832–83); French Impressionist painter, refused to exhibit with Impressionists. Everyday, somewhat sentimental, subjects – *Washing Day* – handled in oils with light, soft touch.

Mann, Thomas (1875–1955); German novelist: *Buddenbrooks* (1901), *Joseph and his Brothers* (1934–44); opposed Nazism and went into exile, 1933; American citizen, 1944; Nobel prize, 1929.

Mao Tse-tung (1893–1976); led Communists to power in China. After quarrelling with CHIANG KAI-SHEK, formed government in Yenan 1927. Assumed power 1949. *Thoughts of Mao Tse-tung* required reading in China. Helped found Chinese Communist party in 1921.

Marat, Jean Paul (1743–93); French physician and revolutionary; whipped up mob violence; leading Jacobin; stabbed in bath by CHARLOTTE CORDAY.

Marconi Marchese Guglielmo (1874–1937); Italian electrical engineer, inventor of radio; shared Nobel physics prize 1909.

Marcus Aurelius (Antoninus) (121–180); Roman emperor and philosopher, born Marcus Annius Verus. Epigrammatic *Meditations* dispensed Stoic philosophy.

Maria Theresa (1717–80); empress of Holy Roman Empire from 1740; defended right to throne in War of Austrian Succession, 1740–8; husband, Francis of Lorraine, recognized as emperor, 1748.

Marie Antoinette (1755–93); queen of France and wife of LOUIS XVI; daughter of Empress MARIA THERESA of Austria. Interfered in politics, hated by French people. Tried and guillotined for treason.

People (contd.)

Mark Antony (Marcus Antonius; *c.*83–30 BC): Roman general and supporter of JULIUS CAESAR. Shared power with Octavian (AUGUSTUS) and Lepidus as *triumvir* 43 BC; became lover of Cleopatra 41 BC; quarrelled with Octavian and defeated by him 30 BC; committed suicide.

Marlborough, Duke of (John Churchill; 1650–1722); British general, commanded English armies, War of Spanish Succession. Victories included Blenheim, Malplaquet.

Marlowe, Christopher (1564–93); Elizabethan English playwright, second only to WILLIAM SHAKESPEARE; *Doctor Faustus, Tamburlaine the Great, Edward II, The Jew of Malta*; killed in tavern brawl.

Marx, Karl Heinrich (1818–83); German philosopher, radical leader, and theorist of socialism, laid foundations of communism. With ENGELS, published *Communist Manifesto* (1848) and later wrote *Das Kapital* (1867). Doctrine of dialectical materialism revolutionized much of political thinking of 20th century. Exile in London from 1849.

Mary, Queen of Scots (1542–87); succeeded father, James V, at age of one week. In 1558 married French dauphin, later king Francis II (d. 1560). Married cousin, Lord Darnley, 1565; he was murdered 1567. Married Earl of Bothwell 1567; forced to abdicate and fled to England 1568; prisoner of Elizabeth I; executed for treason.

Masaryk Two Czech statesmen: **Tomás** (1850–1937), first president of Czechoslovakia, 1918–35. **Jan** (1886–1948), son of Tomás; foreign minister, 1945–8; opposed Communists; died either by suicide or murder.

Mascagni, Pietro (1863–1945); Italian composer and conductor, remembered only for world famous opera *Cavalleria Rusticana*.

Masefield, John (1878–1967); English poet and novelist; ran away to sea, 1891; works include many sea ballads; and novels *Sard Harker* (1924), *Dead Ned* (1938); poet laureate 1930–67; Order of Merit, 1935.

Mata Hari (1876–1917); Dutch dancer, born *Margaretha Gertrud Zelle*; executed as German spy by French.

Matisse, Henri (1869–1954); French painter and sculptor, leader of 'Fauves', used colour in art as he felt light functioned in nature; *Joy of Life* and *Large Red Interior*.

Maugham, W. Somerset (1874–1965); English novelist and playwright; master short-story writer (stories collected as *The World Over*, 1951); novels include *Of Human Bondage* (1916), *The Moon and Sixpence* (1919), *The Razor's Edge* (1944); plays include *The Constant Wife* (1927).

Maupassant, Guy de (1850–93); leading French short-story writer (*Boule de Suif*, 1880), and novelist (*Bel-Ami*, 1885).

Lorenzo de Medici was a patron of writers, artists and scientists. He was known as 'the Magnificent'.

Mauriac, François (1885–1970); French writer; verse *Les Main Jointes* (1909); novels *Le Baiser au Lépreux* (1922), *Le Fin de la Nuit* (1939); essays; plays; Nobel prize for literature 1952.

Maxwell, James Clerk (1831–79); Scottish mathematician and physicist, revolutionized fundamental physics. Developed electromagnetic theory, predicting existence of electromagnetic waves (1864); used statistical methods on kinetic theory of gases.

Mead, Margaret (1901–1979); American anthropologist, studied culture of Pacific Islands. Wrote *Coming of Age in Samoa* (1928), etc.

Mechnikov, Ilya Ilich (also known as Elie Metchnikoff; 1845–1916); Russian-French bacteriologist, shared 1908 Nobel prize for work on white blood corpuscles.

Medici Name of ruling family of Florence, Italy. Founder **Giovanni de' Medici** (1360–1429), wealthy merchant. Sons **Cosimo** (banker); **Lorenzo** ('the Magnificent'), ruler of Florence (1449–92). **Marie de Médicis** (1573–1642) married HENRY IV of France.

Meir, Golda (1898–1978); prime minister of Israel, 1970–4; born Kiev as Golda Mabovitch; brought up in United States; emigrated to Palestine 1921; minister to Moscow, 1948–9; foreign minister, 1956–65; retired; brought back to restore peace to Israeli Labour Party.

Melville, Herman (1819–91); American author; bank clerk, teacher, whaler, customs official; *Moby Dick* (1851); *Billy Budd* (1924).

Mendel, Gregor Johann (1822–84); Austrian botanist and monk, discovered principles of heredity; studied breeding of pea plants and proposed two laws of inheritance, ignored for 30 years.

Mendeleyev, Dmitri Ivanovich (1834–1907); Russian chemist, devised Periodic Table of elements, arranged according to atomic weight and valence.

Mendelssohn (-Bartholdy), (Jacob Ludwig) Felix (1809–47); German composer and conductor, child prodigy, became favourite musician of Victorian England. Works include violin concerto, oratorio *Elijah*, *Scottish* and *Italian* symphonies.

Menuhin, Yehudi (b. 1916); American violinist, made name as child prodigy; renowned for interpretations of Beethoven and Elgar.

Menzies, Sir Robert Gordon (1894–1978); Australian statesman; prime minister 1939–1941, 1949–1966; knighted 1963.

Mercator, Gerardus (Gerhard Kremer; 1512–94); Flemish geographer, made first cylindrical projection map of world to show round surface on flat paper.

Metternich, Prince Clemens von (1773–1859); Austrian foreign minister, 1809–48; tried to keep *status quo* in Europe and resisted change; resigned after revolution of 1848; lived in retirement.

Michelangelo (Buonarroti) (1475–1564); Italian sculptor, painter, and poet, one of greatest figures of Renaissance. Covered vast ceiling of Sistine Chapel with awesome Biblical scenes. Other masterpieces include sculpture (*Pietà* in Rome), huge statues *David*, *Moses*. Appointed chief architect of St Peter's, Rome (1547).

Michelson, Albert Abraham (1852–1931); German-born American physicist, won 1907 Nobel prize for work in optics. Devised interferometer, and made first accurate measurement of star's diameter. With Edward Williams Morley, conducted classic experiment showing no measurable motion of Earth through ether. Worked on accurate measurement of speed of light. Suggested use of red line of cadmium spectrum as new standard of length (adopted 1925).

Mies van der Rohe, Ludwig (1886–1969); German architect, pioneered design of glass-walled skyscrapers. Director of Bauhaus (1930–3); emigrated to US when HITLER came to power.

Mill, John Stuart (1806–73); English philosopher and economist, convinced Utilitarian; advanced theories in widely studied *Principles of Political Economy* (1848).

Dmitri Ivanovich Mendeleyev, the Russian chemist who devised the Periodic Table of Elements.

People (contd.)

Milne, Alan Alexander (1882–1956); English novelist and playwright; created the *Pooh* books for children.
Milton, John (1608–74); English poet, classical scholar, and a staunch Puritan; Latin secretary under Commonwealth; became blind 1652; major poems: *Paradise Lost* (1667), *Paradise Regained* (1671); *Samson Agonistes* (1671); many political pamphlets.
Miró, Joán (b. 1893); Spanish painter, with Dali pioneered Surrealism. Free style and bright colours; murals of UNESCO building, Paris.
Mohammed See MUHAMMAD.
Molière (Jean Baptist Poquelin; 1622–1673); French dramatist; became an actor, 1643; plays include *Tartuffe* (1664), *Le Misanthrope* (1666), *Le Bourgeois Gentilhomme* (1670), *Le Malarde Imaginaire* (1673).
Monet, Claude (1840–1926); French Impressionist painter; open-air subjects – *Rouen Cathedral* – characterized by special lighting effects achieved by use of broken colour.
Montaigne, Michel de (1533–92); French writer; created the essay; strongly influenced French philosophers.
Montesquieu, Baron de (Charles Louis de Secondat; 1689–1755); French philosopher; wrote *The Spirit of Laws* (1748).
Montessori, Maria (1870–1952): the first woman medical graduate of Rome University, she became a famous educator. Her teaching methods of 'free discipline', where children move freely from task to task in the classroom, using simple but stimulating apparatus, apply to children of 3–10 years old and are outlined in the two handbooks she wrote.
Montezuma II (1466–1520); last Aztec emperor of Mexico, surrendered to Spanish adventurer CORTÉS; killed by stone while pacifying mob.
Montgolfier French brothers who invented first balloons capable of carrying men into air. First manned flight 1783. **Joseph Michel** (1740–1810) and **Jacques Étienne** (1745–99), born Vidalon-lez-Annonay.
Montgomery, Bernard Law, 1st Viscount (1887–1976); commanded British Eighth

Monet: *Lady with Umbrella* (Jeu de Paume, Paris). Only impressionist fully recognized in own time.

Army, 1942; spearheaded Normandy invasion, 1944. Victories included Battle of Alamein, 1942.
Moore, Henry (b. 1898); English sculptor, works in stone, bronze, and wood; advocate of direct carving. Massive figures, often reclining, decorate public buildings worldwide.
More, Sir Thomas (1478–1535); English lawyer, statesman, and scholar, became Lord Chancellor under HENRY VIII. After king's divorce, More refused to recognize him as head of Church and was executed for treason. Wrote *Utopia*, describing ideal political state.
Morgan, Sir Henry (*c.*1635–88); Welsh pirate, arrested 1672, pardoned and made lieutenant-governor of Jamaica, 1672–83.
Morris, William (1834–96); English artist, poet, printer, and designer, one of Pre-Raphaelite Brotherhood. Founded firm of furniture-makers, and Kelmscott Press (high-class printers and publishers) to revive fine craftsmanship. Writings, e.g. *A Dream of John Ball*, reflect strong socialist views.
Mountbatten, Lord Louis (1900–1979);

formerly prince; related to British royal family; distinguished naval career; Supreme Allied Commander, South-East Asia, 1943–1946; last viceroy of India, 1947; first governor-general, 1947–8; created Earl Mountbatten, 1947. Murdered by IRA.

Mozart, Wolfgang Amadeus (1756–91); Austrian composer, child prodigy, became one of world's greatest musicians. Mastery of melody, phrasing and rhythm unique. Wrote over 40 symphonies (*Linz, Prague, Jupiter*, etc.), 21 piano concertos, several operas (*The Marriage of Figaro, Don Giovanni, The Magic Flute*, etc.), 24 string quartets, etc. Died in poverty.

Muhammad (*c.*570–632); Arab prophet and founder of Islam. With fanatical followers, conquered Mecca and laid foundations of Islamic Empire. Sayings revealed to him by Allah (God) embodied in *Koran*.

Müller, Paul (1899–1965); Swiss chemist, Nobel medicine and physiology prize (1948) for discovery of insecticidal use of DDT.

Musset, Alfred de (1810–57); French writer, lover of GEORGE SAND; poems *Tales of Spain and Italy* (1830); plays collected in *Comédies et Proverbes* (1840).

Moore: ***Madonna and Child*** (Tate Gallery).

Mussolini, Benito (1883–1945); dictator of Italy from 1922. At first schoolmaster and journalist; founded Fascist party, 1919; conquered Ethiopia (Abyssinia), 1935–6; took Italy into World War II in support of ADOLF HITLER, 1940; overthrown 1943; shot by resistance fighters.

Mussorgski, Modest Petrovich (1839–1881); Russian composer, one of 'The Five' and, like BORODIN, not a professional musician. Realistic approach evident in opera *Boris Godunov*, orchestral pieces *Night on the Bare Mountain* and *Pictures from an Exhibition*.

Nansen, Fridtjof (1861–1930); Norwegian zoologist and statesman, made first crossing of Greenland, 1888, and tried to reach North Pole, 1895. Later Norway's ambassador to London; won Nobel peace prize 1922.

Napier, John (1550–1617); Scottish mathematician, invented logarithms and decimal point.

Napoleon I (1769–1821); Corsican soldier, made himself emperor of French 1804, already holding supreme power. Conquered Italy, Spain, Egypt, Netherlands, most of central Europe. Invasion of Russia failed (1812). Defeated Leipzig (1813), abdicated 1814. Returned to power 1815, defeated at Waterloo, exiled to St Helena. Family name BONAPARTE.

Nash, Ogden (1902–71); American writer of humorous verse; *Hard Lines* (1931).

Nasser, Gamal Abdel (1918–70); Egyptian revolutionary and army officer; helped depose King Farouk, 1952; president from 1956; tried to modernize country; nationalized Suez Canal, 1956.

Nehru, Jawahalal (1889–1964); Indian statesman, worked for Indian independence, 1919–47; India's first prime minister, 1947–64.

Nelson, Horatio (1758–1805); British naval hero, lost eye and arm in battle; destroyed French fleet at Battle of Nile, 1798; won Battle of Copenhagen, 1801; destroyed another French fleet at Trafalgar, 1805, dying in moment of victory. Created viscount, 1801; liaison with Emma, Lady Hamilton, a public scandal.

Nero (Nero Claudius Drusus Germanicus; 37–68); Roman emperor. Feared plots, and had many people murdered, including

People (contd.)

mother, Agrippina. Undeservedly vain of powers as singer and actor. Committed suicide when army revolted.

Newton, Sir Isaac (1642–1727); English scientist, made fundamental and far-reaching contributions to physics, mathematics, and astonomy. In 18 months (1665–7) he derived law of universal gravitation from his laws of motion, he discovered secrets of light and colour (particulate theory of light), and invented calculus. Thanks largely to HALLEY, works published in famous *Mathematical Principles of Natural Philosophy* (1687), known as *Principia*.

Nicholas II (1868–1918); last tsar of Russia; succeeded 1894; corruption of ministers led to revolutions in 1905, 1917; abdicated; killed by Communists 1918.

Niemeyer, Oscar (b. 1907); Brazilian architect, planned city of Brasília.

Nietzche, Friedrich Wilhelm (1844–1900); German philosopher, claimed that driving force of human endeavour was thirst for power. Elaborated ideas in *Thus Spake Zarathustra* (1880).

Nightingale, Florence (1820–1910); English reformer, became nurse; against much opposition organized sanitary barrack hospitals in Crimean War (1854–6); saving thousands of lives; known as 'lady with the lamp'. System adopted worldwide.

Nijinsky, Vaslav (1890–1950); Russian ballet dancer, danced with DIAGHILEV'S Ballets Russes; grace, strength, and prodigious leaps revitalized male dancing in western Europe; insanity cut short career in 1917.

Nixon, Richard Milhous (b. 1913); vice-president of United States, 1953–61; 37th president, 1969–74; resigned to avoid impeachment over Watergate conspiracy scandal.

Nobel, Alfred Bernhard (1833–96); Swedish inventor of dynamite and blasting gelatine, left his fortune to establish annual prizes for peace, literature, physics, chemistry, and physiology and medicine.

Oates, Titus (1649–1705); English conspirator; invented 'Popish plot' to assassinate Charles II; gave much false evidence; flogged and jailed for perjury.

O'Casey, Sean (1880–1964); Irish playwright and major influence in Irish literature; plays *Shadow of a Gunman* (1923), *Juno and the Paycock* (1924), *The Plough and the Stars* (1926); autobiography.

Oersted, Hans Christian (1777–1851); Danish physicist, first showed connection between electricity and magnetism.

Offenbach, Jacques (1819–80); German-born French composer, wrote more than 90 popular light operas: *Orpheus in the Underworld, La Belle Hélène*, etc.; one serious opera, *Tales of Hoffman*.

O'Higgins, Bernardo (1778–1842); Chilean patriot, son of Irish father, led Chilean rebellion against Spaniards, 1814; fled to Argentina; with SAN MARTÍN won victory, 1817; became dictator of Chile; forced to resign, 1823.

Oistrakh, David (1908–74); Russian violinist and conductor, toured Western cities from 1950s. Russian composers such as PROKOFIEV composed for him. Son **Igor Oistrakh** (b. 1931) also violin virtuoso.

Olivier, Laurence Kerr, Lord Olivier of Brighton (b. 1907); English actor, director, and theatre manager. Director of National Theatre; also made outstanding contribution to British acting at Old Vic; directed and starred in films *Henry V, Hamlet, Richard III*.

Tsar Nicholas II of Russia and his family aboard their yacht. During the revolution they were captured and killed by the Bolsheviks.

Omar Khayyám (d. *c.*1123); Persian poet, astronomer, mathematician; poem the *Rubáiyát* ('Collection of Quatrains') freely translated by FITZGERALD (1859).
O'Neill, Eugene (1888–1953); American playwright; *Emperor Jones* (1921), *Mourning Becomes Electra* (1931), *Long Day's Journey into Night* (1957); Pulitzer prize-winner; Nobel prize for literature 1936.
Oppenheimer, J. Robert (1904–67); American physicist, after early work on subatomic particles, headed development of atomic bomb at Los Alamos; opposed development of hydrogen bomb. Controversially labelled 'not a good security risk' by Atomic Energy Commission as 'McCarthyism' swept US.
Orwell, George (Eric Arthur Blair; 1903–1950); English satirical novelist, b. Bengal. Independent radical thinker; fought in Spanish Civil War; main works: *The Road to Wigan Pier* (1937), *Animal Farm* (1945), *Nineteen Eighty-Four* (1949).
Osborne, John (b. 1929); British playwright, actor, and producer; plays include *Look Back in Anger* (1956); *The Entertainer* (1957); first 'angry young man'.
Ovid (Publius Ovidius Naso; 43 BC–*c.* AD 17); Roman poet; narrative poem *Metamorphoses*; elegies; love poems.
Owen, Robert (1771–1858); Welsh social reformer, established in textile mills at New Lanark, Scotland, model co-operative industrial community with ideal housing and working conditions.
Paderewski, Ignace Jan (1860–1941); Polish virtuoso pianist and statesman, became Poland's first prime minister (1919). Works include *Minuet in G*.
Paganini, Niccolo (1782–1840); Italian violinist and composer, possibly greatest of all violinists; 24 caprices for solo violin.
Paine, Thomas (1737–1809); British-born agitator and writer; wrote *Common Sense* (1776) supporting American colonists; *Rights of Man* (1792), supporting French Revolution; fought in American War of Independence; member of French National Convention 1792–3; died in poverty in America.
Palestrina, Giovanni Pierluigi da (*c.* 1525–94); Italian composer, hailed as 'Prince of Music'. Set rigid standards for composition of sacred music in which his

Nijinsky dancing in *Le Spectre de la Rose* (1911).

contrapuntal skill for unaccompanied voices was of highest order.
Palladio, Andrea (1518–80); Italian architect, pioneered modern Italian architecture.
Palmerston, Viscount (Henry John Temple; 1784–1865); British statesman. War secretary, 1809–28; foreign secretary 1830–41, 1846–51; home secretary 1853–1855; prime minister 1855–7, 1859–65. Known for aggressive policies.
Pankhurst, Emmeline (1858–1928); English suffragette, helped obtain vote for British women. With daughters Christabel and Sylvia, encouraged militant action by followers, including arson, chaining themselves to railings, and hunger strikes during imprisonment.
Pascal, Blaise (1623–62); French scientist, philosopher, and writer. Wrote treatise on conic sections at 16, invented calculating machine at 18. Founded, with FERMAT, theory of probability, formulated laws of hydraulics (Pascal's Law relating to pressures in vessel) and atmospheric pressure. Became Jansenist monk (1654), wrote *Provincial Letters* (1656–7), brilliant reply to Jesuits in defence of Jansenism.

People (contd.)

Pasternak, Boris Leonidovich (1890–1960); Russian writer; main novel *Doctor Zhivago* (1957); declined 1958 Nobel prize for literature because of political pressure.

Pasteur, Louis (1822–95); French chemist, established bacteriology as science; devised method of gentle heating (pasteurization) to kill micro-organisms in wine and beer; showed air to contain spores of living organisms; proposed germ theory of disease; developed inoculation of animals against anthrax and rabies.

Patrick, St (*c*.385–461); patron saint of Ireland; born in Wales and sold into slavery in Ireland. After escaping, returned and evangelized Irish.

Patton, George Smith (1885–1945); American general World War II; reckless and outspoken.

Paul, St (d. *c*.AD 64); Christian missionary and apostle, originally Saul, Jewish nationalist and Roman citizen who persecuted Christians. After sudden conversion to Christianity, made many missionary journeys in Mediterranean regions. Author of major epistles in New Testament.

Pauli, Wolfgang (1900–58); Austrian-American physicist, 1945 Nobel prize for earlier discoveries about structure and nature of atoms; exclusion principle of quantum theory, 1925. Postulated existence of new particle (neutrino) in 1931 (detected 1956).

Pauling, Linus Carl (b. 1901); American chemist, revolutionized ideas of structure of molecules and nature of chemical bonds; 1954 Nobel chemistry prize and 1963 Nobel peace prize for work towards nuclear disarmament.

Pavlov, Ivan Petrovich (1849–1936); Russian physiologist, established idea of conditioned reflexes ('Pavlov's dogs'); 1904 Nobel prize for discovery of details of digestion and establishing importance of autonomic system.

Pavlova, Anna Matveyevna (1885–1931); Russian ballerina, danced for DIAGHILEV'S Ballets Russes in Paris. Fokine created role of *The Dying Swan* for her.

Peel, Sir Robert (1788–1850); British statesman, prime minister 1834, 1841–6; founded London police force, 1829.

A statue by the Spanish artist Pablo Picasso, outside the Chicago Civic Centre.

Penn, William (1644–1718); English Quaker leader, founder of Pennsylvania and Philadelphia.

Pepys, Samuel (1633–1703); English civil servant, organizer of modern British naval service; famous for his *Diary* (1660–9); secretary to the Admiralty.

Pericles (*c*.495–429 BC); Athenian statesman, led government of Athens 460–430 BC; known as 'father of democracy'.

Perón, Juan Domingo (1895–1974); twice president of Argentina; in power 1946–55, supported by wife **Eva** (1919–52); exiled; again president, 1973–4; succeeded by second wife, **Maria Estela (Isabel)**, who was vice-president.

Pétain, Henri Philippe (1856–1951); French soldier and statesman; hero of World War I for defence of Verdun; recalled to be premier, 1940, on fall of France in World War II; headed Vichy government, 1940–4; tried and jailed for treason, 1945.

Peter I, the Great (1672–1725); tsar of Russia 1689. Toured western Europe, then modernized Russia. Defeated CHARLES XII of Sweden, 1709. Founded St Petersburg (Leningrad). Enforced law harshly.

Petrarch (Francesco Petrarcha; 1304–74); Italian scholar and poet; perfected the sonnet; *Rime* (poems in Italian); many works in Latin; rediscovered the classics.

Petrie, Sir Flinders (1853–1942); British Egyptologist, excavated many Egyptian sites, also sites in Palestine and Stonehenge. Professor of Egyptology, London, 1892–1933.

Phidias (*c.*500–432 BC); Greek sculptor and architect, constructed Parthenon and gold and ivory *Athene; Zeus*, at Olympia.

Philip, Prince (b. 1921); consort of ELIZABETH II. Son of Prince Andrew of Greece; brought up in England. Served Royal Navy, 1939–50; renounced Greek titles 1947 to marry Elizabeth; created Duke of Edinburgh.

Picasso, Pablo (1881–1974); Spanish artist, strongly influenced many 20th-century movements in art. With BRAQUE, pioneered Cubism. Later turned to pottery and sculpture.

Pindar (*c.*522–443 BC); Greek lyric poet; invented Pindaric ode; many odes and fragments of other poems survive.

Pitt, William, the Elder. See CHATHAM.

Pitt, William, the Younger (1759–1806); British statesman; son of EARL OF CHATHAM. Prime minister 1783–1801, 1804–6; organized opposition to NAPOLEON I; introduced income tax, 1799.

Pizarro, Francisco (*c.*1474–1541); Spanish *conquistador*, settled in Panama 1513; visited Peru 1524; conquered it with 180 men, 1528. Assassinated.

Planck, Max Karl Ernst Ludwig (1858–1947); German physicist, revolutionized physics with quantum theory; 1918 Nobel prize.

Plantagenet Surname of House of Anjou, which ruled England 1154–1399. Founded by Geoffrey, Count of Anjou, who married Matilda, daughter of Henry I of England. First Plantagenet king Henry II; last Richard II. After Richard, split into Houses of York and Lancaster.

Plato (*c.*427–347 BC); Greek philosopher, pupil of SOCRATES and teacher of ARISTOTLE. Teachings contained in written *Dialogues*: *Republic* deals with justice and ideal statesman; *Apology* describes trial of Socrates. Platonism, stressing idea of the good rather than material appearances, has influenced philosophic thought ever since.

Pliny Two Roman authors. **Pliny the Elder** (Gaius Plinius Secondus; 23–79) wrote on history and science; **Pliny the Younger** (Gaius Plinius Caecilius Secondus; *c.*61–*c.*113), his nephew, wrote *Letters* recording life of Rome.

Plutarch (*c.*46–*c.*120); Greek biographer and teacher, wrote *Parallel Lives of Illustrious Greeks and Romans*, important historical source work.

Poe, Edgar Allan (1809–49); American writer, with fascination for morbid and mysterious. Poetry *The Raven and Other Poems* (1845); novels *The Murders in the Rue Morgue* (1841); stories *Tales of the Grotesque and Arabesque* (1840).

Polo, Marco (*c.*1254–1324); Venetian merchant, travelled with father and uncle to court of emperor KUBLAI KHAN in Cathay

This detail from a 14th-century map of Asia shows Marco Polo on one of his long trading journeys.

People (contd.)

(China). Served as travelling envoy for KUBLAI KHAN, returning to Venice 1295, after 24-year absence, a wealthy man.

Pompey the Great (Gnaeus Pompeius Magnus; 106–48 BC); Roman general and statesman, cleared the Mediterranean of pirates; member of First Triumvirate with JULIUS CAESAR and Crassus (60 BC); opposed Caesar 48 BC; defeated; fled to Egypt, where he was murdered.

Pope, Alexander (1688–1744); English poet and satirist, noted for polished heroic couplets; poems include *The Rape of the Lock* (1712), *Dunciad* (1728); *Essay on Man* (1733–4).

Porter, Cole (1893–1964); American jazz and light music composer; hits included *Night and Day*.

Pound, Ezra (1885–1972); American poet; influenced many other poets; lived mostly in London, Paris, Italy; charged with treason after radio broadcasts during World War II on behalf of Italians; in mental hospital 1945–58.

Praxiteles (4th cent. BC); Athenian sculptor, only surviving work marble statue of *Hermes with the Infant Dionysius*. Copies of *Aphrodite of Cnidus* and other works show superb technique of flowing lines and balanced light and shadow.

Priestly, Joseph (1733–1804); English chemist and religious thinker; discoverer of oxygen, ammonia, carbon monoxide, sulphur dioxide, hydrogen chloride, oxides of nitrogen. Accepted 'phlogiston' theory, and discovered 'dephlogisticated air', later called oxygen by LAVOISIER; shared discovery with SCHEELE. One of founders of Unitarian Society. Persecuted for political views; lived in US after 1794.

Prokofiev, Sergei Sergeyevich (1891–1953); Russian composer and pianist, broke new ground with satirical innovations in rhythm and harmony. Children's musical fairytale *Peter and the Wolf*; ballet *Romeo and Juliet*.

Proust, Marcel (1871–1922); French novelist; introspective, asthmatic; wrote seven-volume masterpiece *À la Recherche du Temps Perdu* (*Remembrance of Things Past*, 1913–27).

Ptolemy (*c.* AD 100); Greek astronomer, proposed Earth-centred idea of Universe. Also studied optics and geography.

A 16th-century print showing Ptolemy being guided by the Muse of Astronomy in the use of a quadrant.

Puccini, Giacomo (1858–1924); Italian operatic composer; gift for theatrical effect made works immensely popular; *La Bohème*, *Tosca*, *Madame Butterfly*.

Purcell, Henry (1659–95); English composer and organist, widely regarded as greatest English musical figure. Wrote many beautiful songs, opera *Dido and Aeneas*, much unsurpassed stage music.

Pushkin, Alexandr Sergeyevich (1799–1837); Russian writer and civil servant; play *Boris Godunov* (1826); narrative poems: *Eugene Onegin* (1823–31), *The Bronze Horseman* (1833); novels *The Queen of Spades* (1834); mortally wounded in duel.

Pythagoras (*c.*582–*c.*497 BC); Greek philosopher, founder of Pythagorean cult. Discovered relationship between length of vibrating string and pitch of note emitted. Calculated theorem of right-angled triangles.

Quisling, Vidkun Abraham Lauritz (1887–1945); Norwegian politician and traitor, collaborated with German invaders of Norway, 1940–5; executed for treason at liberation.

Rabelais, François (*c.*1494–1553); French satirist and monk; wrote *Pantagruel* (1533), *Gargantua* (1535), both full of broad, racy 'Rabelaisian' humour.

Rachmaninov, Sergei Vasilyevich (1873–1943); Russian composer and pianist, lived in US after Russian Revolution. *Rhapsody on a Theme by Paganini, Prelude in C♯ Minor*, piano concertos.

Racine, Jean Baptiste (1639–99); French playwright, produced seven tragic masterpieces, including *Phèdre* (1677).

Raleigh, Sir Walter (*c.*1552–1618); English soldier and courtier, established first colony in Virginia. Explored Guiana region of S. America. Jailed for treason by James I, he was freed to find gold, but failed. James had him executed.

Ramsay, Sir William (1852–1916); Scottish chemist, discovered argon (with RAYLEIGH), helium, neon, krypton, and xenon, and calculated atomic weight of radon; 1904 Nobel prize.

Ranke, Leopold von (1795–1886); German historian, founded modern objective method of writing history based on research rather than legend or tradition. Professor of history, Berlin, 1825–71.

Raphael (Raffaello Sanzio; 1483–1520); Italian painter, influenced by work of LEONARDO and MICHELANGELO, painted numerous Madonnas with soft colouring and outline that went perfectly with their dignified pose; *School of Athens* fresco in papal apartments.

Rasputin, Grigori Yefimovich (1871–1916); Russian monk and mystic; gained influence over family of Tsar Nicholas II; murdered by Russian nobles.

Ravel, Maurice (1875–1937); French composer; logical, clear-cut approach to music set new standards in piano composition and orchestration. Works include *Bolero, Le Tombeau de Couperin*, suite *Mother Goose*, and ballet *Daphnis and Chloë*.

Rayleigh, Lord (John William Strutt; 1842–1919); English physicist, 1904 Nobel prize for contribution towards discovery of argon in air; studied wave motions of all types.

Rembrandt (Harmensz van Rijn) (1606–69); Dutch artist, master of light, colour, and mood, particularly in portraiture; *The Night Watch, The Anatomy Lesson*, many self-portraits and fine etchings.

Renoir, Pierre Auguste (1841–1919); French Impressionist painter; pure colour and subtle lighting used mainly for female nude; painted about 6,000 pictures.

Revere, Paul (1735–1818); American silversmith and patriot; rode from Boston to Lexington to warn of British troop movements, 1755.

Rhodes, Cecil John (1853–1902); British statesman, made fortune from diamonds in South Africa, and became premier of Cape Colony, 1890. Masterminded white settlement of Rhodesia, 1890–5. Disgraced over Jameson Raid on Transvaal, 1896.

Ribbentrop, Joachim von (1893–1946); German Nazi leader, ambassador to Britain, 1936–8; foreign minister, 1939–45; executed as war criminal.

Richelieu, Cardinal (Armand Jean du Plessis; 1585–1642); chief minister of Louis XIII, 1624–42, and virtual ruler of France; cardinal from 1622; broke power of Huguenots and curbed that of nobles.

Riemenschneider, Tilman (*c.*1460–1531); German sculptor, leader of late Gothic style, remembered mainly for superbly carved church decorations.

Rimsky-Korsakov, Nikolai Andreyevich

A sketch by Rembrandt of his sleeping wife.

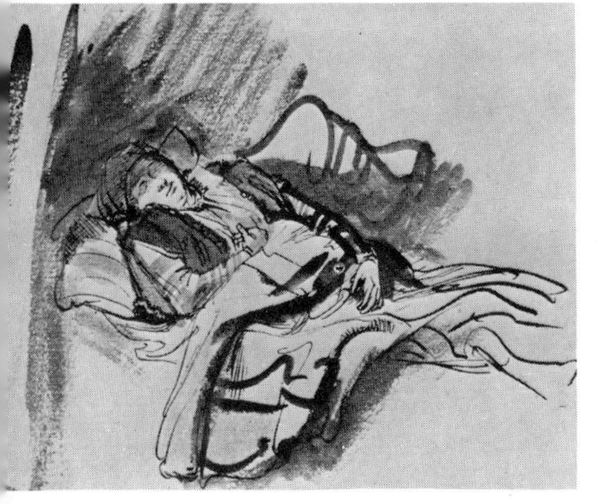

People (contd.)

(1844–1908); Russian composer, one of 'The Five' with BORODIN, MUSSORGSKY, etc. Works include *Flight of the Bumblebee*, suite *Scheherazade*, opera *The Golden Cockerel*.

Robert I, the Bruce (1274–1329); had himself crowned king of Scotland in 1306, when throne was vacant. After many defeats in wars with English, finally won resounding victory at Bannockburn (1314).

Robespierre, Maximilien (1758–94); French lawyer and revolutionary; leader of Jacobins; voted for death of LOUIS XVI; supported Reign of Terror, but himself fell victim to it.

Robin Hood (*c.*1200s); legendary English folk-hero; may have basis in fact.

Rob Roy (Robert MacGregor; 1671–1734); Scottish Highland outlaw and cattle thief; captured by English but pardoned, 1727.

Rockefeller Family of American businessmen and philanthropists; **John Davison** (1839–1937) became world's richest man through oil; began Rockefeller Foundation; **Nelson Aldrich** (1908–1979); became US vice-president to GERALD FORD, 1974.

Rodgers, Richard (b. 1902); American composer of musicals; partnership with Oscar Hammerstein yielded such hits as *The King and I* and *The Sound of Music*.

Rodin, Auguste (1840–1917); French sculptor, worked in bronze and marble; *The Thinker, The Kiss*.

Roentgen, Wilhelm Konrad (1845–1923); German physicist; 1901 Nobel prize for discovery of X-rays.

Romanov Name of Russian dynasty, descended from German nobleman. Romanovs were tsars of Russia 1613–1730 in direct male line, to 1917 in female line. Tsars included PETER I, THE GREAT; NICHOLAS II.

Rommel, Erwin (1891–1944); German field-marshal; commanded Afrika Korps World War II, 1941–3; commanded army in Normandy, 1944; ordered to commit suicide for opposing ADOLF HITLER.

Ronsard, Pierre de (1524–85); French lyric poet; leader of *La Pléide*, new poetic movement following the classics.

Roosevelt, Franklin Delano (1884–1962); 32nd president of United States,

Rousseau's paintings are free from formal restrictions.

1933–45; elected for four terms. Began 'New Deal' reforms to help end 'Great Depression'; led country through World War II; helped draft Atlantic Charter, 1941.

Ross, Sir Ronald (1857–1932); English physician, showed that malarial parasite is carried by mosquito; 1902 Nobel prize.

Rossetti (English brother and sister of Italian parentage): **Dante Gabriel** (1828–82); poet and painter, helped found Pre-Raphaelite Brotherhood (1848). **Christina Georgina** (1830–94); short lyric poems, especially for children.

Rossini, Gioacchino Antonio (1792–1868); Italian composer, mainly operatic; vigour, humour, and gift for melody ensured immediate success of his operas: *The Barber of Seville, La Cenerentola*; also wrote lovely *Stabat Mater* and 15 cantatas.

Rothschild Jewish family of bankers. Founder **Mayer Amschel** (1743–1812), in Frankfurt-am-Main; his five sons opened banks in London, Paris, Vienna, Naples. **Lionel Walter** (1858–1937), distinguished zoologist; **Nathaniel**, third baron (b. 1910), biologist and bomb-disposal expert.

Rousseau, Henri 'Douanier' (1844–1910); French 'primitive' painter who worked as a customs official. No formal art training. Best known for fantasy paintings.

Rousseau, Jean Jacques (1712–78); French writer, philosopher, composer; champion of liberty;. works include novel *Émile* (1762), *The Social Contract* (1762), opera *Les Muses Galantes* (1747), autobiography *Confessions* (1784).

Rubens, Sir Peter Paul (1577–1640); Flemish painter commissioned by several European courts. Vast output only maintained by establishing 'workshop' in which other artists were employed. Rich, sensuous colours and textures characterized his paintings; masterpiece, triptych *Elevation of the Cross* (Antwerp Cathedral). Successful diplomat, knighted by Charles I.

Ruskin, John (1819–1900); English art critic, reformer, philanthropist; *Modern Painters* (1843–60), *Seven Lamps of Architecture* (1849), *Stones of Venice* (1851–53), *Sesame and Lilies* (1865); seeker of beauty in all things, profoundly influenced contemporaries.

Russell, Bertrand, third Earl Russell (1872–1970); English mathematician, philosopher; pacifist, social reformer; *Principles of Mathematics* (1903), *The ABC of Relativity* (1925), *History of Western Philosophy* (1945); Nobel prize for literature 1950.

Rutherford, Ernest, Baron Rutherford of Nelson (1871–1937); New Zealand-born British physicist, first to 'split' atom, 1919. Named and studied alpha- and beta-rays, and discovered gamma-rays. Studied radioactive decay, discovered half-life and proposed idea of isotopes. Discovered nature of alpha-particles, and, using them, evolved theory of nuclear atom for which he received 1914 Nobel chemistry prize.

Saint-Saëns, (Charles) Camille (1835–1921); French composer; opera *Samson & Delilah*, orchestral pieces *Danse Macabre* and *Carnival of the Animals*.

Sand, George (Amandine Aurore Lucie Dupin, Baronne Dudevant; 1804–76); French novelist; mistress of Alfred de Musset and CHOPIN; pioneer of 'women's lib'; novels *Indiana* (1831), *The Miller of Angibault* (1845).

San Martín, José de (1778–1850); Argentinian general, great leader in cause of S. America's struggle for independence against Spain.

Sappho (*c*.600 BC); Greek lyric poet; she wrote nine books of poems, of which one ode survives; headed religious cult.

Sargent, Sir (Harold) Malcolm (1895–1967); British conductor and organist, largely responsible for success of Promenade concerts as conductor-in-chief.

Sartre, Jean-Paul (b. 1905); French philosopher and novelist, leader of Existentialist movement, claiming that man creates a meaning for his existence by taking responsibility for own destiny.

Scarlatti, Alessandro (1659–1725); Italian composer, helped to develop Italian opera, wrote much church music. Son **(Giuseppe) Domenico** (1685–1757), harpsichord virtuoso, composed about 600 harpsichord sonatas.

Scheele, Karl Wilhelm (1742–86); Swedish chemist, prepared and discovered remarkable number of new substances, including several acids, inorganic gases, chlorine (did not recognize it as element), manganese, barium, tungsten, nitrogen, and, most important of all, oxygen, but did not carry work far enough (in case of oxygen, published too late) and others usually got credit.

Schiller, Friedrich von (1759–1805); German poet and playwright; army surgeon, later professor of literature; plays: *Wallenstein* (1799), *Maria Stuart* (1800), *Wilhelm Tell* (1804); books on history and art.

Schliemann, Heinrich (1822–90); German archaeologist, discovered remains of ancient Troy; also ancient Mycenae. Born poor, made fortune as trader; retiring in 1863 to study archaeology. Spoke 13 languages.

Schopenhauer, Arthur (1788–1860); German philosopher, combined German idealism with Oriental fatalism. Taught negation of human will and claimed that strife arose only from conflict of wills; *The World as Will and Idea* (1819).

Schrödinger, Erwin (1887–1961); Austrian physicist, shared 1933 Nobel prize for work on wave (quantum) mechanics; 'Schrödinger equation' put quantum theory on mathematical basis.

Schubert, Franz Peter (1797–1828); Austrian composer, astonishing gift for melody; produced over 600 well-loved songs (*Ave Maria, The Erl King,* etc.). Established German *lieder* ('songs') tradition; numerous chamber works, 2 symphonies including *The Unfinished*. Died of typhus.

Schumann, Robert Alexander (1810–

People (contd.)

56); German composer and pianist, leader of German Romantic school. Turned to composition only after injuring hand through over-zealous piano practice. Wrote piano pieces *Papillons, Carnival*, etc.; cello concerto, 4 symphonies.

Schweitzer, Albert (1875–1965); Alsatian theologian, physician, philosopher, missionary and musician, devoted life to caring for sick in French Equatorial Africa (Lambaréné); raised funds with organ recitals in Europe; Nobel peace prize 1952. Regarded by many as noblest figure of 20th century.

Scipio Name of two Roman generals, father and son. **Publius Scipio the Elder** (*c.*236–*c.*184 BC) defeated HANNIBAL. **Publius Scipio the Younger** (185–129 BC) besieged and captured Carthage.

Scott, Robert Falcon (1868–1912); English naval officer, led an expedition to South Pole in 1911. Hampered by bad weather, Scott reached Pole in January 1912, to find AMUNDSEN had beaten him to it. Scott's party died on return trip.

Scott, Sir Walter (1771–1832); Scottish poet and novelist, became lawyer, won fame with *The Lay of the Last Minstrel* (epic poem; 1805); first novel *Waverley* (1814), instant success; from 1825 worked unceasingly to pay off creditors of firm he had shares in; created baronet 1820.

Scriabin, Alexander Nikolayevich (1872–1915); Russian composer and pianist, a Romantic writer of piano pieces and architect of massive tone poems such as *Prometheus*.

Segovia, Andrés (b. 1893); Spanish guitarist, revived art of classical guitar and pioneered use as concert instrument. Many composers have written for him; transcribed earlier instrumental works for guitar.

Seneca (Lucius Annaeus Seneca; *c.*4 BC–AD 65); Roman statesman, writer, and playwright. Copious essays, including *Moral Letters* urging man's Stoical resignation to divine wisdom. Nero's tutor.

Shackleton, Sir Ernest Henry (1874–1922); British naval officer, led two expeditions to Antarctica, in 1907–8 and 1915–16. Died of heart failure while travelling to lead third expedition.

William Shakespeare, the greatest English playwright.

Shakespeare, William (1564–1616); greatest English dramatist; actor from *c.* 1590; poems *Venus and Adonis, Sonnets*; plays include comedies, histories, tragedies; outstanding are *Hamlet, Macbeth, Othello, King Lear, Romeo and Juliet, A Midsummer Night's Dream, The Tempest, Henry V, Julius Caesar*.

Shapley, Harlow (1885–1972); American astronomer, compiled picture of galaxy that gave relatively true idea of real size, placing Solar System towards edge instead of in centre.

Shaw, George Bernard (1856–1950); Irish-born dramatist, critic, and active Socialist; music and drama critic for newspapers; member of Fabian Society; main plays include *Caesar and Cleopatra* (1901), *Major Barbara* (1905), *Pygmalion* (1912; as a musical, *My Fair Lady*, 1956), *St Joan* (1923).

Shelley, Percy Bysshe (1792–1822); English Romantic poet; rebel against tyranny and convention; poems include *Prometheus Unbound* (1820), *Adonais* (1821); drowned near Leghorn, Italy. Married as second wife **Mary Wollstonecraft Godwin** (1797–1851; author of *Frankenstein*, 1818).

Sheraton, Thomas (1751–1806); English furniture designer; simple lines and elegant proportions.

Sir Walter Scott, pioneer of the historical novel.

Sheridan, Richard Brinsley (1751–1816); British playwright and politician; born in Ireland; theatre manager from 1776; MP 1780–1812; led impeachment of WARREN HASTINGS; plays *The Rivals* (1775), *The School for Scandal* (1777), *The Critic* (1779).

Sherman, William Tecumseh (1820–91); American general, on Union side in Civil War; laid waste much of Georgia, S. Carolina.

Shostakovitch, Dmitri (1906–1975); Russian composer; symphonies, operas, and ballets. Weathered repeated Soviet disapproval without compromising his musical standards.

Sibelius, Jean Julius Christian (1865–1957); Finnish composer, one of leading symphonists of 20th century. Works, inspired by Finnish legends, include tone poem *Finlandia*, 7 symphonies, violin concerto.

Sidney, Sir Philip (1554–86); English soldier, statesman, poet. Mortally wounded at Battle of Zutphen, Netherlands. Poems: *Astrophel and Stella*.

Sinatra, Frank (b. 1917); American singer and film actor; worldwide following built up through radio and records. Starred in *From Here to Eternity*.

Smetana, Friedrich (1824–84); Czech composer, shaped Czech national school of music. Works include tone poem *Ma Vlast*, charming Mozartian opera *The Bartered Bride*.

Smith, Joseph (1805–44); American religious leader, claimed to have translated *Book of Mormon* from ancient language written on golden plates. Murdered by mob in Illinois; his followers established Church of Jesus Christ of Latter-Day Saints (Mormons).

Smuts, Jan Christiaan (1870–1950); South African soldier and statesman, Boer general in war of 1899–1902; fought for Britain, World War I; prime minister South Africa, 1919–24, 1939–48.

Snorri Sturluson (1179–1241); Icelandic poet and historian; head of legislature; wrote *Heimskringla*, poetic chronicles, and *Prose Edda*, textbook of Norse mythology.

Socrates (469–399 BC); Greek philosopher, taught by method of question and answer; acknowledgment of one's own ignorance is beginning of wisdom. Among his pupils were PLATO and Xenophon. Died of hemlock poisoning, after being condemned to death for unpopular political ideas.

Soddy, Frederick (1877–1956); English chemist, 1921 Nobel prize for discovery of isotopes.

Solon (*c*.638–*c*.559 BC); Athenian archon (chief magistrate) and lawmaker; reorganized constitution, law courts, and economic affairs of Athens.

Solzhenitsyn, Alexander I. (b. 1918); Russian author; expelled from Russia 1974 for publication in West of *The Gulag Archipelago*, a denunciation of Russian labour camps; Nobel prize for literature 1970; other major works *One Day in the Life of Ivan Denisovich* (1963), *The First Circle* (1968), *Cancer Ward* (1968), *August 1914* (1972).

Sophocles (*c*.496–*c*.406 BC); Greek tragic playwright; served as treasurer of Athens and army commander; wrote 123 plays, of which 7 survive: *Oedipus Rex, Oedipus at Colonus, Antigone, Electra, Philoctetes, Ajax, Maidens of Trachus*.

Sousa, John Philip (1854–1932); American composer and bandleader, 'march king of the USA'; *Blaze Away, Under the Double Eagle, El Capitan, The Stars and Stripes Forever, Washington Post*.

People (contd.)

Spence, Sir Basil Urwin (1907–1976); Scottish architect, designed the new Coventry cathedral; is also known for his innovative approach in modern university building.

Spengler, Oswald (1880–1936); German historian and philosopher, drew convincing analogy between birth, growth, and death of civilizations and human life-cycles. Doctrine first expounded in famous 2-volume work *Decline of the West* (1918–1922).

Spinoza, Benedict or **Baruch** (1632–77); Dutch-Jewish philosopher, equated God with Nature as basic substance of universe; published ideas in *Ethics* (1677).

Stahl, Georg Ernst (1660–1734); German chemist, proposed phlogiston theory of combustion.

Suleiman the Magnificent and his army capture Rhodes. During his long reign, his empire spread its influence and splendour over much of the eastern Mediterranean.

Stalin, Joseph (1879–1953); Russian revolutionary, succeeded LENIN as ruler of Soviet Union, 1924. Purged political opponents, 1930s. Led country during German invasion of World War II. Name originally *Iosif Dzhugashvili*.

Stanley, Sir Henry Morton (1841–1904); American-British journalist, explored Africa. Sent to find LIVINGSTONE 1871. Explored Lakes Victoria and Tanganyika, 1874, then sailed down Congo (Zaïre). Rescued Emin Pasha in Sudan, 1888.

Stavisky, Serge Alexandre (*c*.1886–1934); Russian-born French swindler, sold millions of worthless bonds to workers; ensuing scandal revealed widespread political corruption and brought downfall of two ministries.

Steele, Sir Richard (1672–1729); Irish-born British writer and editor; founded successively the *Tatler, Spectator, Guardian, Englishman*; wrote many essays, commenting on affairs of day.

Steinbeck, John (1902–68); American novelist and journalist; main works *Of Mice and Men* (1937), *The Grapes of Wrath* (1939), *East of Eden* (1952), *The Winter of Our Discontent* (1961); Nobel prize for literature 1962.

Stendhal (Marie Henri Beyle; 1783–1842); French novelist and soldier; *Le Rouge et le Noir* (1831), *La Chartreuse de Parme* (1839).

Stephenson, George (1781–1848); English inventor of steam locomotive; built Stockton–Darlington Railway (1821–5). Also developed miner's lamp and alarm clock. Son **Robert** (1803–59) built bridges, viaducts, and railways.

Sterne, Laurence (1713–68); Irish-born novelist; clergyman from 1738; main work *The Life and Opinions of Tristram Shandy* (1760–7, unfinished).

Stevenson, Robert Louis (1850–94); Scottish poet and novelist; travelled in search of health; lived in Samoa from 1888; novels include *Treasure Island* (1883), *Dr Jeykll and Mr Hyde* (1886).

Stowe, Harriet (Elizabeth) Beecher (1811–96); American novelist, author of *Uncle Tom's Cabin*, which with its anti-slavery sentiments, inspired abolitionists.

Stradivari, Antonio (1644–1737); Italian musical instrument-maker; superb violins most coveted of all instruments today. With sons set up workshop at Cremona; also made cellos.

Strauss, Johann (the elder, 1804–49; the younger, 1825–99); Austrian composers, father and most famous of 3 sons. Elder wrote *Radetzky March*. Younger known as 'Waltz King'; *The Blue Danube*, operettas such as *Die Fledermaus (The Bat)*.

Strauss, Richard (1864–1949); German composer and conductor, work influenced early by BRAHMS and later by WAGNER. Wrote instrumental and ballet music, operas (*Der Rosenkavalier*), symphonic poems (*Don Juan*).

Stravinsky, Igor Fedorovich (1882–1971); Russian-born American composer; his new music full of dissonances and strange rhythms alienated critics at first. Ballets *The Fire-Bird, Petrouchka*, and *Rite of Spring*; opera *The Rake's Progress*.

Strindberg, August (1849–1912); Swedish writer; also teacher, librarian; plays include *The Father* (1887), *Miss Julie* (1888), *The Ghost Sonata* (1907); novels.

Stuart Name of Scottish royal house from 1371 to 1714; of English royal house 1603–1714. Founder Walter FitzAlan, High Steward (Stewart, Stuart) of Scotland. First king **Robert II** (1316–90). Notable members: James VI (I of England); CHARLES I, Charles II; James VII and II; MARY QUEEN OF SCOTS.

Sturt, Charles (1795–1869); British army officer, discovered Darling, Murray, and Murrumbidgee rivers, Australia.

Suetonius (Gaius Suetonius Tranquillus; *c*.69–140); Roman biographer; wrote *Lives of the Caesars*, valuable source book.

Suleiman I, the Magnificent (*c*.1494–1566); sultan of Ottoman Empire from 1520, conquered Belgrade, Rhodes, part of Hungary, eastern Turkey, Syria; known as *Kanuni*, the Lawgiver, because of reforms.

Sulla, Lucius Cornelius (138–78 BC); successful Roman general, crushed rivals and made himself dictator, 82 BC.

Sullivan, Sir Arthur (1842–1900); English composer, wrote *The Lost Chord* and *Onward Christian Soldiers*. Gained undying fame through collaboration with W. S. Gilbert which produced the Savoy operas (*The Mikado, The Pirates of Penzance*, etc.).

Sun Yat-sen (1866–1925); Chinese revolutionary and statesman; headed Kuomintang (Nationalist) party; president of China 1912, 1921–5.

Sutherland, Joan (b. 1926); Australian operatic coloratura soprano, nicknamed 'La Stupenda' by La Scala audiences. Joined Covent Garden Opera Company (1952) and gained overnight fame for portrayal of Lucia in *Lucia di Lammermoor*. CBE in 1961.

Swedenborg, Emanuel (1688–1772); Swedish scientist, theologian, philosopher, and mystic, writings influenced BLAKE, BALZAC, and others. Followers organized Church of the New Jerusalem after his death.

Swift, Jonathan (1667–1745); Irish-born satirist; clergyman from 1694, Dean of St Patrick's, Dublin, from 1713; main work *Gulliver's Travels* (1726).

Synge, John Millington (1871–1909); Irish dramatist; helped to found Abbey Theatre, Dublin; plays include *Riders to the Sea* (1904), *The Playboy of the Western World* (1907).

Tacitus, Cornelius (*c*.55–*c*.120); Roman historian, wrote *Annals*, Roman history from Tiberius to Nero; *Historiae*, continuing history up to Domitian; works describing life in Germany and Roman Britain.

Talleyrand (Charles Maurice de Talleyrand-Périgord, Prince de Bénévent; 1754–1838); French statesman and cleric, revolutionary; foreign minister 1796–1807; adviser to LOUIS PHILIPPE.

Tamerlane (1336–1405); Mongol chieftain from Samarkand, conquered empire in eastern Asia stretching from Turkey to India and north to Moscow, in Europe. Name means 'Timur the Lame'.

Tasman, Abel Janszoon (*c*.1603–*c*.1659); Dutch trader, discovered Tasmania, New Zealand, Tonga, and Fiji (1642–3).

Tasso, Torquato (1544–95); Italian poet; taught astronomy and mathematics; became deranged, 1577; main works *Gerusalemme Liberata* (1575), *Aminta* (1573).

Tchaikovsky, Piotr Ilyich (1840–93); Russian Romantic composer, most popular of all Russian composers with Western audiences. Fantasy overture *Romeo and Juliet, 1812 Overture, Piano Concerto No. 1;*

People (contd.)

ballets *Swan Lake, Sleeping Beauty, The Nutcracker*.

Tenniel, Sir John (1820–1914); English caricaturist and cartoonist, illustrated *Alice's Adventures in Wonderland* and *Through the Looking Glass*; long-time illustrator for *Punch*.

Tennyson, Alfred, first Lord Tennyson (1809–92); English poet laureate from 1850; poems include *Idylls of the King* (1859), *Locksley Hall, In Memoriam*; plays.

Terence (Publius Terentius Afer; 185–159 BC); Roman playwright; born in Carthage; at first a slave, but freed; his six surviving plays are *Andria, Heautontimoroumenos, Eunuchus, Phormio, Hecyra, Adelphi*.

Tereshkova, Valentina Vladimirova (b. 1937); the first woman in space. Formerly a Russian textile worker, she was launched in the spacecraft *Vostok 6* in June 1963, and returned to Earth three days later after completing 48 orbits.

Thackeray, William Makepeace (1811–1863); English novelist and satirist, b. Calcutta; novels include *Vanity Fair* (1848), *Henry Esmond* (1852), *The Newcombes* (1855).

Thant, U (1909–75); Burmese diplomat; UN secretary-general 1961–71.

Thatcher, Margaret Hilda (b. 1925); British politician, first woman to lead Conservative party (1975); Secretary for Education, 1970–1974. Became Europe's first woman prime minister in 1979.

Thomas, Dylan (1914–53); Welsh poet; outstanding work *Under Milk Wood* (1954), a play for radio; novel *Portrait of the Artist as a Young Dog* (1940); lecturer, broadcaster; tempestuous life, early death due to alcoholism.

Thomas à Becket, St (1118–70); Archbishop of Canterbury; murdered in Canterbury Cathedral at instigation of former friend and patron Henry II. The two quarrelled repeatedly over respective jurisdiction of church and state.

Thomas à Kempis (*c.*1380–1471); German theologian, believed to be author of *The Imitation of Christ*, one of most widely read Christian devotional works.

Thomas Aquinas, St (1225–74); Catholic theologian and philosopher, became a Dominican and later taught at Paris.

Tenniel's illustrations to Lewis Carroll's *Alice* books have become a familiar part of childhood.

Systemized Catholic theology and published doctrine of Thomism in *Summa Theologica*.

Thomson, Sir Joseph John (1856–1940); English physicist, studied cathode rays and thus discovered electron. Measured its mass-to-charge ratio; 1906 Nobel prize.

Thoreau, Henry David (1817–62); American writer; *A Week on the Concord and Merrimack Rivers* (1849); *Walden* (1854); 20-vol. collection of writings published 1906.

Thurber, James (1894–1961); American humorist and artist; collections of sketches *The Owl in the Attic* (1931), *My Life and Hard Times* (1934), *Let Your Mind Alone* (1937).

Tiglath Pileser III (d. 728 BC); originally named *Pul*, usurped throne of Assyria 745 BC. Occupied most of Israel (734 BC), and annexed Babylon.

Tintoretto (Jacopo Robusti; 1518–94); Italian painter; elongated figures, impressionistically exaggerated, are feature of his many religious subjects; *Paradise*, painted for Doge's Palace.

Titian (Tiziano Vecellio; *c.*1487–1576); Italian painter, greatest of Venetian painters of High Renaissance; early influenced by work of Giorgione. Pictures, mythological and religious, characterized by rich, warm colour.

Tito (Josip Broz; b. 1892); Yugoslav partisan, led Communist resistance in Yugoslavia during World War II; prime minister 1945–53; president from 1953.

Tolstoy, Leo Nicolayevich, Count Tolstoy (1828–1910); Russian writer, philosopher, and reformer; in 1890 gave up his wealth and worked as peasant; novels include *War and Peace* (1866), *Anna Karenina* (1877); other works: *What I Believe* (1884).

Torricelli, Evangelista (1608–47); Italian physicist, invented first barometer (1643); first proposed atmosphere to be finite and space to be a vacuum.

Toscanini, Arturo (1867–1957); Italian conductor, became best known of all conductors. Musical director at La Scala, Milan; left fascist Italy, settled in US, where NBC Symphony Orchestra was created specially for him.

Townes, Charles Hard (b. 1915); American physicist, shared 1964 Nobel prize for invention and development of maser and laser.

Trevithick, Richard (1771–1833); English inventor, built steam locomotives, though not as successfully as STEPHENSON.

Trotsky, Leon (Lev Davidovich Bronstein; 1879–1940); Russian revolutionary, Minister under LENIN, 1917; organized Red Army, civil war of 1918–21; opposed STALIN; exiled 1929; assassinated by a Stalin agent in Mexico.

Richard Trevithick designed the first practical high-pressure steam engine and introduced rails into steam transport, but gained little recognition.

Truman, Harry S (1884–1972); succeeded Franklin D. Roosevelt as 33rd president of the United States, 1945; took decision to drop atomic bomb on Japan; sent US troops to fight in Korean War, 1950; retired 1953. Vice-president 1945.

Tudor Name of family that ruled England 1485–1603. Founder Owen Tudor, Welsh gentleman who married Catherine of France, widow of Henry V of England. Sovereigns: Henry VII, HENRY VIII, Edward VI, Mary I, ELIZABETH I.

Tull, Jethro (1674–1741); English farmer; invented drill for sowing seed.

Turgenev, Ivan Sergeyevich (1818–83); Russian novelist; gave up civil service to travel; novels include *On the Eve* (1860), *Fathers and Sons* (1862); plays *A Month in the Country* (1850), *A Provincial Lady* (1851).

People (contd.)

Turner, Joseph Mallord William (1775–1851); England's greatest painter, specialized in watercolour landscapes; mastery of light, achieved with broken colour, foreshadowed art of Impressionists; *The Fighting Temeraire* and *Rain, Steam, and Speed*.

Twain, Mark (Samuel Langhorne Clemens; 1835–1910); American author, printer, river pilot, journalist; *The Adventures of Tom Sawyer* (1876), *Adventures of Huckleberry Finn* (1885), *A Connecticut Yankee at King Arthur's Court* (1889); travel books, sketches.

Ulanova, Galina (b. 1910); Russian prima ballerina, ballet mistress of Bolshoi Theatre. Début in *Les Sylphides* (1928); starred particularly in *Giselle* with Bolshoi Ballet in 1950s.

Valentino, Rudolph (Rodolpho d'Antonguolla; 1895–1926); Italian-born American film star of silent screen; object of hysterical female adulation; best known for romantic lead in *The Sheik*.

Van Gogh, Vincent (1853–90); Dutch painter, specialized in vivid, colourful landscapes and portraits with simple form and passionate use of colour. Suffered intermittent periods of insanity; finally committed suicide.

Vaughan Williams, Ralph (1872–1958); English composer, collector of folk and Tudor music. Wrote 6 symphonies, ballad opera *Hugh the Drover, Fantasia on a Theme by Thomas Tallis*, ballet music, many songs.

Vega, Lope de (1562–1635); one of Spain's greatest writers; created Spanish national drama; 470 surviving plays; many poems; sailed with Spanish Armada, 1588; later became a priest.

Velázquez, Diego Rodriguez de Silva y (1599–1660); Spanish artist, court painter to Spanish royal family. Experimented with properties of light; *Rokeby Venus* and *Las Meniñas*.

Verdi, Giuseppe (1813–1901); Italian operatic composer; sense of theatre and gift for melody established new era in Italian opera. Operas *Rigoletto, Il Trovatore*, and *La Traviata*; also wrote superb *Requiem*.

Vermeer, Jan (1632–75); Dutch painter; calm, peaceful interiors typified by *Young Woman with a Water Jug* and *The Lady Standing at the Virginals*.

Verne did not know about weightlessness in space when he described this cluttered, homely rocket.

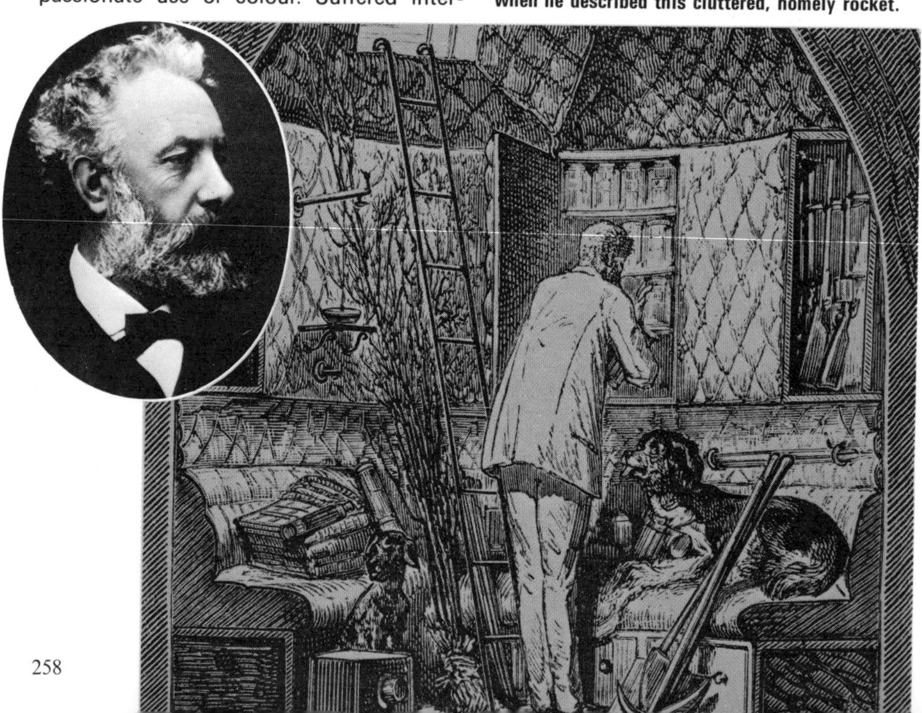

George Washington, first president of America.

Verne, Jules (1828–1905); French science fiction writer; novels include *Voyage to the Centre of the Earth* (1864), *Twenty Thousand Leagues under the Sea* (1870), *Around the World in Eighty Days* (1873).
Vesalius, Andreas (1514–64); Flemish anatomist, wrote *De Corporis Humani Fabrica* (1543), most accurate and well illustrated book on anatomy until then.
Vespucci, Amerigo (1451–1512); Florentine merchant, made several voyages to New World, exploring coast of South America, claiming to be first to sight it. It was named after him.
Victoria (1819–1901); became queen 1837 and had longest reign of any British monarch. After death of husband, Prince Albert, in 1861, became partial recluse. High moral tone she and Albert set helped restore people's confidence in monarchy.
Villa, Pancho (Doroteo Arango; 1877–1923); Mexican bandit and revolutionary, brutal killer; assassinated.
Villon, François (1431–*c.*1563); French lyric poet; led wild life, in and out of jail; condemned to death for murder but reprieved; main work *Grand Testament* (1461).
Virgil (Publius Vergilius Maro; 70–19 BC); major Roman poet; wrote epic *The Aeneid*; *Eclogues*; *Georgics*.
Volta, Alessandro Giuseppe Antonio Anastasio, Count (1745–1827); Italian physicist, invented electrophorus (basis of electrical condenser) and first battery, 'Voltaic pile' (1800); *volt* named after him.
Voltaire (François Marie Arouet; 1694–1778); French author, philosopher and acidulous critic; attacked organized religion, oppression, and civil injustices with wit and scorn; admired English liberalism. *Candide* (1759), famous satirical novel; tragedies, poems, histories.
Voroshilov, Kliment Efremovich (1881–1969); Russian soldier and statesman, commissar for defence (1925–40), command of Leningrad front 1941 and with ZHUKOV broke German siege 1943; president USSR 1953–60.
Wagner, Wilhelm Richard (1813–83); German operatic composer and conductor, regarded his monumental Romantic operas as 'music dramas'. Built Festival Opera at Bayreuth, Bavaria, to stage own productions. Works include *The Flying Dutchman*, *Tannhaüser, Ring of the Nibelung* (4-opera cycle).
Waldheim, Kurt (b. 1918); Austrian diplomat; foreign minister 1968–70; elected UN secretary-general, 1972.
Wallis, Sir Barnes Neville (1887–1979); British scientist and inventor who made numerous important contributions in the field of aviation design, including swing-wing aircraft; developed the famous 'bouncing bomb' that breached the Ruhr dams in World War II.
Walpole, Sir Robert (1676–1745); Britain's first prime minister (1721–42); served under George I and George II; created Earl of Orford, 1742.
Warwick the Kingmaker (Richard Neville, Earl of Warwick; 1428–71); leading Yorkist in Wars of Roses, supporting Edward IV; later supported Lancastrian Henry VI; killed in battle.
Washington, George (1732–99); commanded colonial armies during American War of Independence (1755–83); elected country's first president, 1789; retired 1797.
Watson, James Dewey (b. 1928); American biochemist, shared 1962 Nobel prize for discovery of structure of DNA molecule.
Watson-Watt, Sir Robert Alexander (1892–1973); Scottish electronics engin-

People (contd.)

James Watt, inventor of the first practical steam engine. The unit of power was named after him.

eer, developed the reflection of radio waves into practical 'radar' system (mid-1930s), decisive 'weapon' in Battle of Britain. Knighted 1942.

Watt, James (1736–1819); Scottish engineer, invented steam engine more efficient than previous ones, and which transferred longitudinal motion of piston into rotary motion of wheel. Also invented centrifugal governor to control speed of engine automatically.

Wedgwood, Josiah (1730–95); English potter, developed new processes in Staffordshire industry with blue or black unglazed ware decorated with white relief designs.

Wegener, Alfred Lothar (1880–1930); German geologist, first proposed continental drift theory.

Weizmann, Chaim (1874–1952); Russian-born Jewish research chemist; Zionist leader from 1898; first president of Israel, 1948–52.

Wellington, Duke of (Arthur Wellesley; 1769–1852); British soldier and statesman, defeated French in Peninsular War, 1808–14; defeated NAPOLEON I at Battle of Waterloo, 1815; prime minister, 1828–30.

Wells, Herbert George (1866–1946); English writer; radical campaigner; works include science fiction *The Invisible Man* (1897), the far-sighted *The War of the Worlds* (1898), and novels *Kipps* (1905) and *The History of Mr Polly* (1910).

Wesley, John (1703–91); English theologian, evangelist, and founder of Methodism; travelled many thousands of miles preaching in open his message of salvation through faith in Christ. Brother **Charles Wesley** (1707–88) wrote over 6,000 hymns.

Whistler, James Abbott McNeill (1834–1903); American artist, lived in Paris and London. Won farthing damages in famous lawsuit against Ruskin. Best known painting *The Artist's Mother*.

White, Patrick (b. 1912); Australian writer; *The Tree of Man* (1956), *Voss* (1957), *The Eye of the Storm* (1973); Nobel prize for literature 1973.

Whitman, Walt (1819–92); American poet; his free verse caused a sensation; poems published under title *Leaves of Grass* (1855–92).

Whittington, Richard 'Dick' (*c*.1358–1423); English merchant, three times lord mayor of London; subject of legends.

Wilberforce, William (1759–1833); English MP, reformer, and philanthropist, campaigned ceaselessly against slavery and slave trade. Achieved abolition and emancipation throughout British colonies by 1834.

Wilde, Oscar Fingal O'Flahertie Wills (1854–1900); Irish poet, dramatist, wit; loved beauty for its own sake; jailed for homosexual crimes, 1895–7; plays include *Lady Windermere's Fan* (1892), *The Importance of Being Earnest* (1895); poems *The Ballad of Reading Gaol*; novels *The Picture of Dorian Gray* (1891).

Wilhelm II (1859–1941); third and last Kaiser of Germany. Arrogant and tactless; allowed army leaders to run country. Deposed 1918 after World War I; died in exile.

William I, the Conqueror (*c*.1027–87); inherited dukedom of Normandy 1035, and in 1066 invaded and conquered England. Brought strong rule to England, and had first national survey made (*Domesday Book*, 1086).

William III of Orange (1650–1702); Stadtholder of Netherlands 1671; king of England (jointly with wife, Mary II) by invitation of parliament from 1689, deposing Roman Catholic father-in-law James II.

Wilson, (James) Harold (b. 1916);

British statesman, leader of Labour party 1963–1976; prime minister 1964–1970 and 1974–1976.

Windsor, Duke of. See EDWARD VIII.

Wolfe, James (1727–59); British soldier. Victory over French at Quebec, at which he was killed, won Canada.

Wolsey, Thomas (*c.*1475–1530); English cleric and statesman, minister to Henry VII and HENRY VIII; archbishop of York, 1514, cardinal 1515, lord chancellor 1515; failed to secure Henry's divorce from Catherine of Aragon; fell from power 1529; died before trial for treason.

Woolf, (Adeline) Virginia (1882–1941); English novelist: *Mrs Dalloway* (1925), *To the Lighthouse* (1925), *Between the Acts* (1941); and essayist; born Virginia Stephen, married Leonard Woolf (1912); leader of 'Bloomsbury Group'; committed suicide.

Wordsworth, William (1770–1850); major English poet, settled in Lake District after European travels, 1813; poet laureate 1843; *The Prelude* (1805), *The Excursion* (1814), many shorter poems and sonnets.

Wren, Sir Christopher (1632–1723); English architect, astronomer, and mathematician. St Paul's Cathedral one of more than 50 churches he built in London.

Whitman began a new tradition of American verse.

Wright, Frank Lloyd (1869–1959); American architect, pioneered use of new materials (e.g. reinforced concrete) in building; aimed always to integrate buildings with environment.

Wright (brothers): **Orville** (1871–1948) and **Wilbur** (1866–1919); American inventors, built and flew first aeroplane.

Wycliffe, John (*c.*1328–84); English reformer, accepted authority of Scriptures implicitly and rejected much of teachings of Church. Began first translation of Bible into English.

Xavier, St Francis (1506–52); Spanish RC missionary, helped to found Jesuits. Called 'Apostle to the Indies'; made missionary journeys to India, E. Indies, China, and Japan.

Xerxes I, the Great (*c.*519–465 BC); king of Persia. Attacked Greece, 480 BC, won victory at Thermopylae, burned Athens; fleet defeated at Salamis. Murdered.

Yeats, William Butler (1865–1939); Irish poet and dramatist; led Irish literary revival; founded Abbey Theatre, Dublin; plays include *The Countess Cathleen* (1892); essays include *Celtic Twilight* (1893); Nobel prize for literature 1923.

Young, Brigham (1801–77); American religious leader, replaced murdered JOSEPH SMITH as head of Mormons. Led followers through many hardships to final settlement at Salt Lake City.

Zhukov, Georgi Konstantinovich (1896–1974); Russian general in World War II, led defence of Moscow and Stalingrad, broke German siege of Leningrad, led armies through Poland into Germany; captured Berlin; accepted German surrender 1945.

Zola, Émile (1840–1902); French novelist; *Les Rougon-Macquart* (20 volumes); intervened in DREYFUS case with *J'Accuse* (1898).

Zoroaster (Zarathustra) (*c.*600s BC); Persian religious leader, founded Zoroastrianism; said to have written its sacred book, *Avesta*.

Zwingli, Ulrich (1484–1531); Swiss religious leader, prominent in Swiss Reformation. In *Concerning True and False Religion*, attacked monasticism and idolatry. Killed in attack on Zurich by citizens of anti-Protestant cantons.

Sport

Olympic Games

1896 Athens
1900 Paris
1904 St Louis
1906 Athens (Intercalated Games)
1908 London
1912 Stockholm
1920 Antwerp
1924 Paris
1928 Amsterdam
1932 Los Angeles
1936 Berlin
1948 London
1952 Helsinki
1956 Melbourne
1960 Rome
1964 Tokyo
1968 Mexico City
1972 Munich
1976 Montreal
1980 Moscow
1984 Los Angeles

Winter Olympics

1924 Chamonix, France
1928 St Moritz, Switzerland
1932 Lake Placid, USA
1936 Garmisch, Germany
1948 St Moritz, Switzerland
1952 Oslo, Norway
1956 Cortina, Italy
1960 Squaw Valley, USA
1964 Innsbruck, Austria
1968 Grenoble, France
1972 Sapporo, Japan
1976 Innsbruck, Austria
1980 Lake Placid, USA
1984 Sarajevo, Yugoslavia

The closing ceremony of the Montreal Olympic Games in 1976.

Commonwealth Games

1930 Hamilton, Canada
1934 London, England
1938 Sydney, Australia
1950 Auckland, New Zealand
1954 Vancouver, Canada
1958 Cardiff, Wales
1962 Perth, Australia
1966 Kingston, Jamaica
1970 Edinburgh, Scotland
1974 Christchurch, New Zealand
1978 Edmonton, Canada
1982 Brisbane, Australia

Left: **The Olympic flame is carried to the site of each Games by runners from Greece.**

Association Football

World Cup Finals

Year	Venue	Winner		Runner-up	
1930	Montevideo, Uruguay (100,000)	Uruguay	4	Argentina	2
1934	Rome, Italy (55,000)	Italy	2	Czechoslovakia	1
1938	Paris, France (65,000)	Italy	4	Hungary	2
1950	Rio de Janeiro, Brazil (199,850)	Uruguay	2	Brazil	1
1954	Berne, Switzerland (55,000)	W. Germany	3	Hungary	2
1958	Stockholm, Sweden (49,737)	Brazil	5	Sweden	2
1962	Santiago, Chile (69,068)	Brazil	3	Czechoslovakia	1
1966	Wembley, England (93,000)	England	4	W. Germany	2
1970	Mexico City, Mexico (110,000)	Brazil	4	Italy	1
1974	Munich, W. Germany (75,000)	W. Germany	2	Netherlands	1
1978	Buenos Aires, Argentina (77,000)	Argentina	3	Netherlands	1

European Cup Finals

Year	Venue	Winner		Runner-up	
1956	Paris (38,329)	Real Madrid (Spain)	4	Stade de Reims (France)	3
1957	Madrid (125,000)	Real Madrid (Spain)	2	Fiorentina (Italy)	0
1958	Brussels (67,000)	Real Madrid (Spain)	3	AC Milan (Italy)	2
1959	Stuttgart (80,000)	Real Madrid (Spain)	2	Stade de Reims (France)	0
1960	Glasgow (127,621)	Real Madrid (Spain)	7	Eintracht Frankfurt (W. Ger)	3
1961	Berne (33,000)	Benfica (Portugal)	3	Barcelona (Spain)	2
1962	Amsterdam (68,000)	Benfica (Portugal)	5	Real Madrid (Spain)	3
1963	Wembley (45,000)	AC Milan (Italy)	2	Benfica (Portugal)	1
1964	Vienna (72,000)	Internazionale (Italy)	3	Real Madrid (Spain)	1
1965	Milan (80,000)	Internazionale (Italy)	1	Benfica (Portugal)	0
1966	Brussels (60,000)	Real Madrid (Spain)	2	Partizan Belgrade (Yug)	1
1967	Lisbon (45,000)	Celtic (Scotland)	2	Internazionale (Italy)	1
1968	Wembley (100,000)	Manchester U. (England)	4	Benfica (Portugal)	1
1969	Madrid (50,000)	AC Milan (Italy)	4	Ajax (Netherlands)	1
1970	Milan (50,000)	Feyenoord (Netherlands)	2	Celtic (Scotland)	1
1971	Wembley (90,000)	Ajax (Netherlands)	2	Panathinaikos (Greece)	0
1972	Rotterdam (67,000)	Ajax (Netherlands)	2	Internazionale (Italy)	0
1973	Belgrade (93,500)	Ajax (Netherlands)	1	Juventus (Italy)	0
1974	Brussels (65,000)	Bayern Munich (W. Ger)	1	Atlético Madrid (Spain)	1
	Replay (30,000)		4		0
1975	Paris (50,000)	Bayern Munich (W. Ger)	2	Leeds United (England)	0
1976	Rome (57,000)	Liverpool (England)	3	Borussia Moenchengladbach (W. Germany)	1
1977	Wembley (92,000)	Liverpool (England)	1	Bruges (Belgium)	0
1978	Munich (58,000)	Nottingham Forest (England)	1	Malmo (Sweden)	0

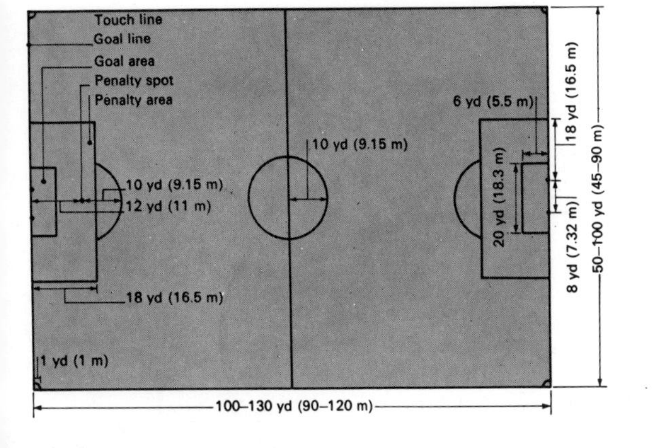

Facts

Ball—circum. 27–28 in (68–71 cm), weight 14–16 oz (400–450 gm)
Duration of game—90 min (2×45) plus 2×15 min extra in certain cup games
Number per side—11 (1 or 2 substitutes, depending on competition)
Ruling body—Fédération Internationale de Football Association (FIFA)

A–Z of sports (contd.)

Badminton

Court – 44×20 ft (13.4×6.1 m), singles – 44×17 ft (13.4×5.2 m)
Height of net – 5 ft 1 in (1.55 m)
Weight of shuttlecock – 4.73–5.50 gm
Scoring – best of 3 or 5 15-pt. games, men; best of 3 11-pt. games, women
Ruling body – International Badminton Federation (IBF)
World team championships – Thomas Cup (men); Uber Cup (women)
Leading individual tournament – All-England Championships

Baseball

Pitching distance – 60 ft 6 in (18.4 m)
Side of 'diamond' – 90 ft (27.4 m)
Max. length of bat – 3 ft 6 in (1.07 m)
Diameter of ball – $2\frac{3}{4}$ in (7 cm)
Weight of ball – 5–$5\frac{1}{2}$ oz (142–156 gm)
Number per side – 9 (substitutes allowed)
No. of innings – 9 or more (played to finish)

Basketball

Court – 85×46 ft (26×14 m)
Height of baskets – 10 ft (3 m)
Diameter of baskets – 18 in (45.7 cm)
Circumference of ball – $29\frac{1}{2}$–$30\frac{1}{2}$ in (75–78 cm)
Weight of ball – 21–23 oz (600–650 gm)
Duration – 40 min actual play (2×20) plus periods of 5 min until result is obtained
No. per side – 5 (up to 5 substitutes)
Ruling body – Fédération Internationale de Basketball Amateur (FIBA)
Major competitions – World championships (men and women) and Olympic Games

Billiards and Snooker

Table – 12 ft×6 ft $1\frac{1}{2}$ in (3.66×1.87 m)
Diameter of balls – $2\frac{1}{16}$ in (5.2 cm)
Billiards – red, white, spot white
Billiards scoring – pot or in-off red 3, white 2; cannon 2
Snooker balls (value) – black (7), pink (6), blue (5), brown (4), green (3), yellow (2), 15 reds (1 each), white (cue-ball)

Bowls (flat green)

Rink (max.) – 132 × 19 ft (40.2 × 5.8 m)
Bowls – diam. (max.) $5\frac{3}{4}$ in (14.6 cm) biased, weight (max.) $3\frac{1}{2}$ lb (1.59 kg), black or brown, made of wood, rubber, or composition
Jack – diam. $2\frac{1}{2}$ in (6.35 cm), weight 8–10 oz (227–284 gm)
Ruling body – International Bowling Board
Events – singles (4 bowls each, 21 *shots* up), pairs (2–4 bowls each, 21 *ends*), triples (2 or 3 bowls each, 18 *ends*), fours (2 bowls each, 21 *ends*)
World championships – every 4 years

Boxing

Professional

Ring – 14–20 ft (4.27–6.10 m) square
Gloves – 6 oz (170 gm) fly to welterweight, 8 oz (227 gm) light-middleweight and above
Duration – 6, 8, 10, 12, or 15 (title) 3-min rounds
Ruling body – World Boxing Council (WBC)

Amateur

Ring – 12–16 ft (3.66–4.88 m) square
Gloves – 8 oz (227 gm)
Duration – 3 3-min rounds (seniors)
Ruling body – Amateur International Boxing Association (AIBA)

Cricket is played throughout the world, but its rules are fixed by one governing body so there need be no disputes between players.

Weight limits

event	WBC st-lb	WBC kg	AIBA st-lb	AIBA kg
Light-fly	—	—	7–07	47.63
Fly	8–00	50.80	8–00	50.80
Bantam	8–06	53.52	8–07	53.98
Feather	9–00	57.15	9–00	57.15
Junior light	9–04	58.97	—	—
Light	9–09	61.24	9–07	60.33
Junior welter	10–00	63.50	10–00	63.50
Welter	10–07	66.68	10–08	67.13
Junior middle	11–00	69.85	11–02	70.76
Middle	11–06	72.58	11–11	78.84
Light-heavy	12–07	79.38	12–10	80.74
Heavy	no limit			

Cricket

Pitch – wicket to wicket 22 yd (20 m), bowling crease 8 ft 8 in (2.64 m) long
Stumps – 28 in (71.1 cm) high, 9 in (22.9 cm) overall width
Bat (max.) – 38 in (96.5 cm) long, $4\frac{1}{4}$ in (10.8 cm) wide
Ball – circum. $8\frac{13}{16}$–9 in (22.4–22.9 cm), weight $5\frac{1}{2}$–$5\frac{3}{4}$ oz (156–163 gm)
No. per side – 11 (subs. only for fielding
Ruling body – International Cricket Conference (ICC)

Croquet

Court – 35 × 28 yd (32 × 25.6 m)
Players – 2 or 4
Balls – 4 (blue and black *v* red and yellow), diam. $3\frac{5}{8}$ in (9.2 cm), weight 1 lb (454 gm)
Hoops – 6 (twice each) plus *peg*; diam. $3\frac{3}{4}$ in (9.5 cm)
International team competition – MacRobertson Shield

Cycle Racing

Ruling body – Union Cycliste Internationale
Major competitions: *Road racing* – Tour de France, Olympic 100-km (62-mile) race
Track racing – Olympics and world championships (sprint, pursuit, 1-km time trial, motor-paced)
Other cycle sports – six-day racing, cyclo-cross, cycle speedway, bicycle polo, time trials

Equestrian sports

Ruling body – Fédération Equestre Internationale (FEI)
Major competitions: *Show jumping* – world championships (men's and women's) every 4 years, alternating with Olympics; President's Cup (world team championship) based on Nations Cup results; 2-yearly European Championships (men's and women's); King George V Gold Cup; Queen Elizabeth II Gold Cup
Three-day event (1 Dressage, 2 Endurance or Cross-country, 3 Show jumping) – 4-yearly world championships and Olympics; 2-yearly European Championships; Badminton Horse Trials
Dressage – Olympics

Fencing

Ruling body – Fédération Internationale d'Escrimé (FIE)
Events – foil, épée, sabre; foil (women)
Major competitions – annual world championships (including Olympics)
Duration of bout – first to 5 hits (or 6 min) men; 4 hits (or 5 min) women

There are three fencing weapons: foil (left), épée (centre), and sabre (right). The target areas are shown shaded. Women fence only the foil.

Football, American

Pitch – 360 × 160 ft (110 × 49 m)
Goals – 20 ft (6 m) high, $18\frac{1}{2}$ ft (5.6 m) wide, 10 ft (3 m) off ground
Ball – length 11 in (28 cm), short circum.

A–Z of sports (contd.)

21¼ in (54 cm), weight 14–15 oz (397–425 gm)
Duration – 60 min (4 × 15) playing time
No. per side – 11 (max. 40 on team)
Scoring – *touchdown* 6 pts., *extra point* 1, *field goal* 3, *safety* 2

Football, Australian Rules

Pitch – oval 135–185 m (148–202 yd) by 110–155 m (120–170 yd)
Goal posts – 6.4 m (21 ft) wide, *behind posts* 6.4 m either side of goal posts
Ball – short circum. 57.2 cm (22½ in), weight 454–482 gm (16–17 oz)
Duration – 100 min (4 × 25)
No. per side – 18 (2 substitutes)
Scoring – *goal* 6 pts., *behind* 1

Football, Gaelic

Pitch – 140–160 yd (128–146 m) by 84–100 yd (77–91 m)
Goal posts – 21 ft (6.4 m) wide, 16 ft (4.9 m) high, crossbar at 8 ft (2.4 m)
Ball – circum. 27–29 in (69–74 cm), weight 13–15 oz (369–425 gm)
Duration – 60 min (2 × 30)
No. per side – 15 (3 substitutes)
Scoring – *goal* 3 pts., ball over crossbar 1
Ruling body – Gaelic Athletic Association

Golf

Ball – max. weight 1.62 oz (46 gm), min. diam. 1.62 in (4.11 cm), US 1.68 in (4.27 cm)
Hole – diam. 4¼ in (10.8 cm)
No. of clubs carried – 14 maximum
Ruling body – Royal and Ancient Golf Club
Major competitions: Individual – British Open, US Open, US Masters, US PGA
Team – World Cup (international teams of 2, annual), Eisenhower Trophy (world amateur, teams of 4, 2-yearly), Ryder Cup (US v GB, 2-yearly)

Golf Terms

Birdie One under par for hole.
Bogey One over par for hole.

Olga Korbut, the young Russian gymnast, won the hearts of the world during the Munich Games, 1972.

Dormie In match play, leading by numbers of holes left.
Double bogey Two over par for hole.
Eagle Two under par for hole.
Fairway Smooth turf between tee and green
Fourball Match in which pairs score their 'better ball' at each hole.
Foursome Match in which pair play same ball, alternately.
Green Specially prepared surface in which hole is situated.
Match play In which player or pair play each other and winner is determined by holes won.
Medal play In which number of strokes taken determines winner.
Par Standard score (assessed on first-class play) for hole or holes.
Rough Unprepared part of course.
Stroke play Medal play.
Tee Starting place for hole, or peg on which ball is placed.

Gymnastics

Ruling body – Fédération Internationale de Gymnastique
Events: men's – floor exercises, rings, parallel bars, pommel horse, vault (lengthwise), horizontal bar; overall; team; women's – floor exercises (to music), vault, asymmetrical bars, beam; overall; team
Major competitions – World and Olympic championships, alternately every 4 years

Handball (team)

Court – 38–44 m (125–144 ft) by 18–22 m (59–72 ft)
Goals – 3 m (9.8 ft) wide, 2 m (6.6 ft) high
Ball – circum. 58–60 cm (23–24 in) men's, 54–56 cm (21–22 in) women's; weight 425–475 gm (15–16¾ oz) men's, 325–400 gm (11½–14 oz) women's
Duration – 60 min (2 × 30) men's, 50 min (2 × 25) women's; in tournaments 2 × 15 and 2 × 10, respectively, without the 10-min interval
No. per side – 7 (max. 12 on team)
Ruling body – International Handball Federation

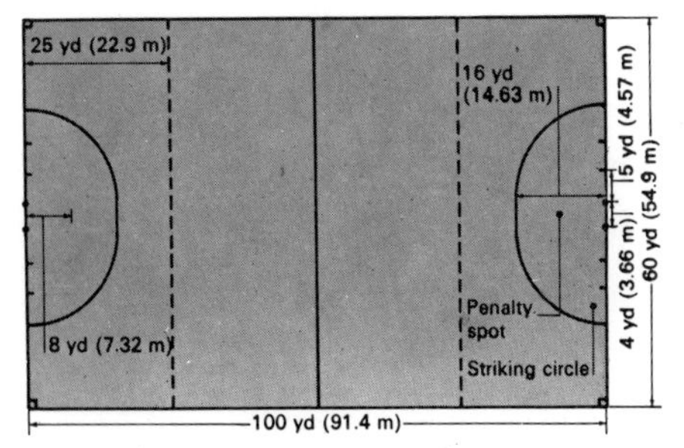

Above: **The layout of a hockey pitch.**

Hockey

Goals – 12 ft (3.66 m) wide, 7 ft (2.13 m) high
Ball – circum. 9 in (23 cm), weight 5½–5¾ oz (156–163 gm), made of cork and twine covered in leather
Duration of game – 70 min (2 × 35)
No. per side – 11 (2 subs. in men's game)
Ruling bodies: men's – Fédération Internationale de Hockey (FIH); women's – International Hockey Rules Board
Major competitions – Olympic Games and World Cup (4-yearly), both men's

Horse Racing

Major races

England – Derby, Oaks, St Leger, 1,000 and 2,000 Guineas (the 5 Classics), King George VI & Queen Elizabeth Stakes, Ascot Gold Cup; Grand National (steeplechase), Cheltenham Gold Cup ('chase), Champion Hurdle
Ireland – Irish Sweeps Derby
France – Prix de l'Arc de Triomphe
Australia – Melbourne Cup, Caulfield Cup
South Africa – Durban July Handicap
USA – Kentucky Derby, Preakness Stakes, Belmont Stakes (Triple Crown); Washington International

Lacrosse

Pitch – 110 × 70 yd (100 × 64 m) max.
Goals – 6 × 6 ft (1.8 × 1.8 m)
Ball – circum. 7¾–8 in (19.7–20.3 cm), weight 4½–5 oz (128–142 gm), made of rubber
Duration – 60 min (4 × 15) men, 50 min (2 × 25) women
No. per side – 10 (9 subs.) men, 12 (1 sub.) women

Modern Pentathlon

Order of events – riding, fencing, shooting, swimming, running
Ruling body – Union Internationale de Pentathlon Moderne et Biathlon
Major competitions – annual world championships (including Olympics)

Motor Sport

Ruling body – Fédération Internationale de l'Automobile (FIA)
Major events and competitions: Formula One – World Drivers Championship

A–Z of sports (contd.)

(based on points gained in individual grands prix: 9, 6, 4, 3, 2, 1 for first 6
Sports car racing – Le Mans, Targa Florio
Rally driving – Monte Carlo Rally
Other motor sports – drag racing, karting, hillclimbing, trials, autocross, rallycross, autotests, stock-car racing, vintage-car racing

Motor Sport – World Champions

1950 Giuseppe Farina (Italy)
1951 Juan Manuel Fangio (Argentina)
1952 Alberto Ascari (Italy)
1953 Alberto Ascari (Italy)
1954 Juan Manuel Fangio (Argentina)
1955 Juan Manuel Fangio (Argentina)
1956 Juan Manuel Fangio (Argentina)
1957 Juan Manuel Fangio (Argentina)
1958 Mike Hawthorn (England)
1959 Jack Brabham (Australia)
1960 Jack Brabham (Australia)
1961 Phil Hill (USA)
1962 Graham Hill (England)
1963 Jim Clark (Scotland)
1964 John Surtees (England)
1965 Jim Clark (Scotland)
1966 Jack Brabham (Australia)
1967 Denis Hulme (New Zealand)
1968 Graham Hill (England)
1969 Jackie Stewart (Scotland)
1970 Jochen Rindt (Austria)
1971 Jackie Stewart (Scotland)
1972 Emerson Fittipaldi (Brazil)
1973 Jackie Stewart (Scotland)
1974 Emerson Fittipaldi (Brazil)
1975 Nicki Lauda (Austria)
1976 James Hunt (England)
1977 Nicki Lauda (Austria)
1978 Mario Andretti (Italy)
1979 Jody Scheckter (South Africa)

Emerson Fittipaldi in a JPS-Ford at Brands Hatch.

Motorcycling Sport

Ruling body – Fédération Internationale Motorcycliste (FIM)
Classes – 50 cc, 125 cc, 250 cc, 350 cc (junior), 500 cc (senior), 750 cc, unlimited; sidecar
Major competitions – world championships (based on points gained in individual grands prix), including Isle of Man TT
Other motorcycle sports – scrambling (motorcross), trials, grasstrack racing

Netball

Court – 100 × 50 ft (30.5 × 15.2 m)
Net – 10 ft (3.05 m) high; ring diam. 15 in (38 cm)
Ball – as for soccer
Duration of game – 60 min (4 × 15)
No. per side – 7 (subs. for injuries)
Ruling body – International Federation of Netball Associations
World championships – every 4 years

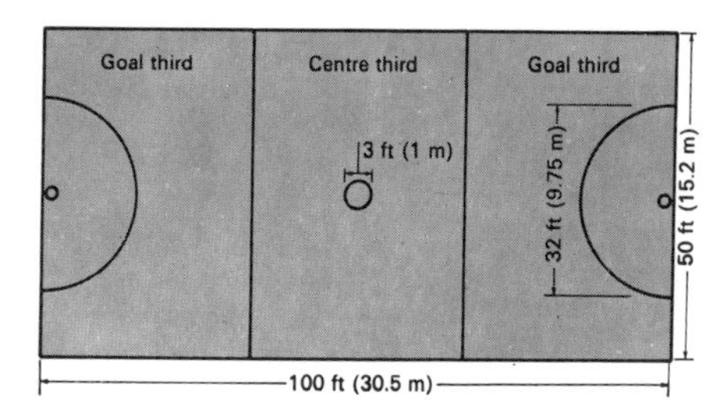

Above: **The layout of a netball court.**

Rowing

Ruling body – Fédération Internationale des Sociétés d'Aviron (FISA)
International events: men – eights, fours and pairs (both coxed and coxless), single, double, and quadruple sculls; women – eights, coxed fours, single, double, and quadruple sculls
Major competitions – World championships every 4 years, alternating with Olympics; Henley Regatta (including Grand Challenge Cup and Diamond Sculls)
Standard course – men 2,000 m (2,187 yd), boys 1,500 m (1,640 yd), women 1,000 m (1,094 yd)

Terms

Bow Front part of boat.
Catch a crab Feather blade in water, usually disrupting boat.
Cox or *coxswain* One who sits at stern, facing oarsmen, and steers.
Coxless Without cox, steered by one of the oarsmen.
Feathering Turning blade flat between strokes to reduce air resistance.
Repechage Race in which losing crews in heats have second chance to qualify for next round.
Sculls Boats in which each oarsman (sculler) has two oars.
Stern Rear end of boat.
Stroke Oarsman nearest stern (with back to others) who sets rhythm and rate; complete cycle of rowing action.

Rugby League

Pitch (max.) – 75 yd (69 m) wide, 110 yd (100 m) between goals, 6–12 yd (5.5–11 m) behind goals
Goal posts – as for rugby union
Ball – slightly smaller than for union
Duration of game – 80 min (2 × 40)
No. per side – 13 (2 substitutes)
Scoring – *try* 3 pts., *conversion* 2, *penalty goal* 2, *dropped goal* 2 (1 in internationals)
Ruling body – International Rugby League Board
Major competition – World Cup

Rugby Union

Pitch (max.) – 75 yd (69 m) wide, 110 yd (100 m) between goals, 25 yd (23 m) behind goals
Goal posts – 18½ ft (5.6 m) wide, no height limit, crossbar 10 ft (3 m) above ground
Ball – length 11 in (28 cm), short circum. 24–25½ in (61–65 cm), weight 13½–15 oz (383–425 gm)
Duration of game – 80 min (2 × 40)
No. per side – 15 (2 subs. in internationals)
Scoring – *try* 4 pts., *conversion* 2, *penalty goal* 3, *dropped goal* 3
Ruling body – International Rugby Football Board
Major competitions – Five Nations Championship (England, France, Ireland, Scotland, Wales), Ranfurly Shield (New Zealand), Currie Cup (South Africa)
Touring sides – Lions (GB), All Blacks (New Zealand), Springboks (South Africa), Wallabies (Australia), Tricolours (France)

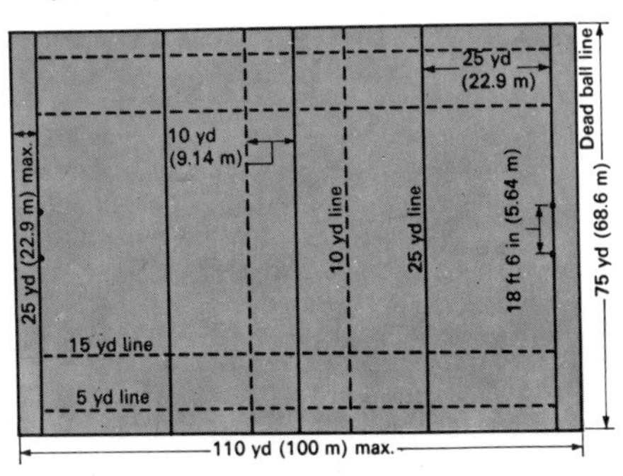

Speedway

Track – 4 laps of 300–450 yd (274–411 m) surface – red shale or granite dust
Meeting – 20 races, 4 riders in race, each getting 5 rides
Scoring – 1st 3 pts., 2nd 2, 3rd 1
Machines – Brakeless 500 cc motorcycles
Ruling body – Fédération Internationale de Motorcycliste (FIM)
Major competitions – World Championship (individual), World Team Cup, World Pairs Championship

World Champions

1936	Lionel Van Praag (Australia)
1937	Jack Milne (USA)
1938	Bluey Wilkinson (Australia)
1949	Tommy Price (England)
1950	Freddie Williams (Wales)
1951	Jack Young (Australia)
1952	Jack Young (Australia)
1953	Freddie Williams (Wales)
1954	Ronnie Moore (New Zealand)
1955	Peter Craven (England)
1956	Ove Fundin (Sweden)
1957	Barry Briggs (New Zealand)
1958	Barry Briggs (New Zealand)
1959	Ronnie Moore (New Zealand)
1960	Ove Fundin (Sweden)
1961	Ove Fundin (Sweden)

A–Z of sports (contd.)

1962 Peter Craven (England)
1963 Ove Fundin (Sweden)
1964 Barry Briggs (New Zealand)
1965 Bjorn Knuttsson (Sweden)
1966 Barry Briggs (New Zealand)
1967 Ove Fundin (Sweden)
1968 Ivan Mauger (New Zealand)
1969 Ivan Mauger (New Zealand)
1970 Ivan Mauger (New Zealand)
1971 Ole Olsen (Denmark)
1972 Ivan Mauger (New Zealand)
1973 Jerzy Szczakiel (Poland)
1974 Anders Michanek (Sweden)
1975 Ole Olsen (Denmark)
1976 P. Collins (England)
1977 Ivan Mauger (New Zealand)
1978 Ole Olsen (Denmark)

Squash

Ball – diam. 39.5–41.5 mm (1.56–1.63 in weight 23.3–24.6 gm (0.82–0.87 oz), made of matt-surface rubber
Racket (max.) – length 27 in (68.6 cm), head 8½ in (21.6 cm) long by 7¼ in (18.4 cm) wide
Scoring – best of 5 9-up games
Ruling body – International Squash Rackets Federation (ISRF)
Major competitions – World Open, Women's Open

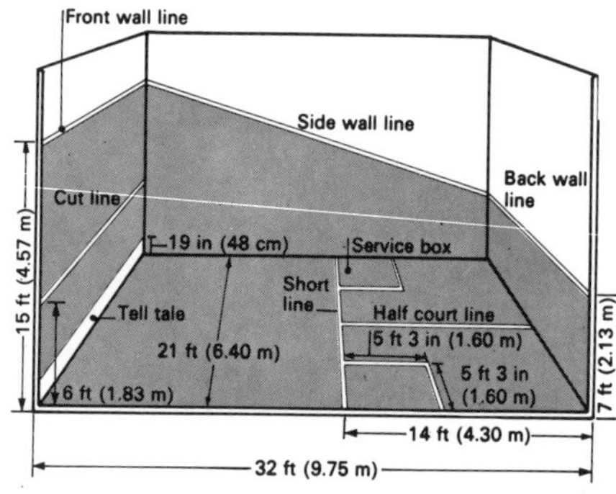

A squash court, not showing one of the two side walls, which have the same dimensions.

Swimming and Diving

Standard Olympic pool – 50 m (54.7 yd) long, 8 lanes
Ruling body – Fédération Internationale de Natation Amateur (FINA)
Competitive strokes – freestyle (front crawl), backstroke, breaststroke, butterfly; individual medley (butterfly, backstroke, breaststroke, freestyle legs), medley relay (backstroke, breaststroke, butterfly, freestyle)
Diving events – men's and women's springboard at 3 m (9¾ ft), highboard at 10 m (33 ft) (lower boards also used)
Major competitions – Olympics and world championships
Major long-distance swims – English Channel, Cook Strait (NZ), Atlantic City Marathon (US)

American Mark Spitz 'swam to immortality' in the 1972 Munich Olympics, winning seven gold medals.

Table Tennis

Table – 9 × 5 ft (2.74 × 1.52 m), 2½ ft (76 cm) off floor
Net – height 6 in (15.2 cm), length 6 ft (1.83 m)
Ball – diam. 1.46–1.50 in (37–38 mm), weight 2.40–2.53 gm (0.085–0.089 oz), made of celluloid-type plastic, white or yellow
Bat surface – max. thickness 2 mm (0.08 in) pimpled rubber or 4 mm (0.16 in) sandwich rubber
Scoring – best of 3 or 5 21-pt games

Ruling body – International Table Tennis Federation

Major competitions – world championships, Swaythling Cup (men's team), Corbillon Cup (women's team), all two-yearly

Tennis

Ball – diam. $2\frac{5}{8}$ in (6.67 cm), weight $2–2\frac{1}{16}$ oz (56.7–58.5 gm), made of wool-covered rubber, white or yellow

Rackets – no limits, wood or metal frames, strung with lamb's gut or nylon, weighing max. of about 14 oz (397 gm)

Scoring – best of 3 or 5 6-game sets, with tiebreaker at 6–6 (or first to lead by 2) or 8–8; games of 4 pts. (15, 30, 40, game), 40–40 being *deuce* and 2-pt. lead required; tiebreaker game usually first to 7 pts. with 2-pt. lead

Ruling body – International Lawn Tennis Federation (ILTF)

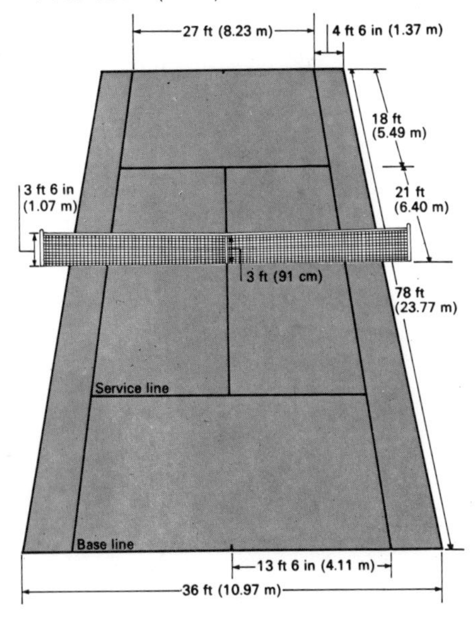

Dimensions of a tennis court as for a doubles match. For singles, the inner sidelines are used, with the posts situated 3 ft outside them.

Major competitions – Wimbledon, Australian Open, US Open, French Open (the four constituting 'Grand Slam'), Davis Cup (world team championship), Federation Cup (Women's World Cup), Wightman Cup (US v GB women)

Wimbledon Champions (since 1946)

	men	women
1946	Yvon Petra (Fr)	Pauline Betz (US)
1947	Jack Kramer (US)	Margaret Osborne (US)
1948	Bob Falkenburg (US)	Louise Brough (US)
1949	Fred Schroeder (US)	Louise Brough (US)
1950	Budge Patty (US)	Louise Brough (US)
1951	Dick Savitt (US)	Doris Hart (US)
1952	Frank Sedgman (Aus)	Maureen Connolly (US)
1953	Victor Seixas (US)	Maureen Connolly (US)
1954	Jaroslav Drobny (Cz)	Maureen Connolly (US)
1955	Tony Trabert (US)	Louise Brough (US)
1956	Lew Hoad (Aus)	Shirley Fry (US)
1957	Lew Hoad (Aus)	Althea Gibson (US)
1958	Ashley Cooper (Aus)	Althea Gibson (US)
1959	Alex Olmedo (Peru)	Maria Bueno (Brazil)
1960	Neale Fraser (Aus)	Maria Bueno (Brazil)
1961	Rod Laver (Aus)	Angela Mortimer (GB)
1962	Rod Laver (Aus)	Karen Susman (US)
1963	Chuck McKinley (US)	Margaret Smith (Aus)
1964	Roy Emerson (Aus)	Maria Bueno (Brazil)
1965	Roy Emerson (Aus)	Margaret Smith (Aus)
1966	Manuel Santana (Sp)	Billie Jean King (US)
1967	John Newcombe (Aus)	Billie Jean King (US)
1968	Rod Laver (Aus)	Billie Jean King (US)
1969	Rod Laver (Aus)	Ann Jones (GB)
1970	John Newcombe (Aus)	Margaret Court (Aus)
1971	John Newcombe (Aus)	Evonne Goolagong (Aus)
1972	Stan Smith (US)	Billie Jean King (US)
1973	Jan Kodes (Cz)	Billie Jean King (US)
1974	Jimmy Connors (US)	Chris Evert (US)
1975	Arthur Ashe (US)	Billie Jean King (US)
1976	Bjorn Borg (Sweden)	Chris Evert (USA)
1977	Bjorn Borg (Sweden)	Virginia Wade (GB)
1978	Bjorn Borg (Sweden)	Martina Navratilova (Czech)
1979	Bjorn Borg (Sweden)	Martina Navratilova (Czech)

Tenpin Bowling

Lane – 60 ft (18.3 m) long, $3\frac{1}{2}$ ft (1.07 m) wide

Pins – $1\frac{1}{4}$ ft (38 cm) high, of maple wood, standing in 3 ft (91 cm) triangle

Bowls – diam. $8\frac{1}{2}$ in (21.6 cm), weight (max.) 16 lb ($7\frac{1}{4}$ kg)

Scoring – 10 *frames* of 2 bowls; *strike* (10 pins down with 1st bowl) scores 10 plus score with next 2 bowls, *spare* (10 down with 2 bowls) scores 10 plus score with next bowl; max. game score 300 (12 strikes)

Ruling body – Fédération Internationale des Quilleurs (FIQ)

Major competition – world championships

Volleyball

Court – 18 × 9 m (59 × $29\frac{1}{2}$ ft)

A–Z of sports (contd.)

Net height – 2.43 m (7 ft 11.7 in) for men, 2.21 m (7 ft 3 in) for women
Ball – circum. 65–67 cm (25.6–26.4 in), weight 260–280 gm (9–10 oz)
No. per side – 6 (6 substitutes)
Scoring – best of 3 or 5 15-pt. sets
Ruling body – Fédération Internationale de Volleyball (FIV)
Major competitions – Olympics and world championships, alternately every 4 years (men and women)

Water Polo

Pool – 20–30 m (22–33 yd) by 8–20 m (8¾–22 yd); min. depth 1 m (1.8 m for international competition)
Goals – 3 × 0.9 m (9¾ × 3 ft) for depths over 1.5 m (4 ft 11 in); for shallower pool, crossbar 2.4 m (7 ft 10 in) above bottom
Ball – circum. 68–71 cm (26¾–28 in), weight 400–450 gm (14–16 oz)
Duration of game – 20 min (4 × 5)
No. per side – 7 (4 substitutes)
Ruling body – FINA (see *Swimming*)
Major competitions – as for *Swimming*

Water Skiing

Ruling body – World Water Ski Union
Events – slalom, jumping, figures (free-style tricks), and overall title
World championships – every 2 years

Weightlifting

Ruling body – International Weightlifting Federation (IWF)
Lifts – *Snatch* (bar pulled overhead in one movement) and *(clean and) jerk* (bar raised to shoulders first, then driven aloft as legs are straightened); (non-Olympic) *bench press, squat, dead lift*
World championships – annual (including Olympics)
Classes – flyweight (52 kg/114½ lb limit), bantam (56 kg/123¼ lb), feather (60 kg/132¼ lb), light (67.5 kg/148¾ lb), middle (75 kg/165¼ lb), light-heavy 82.5 kg/181¾ lb), middle-heavy (90 kg/198¼ lb), heavy (110 kg/242½ lb), super-heavy (over 110 kg)

Winter Sports

Ice Skating

Ruling body – International Skating Union (ISU)
World championships – annual (including Olympics)
Figure skating events – men's, women's, pairs, (pairs) dancing (all with compulsory and 'free' sections); two sets of marks, for technical merit and artistic impression
Speed skating events (on oval 400-m circuits) – men's 500, 1,500, 5,000, and 10,000 m; women's 500, 1,000, 1,500, and 3,000 m; overall titles in world and international events

Ice Hockey

Rink – max. 200 × 100 ft (61 × 30.5 m)
Surround – max. 4 ft (1.22 m) high boards
Goals – 6 × 4 ft (1.83 × 1.22 m)
Puck – diam. 3 in (7.6 cm), thickness 1 in (2.5 cm), weight 5½–6 oz (156–170 gm), made of vulcanized rubber or similar material
Duration – 60 min (3 × 20) playing time
No. per side – 6 (max. 17 on team)
Ruling body – International Ice Hockey Federation
Major competitions (amateur) – annual world championships (incl. Olympics)

Pair skating: Russian world champions Irena Rodnina and Alexei Ulanov.

Curling
Rink – 138 × 14 ft (42 × 4.27 m)
Houses (targets) – diam. 12 ft (3.66 m), dist. between centres 114 ft (34.75 m)
Stones (max.) – circum. 36 in (91.4 cm), thickness 4½ in (11.4 cm), weight 44 lb (20 kg), made of granite or similar
No. per team – 4 (2 stones each)
No. of *heads* (or *ends*) – 10 or 12 (or time limit)
Ruling body – Royal Caledonian Curling Club
World championships – Silver Broom Trophy (annual)

Bobsleigh
Course – min. length 1,500 m (1,640 yd), with at least 15 banked turns; agg. time for 4 descents
Events – 2- and 4-man bobs
Ruling body – International Bobsleigh Federation
World championships – annual (including Olympics)

Luge Tobogganing
Course – 1,000–1,500 m (1,094–1,640 yd); agg. time for 4 descents
Events – 1- and 2-man luge, 1-woman luge; ridden in sitting position
Ruling body – International Luge Federation
World championships – annual (including Olympics)

Cresta Run
Course – unique to St Moritz, 1,213 m (1,326.6 yd); agg. time for 3 descents
Event – single seater, ridden face down
Ruling body – St Moritz Tobogganing Club
Major competitions – Grand National (full course, from Top), Curzon Cup (from Junction, 888 m or 971 yd); Olympic event (full course) in 1928 and 1948

Alpine Ski Racing
Events – downhill, slalom, giant slalom, combined
Downhill – vert. drop 850–1,000 m (2,789–3,281 ft) men; 400–700 m (1,312–2,297 ft) women
Slalom – 55–75 gates men, 40–60 gates women; alternate gates (pairs of poles 4–5 m, 13–16 ft, apart) have blue or red flags and are 0.75–15 m (2.5–49 ft) apart
Giant slalom – min. 30 gates 4–8 m (13–26 ft) wide, at least 5 m (16 ft) apart

Alpine ski racing: taking a gate in the slalom.

Ruling body – Fédération Internationale de Ski (FIS)
Major competitions – 2-yearly world championships (including Olympics, which has no combined title), annual World Cup (men's and women's, individuals scoring in 15 of 21 top international events, first 10 scoring 25, 20, 15, 11, 8, 6, 4, 3, 2, 1 pts.), annual Arlberg-Kandahar

Ski-Bob Racing
Events – downhill, giant slalom, special slalom, combined
Ruling body – Fédération Internationale de Skibob (FISB)
World championships – two-yearly (men's and women's)

Nordic Ski Competition
Events – 15, 30, 50 km (9.3, 18.6, 31 miles) men's, 5, 10 km (3.1, 6.2 miles) women's; 4 × 10 km relay (men), 3 × 5 km relay (women); nordic combination (15 km cross-country and ski jumping, men's); men's 70 and 90 m (230 and 295 ft) ski jumping (points awarded for style and distance)
Ruling body – Fédération Internationale de Ski (FIS)
Major competitions – 2-yearly world championships (including Olympics); 90-m ski jumping and biathlon, annually

General Information

Flags of the nations

Afghanistan

Albania

Algeria

Argentina

Australia

Austria

Belgium

Bolivia

Brazil

Bulgaria

Burma

Canada

Chile

China

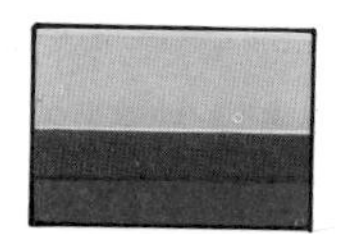
Colombia

Cuba

Cyprus

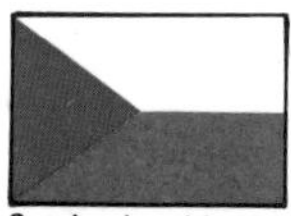
Czechoslovakia

Denmark

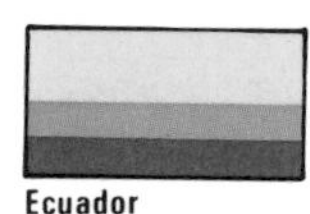
Ecuador

Ethiopia

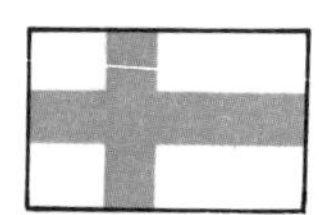
Finland

France

East Germany

West Germany

Ghana

Greece

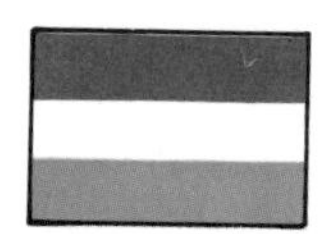
Hungary

Iceland

India

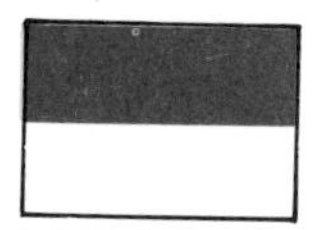
Indonesia

Iran

Iraq

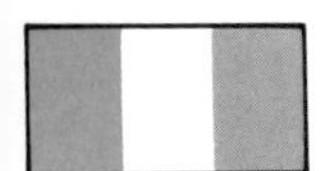
Ireland

Israel

Italy

Jamaica

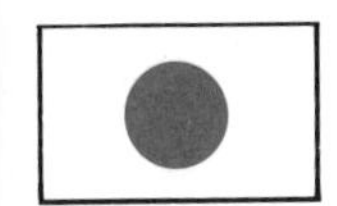
Japan

North Korea

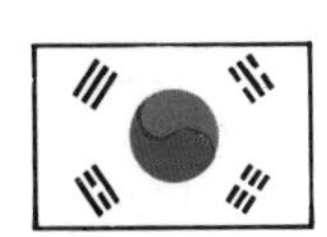
South Korea

Lebanon

Malaysia

Mexico

Morocco

Netherlands

New Zealand

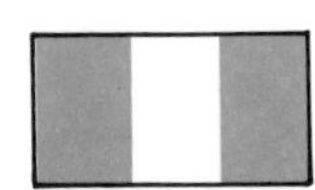
Nigeria

Norway

Pakistan

Peru

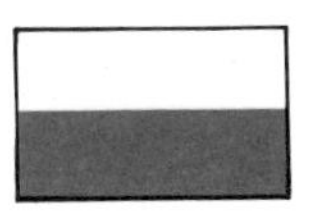
Poland

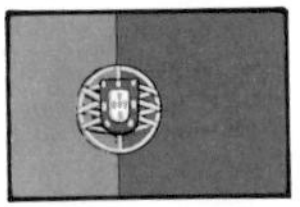
Portugal

Romania

Saudi Arabia

Singapore

South Africa

Spain

Sri Lanka (Ceylon)

Sweden

Switzerland

Thailand

Tunisia

Turkey

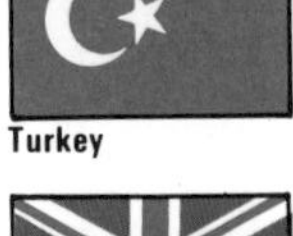
United Kingdom

United States

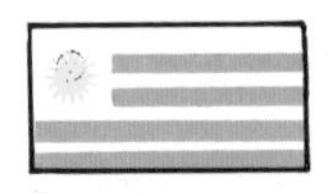
Uruquay

USSR

Venezuela

Yugoslavia

Zaïre

Cooking

Cookery terms

anglaise Garnish of boiled vegetables such as turnips, carrots, and celery hearts; used with boiled salt beef.
au bain marie Cook by standing container of food in hot-water bath to protect from fierce heat; can also be used to keep food warm.
au beurre Cooked with butter, either by itself or in sauce.
au gratin Cooked with crumbed bread or cheese on top, then browned under grill.
bake Cook in enclosed space using dry heat only.
bake blind Bake pastry case having filled it completely with beans to keep it from rising.
bard Cover fatless meat or game with large piece of fat or bacon to keep it moist in cooking.
baste Spoon hot fat or liquid over food being roasted or poached.
bat Flatten (with heavy object) fillet of sole, lamb cutlet, or veal escalope.
bechamel White sauce made from *roux* of butter and flour, mixed with milk, with herbs and diced vegetables.
beurre manié Kneaded butter used for thickening soups and sauces.
beurre noisette Butter cooked to nut brown colour, with herbs and lemon juice then added; served with fish or meat.
beat Mix using strong implement without including air into mixture.
blanch Put food, usually onions or some meats, into cold water, bring to boil, and remove. Or put green vegetables into boiling water for ½ minute, drain, and refresh with cold water.
blanquette Dish cooked with white sauce, e.g. *blanquette de veau* – white veal stew.
blend Mix ingredients together to form homogeneous mixture.
bind Hold together and solidify mixture by adding another ingredient, usually eggs.
boil Cook food in boiling water or water-based liquid.
bonne femme Garnish of bacon *lardons*, button onions, button mushrooms, and small potatoes.
bouchée Small vol-au-vent.
bouillon Broth.
bouquet garni Parsley, bayleaf, and thyme with other herbs, all tied together. Used to flavour stews and casseroles; removed after cooking.
bourgignon Sauce containing red burgundy, button mushrooms, and small onions; served with beef.
braise Cook slowly to tenderness in oven.
brochettes Pieces of meat cooked with herbs on skewers.
broil Cook meat directly over fire.
brunoise Garnish of root vegetables; as julienne, but very finely diced before cooking.
canapés Fried bread, cheese, or short-crust pastry cut into small shapes and covered with savoury mixture.
casserole Cook meat, game, or poultry, and sometimes vegetables, together in an enclosed container in an oven.
chasseur Sautéed mushrooms added to sauté of game, chicken, or veal.
clarify Clean out impurities in butter by heating, or in broth by using the white of an egg.
colbert Sauce containing meat or fish glaze, light stock, softened butter, lemon juice, Madeira, and parsley.
compote Fruit poached in sugar syrup.
concasser Skin and seed tomatoes and cut into thin strips.
consommé Strong, clear bouillon.
court bouillon Slightly acid stock made from water, root vegetables, and white wine or vinegar.
cream Beat ingredients to a cream-like consistency.
croûtes Pieces of fried bread used as base for savouries, tournedos, or eggs.
croûtons Very small cubes of fried bread served with soups.
cuisson Natural cooked juices from fish, chicken, or meat.
cut and fold Cut to bottom of air-containing mixture and fold over so as to mix in other ingredients without losing the air.
deglaze Scrape down meat juices from roasting tin with metal spoon.
degorger Remove unwanted substances from certain foods; e.g. salt from anchovies by soaking in milk; bitter juices from aubergines by sprinkling with salt.

demi-glace Brown sauce made from mirepoix, tomato purée, mushrooms, and bouquet garni.
depouiller Remove fat from sauce by dropping in cold liquid to solidify fat, which can then be skimmed off.
dice Cut food into small, neat cubes.
doria Garnish of cucumber.
dredge Sprinkle liberally with flour or sugar.
dripping Beef fat that is left after roasting beef.
dropping consistency Consistency of a mixture that, when lifted up on a spoon, drops easily back into the bowl.
dubarry Cauliflower flowerets coated with mornay sauce and cooked *au gratin*.
duxelles Finely chopped mushrooms and shallots, often used in stuffings.
escalope Slice of veal, $\frac{1}{4}$–$\frac{1}{2}$ in (6–13 mm) thick, preferably cut across best part of leg. Can also be taken from neck or loin and well beaten.
flamande Garnish of red cabbage and glazed small onions; used with pork or beef.
flamber Set light to, using brandy or fortified wine.
florentine Garnish of spinach. Also old name for apple pie.
fricassée Pieces of cooked white meat reheated in creamy white sauce.
frit Fried.
fry Cook in hot fat in open pan over heat.

APPROXIMATE OVEN TEMPERATURES

description	electric °F	electric °C	gas no.*
very cool	225°	107°	$\frac{1}{4}$ (240°)
	250°	121°	$\frac{1}{2}$ (265°)
cool	275°	135°	1 (290°)
	300°	149°	2 (310°)
warm	325°	163°	3 (335°)
moderate	350°	177°	4 (355°)
fairly hot	375°	191°	5 (375°)
	400°	204°	6 (400°)
hot	425°	218°	7 (425°)
very hot	450°	232°	8 (450°)
	475°	246°	9 (470°)

*Temperature equivalents of the gas numbers are given in °F in parentheses.

A selection of the many herbs commonly used in cooking to improve flavour.

fumet Strong stock made from fish or game and well reduced.
garni Garnished.
garnish Decorate with complementary foodstuffs.
glaze Brush with liquid substance that cooks or dries to shiny finish.
grate Reduce to small particles by rubbing against rough surface.
grill Cook underneath direct heat.
hollandaise Hot emulsified sauce containing mainly butter and egg yolks.
indienne Mayonnaise seasoned with curry and chopped chives.
jardinière Groups of different vegetables, or a macedoine, used to garnish meat dishes, usually with demi-glace sauce.
joinville Garnish of sliced truffles, crayfish tails, and mushrooms, with a sauce Nantua.
julienne Vegetables cut into very thin strips and cooked slowly in butter.
knead Work and blend moist dough to homogeneous consistency.
lard Thread strips of fat through fatless meat to moisten it in cooking.
lardons Approximately finger-sized strips of bacon used for flavouring.
liaison Thickening and enriching agent added to soup or sauce towards end of cooking time.
lyonnaise Garnish of fried onions.

Cooking terms (contd.)

macedoine Mixture of vegetables or fruit cut into large dice.
macerer Soak fruit in liqueur or syrup.
marinate Soak food for some hours in suitable liquid; e.g. meat in red wine with herbs and spices; fruit in sugar and liqueur syrup.
mayonnaise Cold emulsified sauce made with egg yolks, oil, and a little vinegar, and/or lemon juice and seasoning.
meunière Finish of *beurre noisette* with lemon juice.
milanese Pasta with tomato sauce, shredded ham, and mushrooms.
mirepoix Selection of $\frac{1}{4}$-in (6-mm) diced vegetables in equal quantities, including carrots, turnips, onions, and celery.
mornay Bechamel sauce flavoured with cheese.
nantua Garnish of prawns, lobster, or crayfish, and sometimes tomato.
Napolitaine Garnish or sauce of tomatoes and parmesan cheese. Also a 3-coloured ice cream.
navarin Brown lamb or mutton stew with root vegetables.
noisette Best end of neck of lamb or mutton, boned, seasoned, tied into a roll, and cut into $1\frac{1}{2}$-in (4-cm) thick slices.
normande Garnish of cider, apples, butter, and cream. Or, with sole, garnish of mussels, oysters, shrimps, and mushrooms.
panade Very thick white sauce, or bread crumbs soaked in milk and beaten smooth.
parboil Partially cook by boiling.
pickle Soak for long time in strong preservative liquid.
poach Cook very gently in shallow pan in water-based liquid at 170°–186°F (77°–86°C).
portuguese Rich tomato sauce, or garnish of tomatoes.
pot au feu Beef broth, possibly thickened with rice or pasta, or served as clear consommé. Or the boiled beef that has been used in making the former.
pot roast Cook very slowly in covered pan with fat herbs and onion.
princesse Denotes use of chicken.
pulses Seeds of leguminous plant that can be eaten, e.g. peas, beans, lentils.
purée Boil food substance to pulp, and strain.

ragoût Brown stew in which meat is cut into large pieces, with some fat left on, and cooked with vegetables.
revenir Pass vegetables through hot oil to glaze, but not to cook them.
ribbon, beat to the Beat until mixture, when lifted up on a spoon, forms a long continuous ribbon-like stream without dropping back into the bowl.
rissoler Brown slowly in fat.
roast Cook in enclosed space using fat; *French roast* by using small quantity of liquid to provide extra moisture.
robert Usually denotes use of mustard.
rôti Roast.
roux Mixture of butter and fat used as base for flour sauce or soup.
St Germain Garnish of peas and sometimes pommes noisette. Also a cream of pea soup.
salpicon Savoury filling of largish pieces of sliced vegetables, meat, or fish.
sauté Cook in small quantity of fat in open pan; fat is absorbed completely into food.
scald Bring milk or cream to near boiling point.

Left: **A master chef prepares to serve from a rich selection of dishes.**

sear Brown and seal outside of meat very quickly.
sift Shake dry ingredients through fine mesh to remove lumps.
simmer Cook in liquid at temperature of about 185°–200°F (85°–93°C) so that liquid shows slight movement but does not actually boil.
slake Mix, usually arrowroot or cornflour, with small amount of cold water before using as thickening for sauce, soup, or gravy.
soubise Onion purée, often mixed with white sauce.
steam Cook slowly by exposing food to concentrated steam.
suprême Of chicken breast.
tournedos Fillet of beef, 1–1½ in (25–40 mm) thick, cut from heart of fillet.
valentino Denotes asparagus and sometimes cheese.
whip Mix thoroughly and quickly with whisk to include as much air as possible into mixture.

USEFUL MEASURES

Imperial

2 teaspoons	=	1 dessertspoon
2 dessertspoons	=	1 tablespoon
16 tablespoons	=	1 cup
2 cups	=	1 pint
1 pint	=	20 fl. oz

American

1 Amer. pint	=	16 fl. oz
1 Amer. cup	=	8 fl. oz

Metric (working) equivalents

1 teaspoon	=	5 ml
1 Amer. teaspoon	=	4 ml
1 pint	=	½ litre (approx.)
1 litre	=	1¾ pints (approx.)
1 lb	=	½ kilo (approx.)

Level teaspoons per oz (approx.)

Breadcrumbs (dry)	3–4
Cheese (grated)	3–4
Flour	2
Gelatine	2
Raisins, etc.	2
Rice	2
Sugar (granulated)	1

Wine

Types of wine glasses: 1 *Tulip*, general purpose glass. 2 *Balloon*, for fine Burgundy (or brandy). 3 *Flute*, for Champagne. 4 *Port*. 5 *Copita*, for Sherry. 6 *Roemer*, for Hock, Moselle, etc.

Glossary

Alsace Province of eastern France between Vosges and Rhine, best known for white wines named after grape (*Riesling*, Sylvaner, etc.).
Amontillado Pale, medium-dry *Sherry*.
Amoroso Golden, fairly rich, dessert *Sherry*.
Appellation Contrôlée Term used on labels of superior French wines, indicating registered trade name and that wine conforms with description on label. See *VDQS*.
Asti Spumante Sparkling, white Italian wine, made in Piedmont; highly scented and usually medium-sweet.
Barsac Luscious French white wine, nearly as sweet as *Sauternes* (in which district it lies); some labelled *Sauternes*.
Beaujolais Large district in *Burgundy*, producing light, fresh, and fruity wines. Most of vast output is red.
Bordeaux Major wine-producing area in south-western France: *red Bordeaux* (*claret*) includes wine from major districts *Médoc*, St Emilion, Pomerol, *Graves*; *white Bordeaux* from *Sauternes*, *Graves*, Entre

Wine glossary (contd.)

Deux Mers, etc. Least distinguished Bordeaux sold simply as *Bordeaux rouge* or *Bordeaux blanc*.
bouquet Perfume given off by wine.
bourgeois Term for high-quality wine, not quite in top bracket.
brut Of Champagne, etc., very dry.
Burgundy Former province of eastern France, famous for the red wines of the Côte d'Or, *Beaujolais*, Mâcon, etc., and white wines of Côte d'Or (Côte de Beaune), Chablis, etc.
chambré Brought to room temperature.
Champagne Former province of northern France where the famous sparkling wine is produced (mostly white, but also rosé). *Méthode Champenoise* puts sparkle in by inducing second fermentation in bottle.
château In *Bordeaux*, a wine-producing estate or farm, seldom with a castle.
Chianti Italian red wine from Tuscany; young medium-bodied kind in familiar wicker-covered *fiascos* or matured full-bodied kind.
claret Term often used in Britain for red *Bordeaux*.
corky Spoilt by diseased cork.
demi-sec Of Champagne, sweet.
dry Unsweetened.
extra-sec Of Champagne, very dry.
Fino Pale, dry, delicate *Sherry*.
fortified wines Strengthened at some stage of production with brandy or spirit (e.g. *Sherry*, *Port*, *Madeira*).
Graves Large district in *Bordeaux* area, producing mainly white wines, the best being dry. The finest Graves are red, and include Haut-Brion.
Hock Term often used in Britain for German Rhine wines.
Kabinett German label term indicating high-quality wine (made without added sugar).
Liebfraumilch Name permitted by law for any indeterminate *Hock of QbA* standard.
Loire Major wine-producing area extending from Bay of Biscay to central France; mostly white wines.
Madeira *Fortified wines* of island of Madeira: Sercial, Verdelho, Bual, Malmsey.
Manzanilla Very pale, tart *Sherry*, with distinctive nutty taste.
Marsala Dark brown *fortified wine* of Sicily, with burnt-caramel flavour.
Médoc Major district of *Bordeaux*, producing many great red wines.
Moselle Name commonly given in Britain to German Mosel-Saar-Ruwer wines, mostly delicate white (pale greenish), made from Riesling grape, with deliciously fresh acidity (e.g. Piesporter).
Mousseux French sparkling wines, mostly white, but some red and rosé.
Oloroso Full-bodied, dark, sweet *Sherry*.
Orvieto White Italian wines, dry (*secco*) or full-flavoured medium-sweet (*abboccato*).
Port *Fortified wine* of Portugal, mostly red, but some white (used for blending or drunk as apéritif); *Wood Port* is blended and matures in wood; *Vintage Port* is from one good vintage, and after 2 years in wood is matured in bottle for further 10–20; *Ruby Port* is young Wood Port, sweet,

WHICH WINE? – A ROUGH GUIDE

food	type of wine*
Hors d'oeuvre	dry white or dry Sherry
Soup (clear)	dry Sherry or Madeira
Pasta	light red
Egg dishes	medium quality dry wine†
Seafood‡	dry white
Fish	dry or medium white, sparkling, or rosé
Red meat, liver, kidney, game§	full-bodied red
Poultry	dry white or light red¶
Veal, pork	white
Curry, goulash, etc.	full-flavoured (or, preferably, beer)
Puddings	Champagne or sweet white
Dessert (fresh fruit, nuts)	sweet white or sweet fortified
Cheese	red or Port

* Dry Champagne or a white Burgundy will go with anything.
† Red, white, or rosé, depending on what is cooked with the eggs.
‡ Rosé possible with shellfish; Sherry with lobster; classic wine to drink with oysters is Chablis.
§ Dry white wines suitable with cold game.
¶ For roast birds with rich sauce or stuffing, red is preferable.

fruity, full-bodied, and brilliant purple; *Tawny Port* is a paler, russet colour (as result of age or blending), with lighter body and subtle taste, drier and nuttier.

QbA (Qualitätswein bestimmter Anbangebiete) Good-quality German wine made to standard laid down by law.

Qualitätswein mit Prädikat Highest-quality German wine.

red wine Made by leaving skin and juice together during fermentation; colour comes from pips and skins. Usually served at room temperature.

Retsina Greek wine with turpentine flavour caused by addition of resin.

Rhine (Rhein) Area in Germany that produces *Hock*, in valleys of Rhine and some of its tributaries.

Rhône Major wine-producing area of France, stretching from Lyon to Avignon, particularly noted for red wines (Côtes du Rhône, Châteauneuf du Pape, etc.); also rosé (the dry, fruity Tavel Rosé) and white.

Riesling Type of grape from which many fine German wines are made (most *Moselles*, some *Hocks*); also used in Alsace, Yugoslavia, etc.

rosé Made like *red wine*, but juice run off sooner, giving it lighter colour and taste; usually served chilled.

Sauternes Major district of *Bordeaux*, producing rich, sweet wines, made from grape with high sugar content encouraged by growth of mould – the 'noble rot'.

ALCOHOL CONTENT: PROOF SYSTEMS

°proof GB	°proof US	per cent alcohol
175	200	100
100	114.3	57.1
87.5	100	50
85	97.1	48.6
80	91.4	45.7
75	85.7	42.9
70	80	40
65	74.3	37.1
60	68.6	34.3
52.5	60	30
50	57.1	28.6
35	40	20
26.3	30	15
21	24	12
17.5	20	10

Grape harvesting in South Africa, which has become a prolific producer of wine.

sec Of Champagne, etc., dry.

Sekt German sparkling wines, usually made by *méthode Champenoise*.

Sherry Famous *fortified wine* of Spain (imitated in Cyprus, South Africa, etc.); *cream* is smooth, sweet blend; *brown*, sweet with rich, full flavour. See *Amontillado, Fino, Manzanilla, Oloroso*.

sparkling wines 'Sparkle' results from presence of free carbon dioxide, either from second fermentation (*méthode Champenoise*) or artificially introduced. They include French *Champagnes* and *Mousseux*, Italian *Asti Spumantes*, *Sekt* (German), Perelada (Spanish), *Vinho Verdes* (Portuguese).

spätlese High-quality German wines made from late-picked (hence more delicate and fruity) grapes.

Tokay Rich Hungarian wines of high quality; Aszu, a sweet dessert wine, golden orange with a 'bready' flavour; Szamorodni, golden wine, dry or sweet.

VDQS wines (Vins Délimités de Qualité Supérieure) French wines not quite up to *Appellation Controlée* standard; guarantee of origin and quality.

The picked grapes are carefully divided into different varieties and qualities. Some will be made into a simple *vin ordinaire.* Others will go to make the finest vintage wines.

WINE: VINTAGE GRADINGS

	Claret (Red Bordeaux)	White Bordeaux (sweet)	Red Burgundy	White Burgundy	Rhone	Loire	Rhine	Moselle
1945	10	9	6	–	9	–	–	–
1946	1	1	1	–	4	–	–	–
1947	7	7	6	–	9	6	–	–
1948	7	7	6	–	6	–	–	–
1949	9	9	7	–	9	–	–	–
1950	6	9	1	–	7	–	–	–
1951	0	1	0	–	3	–	–	–
1952	6	7	7	4	9	–	–	–
1953	7	9	6	4	9	–	9	7
1954	4	1	3	1	4	–	1	–
1955	7	10	6	4	9	–	6	6
1956	0	1	0	0	4	–	–	–
1957	6	6	7	6	9	–	4	4
1958	6	6	3	4	6	–	4	4
1959	9	9	9	6	9	–	9	9
1960	6	4	0	0	9	–	1	1
1961	10	10	7	7	10	–	7	6
1962	9	9	7	9	9	–	4	4
1963	1	0	1	1	3	–	3	3
1964	7	4	9	9	9	6	9	9
1965	0	0	0	0	3	–	1	0
1966	10	6	9	10	9	6	9	7
1967	9	7	6	9	9	7	7	6
1968	1	0	1	3	3	1	4	3
1969	7	7	10	10	7	10	9	9
1970	10	10	7	10	7	9	7	6
1971	7	9	10	10	7	9	10	10
1972	4	4	6	6	7	9	1	1
1973	6	6	4	4	6	9	6	7
1974	5	0	3	8	6	9	5	3
1975	10	10	3	6	3	9	10	10
1976	7	7	10	8	9	9	10	10
1977	4	3	3	5	6	5	6	5

Wine glossary (contd.)

Vermouth A wine 'manufactured' in Italy and France, not quite a *fortified wine*; 'French' is dry, 'Italian' or 'It' sweetish and red (*rosso*); *bianco* is sweet white; various kinds now made in both Italy and France; complex mixture of herbal ingredients with filtered white wine, fortified with grape brandy; drunk as apéritif, alone or in cocktails.

vin de pays (du pays) Ordinary but identified wine, more respectable than *vin ordinaire*.

vin ordinaire Term used in Britain to denote everyday table wine; in France, anonymous wine usually priced according to alcoholic strength.

Vinho Verdes Light and fresh medium-dry Portuguese wines, red or white, with slight sparkle to tongue.

vintage wine One made entirely from grapes picked from 'vintage' (harvest) of single year.

white wines Made without pips and by removing skins before fermentation.

Incidental intelligence

CHESS NOTATION

BLACK

	a	b	c	d	e	f	g	h
8	QR1 / QR8	QKt1 / QKt8	QB1 / QB8	Q1 / Q8	K1 / K8	KB1 / KB8	KKt1 / KKt8	KR1 / KR8
7	QR2 / QR7	QKt2 / QKt7	QB2 / QB7	Q2 / Q7	K2 / K7	KB2 / KB7	KKt2 / KKt7	KR2 / KR7
6	QR3 / QR6	QKt3 / QKt6	QB3 / QB6	Q3 / Q6	K3 / K6	KB3 / KB6	KKt3 / KKt6	KR3 / KR6
5	QR4 / QR5	QKt4 / QKt5	QB4 / QB5	Q4 / Q5	K4 / K5	KB4 / KB5	KKt4 / KKt5	KR4 / KR5
4	QR5 / QR4	QKt5 / QKt4	QB5 / QB4	Q5 / Q4	K5 / K4	KB5 / KB4	KKt5 / KKt4	KR5 / KR4
3	QR6 / QR3	QKt6 / QKt3	QB6 / QB3	Q6 / Q3	K6 / K3	KB6 / KB3	KKt6 / KKt3	KR6 / KR3
2	QR7 / QR2	QKt7 / QKt2	QB7 / QB2	Q7 / Q2	K7 / K2	KB7 / KB2	KKt7 / KKt2	KR7 / KR2
1	QR8 / QR1	QKt8 / QKt1	QB8 / QB1	Q8 / Q1	K8 / K1	KB8 / KB1	KKt8 / KKt1	KR8 / KR1

WHITE

The chess board with pieces positioned for the start of a game. The bottom right-hand square must be a white one. In a description of a game, White's moves are shown on the left, Black's on the right.

BLACK

♜	♞	♝	♛	♚	♝	♞	♜
♟	♟	♟	♟	♟	♟	♟	♟
♙	♙	♙	♙	♙	♙	♙	♙
♖	♘	♗	♕	♔	♗	♘	♖

WHITE

There are two systems of notation: ***descriptive*** **(most English-speaking countries) has different square names for white and black (shown within board);** ***algebraic*** **is shown outside board (a1, etc).**

♔	King, K
♕	Queen, Q
♖	Rook, R
♗	Bishop, B
♘	Knight, Kt or N
♙	Pawn, P
x	takes
ch	check
O-O	castles on King's side
O-O-O	castles on Queen's side
!	fine move, 'brilliancy'
?	questionable move, mistake

TRADITIONAL ANNIVERSARY NAMES

year	name
1	paper
2	cotton
3	leather
4	fruit, flowers
5	wood
6	iron, sugar
7	wool, copper
8	bronze
9	pottery
10	tin, aluminium
11	steel
12	silk, fine linen
13	lace
14	ivory
15	crystal
20	china
25	silver
30	pearl
35	coral
40	ruby
45	sapphire
50	golden
55	emerald
60	diamond
75	diamond

Incidental information (contd.)

BIRTHSTONES

month	Hebrew (Biblical)	present day
January	garnet	garnet
February	amethyst	amethyst
March	jasper	aquamarine bloodstone
April	sapphire	diamond
May	chalcedony carnelian agate	emerald chrysoprase
June	emerald	pearl moonstone alexandrite
July	onyx	ruby carnelian
August	carnelian	peridot sardonyx
September	chrysolite	sapphire lapis lazuli
October	aquamarine beryl	opal tourmaline
November	topaz	topaz
December	ruby	turquoise zircon

DERIVATION OF DAYS AND MONTHS

day	named after
Sunday	the Sun
Monday	the Moon
Tuesday	Tiu, Norse god of war
Wednesday	Woden, Anglo-Saxon chief of gods
Thursday	Thor, Norse god of thunder
Friday	Frigg, Norse goddess
Saturday	Saturn, Roman god of harvests
January	Janus, Roman god of doors and gates
February	Februa, Roman period of purification
March	Mars, Roman god of war
April	aperire, Latin 'to open'
May*	Maia, Roman goddess of spring and growth
June*	Juno, Roman goddess of marriage
July	Julius Caesar
August	Augustus, first emperor of Rome
September	septem, Latin 'seven'
October	octo, Latin 'eight'
November	novem, Latin 'nine'
December	decem, Latin 'ten'

* According to some scholars, May comes from *majores* (older men), June from *juniores* (young men), to whom months were held to be sacred.

Left: **Julius Caesar after whom the month of July was named. In 46 BC, Caesar asked an astronomer to review the calendar. The resulting Julian Calendar lasted until 1582, when Pope Gregory XIII corrected the accumulated errors by dropping October 5-14. The Gregorian Calendar gradually came into worldwide use.**

NOBEL PRIZEWINNERS: PEACE

1901 Henri Dunant (Swiss) & Frédéric Passy (French)
1902 Elie Ducommun and Albert Gobat (Swiss)
1903 Sir William Cremer (British)
1904 Institute of International Law
1905 Baroness Bertha von Suttner (Austrian)
1906 Theodore Roosevelt (American)
1907 Ernesto Moneta (Italian) & Louis Renault (French)
1908 Klas Arnoldson (Swedish) & Fredrik Bajer (Danish)
1909 Auguste Beernaert (Belgian) & Paul d'Estournelles (French)
1910 Permanent International Peace Bureau
1911 Tobias Asser (Dutch) & Alfred Fried (Austrian)
1912 Elihu Root (American)
1913 Henri La Fontaine (Belgian)
1914–16 *No award*
1917 International Red Cross
1918 *No award*
1919 Woodrow Wilson (American)
1920 Léon Bourgeois (French)
1921 Karl Branting (Swedish) & Christian Lange (Norwegian)
1922 Fridtjof Nansen (Norwegian)
1923–24 *No award*
1925 Sir Austen Chamberlain (British) & Charles Dawes (American)
1926 Aristide Briand (French) & Gustav Stresemann (German)
1927 Ferdinand Buisson (French) & Ludwig Quidde (German)
1928 *No award*
1929 Frank Kellog (American)
1930 Nathan Söderblom (Swedish)
1931 Jane Addams & Nicholas Butler (American)
1932 *No award*
1933 Sir Norman Angell (British)
1934 Arthur Henderson (British)
1935 Carl von Ossietzky (German)
1936 Carlos de Saavedra Lamas (Argentinian)
1937 Viscount Cecil of Chelwood (British)
1938 Nansen International Office for Refugees
1939–43 *No award*
1944 International Red Cross
1945 Cordell Hull (American)
1946 Emily Balch & John Mott (American)
1947 Friends Service Council (British) & American Friends Service Committee
1948 *No award*
1949 Lord John Boyd Orr (British)

Eisaku Sato, ex-premier of Japan (1974 prize).

1950 Ralph Bunche (American)
1951 Léon Jouhaux (French)
1952 Albert Schweitzer (Alsatian)
1953 George C. Marshall (American)
1954 Office of the UN High Commissioner for Refugees
1955–56 *No award*
1957 Lester Pearson (Canada)
1958 Dominique Georges Pire (Belgian)
1959 Philip Noel-Baker (British)
1960 Albert Luthuli (South African)
1961 Dag Hammarskjöld (Swedish)
1962 Linus Pauling (American)
1963 International Red Cross & League of Red Cross Societies
1964 Martin Luther King Jr (American)
1965 UNICEF (UN Children's Fund)
1966–67 *No award*
1968 René Cassin (French)
1969 International Labour Organization
1970 Norman Borlaug (American)
1971 Willy Brandt (West German)
1972 *No award*
1973 Henry Kissinger (American); Le Duc Tho (North Vietnamese) – declined
1974 Sean MacBride (Irish) & Eisaku Sato (Japanese)
1975 Andrei Sakharov (Russian)
1976 Betty Williams & Mairead Corrigan (British)
1977 Amnesty International
1978 Mohammed Anwar El Sadat (Egyptian) & Menachem Begin (Israeli)
1979 Mother Teresa of Calcutta (Indian)

POPES

List of popes and their dates of accession. Antipopes and doubtful popes are not included.

St Peter	42
St Linus	67
St Anacletus (Cletus)	76
St Clement I	88
St Evaristus	97
St Alexander I	105
St Sixtus I	115
St Telesphorus	125
St Hyginus	136
St Pius I	140
St Anicetus	155
St Soterus	166
St Eleutherius	175
St Victor I	189
St Zephyrinus	199
St Callistus I	217
St Urban I	222
St Pontian	230
St Anterus	235
St Fabian	236
St Cornelius	251
St Lucius I	253
St Stephen I	254
St Sixtus II	257
St Dionysius	259
St Felix I	269
St Eutychian	275
St Caius	283
St Marcellinus	296
St Marcellus I	308
St Eusebius	309
St Melchiades	311
St Sylvester I	314
St Marcus	336
St Julius I	337
Liberius	352
St Damasus I	366
St Siricius	384
St Anastasius I	399
St Innocent I	401
St Zosimus	417
St Boniface I	418
St Celestine I	422
St Sixtus III	432
St Leo I (the Great)	440
St Hilary	461
St Simplicius	468
St Felix III	483
St Gelasius I	492
Anastasius II	496
St Symmachus	498
St Hormisdas	514
St John I	523
St Felix IV	526
Boniface II	530
John II	533
St Agapetus I	535
St Silverius	536
Vigilius	537
Pelagius I	556
John III	561
Benedict I	575
Pelagius II	579
St Gregory I (the Great)	590
Sabinianus	604
Boniface III	607
St Boniface IV	608
St Deusdedit (Adeodatus I)	615
Boniface V	619
Honorius I	625
Severinus	640
John IV	640
Theodore I	642
St Martin I	649
St Eugene I	654
St Vitalian	657
Adeodatus II	672
Donus	676
St Agatho	678
St Leo II	682
St Benedict II	684
John V	685
Conon	686
St Sergius I	687
John VI	701
John VII	705
Sisinnius	708
Constantine	708
St Gregory II	715
St Gregory III	731
St Zachary	741
Stephen II (III)*	752
St Paul I	757
Stephen III (IV)	768
Adrian I	772
St Leo III	795
Stephen IV (V)	816
St Paschal I	817
Eugene II	824
Valentine	827
Gregory IV	827
Sergius II	844
St Leo IV	847
Benedict III	855
St Nicholas I	858
Adrian II	867
John VIII	872
Marinus I	882
St Adrian III	884
Stephen V (VI)	885
Formosus	891
Boniface VI	896
Stephen VI (VII)	896
Romanus	897
Theodore II	897
John IX	898
Benedict IV	900
Leo V	903
Sergius III	904
Anastasius III	911
Landus	913
John X	914
Leo VI	928
Stephen VII (VIII)	928
John XI	931
Leo VII	936
Stephen VIII (IX)	939
Marinus II	942
Agapetus II	946
John XII	955
Leo VIII	963
Benedict V	964
John XIII	965
Benedict VI	973
Benedict VII	974
John XIV	983
John XV	985
Gregory V	996
Sylvester II	999
John XVII	1003
John XVIII	1004
Sergius IV	1009
Benedict VIII	1012
John XIX	1024
Benedict IX	1032
Gregory VI	1045
Clement II	1046
Benedict IX†	1047
Damasus II	1048
St Leo IX	1049
Victor II	1055
Stephen IX (X)	1057
Nicholas II	1059
Alexander II	1061
St Gregory VII	1073
Victor III	1086
Urban II	1088
Paschal II	1099
Gelasius II	1118
Callistus II	1119
Honorius II	1124
Innocent II	1130
Celestine II	1143
Lucius II	1144
Eugene III	1145
Anastasius IV	1153
Adrian IV	1154
Alexander III	1159
Lucius III	1181
Urban III	1185
Gregory VIII	1187
Clement III	1187
Celestine III	1191
Innocent III	1198
Honorius III	1216
Gregory IX	1227
Celestine IV	1241
Innocent IV	1243
Alexander IV	1254
Urban IV	1261
Clement IV	1265
Gregory X	1271
Innocent V	1276
Adrian V	1276
John XXI	1276
Nicholas III	1277
Martin IV	1281
Honorius IV	1285

Nicholas IV	1288	Julius II	1503	Alexander VIII	1689
St Celestine V	1294	Leo X	1513	Innocent XII	1691
Boniface VIII	1294	Adrian VI	1522	Clement XI	1700
Benedict XI	1303	Clement VII	1523	Innocent XIII	1721
Clement V	1305	Paul III	1534	Benedict XIII	1724
John XXII	1316	Julius III	1550	Clement XII	1730
Benedict XII	1334	Marcellus II	1555	Benedict XIV	1740
Clement VI	1342	Paul IV	1555	Clement XIII	1758
Innocent VI	1352	Pius IV	1559	Clement XIV	1769
Urban V	1362	St Pius V	1566	Pius VI	1775
Gregory XI	1370	Gregory XIII	1572	Pius VII	1800
Urban VI	1378	Sixtus V	1585	Leo XII	1823
Boniface IX	1389	Urban VII	1590	Pius VIII	1829
Innocent VII	1404	Gregory XIV	1590	Gregory XVI	1831
Gregory XII	1406	Innocent IX	1591	Pius IX	1846
Martin V	1417	Clement VIII	1592	Leo XIII	1878
Eugene IV	1431	Leo XI	1605	St Pius X	1903
Nicholas V	1447	Paul V	1605	Benedict XV	1914
Callistus III	1455	Gregory XV	1621	Pius XI	1922
Pius II	1458	Urban VIII	1623	Pius XII	1939
Paul II	1464	Innocent X	1644	John XXIII	1958
Sixtus IV	1471	Alexander VII	1655	Paul VI	1963
Innocent VIII	1484	Clement IX	1667	John Paul I‡	1978
Alexander VI	1492	Clement X	1670	John Paul II	1978
Pius III	1503	Innocent XI	1676		

‡John Paul I died after only 33 days as pontiff.

St Peter's in Rome is the heart of the Roman Catholic Church. As Bishops of Rome, Popes claim spiritual descent from St Peter, martyred in Rome in the reign of the Emperor Nero.

HISTORIC ASSASSINATIONS

victim	details of assassination	date
Philip II, king of Macedonia	Pausanias, young noble with a grudge	336 B.C.
Julius Caesar, Roman dictator	Stabbed by Brutus, Cassius *et al.* in Senate	44 B.C.
St Thomas à Becket, English archbishop	Slain by four knights in cathedral	29.12.1170
Albert I, German king	By nephew, John 'the Parricide'	1.5.1308
James I of Scotland	Plot: Sir Robert Graham *et al.*	21.2.1437
David Beaton, Scottish chancellor/cardinal	Band of Protestant nobles in St Andrews Castle	29.5.1546
Lord Darnley, husband of Mary Queen of Scots	Blown up; plot	10.2.1567
William the Silent, Prince of Orange	Shot by Balthasar Gérard	10.7.1584
Henry III of France	Stabbed by fanatic monk (Jacques Clément)	2.8.1589
Henry IV of France (de Navarre)	Stabbed by fanatic (François Ravaillac)	14.5.1610
Albrecht von Wallenstein, Austrian general	Irish and Scottish officers	25.2.1634
Gustavus III of Sweden	Plot: shot by Johan Ankarström	29.3.1792
Jean Marat, French revolutionary	Stabbed in bath by Charlotte Corday	13.7.1793
Jean Baptiste Kléber, French general	By Turkish fanatic, in Cairo	14.6.1800
Abraham Lincoln, US president	Shot by actor, J. Wilkes Booth, in theatre	14.4.1865
Alexander II, emperor of Russia	Nihilist bomb	13.3.1881
James Garfield, US president	Shot at station by Charles Guiteau (grudge)	2.7.1881†
Sadi Carnot, French president	Stabbed by anarchist	24.6.1894
Antonio Cánovas del Castillo, Spanish premier	Shot by anarchist	8.8.1897
Elizabeth, empress of Austria	By Italian anarchist at Geneva	10.9.1898
Humbert I, king of Italy	By anarchist at Monza	29.7.1900
William McKinley, US president	Shot by anarchist, Leon Czolgosz, at Buffalo	6.9.1901‡
Pyotr Stolypin, Russian premier	Shot by revolutionary, Dmitri Bogrov	14.9.1911§
George I, king of Greece	At Salonika	18.3.1913
Francis Ferdinand, archduke of Austria	Alleged Serbian plot: shot in car by Gavrilo Princip at Sarajevo (sparked World War I)	28.6.1914
Jean Jaurès, French socialist	By nationalist, in café	31.7.1914
Rasputin, powerful Russian monk	By Russian noblemen	31.12.1916
Walter Rathenau, German foreign minister	By reactionaries	24.6.1922
Michael Collins, Irish Sinn Fein leader	Ambushed and shot	22.8.1922
'Pancho' Villa, former Mexican bandit/rebel	Ambushed in car	20.7.1923
Álvaro Obregón, Mexican president	Shot while dining, by José Toral	17.7.1928
Paul Doumer, French president	Shot by mad Russian émigré, Paul Gorgoulov	6.5.1932*
Anton Cermak, mayor of Chicago	By anarchist Joseph Zangara, with bullet intended for president-elect F. D. Roosevelt	15.2.1933¶
Engelbert Dollfuss, Austrian chancellor	Shot by Nazis in chancellery	25.7.1934
Alexander I of Yugoslavia; Jean Louis Barthou, French foreign minister	By Macedonian terrorist at Marseille	9.10.1934
Sergei Kirov, Russian political leader	By young party member, Leonid Nikolayev	1.12.1934
Huey Long, corrupt American politician	By Dr Carl Austin Weiss	8.9.1935**
Armand Calinescu, Romanian premier	By pro-Nazi Iron Guards	21.9.1939
Leon Trotsky, exiled Russian communist leader	Axed in Mexico by Ramon del Rio	21.8.1940
Jean Darlan, French admiral/political leader	In N. Africa; anti-Vichy motive	24.12.1942
Mahatma Gandhi, Indian nationalist leader	Shot by Hindu fanatic, Nathuran Godse	30.1.1948
Count Folke Bernadotte, Swedish diplomat	Ambushed in Jerusalem by Jewish extremists	17.9.1948
Abdullah ibn Hussein, king of Jordan	In Jerusalem mosque	20.7.1951
Liaquat Ali Khan, Pakistani premier	By fanatics at Rawalpindi	16.10.1951
Anastasio Somoza, Nicaraguan president	Shot by Rigoberto López Pérez, in León	21.9.1956††
Carlos Castillo Armas, Guatemalan president	By one of own guards	26.7.1957
Faisal II of Iraq	Military coup in Baghdad	14.7.1958
S.W.R.D. Bandaranaike, Ceylonese premier	By Buddhist monk in Colombo	25.9.1959*
Patrice Lumumba, deposed Congolese premier	Katanga secessionist regime	Jan/Feb 1961
Rafael Trujillo Molina, Dominican Republic dictator	Car machine-gunned	30.5.1961
Sylvanus Olympio, Togolese president	Army coup	13.1.1963
Ngo Dinh Diem, S. Vietnamese president	By generals in coup	2.11.1963

Above: **Robert Kennedy lies fatally wounded on the floor of a hotel lobby in Los Angeles.**
Left: **Archbishop Thomas à Becket is struck down at the altar of Canterbury Cathedral in 1170.**

John F. Kennedy, US president	Shot in car, in Dallas, Texas‡‡	22.11.1963
Malcolm X (Little), US Black Muslim leader	Shot at rally	21.2.1965
Sir Abubakar Tafawa Balewa, Nigerian premier	Army coup	15.1.1966
Hendrik Verwoerd, South African premier	Stabbed by parliamentary messenger, Dimitri Tsafendas (later ruled mentally disordered)	6.9.1966
Rev. Martin Luther King Jr., US Negro Civil Rights leader	Shot on hotel balcony by James Earl Ray, in Memphis, Tennessee	4.4.1968
Robert F. Kennedy, US senator	Shot by Arab immigrant, Sirhan Sirhan, in Los Angeles (Hotel Ambassador)	5.6.1968*
Tom Mboya, Kenyan economics minister	In Nairobi	5.7.1969
Abdirashid Ali Shermarke, Somalian president	Shot by security guard, Yussuf Ismail	15.10.1969
Wasfi Tal, Jordanian premier	By Palestinian guerrillas, in Cairo	28.11.1971
Louis Carrero Blanco, Spanish premier	Explosion under car; Basque terrorists (ETA)	20.12.1973
Mrs Park (Yook Young Soo), wife of South Korean president Park Chung Hee	By Mun Se Kwang (member of youth organization) with bullet intended for president	15.8.1974
Lalit Mishra, Indian railways minister	Bomb explosion at inauguration of new line	2.1.1975*
King Faisal of Saudi Arabia	Shot by nephew Prince Faisal ibn Masaed	25.3.1975
Ngarta Tombalbaye, Chad president	Military coup	13.4.1975
General Murtala Mohammed, Nigerian head of state	Unsuccessful coup	13.2.1976
Christopher Ewart-Biggs, British ambassador to Republic of Ireland	Car blown up by landmine planted by IRA	21.7.1976
Aldo Moro, president of Italy's Christian Democrats and five times prime minister of Italy	Kidnapped by 'Red Brigade' terrorists (16.3.78) and later found dead	9.5.1978
Sir Richard Sykes, British ambassador in The Hague	Shot by IRA	22.3.1979
Airey Neave, British Conservative MP and Northern Ireland spokesman	Explosion under car while leaving House of Commons car park; IRA	30.3.1979
Lord Louis, 1st Earl Mountbatten of Burma, uncle of Queen Elizabeth II	Explosion in sailing boat off coast of Ireland; IRA	27.8.1979
Park Chung Hee, president of South Korea	Shot in restaurant by chief of Korean Central Intelligence Agency	26.10.1979

*Died next day. †Died 19 Sep. ‡Died 14 Sep. §Died 18 Sep. ¶Died 6 Mar. **Died 10 Sep. ††Died 29 Sep.
‡‡Accused, Lee Harvey Oswald, himself shot by Jack Ruby (24 Nov.) while awaiting trial.

Index

In a work of this kind it is not possible to index every entry; otherwise the index would be almost as long as the book itself. For this reason, look for terms and definitions in the relevant glossaries, such as the Science A-Z and the Glossary of Musical Terms.

A

C

G

I

J

M

O

P

U

V

W

X

Y

ACKNOWLEDGEMENTS

Allsport 266, 270; Associated Press 289 TR; ATA Stockholm 165; Atomic Energy Authority 99; Australian News and Information Bureau 129; B.A.C. 174 TL; B.B.C. 115 TR; Bank of England 191; Bettman Archive 145, 259; Bibliothek Nationale 139; Martin Borland 246; British Hovercraft Ltd. 170; British Museum 134, 190, 195, 221, 249; British Oxygen Company 34 BR; British Petroleum 28; British Tourist Authority 12, 23; Canadian Union Pacific 172; J. Allan Cash 187 TL; Michael Chinery 55; Colorsport 58, 262, 264, 268, 272, 273; Mary Evans Picture Library 35 BR, 141 BL, 145 BR, 169 BR, 229; Freeman, Fox and Partners 80; French Government Tourist Office 278; Giraudon 157; Sonia Halliday 8 TR, 29, 66, 103, 119 TR, 138, 140, 206, 234, 254, Robert Harding 131; Harland & Wolf 53; Brian Hawkes 19; Michael Holford 102 BR, 162, 163, 213; Imperial War Museum 147; India Office 143; India Tourist Office 8 BR; Institute of Geological Sciences 25, 26, 27; Italian Institute 108; Italian State Tourist Office 126; Japan Information Service 119 BL, 285; Keystone 146 BL, 148; London Art Technical 179; London Museum 155 TR; Louvre 105, 107 TR; Mansell 35 TR, 85, 96, 104, 118, 124, 125 BL, 136, 141 TR, 144, 164, 174, 175, 201, 202, 208, 209, 212, 220, 228, 232, 233, 237, 240, 244, 245, 253, 257, 261, 284, 259 TL; Metropolitan Museum of Art 100–101; Middlesex Hospital 57; Ministry of Agriculture 84 BL; Musée du Jeu de Paume, Paris 226, 242; N.A.S.A. 20, 46–47, 73 BR, 74, 76; National Film Archive 118; National Gallery 102 T, 106 TR, 218, 231, 250; National Maritime Museum 142, 151, 220; National Monuments Collection, Crown Copyright 155 BR; National Motor Museum 162; National Museum, Copenhagen 165; National Portrait Gallery 126, 127, 214, 215, 223, 224, 252, 259, 260; Nobelstifelsen 93; Novosti 72, 73 BL, 147 BR, 187 TR, 241; Popperfoto 77, 117, 239; Press Association 222; R.A.S. 65; Radio Times Hulton Picture Library 84 TR, 132, 146, 256, 258; Ronan Picture Library 248, 283; Royal Copenhagen 122–123; Royal Free Hospital 97; Royal Marsden Hospital 95; S.N.C.F. 173; Christian Sappa 282; S.A.T.O.R. 281; Scala 137, 211, 219, 227; Science Museum 34 TR, 217, 236; Seaphot 10 BL; Stadelisches Kunstitute 125 TR; Crown Copyright, reproduced with permission of the Controller of Her Majesty's Stationery Office 187 BL; Swiss Tourist Office 21; Syndication 115 TL, 207; Tate Gallery 107 TL, 243; Daily Telegraph Colour Library 183; Twentieth Century Fox 121; United Nations 184, 188; U.S. Information Service 13 BR; U.S. Naval Observatory 67; Victoria and Albert Museum 108 BL; Watneys 44; Wellington Museum 210; K. Wicks 39 BL; Zefa 5, 10–11, 11, 14–15, 22, 78, 112, 133, 185, 238, 257.